· 2017 ·

何 梁 何 利 奖

HLHL PRIZE

何梁何利基金评选委员会　编

THE SELECTION BOARD OF HO LEUNG HO LEE FOUNDATION

中国科学技术出版社
·北　京·

图书在版编目(CIP)数据

2017何梁何利奖 / 何梁何利基金评选委员会编.—北京:
中国科学技术出版社,2018.10

ISBN 978-7-5046-8143-0

Ⅰ.①2… Ⅱ.①何… Ⅲ.①自然科学－科学家－生
平事迹－中国－2017 Ⅳ.①K826.1

中国版本图书馆CIP数据核字(2018)第217877号

责任编辑	韩　颖	
责任校对	焦　宁	
责任印制	李晓霖	

出　　版	中国科学技术出版社
发　　行	中国科学技术出版社发行部
地　　址	北京市海淀区中关村南大街16号
邮　　编	100081
发行电话	010-62173865
传　　真	010-62179148
网　　址	http://www.cspbooks.com.cn

开　　本	787mm×1092mm　1/16
字　　数	448千字
印　　张	21
插　　页	4
印　　数	1-3000册
版　　次	2018年10月第1版
印　　次	2018年10月第1次印刷
印　　刷	北京华联印刷有限公司

书　　号	ISBN 978-7-5046-8143-0/K·245
定　　价	80.00元

(凡购买本社图书,如有缺页、倒页、脱页者,本社发行部负责调换)

内 容 提 要

　　本书是何梁何利基金出版物——《何梁何利奖》的第二十四集。书中简要介绍了 2017 年度何梁何利基金 52 位获奖人的生平经历和主要科技成就。为了便于海内外人士了解本奖背景，书中同时收入了反映何梁何利基金及其科技奖励情况的资料，作为附录刊出。

This is the twenty-four collection of the publications of Ho Leung Ho Lee Foundation—*Ho Leung Ho Lee Prize.* In this book, the biographical notes on the 52 awardees of the year 2017 and their main scientific and technological achievements are accounted briefly. This collection includes appendices concerning Ho Leung Ho Lee Foundation and its scientific and technological award in order to help the readers both in China and abroad to understand the background of this prize.

2017 年 10 月 25 日，何梁何利基金 2017 年度颁奖大会（第二十四届）在北京钓鱼台国宾馆举行。全国人大常委会副委员长张宝文，全国政协副主席、科技部部长万钢等在主席台上。

On October 25, 2017, the 2017 Award Ceremony (24th) of Ho Leung Ho Lee Foundation is held at the Beijing Diaoyutai State Guesthouse. Zhang Baowen, Vice Chairman of the Standing Committee of National People's Congress, and Wan Gang, Vice Chairman of the Chinese People's Political Consultative Conference and Minister of the Ministry for Science and Technology, are on the rostrum.

国家领导人、各界嘉宾、捐款人代表与何梁何利基金 2017 年度获奖人合影。

The state leaders, the honored guests, and the representatives of the donors have a group photo taken with the winners of 2017 HLHL Prize.

全国人大常委会副委员长张宝文在何梁何利基金 2017 年度颁奖大会主席台上。
Zhang Baowen, Vice Chairman of the Standing Committee of National People's Congress, is on the rostrum of the 2017 Award Ceremony of Ho Leung Ho Lee Foundation.

全国人大常委会副委员长张宝文在何梁何利基金 2017 年度颁奖大会上讲话。
Zhang Baowen, Vice Chairman of the Standing Committee of National People's Congress, addresses at the 2017 Award Ceremony of Ho Leung Ho Lee Foundation.

全国政协副主席、科技部部长万钢在何梁何利基金 2017 年度颁奖大会上讲话。
Wan Gang, Vice Chairman of the Chinese People's Political Consultative Conference and Minister of the Ministry for Science and Technology, addresses at the 2017 Award Ceremony of Ho Leung Ho Lee Foundation.

何梁何利基金信托委员会主席、评选委员会主任朱丽兰在何梁何利基金 2017 年度颁奖大会上作评选委员会工作报告。
Zhu Lilan, Chairwoman of the Board of Trustees and Director of the Selection Board of HLHL Foundation, delivers a report on the work of the Selection Board at the 2017 Award Ceremony of Ho Leung Ho Lee Foundation.

何梁何利基金评选委员会秘书长段瑞春宣布获奖人名单。

Duan Ruichun, the Secretary–General of the Selection Board of HLHL Foundation, announces the list of the winners of 2017 HLHL Prize.

全国人大常委会副委员长张宝文为何梁何利基金 2017 年度科学与技术成就奖获奖科学家黄旭华颁奖，并与其合影留念。

Zhang Baowen, Vice Chairman of the Standing Committee of National People's Congress, presents prize to Huang Xuhua, the winner of 2017 HLHL Prize for Science and Technology Achievements, and has a photo taken with him.

何梁何利基金捐款人代表梁祥彪先生为获奖人颁奖。

Mr. Thomas Liang Cheung Biu, the representative of the donors of HLHL Foundation, presents prize to the winners.

何梁何利基金捐款人代表梁洁华博士（右三）、梁祥彪先生（左二）、何厚锵先生（右一）、何乃威先生（左一）与获奖代表合影。

Dr. Leung Kit–Wah (right3), Mr. Thomas Liang Cheung Biu (left2), Mr. Norman Ho Hau Chong (right1) and Mr. Thomas Ho Lai Wai (left1), the representatives of the donors of HLHL Foundation, have a photo taken with the winners of 2017 HLHL Prize.

何梁何利基金 2017 年度科学与技术成就奖获奖者黄旭华教授在颁奖大会上发言。
Prof. Huang Xuhua, the winner of 2017 HLHL Prize for Science and Technology Achievements, makes a speech at the 2017 Award Ceremony of Ho Leung Ho Lee Foundation.

何梁何利基金 2017 年度颁奖大会会场。
The meeting hall of the 2017 Award Ceremony of Ho Leung Ho Lee Foundation.

在何梁何利基金 2017 年度颁奖大会上的讲话

全国人大常委会副委员长　张宝文

（2017 年 10 月 25 日）

各位来宾，同志们，朋友们：

在举国上下欢庆党的第十九次全国代表大会胜利闭幕之际，我们在此隆重集会，举行何梁何利基金 2017 年度颁奖大会，向荣获何梁何利"科学与技术成就奖"的杰出科学家彭士禄院士、黄旭华院士，向 34 位荣获"科学与技术进步奖"、16 位荣获"科学与技术创新奖"的优秀科技工作者颁奖，这是我国科技界、教育界和社会各界的一大盛事。值此喜庆时刻，让我们向全体获奖科学家表示热烈的祝贺！向何梁何利基金创立者和捐款人代表表示崇高的敬意！向基金信托委员会、评选委员会、投资委员会表示由衷的感谢！

1994 年，香港爱国金融实业家何善衡、梁銶琚、何添、利国伟先生共同捐资创立了何梁何利基金，这项创举、义举和善举开辟了我国社会力量重奖杰出科技人才的先河，同时为香港回归祖国献上了一份厚礼。多年来，基金坚持制度透明、阳光操作、科学管理、规范运行，已遴选、奖励祖国优秀科学家、工程师和产业领军人才 1250 人，在激励自主创新、激发人才活力、营造良好创新环境等方面发挥了重要作用，为推动我国科技进步与创新，弘扬崇尚科学、尊重创造的精神做出了重要贡献，已经成为我国社会力量创办科技奖励的杰出代表和特色品牌。

刚才，朱丽兰同志作了一个很好的工作报告，我完全赞同。何梁何利基金最高奖项获奖人黄旭华院士和彭士禄院士的女儿彭洁同志的发言感人肺腑、催人奋进。两位"科学与技术成就奖"的获奖人在极其艰辛的条件下做隐姓埋名人、干惊天动地事，为我国核潜艇从无到有、从跟跑到跻身世界先进行列，为我国核电站在引进、消化、吸收、改造和再创新，取得跨越发展，达到世界先进水平，做出了彪炳史册的重大贡献，成为万众景仰的楷模。核潜艇是国之重器，从当年面对国际封锁，毛泽东主席发出"核潜艇一万年也要搞出来"的豪迈誓言，到启动建造核潜艇工程，艰苦奋斗，攻坚克难，仅6年时间，我国首艘核潜艇下水，与彭士禄、黄旭华同志并肩作战、创造这项科技奇迹的还有赵仁恺、黄纬禄等已故杰出科学家以及无怨无悔、献身国防科技事业的一大批科技工作者。在此，我们也向他们表达深切的缅怀，致以崇高的敬意！

今年荣获科学与技术进步奖、科学与技术创新奖的50位科技工作者中，有在基础科学前沿领域毕生耕耘的老一辈科学大家，有在高科技研究领域取得重大突破的领军人物，也有新科技革命和产业革新大潮中涌现出的青年才俊。他们有的来自高等院校和科研院所，有的来自创新型企业，有的来自香港著名大学或本地与香港合作机构，也有的来自西部艰苦地区或少数民族地区。经过海内外评委科学评议、优中选优、无记名投票所产生的50位获奖科学家，是我国科技人员的杰出代表，是科技界、教育界和全社会学习的榜样。让我们再次以热烈的掌声，对他们获得何梁何利科学与技术奖表示衷心的祝贺！

当今世界，全球新一轮科技革命和产业变革方兴未艾，科技创新正加速推进，并深度融合、广泛渗透到人类社会的各个方面，成为重塑世界格局、创造人类未来的主导力量。世界科技发展呈现出新的趋势：**一是前沿基础研究向宏观拓展、微观深入**。随着技术手段的不断进步，人类对客观物质世界的认识提升到前所未有的新高度。合成生物学进入快速发展阶段，将掀起新一轮生物技术进步的浪潮。脑科学研究有望描绘出人脑活动图谱和工作机理。前沿基础研究的重大突破可能改变和丰富人类对客观世界与主观世界的基本认知，催生新的重大科学思想和科学理论。**二是颠覆性技术突破层出不穷**。信息网络、生物科技、清洁能源、新材料与先进制造等正孕育一批颠覆性技术。量子计算机与量子通信、干细胞与再生医学、纳米科技和量子点技术、石墨烯材料等已展现出诱人的应用前景，将为经济社会发展提供前所未有的驱动力，推动经济格局和产业形态深刻调整，成为创新驱动发展和国家竞争力的关键所在。**三是"互联网＋"将全方位、多要素地改变人类生产和生活。**随着大数据技术普及，人类活动将全面数据化。工业互联网、能源互联网、车联网、物联网、太空互联网等新网络形态不断涌现，将推动人类生产方式、商业模式、生活方式、学习和思维方式等发生深刻变革。互联网的力量将借此全面重塑世界，使人类文明继农业革命、工业革命之后迈向新的"智业革命"时代。**四是科技制高点向深空、深海、深地、深蓝拓进。**天基与地基相结合的观测系统等将有效提升对地观测、深空探测、综合信息利用能力。海洋新技术突破正催生新型蓝色经济的兴起与发展。地质勘探技术和装备研制技术将为开辟新的资源能源提供条件。量子计算机、非硅信息功能材料、第五代移动通信技术（5G）有望帮助人类实现"信息随心至、万物触手及"，并带来一系列产业创新和巨大经济及战略利益。**五是国际科技合作向更高层次和更大范围发展。**全球气候变化、网络信息安全、重大自然灾害等一系列重要问题事关人类共同安危。氢能和核聚变能可望成为解决人类基本能源需求的主要方向。人类面临共同挑战的复杂性和风险性、科学研究的艰巨性和成本之高昂，将大大促进合作研究和资源共享，推动高水平科技合作广泛深入开展。**六是新型研发组织和创新模式将显著改变创新生态。**网络信息技术、大型科研设施开放共享、智能制造技术提供了功能强大的研发工具和前所未有的创新平台，催生越来越多的新型科研机构和组织。以"创客运动"为代表的小微型创新正在全球范围掀起新一轮创新创业热潮，这些趋势将带来人类科研和创新活动理念及组织模式的深刻变革，激发出前所未有的创新活力。**七是优秀科技人才成为竞相争夺的焦点。**经济全球化对创新资源配置日益产生重大影响，人才全球流动速度、范围和规模都将达到空前水平。发达国家利用优势地位，通过开放国民教育、设立合作研究项目、提供丰厚薪酬待遇等方式，持续增强对全球优秀科技人才的吸引力。新兴国家也积极参与科技资源和优秀人才的全球化竞争，优秀科技人才竞争已经成为焦点。**八是全球科技创新格局出现重大调整**。国际金融危机以来，全球科技创新力量开始从发达国家向发展中国家扩散。从 2001 年到 2011 年，美国研发投入占全球比重由 37% 下降到 30%，欧洲从 26% 下降到 22%。虽然以美国为代表的发达国家目前在科技创新上仍处于无可争议的领先地位，但中国、印度、巴西、俄罗斯等新兴经济体对世界科技创新的贡献率也快速上升。未来 20 — 30 年，北美、东亚、欧盟三个世界科技中心将鼎足而立，主导全球创新格局。

十八大以来，以习近平同志为核心的党中央顺应世界科技发展潮流，高度重视科技创新，以历史纵深和全球视野，从时代发展前沿和国家战略高度，提出了"五位一体"的总体布局、"四个全面"的战略布局和创新、协调、绿色、开放、共享的发展理念，将实施创新驱动发展战略提升到事关"两个一百年"奋斗目标和实现中国梦的全局高度，陆续出台《深化科技体制改革实施方案》《国家创新驱动发展战略纲要》《"十三五"国家科技创新规划》等文件，修订《促进科技成果转化法》，启动面向 2030 年的科技创新重大项目部署，召开"科技三会"，向全党全国发出了建设世界科技强国的号召。

在党和国家的高度重视和领导下，在广大科技工作者的共同努力下，我国科技整体能力持续提升，科技体制改革加速推进，科技服务经济社会发展的能力不断增强，一些重要科技领域跻身世界领先行列，某些前沿方向开始进入并行、领跑阶段，我国已经发展成为具有重要影响力的科技大国。高温超导、中微子物理、量子反常霍尔效应、纳米科技、干细胞研究、肿瘤早期诊断标志物、人类基因组测序等基础研究成果呈"井喷式"爆发；载人航天、探月工程、北斗导航、载人深潜、高速铁路、航空母舰等战略高技术取得重大突破；全社会研究与试验发展经费持续高速增长，2016 年占 GDP 比重为 2.1%；科技创新人才队伍持续壮大，研发人员总量居世界第一位；国际科技论文数量稳居世界第二，科学研究的国际

全国政协副主席、科技部部长万钢为获奖人颁奖。
Wan Gang, Vice Chairman of the Chinese People's Political Consultative Conference and Minister of the Ministry for Science and Technology, presents prize to the winners.

何梁何利基金捐款人代表梁洁华博士为获奖人颁奖。
Dr. Leung Kit–Wah, the representative of the donors of HLHL Foundation, presents prize to the winners.

全国人大常委会副委员长张宝文与何梁何利基金2017年度科学与技术成就奖获奖科学家黄旭华及其夫人李世英合影留念。

Zhang Baowen, Vice Chairman of the Standing Committee of National People's Congress, has a photo taken with Huang Xuhua, the winner of 2017 HLHL Prize for Science and Technology Achievements, and his wife Li Shiying.

全国人大常委会副委员长张宝文为何梁何利基金2017年度科学与技术成就奖获奖科学家彭士禄颁奖，由其女儿彭洁代领，并与彭洁合影留念。

Zhang Baowen, Vice Chairman of the Standing Committee of National People's Congress, presents prize to Peng Shilu, the winner of 2017 HLHL Prize for Science and Technology Achievements. Peng Jie, the daughter of Peng Shilu, received the prize on behalf of her father. Zhang Baowen has a photo taken with Peng Jie.

影响力大幅提升；科技进步贡献率增至56.2%，创新型国家建设取得重要进展；科技创新成果加速转化，大众创业、万众创新蓬勃兴起，蕴藏在亿万人民中间的创新智慧被充分释放，中华大地展现出一片创新发展的勃勃生机。这些成绩来之不易，是全党全国各族人民团结奋斗、迎难而上的结果，是广大科技工作者攻坚克难、砥砺奋进的结果。今天我们在这里举行何梁何利基金颁奖大会，回顾和总结过去，表彰和激励先进，希望大家鼓足干劲、与时俱进、扎实工作，为建设创新型国家、建成世界科技强国做出新的更大的贡献。

同志们，朋友们！

中国共产党第十九次全国代表大会刚刚闭幕，本次大会是在全面建成小康社会决胜阶段、中国特色社会主义发展关键时期召开的一次十分重要的大会，承担着谋划决胜全面建成小康社会、深入推进社会主义现代化建设的重大任务，具有非常重大的意义。习近平总书记的报告高屋建瓴，博大精深，催人奋进，倍受鼓舞。报告立足历史发展、当今世界和当代中国，做出了中国特色社会主义进入新时代的科学判断，确立了新时代中国特色社会主义思想，提出了实现新目标、迈向新征程的基本方略，科技界全体同人应该精神更加振奋、斗志更加昂扬、信心更加坚定。让我们更加紧密地团结在以习近平同志为核心的新一届党中央周围，牢固树立创新发展理念，着力推进科技体制改革，增强发展动力，厚植人才优势，让创新创业在全社会蔚然成风，为实现"两个一百年"奋斗目标、中华民族伟大复兴的"中国梦"，建成富强民主文明和谐美丽的社会主义现代化强国再谱新华章、再写新辉煌！

ADDRESS AT THE 2017 AWARD CEREMONY OF HO LEUNG HO LEE FOUNDATION

Zhang Baowen, Vice Chairman of the Standing Committee of National People's Congress

(October 25, 2017)

Distinguished guests, friends and comrades:

At the moment when people throughout China are celebrating the successful conclusion of the 19th CPC National Congress, we gather here to solemnly hold the 2017 Annual Award Ceremony of the Ho Leung Ho Lee Foundation and to award the HLHL Prize for Scientific and Technological Achievements to the two eminent scientists/Academicians Peng Shilu and Huang Xuhua, to award the HLHL Prize for Scientific and Technological Progress to 34 outstanding scientists, and to award the HLHL Prize for Scientific and Technological Innovation to 16 outstanding scientists. This is a big event for the circles of science, technology and education in particular and for the society in general. At this moment of celebration, let us give our warm congratulations to all the prize-winning scientists, our high respect to the founders and donors of the Ho Leung Ho Lee Foundation, and our heart-felt gratitude to the Board of Trustees, the Selection Board and the Investment Committee of the foundation!

In 1994, Hong Kong patriotic financial industrialists Ho Sin-Hang, Leung Kau-Kui, Ho Tim and Lee Quo-Wei jointly founded the HLHL Foundation. This unprecedented act of integrity and charity pioneered in using non-governmental resources to give substantial rewards to eminent scientific and technological talents— a generous gift to Hong Kong just before it was returned to the motherland. Over the years, the HLHL Foundation has adhered to the principle of making all the rules and regulations known to the public, transparency in all practices, scientific management and standardized operation. A total of 1250 scientists and engineers and industrial leaders have been selected to receive the prizes. The HLHL Foundation has played an important role in encouraging independent innovation, stimulating the vitality of talents, and creating a good environment for innovation. It has made an important contribution to promoting the progress and innovation in science and technology in China and to carrying forward the spirit of respecting and promoting science and respecting creativity. And it has become an outstanding representative and a distinctive brand in using non-governmental resources to establish scientific and technological awards in China.

Just now, Comrade Zhu Lilan made a very good work report and I completely approve of what she has said. Academician Huang Xuhua and Peng Jie, the daughter of Peng Shilu, representing the winners of the foundation's highest prize, delivered very touching and inspiring speeches. These two laureates of the HLHL Prize for Scientific and Technological Achievements have worked very hard under extremely arduous conditions and made great achievements. Thanks to their efforts, China has made rapid progress in the development of its nuclear submarine industry, from virtually non-existence to a world leader in this area. Their work has also helped China's nuclear power plant achieve a big stride in development in the process of introduction (of foreign technology), digestion, absorption, transformation and re-innovation, and finally reaching advanced international level. Their important contributions will be written down in the chapters of modern Chinese history and they are role models for all. Nuclear submarine is an important element to a country's military strength. In the early days of the Republic, Chairman Mao Zedong, facing international blockade, made the heroic statement "we will build our own nuclear submarines even if it will take ten thousand years." After the project of building nuclear submarine was initiated, it took only six years of arduous work and struggle in tackling and cracking difficulties before China's first nuclear submarine was launched. In addition to Peng Shilu and Huang Xuhua, a large number of scientists dedicated their lives to the project, notably the late eminent scientists Zhao Renkai and Huang Weilu. Here we greatly cherish the memories of these scientists and pay our highest respect to them.

Of the 50 scientists who won the HLHL Prize for Scientific and Technological Progress and the HLHL Prize for Scientific and Technological Innovation, some are senior scientists who have worked hard all their life in the frontiers of basic sciences, some are leading figures who have achieved important breakthroughs in the areas of high technology research, and others are young talents who have risen in the revolution of new science and technology and industrial innovation. Some of them come from institutions of higher learning or scientific research institutions, some from innovative enterprises, some from prestigious universities in Hong Kong and/or local institutions in cooperation with Hong Kong, and some from western regions and/or regions mainly inhabited by minority ethnic groups where conditions are relatively poor. These 50 prize-winning scientists, who have been selected from among the best of the best through a secret ballot after the sound reviews and evaluations of the judges in China and overseas, are the outstanding representatives of Chinese scientific and technological workers and the role models for people working in the fields of science and technology and of education and the entire society as well. Let us express our sincere congratulations to the prize winners with a big round of applause.

In the present world, a new round of science and technology revolution and industrial transformation is on the rise. Scientific and technological innovation has been pushed forward at an accelerated pace. It merges deeply with and permeates various aspects of the human society. It is becoming a leading force that will reshape the world and the future of mankind. Many new trends emerge in the development of science and technology in the world.

First, the frontier basic research is extending far into macroscopic realms and reaching deeply into the microscopic realms. With constant progress in the use of technical means, our understanding of the physical world has been elevated to an unprecedented new height. Synthetic biology has entered a stage of rapid development and it will set off a new round of development waves in biological technology. Hopefully, the research in brain science will draw a brain activity map and describe its working mechanism. Important breakthroughs in frontier basic research may change and enrich our basic understanding of the objective and subjective worlds and contribute to the creation of new important scientific thought and theory.

Second, breakthroughs in disruptive technology have been made one after another. A group of disruptive technologies are about to be born in information network, biological technology, clean energy, new materials and advanced manufacturing. Quantum computer and quantum communication, stem cell and regenerative medicine, nanotechnology and quantum dot technology, and graphene materials have already showed attractive prospects in application. They will provide unprecedented driving power to economic and social development, promote profound adjustments in economic landscape and industrial forms, and become the key areas in innovation-driven development and national competitiveness.

Third, "Internet⁺" will change the production activity and life of mankind in an all-round and multifactorial manner. With the spreading of big data services, people's activities will be digitized comprehensively. New network forms, such as industrial internet, internet of energy, internet of vehicles, internet of things, and orbital internet, are emerging one after another. These networks will push forward the profound transformation of the mode of production, business model, lifestyle, and ways of learning and thinking of mankind. The force of the internet will comprehensively reshape the world with such developments so that human civilization will enter a new era of "intelligence industry revolution" after the agricultural and industrial revolutions.

Fourth, the vintage points in science and technology are extending deeper into outer space, the sea, the earth and deep blue. Sky-and ground-based integrated observation systems will effectively improve man's ability in earth observation, outer space exploration and comprehensive information utilization. Breakthroughs in new marine technology are now promoting the rise and development of new-type blue economy. Geological prospecting technology and equipment research and development technology will provide conditions for finding new resources and energies. Quantum computer, non-silicon information functional materials, and the 5th-generation mobile communication technology (5G) are expected to help mankind to realize the situation that "information comes at will and everything comes within the reach of your hand". They will also bring a series of industrial innovations and create huge economic and strategic interests.

Fifth, international scientific and technological cooperation will develop at higher levels and in a greater scope. A series of important issues, such as global climate change, web information security and major natural disasters, concern the common safety of mankind. Hydrogen energy and nuclear fusion energy are expected to become the main solutions to the basic energy demand of mankind. The complexities and risks of the challenges facing mankind as well as the difficulties and high costs of scientific research will facilitate cooperation in research and resource sharing, promoting extensive and in-depth scientific and technological cooperation at higher levels.

Sixth, new-type research and development organizations and innovation models will noticeably change innovation landscape. Web information technology, opening and sharing of large scientific research facilities, and intelligent manufacturing technology provide powerful research and development tools and unprecedented innovation platforms and facilitate the establishment of more and more new-type scientific research institutions and organizations. Micro and small-sized innovations, represented by the Maker Movement, are setting off a new round of innovation on the globe. These trends will bring about profound changes in the philosophy and organization models of the scientific research and innovation of mankind and stimulate unprecedented vitality for innovation.

Seventh, excellent scientific and technological talents will become the focus of competition. Economic globalization will exert increasingly important influence on the allocation of innovation resources. The speed, range and size of global talent flow will reach an unprecedented level. Utilizing their advantageous statuses, developed countries keep enhancing their attraction to excellent scientific and technological talents on the globe through opening national education, establishing cooperative research projects, and offering generous salaries and benefits. Emerging countries also take an active part in the global competition for scientific and technological resources and talents. The competition for excellent scientific and technological talents has become the focus.

And eighth, important adjustments have occurred to the global landscape of scientific and technological innovation. Since the International Financial Crisis, scientific and technological innovation forces have spread from developed countries to developing countries around the globe. From 2001 to 2011, the proportion of the research and development spending of the USA to the global total decreased from 37% to 30% and that of Europe from 26% to 22%. Although developed countries, represented by the USA, still hold an undisputable leading position in scientific and technological innovation, the contribution of emerging economies, such as China, India, Brazil and Russia, to the world's scientific and technological innovation is increasing quickly. In the next 20 ~ 30 years, the three centers of science and technology in the world, namely North America, East Asia and the EU, will define the global innovation landscape together.

Since the 18th CPC National Congress, the Central Committee with Xi Jinping at the core has followed the development trend of science and technology in the world and attached great importance to scientific and technological innovation. By considering historical experiences and the frontiers development of our time, with reference to China's national strategy and from a global perspective, the Central Committee has adopted the Five-sphere Integrated Plan and the Four-pronged Comprehensive Strategy, and the philosophies of innovative, balanced, green, open and shared development. It raised implementing innovation-driven development strategy to such height that its success or failure will be closely linked to the realization of the Two Centenary Goals and the Chinese Dream. It successively promulgated the *Plan for Implementation of Deepening the Reform of Scientific and Technological System*, the *Outline of the State Strategy on Innovation-Driven Development*, and the *State Plan of Scientific and Technological Innovation in the 13th Five Year Plan* and amended the *Law of Promoting the Transformation of Scientific and Technological Research Results*. It has made plans and arrangements for important scientific and technological projects oriented to 2030 and held the Three Conferences of Science and Technology to call on the whole CPC and the general public to build China into a powerful country in science and technology in the world.

Under the strong leadership of the CPC and the government and with joint efforts of all scientific and technological workers, China's overall scientific and technological capacities keep improving. The reform of scientific and technological system has been accelerated and the ability of science and technology in serving economic and social development keeps enhancing. China becomes one of the world leaders in some important scientific and technological areas and in some frontier directions China is the sole or shared leaders. Generally speaking, China has developed into a major country of science and technology with important influence. We have seen substantial results in basic research areas such as high temperature superconductor, neutrino physics, quantum anomalous Hall effect, nanotechnology, stem cell study, tumor biomarker in early diagnosis, and human genome sequencing. There have been important breakthroughs in strategic high technologies such as manned space flight, lunar exploration program, Beidou navigation satellite system, manned deep-sea research submersibles, high speed railway, and aircraft carriers. The funds for the development of research and experimentation show continuous growth in the whole society. In 2016, its weight in GDP reached 2.1%. The contingent of scientific and technological innovation personnel keeps growing. The total number of research and development personnel ranks first in the world. The number of scientific and technological papers published internationally ranks steadily in second place. China's scientific research has increased its international influence greatly. In China the contribution rate of scientific and technological progress has risen to 56.2%. Important progress has been achieved in building an innovative country. The transformation of the research results of scientific and technological innovation has sped up. The trend of mass entrepreneurship and innovation has risen and thriven. The innovation wisdom among more than one billion people has been fully released. Innovation and development are the byword in today's China. These achievements have been made through hard work. They are the results of hard struggles fought together by the whole Party and all the Chinese people, and the results after a large number of scientific and technological workers tenaciously tackled one difficulty after another. Today, we hold the award ceremony of the HLHL Foundation here to review and summarize the past and to commend and encourage leading scientists. We hope that all the people will exert their utmost effort, advance with the time, and work conscientiously to make new and greater contributions to building China into an innovative country and a powerful country of science and technology in the world.

Friends and comrades, the 19th National Congress of the Communist Party of China has just concluded. It is a very important meeting held at the decisive stage of completing the building of a moderately prosperous society in all respects and at the critical period of the development of socialism with Chinese characteristics. It undertakes the important task of planning the decisive move in comprehensively completing the building of a moderately prosperous society and pushing forward socialist modernization construction and thus it is of very important significance. The report of the General Secretary exhibits extensive and profound thought from a higher perspective and it is both inspiring and encouraging. The report takes historical development and the situation in the current world and China in the contemporary time as its start point. It makes the scientific judgment that socialism with Chinese characteristics has entered a new era. It establishes the thought of socialism with Chinese characteristics in a new era and proposes the basic policies to achieve new goals and embark on new journeys. All our colleagues in the circle of science and technology feel more energized and motivated and are full of confidence in our endeavor. Let us unite more closely around the new CPC Central Committee with Comrade Xi Jinping at the core, firmly establish the concept of innovation and development, make more efforts to push forward the reform of scientific and technological system, strengthen the driving power of development, and build up the advantages in human resources. We should make innovation and entrepreneurship a popular trend in the whole society and write a new, brilliant chapter in history on realizing the Two Centenary Goals and the Chinese Dream of the great rejuvenation of the Chinese nation and building China into a wealthy, powerful, democratic, culturally-advanced, harmonious and beautiful modern socialist country.

序

时光流转，何梁何利基金的运作已迈向第二十五年。过去一年，基金在信托委员会朱丽兰主席、岳毅副主席、杜占元委员、杨纲凯教授和郑慧敏委员的带领下，在评选委员会同人和全体义务工作人员的忠诚合作以及基金顾问的指导下，继续有满意的发展，各捐款人对此衷心感谢。

从评选委员会的工作报告中，可以看到去年基金的得奖人年龄分布和结构更加优化，中青年人才和海外归国人员已经成为我国科学研究和技术创新的生力军。

根据去年7月我国首次发表的《中国国际科技合作现状报告》显示，从2006年到2015年，中国在国际科研合作的规模已经提升到全球第4位。中国近年的科研成就获得国际的广泛认同，去年9月，美国《福布斯》杂志指出，经过政府多年的支持、国内生产总值的强劲增长和对教育的大力投入，中国已经从以前的科技模仿者转变为创新者。中国只用了30年时间走完西方200年才完成的三次工业革命，是很了不起的成就。在金融、生物和智能机器人技术快速发展的新时代，中国将会负起全球科技的领导角色。

今年年初，国家主席习近平在主持中央政治局一次学习会议时指出："现代化经济体系是由社会经济活动各个环节、各个层面、各个领域的相互关系和内在联系构成的一个有机整体。要建设创新引领、协同发展的产业体系，实现实体经济、科技创新、现代金融、人力资源协同发展，使科技创新在实体经济发展中的贡献份额不断提高，现代金融服务实体经济的能力不断增强，人力资源支撑实体经济发展的作用不断优化。""要加快实施创新驱动发展战略，强化现代化经济体系的战略支撑，加强国家创新体系建设，强化战略科技力量，推动科技创新和经济社会发展深度融合，塑造更多依靠创新驱动、更多发挥先发优势的引领型发展。"

何梁何利基金成立的原旨就是推动国家的科技进步和创新发展，回顾自从基金成立这四分之一个世纪，中国无论在经济还是科技方面均有飞跃的成就，基金同人亦与有荣焉。何梁何利基金定会再接再厉，继续透过奖励科技工作者，为中国的繁荣昌盛以及成为世界科技强国的目标尽力。

何梁何利基金捐款人

何善衡慈善基金会有限公司　　梁铼琚慈善基金会有限公司
何添基金有限公司　　　　　　伟伦基金有限公司

2018 年 5 月于香港

PREFACE

During the quarter of a century since its establishment, the unwavering mission of the Ho Leung Ho Lee Foundation has been to encourage and support China's development as a global leader in the areas of science and technology. The donors wish to express their sincere gratitude to Chairman Zhu Lilan, Vice Chairman Yue Yi, Professor Du Zhanyuan, Professor Kenneth Young and Ms Louisa Cheang Wai Wan of the Trustee Committee– as well as the Selection Board Members, volunteers and Advisors– for their wise guidance, commitment, and hard work, which has led to the continued flourishing of the Foundation.

As stated in the working report of the Selection Board, the diversity and age distribution of Foundation awardees has been further enhanced over the past year, with young and middle–aged talent and individuals returning from overseas becoming key drivers of scientific research and technological innovation in China.

According to the report *China's International Scientific Research Collaboration* published in July 2017, China's scale of international scientific research cooperation saw an upward trend from 2006 to 2015 and ranked 4th in the world. China is continuing to gain greater global recognition for its scientific achievements. In September last year, Forbes magazine noted that following years of government support, strong GDP growth and significant investment in education, China has moved from imitator to innovator. In just 30 years, our country has successfully undertaken three 'Industrial Revolutions' that took nations in the West 200 years to complete. China is now took a global leading role in the new era of fintech, biotech and machine learning.

During a group study of the Political Bureau of the Central Committee earlier this year, President Xi Jinping pointed out that the modern economic system is an organic entity composed of the interrelationships and intrinsic connections between all aspects, levels, and fields of social and economic activities. It is necessary to build an industrial system that is innovation–driven with synergistic development, that achieves the coordinated development of the real economy, scientific and technological innovation, modern finance, and manpower, so that scientific and technological innovation can continue to contribute to an ever–growing portion of the real economy development, capabilities of the modern financial service of the real economy can continue to grow, and the role of manpower in supporting the economic development of the entity can continuously be optimised.

It is necessary to accelerate the implementation of innovation–driven development strategies and strengthen the strategic support of the modern economic system, fortify the national innovation system, brace strategic scientific and technological capabilities, promote deep integration of scientific and technological innovation and economic and social development, and to create more guided developments that are innovation–driven and display advantages.

The founding principle of the Ho Leung Ho Lee Foundation was to promote national scientific and technological advancement and innovative development. Looking back at the 25 years since the Foundation was established, China has achieved momentous advancements on economic, scientific, and technological fronts. Everyone involved with the Foundation takes pride in these achievements. The Foundation will continue to support our nation in its mission to become a global powerhouse in the fields of science and technology and attain sustainable prosperity for all in China.

Donors of Ho Leung Ho Lee Foundation

S. H. Ho Foundation Limited   Leung Kau Kui Foundation Limited

Ho Tim Foundation Limited   Wei Lun Foundation Limited

May 2018, Hong Kong

何梁何利基金评选委员会 2017 年度工作报告

信托委员会主席、评选委员会主任　朱丽兰

（2017 年 10 月 25 日）

尊敬的全国人大常委会副委员长张宝文同志，

尊敬的全国政协副主席、科技部部长万钢同志，

各位嘉宾，同志们，朋友们：

十月的北京，秋高气爽，硕果飘香。今天，在举国上下欢庆党的第十九次全国代表大会胜利闭幕的喜庆时刻，在香港回归祖国 20 周年的重要年份，在中国特色社会主义进入新时代的历史性进程中，我们在北京钓鱼台国宾馆隆重举行何梁何利基金 2017 年度颁奖大会，向 52 位杰出科技工作者授予何梁何利科学与技术奖励的崇高荣誉，具有重要意义。国务院副总理刘延东同志致函热烈祝贺本次颁奖大会的召开，代表国务院向获奖科学家表示衷心祝贺，向捐款人代表致以崇高敬意，向广大科技工作者致以亲切问候。全国人大常委会张宝文副委员长，全国政协副主席、科技部部长万钢同志亲临大会指导，给予我们莫大鼓舞。在此，我谨代表基金全体同人，对党和国家领导同志的亲切关怀和悉心指导表示衷心感谢，对捐款人代表和内地以及香港科技界、教育界和社会各界嘉宾出席本次盛典表示热烈的欢迎！

下面，我代表评选委员会作工作报告。

一、关于基金 2017 年度评选工作

今年 6 月 6 日，何梁何利基金信托委员会在中银香港举行全体会议，审议并接受基金投资委员会去年的投资情况报告，审议并通过基金评选委员会 2016 年度工作报告和 2017 年工作设想。2016

年，虽然全球经济环境很不明朗，世界经济复苏乏力，但基金财务状况总体稳定，截至 2017 年 3 月底，基金的投资市值为 6.83 亿港元，与 1994 年 3 月成立之初总共 3.9 亿港元相比，23 年来，在保障每年奖励活动正常运作的同时，基金市值增值 75%，平均每年的增长率为 3.27%。尽管受全球经济影响，短期内尚难期待基金收入有很大突破，但在基金投资委员会审慎管理和智慧应对之下，维持一定水平的投资收益，保障奖励工作正常运行，我们充满信心。

根据综合经济预期评估，信托委员会决定今年用于发放奖金的预算总金额比去年略有增加，确定为 1200 万港元。这笔资金来之不易，我们要感谢基金投资委员会在十分困难的条件下所做出的宝贵贡献。

今年年初，评选委员会办公室向国内外有效提名人共发出提名推荐书 2200 多份。在规定的期限内收到推荐材料 683 份，有效被提名人 627 人，再创历史新高。特别是"科学与技术创新奖"，今年推荐材料和有效被提名人均突破 200，双双刷新历史纪录。这从一个侧面反映出何梁何利科技奖的权威性、影响力及其在科技人员心目中的分量与日俱增。这也对我们进一步做好评审工作提出了新的挑战。

今年 7 月 3—7 日，何梁何利基金专业评审会在北京铁道大厦举行。经过专家初评，产生"科学与技术进步奖"候选人 72 名、"科学与技术创新奖"候选人 28 名。"科学与技术成就奖"是何梁何利基金的大奖，是评选工作的重中之重。根据《评选章程》规定，评选委员会成立由段瑞春秘书长牵头、内地评选委员会委员和部分专业评委参加的预审小组，经过实地考察、听证和综合评议，产生"科学与技术成就奖"候选人 2 名。上述候选人一并提请评选委员会全体会议审议。

8 月 29 日，何梁何利基金评选委员会在北京友谊宾馆举行全体会议，经过科学评价、优中选优、无记名投票表决，评选产生"科学与技术成就奖"得主 2 名、"科学与技术进步奖"得主 34 名、"科学与技术创新奖"得主 16 名，圆满完成了今年三大奖项评选工作。

二、关于今年获奖科学家总体情况

今年是中国人民解放军建军 90 周年。何梁何利基金最高奖项——"科学与技术成就奖"授予两位为我国的国之重器——核潜艇、核电站事业毕生奉献、成就卓著的杰出科学家。一位是我国著名核动力专家，先后任我国核潜艇的首任总设计师和核电站引进、改造、自主设计和创新的领军人物；一位是我国著名核潜艇总体设计研究专家，多年出任我国核潜艇总设计师，为核潜艇第一代的创建升级、第二代的飞跃赶超和第三代的跨越发展做出重大建树。他们在极其艰苦的条件下，数十年做隐姓埋名人，干惊天动地事，无怨无悔献身国防科技事业，其卓越成就和崇高品德将彪炳共和国科技发展与创新的千秋史册。

从整体来说，在创新驱动发展战略的指引下，在大众创业、万众创新浪潮中脱颖而出的 50 位"科学与技术进步奖""科学与技术创新奖"获奖人科技成果丰硕、创新业绩喜人，都有一张十分靓丽的成绩单。他们是我国优秀科技人才、战略科技人才、领军科技人才、青年科技人才的缩影。与往年相比，有几个特点：

一是国防科技领域重大成果彰显大国实力。无人自主水下航行器的技术研究，实现了我国自航水雷技术的跨越式发展；"长征七号"运载火箭的成功发射，为我国空间站建设打下坚实基础；歼-20 战斗机的成功研制，实现了我国航空武器装备创新能力的历史性跨越，使我国拥有了真正意义上的制空权。

二是基础研究原创性成果突出。例如，Sp 杂化的二维石墨炔材料，引领了国际上二维碳材料的发展新方向；二维黑磷晶体场效应管，在少量黑磷晶体观察到量子振荡现象和整数量子霍尔效应，使得磷烯成为继石墨烯之后的又一个二维晶体量子材料体系。

三是产学研合作激发创新创业热情。例如，环保型阻燃热塑性树脂关键技术的突破，从根本上扭转了国外相关产品的垄断局面；流波束赋形无线传输技术成为 TD-LTE 4G 国际标准的标志性核心技术，为移动通信成为具有国际竞争力的高科技领域之一做出了突出贡献。

四是科技成果转化效益突出。例如，集成电路非易失存储器的研究和开发，改变了我国集成电路高端产品研发依赖国外技术的被动局面；特种污染水防控和密闭空间生命保障的理论及环境工程技术研究，构建了特殊区域环境污染控制体系，对推动我国特种污染防治事业做出了重要贡献。

五是区域创新全面服务地方发展。例如，我国优秀科技工作者不忘初心，28 年扎根西北边疆，树立起国家生态屏障，改变恶劣环境，创造了巨大的生态和经济效益。

六是医学药学领域群英荟萃竞争激烈。今年从 100 多名被提名人中脱颖而出的 8 名获奖科学家均是我国医学、药学和生命科学领域的领军人物。其中，有成功研制基因型新兴"重组埃博拉疫苗"，进军生物危害防控前沿领域，实现重大突破的巾帼科学家；有在眼科、口腔、基因诊断、创伤修复等小学科领域奋发有为、科研成果大放异彩的优秀人才。

七是香港杰出人才脱颖而出，内地与香港合作成果喜人。在聚集诱导发光前沿领域取得了一系列原创性和引领性的研究成果，开创了由我国香港科学家引领、多国科学家竞相跟进的崭新领域。再有，由基金捐款人代表创建的梁铼琚脑科学研究中心，从事培养高端神经解剖学人才，研究痛与镇痛神经机制，也取得一系列原创成果。

八是中青年人才和海归人才成创新主要力量。今年获奖人年龄最大的 92 岁，年龄最小的 40 岁，平均年龄为 56 岁，50 岁以下的约占 13.5%，50～60 岁的约占 71.2%，60 岁以上的约占 15.3%，获奖人员年龄梯次和结构更加优化。海外归国人员比例达到 69.2%，中青年人才和海外归国人员已经成为科技创新的主要力量。他们在产学研合作创新、在军民深度融合创新、在科技成果转化和推进产业转型升级方面所做出的贡献，得到我国科技界、教育界和社会各界的高度认同。

值得一提的是，今年获奖科学家科学论文、发明专利等业绩良好。"科学与技术进步奖"34 位获奖人发表论文 5804 篇，人均 170.7 篇；"科学与技术创新奖"16 位获奖人发表论文 784 篇，人均 49 篇，与去年基本持平。在授权发明专利方面，今年 52 位获奖科学家拥有专利 1653 项，人均 31.8 项，比去年人均专利数提高 13.1%。

我每年作工作报告，讲到这里，总想说两句肺腑感言。这些年，每年被提名人数从 400 增加到 500，去年突破 600，今年增加到 627 人。何梁何利基金科技奖影响大、人气旺、含金量高，提名踊跃，这是好事。但由于全球经济低迷，通过资本运营的新增盈余作为奖金，今年较去年虽略有增加，也只有 1200 万港元。面对提名人数增多和奖金总额有限这一矛盾，评选委员会的唯一办法只能是优中选优，在充分评议的基础上，由评委独立判断，用选票形成评委会的最终决定。今年初评按 6：1 产生候选人，终评按 2：1 评出获奖人，总的入选率为（12～13）：1。这中间难免留下一些遗憾。有些优秀科技工作者落选，确实令人惋惜。不过，我想说的是：第一，欢迎提名，欢迎参评，这是勇于挑战自我的表现，也是对何梁何利基金的支持；第二，理性乐见两种可能的参评结果，入选欣然，落选坦然，顺其自然；第三，何梁何利科技奖一年一届，可以年年参评，年年有机会。何梁何利科技奖的大门，永远向投身祖国科技事业的杰出科技人才敞开。

同志们，朋友们！

1994 年春天，在香港回归祖国的前夜，香港爱国金融实业家何善衡、梁銶琚、何添和利国伟先生共同捐款 4 亿港币，于香港注册成立以他们姓氏命名的慈善基金——何梁何利基金。光阴荏苒，岁月如梭，弹指间 20 多年过去了，四位基金创立者均在 90 多岁高龄驾鹤西去，我们深深地怀念他们。令人高兴的是，四位捐款人的家属、子女秉承父辈志向，继续推进这项崇高的奖励事业，砥砺前行。20 多年来，基金信托委员会、评选委员会、投资委员会及广大境内外同人不忘初心，牢记使命，同心协力，开拓进取，恪守公平公正公开的评选原则，努力打造具有权威性和公信力的中国特色奖励品牌，如穿石之水滴、断木之绳锯，使得何梁何利基金成为我国社会力量设立科技奖励的杰出代表和成功典范，受到社会各界的广泛关注和普遍赞誉，这是我国科技界、教育界和社会各界共同努力的结果。今后，基金同人将铭记刘延东副总理和各位领导的殷切期望和重要指示，不负众望，不辱使命，承前启后，继往开来，努力把何梁何利奖办成国际一流的科技大奖，为建设创新型国家再立新功。

各位嘉宾、同志们、朋友们，党的第十九次全国代表大会已胜利闭幕，建设中国特色社会主义强国的航程已经开启。党的十九大报告指出：创新是引领发展的第一动力，是建设现代化经济体系的战略支撑。让我们紧密团结在以习近平同志为核心的党中央周围，认真地学习和贯彻党的十九大精神，为推进创新驱动发展战略、决胜全面建成小康社会、实现中华民族伟大复兴的中国梦做出更大贡献。

谢谢大家！

2017 WORK REPORT OF THE SELECTION BOARD OF HO LEUNG HO LEE FOUNDATION

Zhu Lilan, Chairwoman of the Trust Board and Director of the Selection Board

（October 25, 2017）

Dear Mr. Zhang Baowen, Vice Chairman of the Standing Committee of the National People's Congress:

Dear Mr. Wan Gang, Vice Chairman of the Chinese People's Political Consultative Conference and Minister of Science and Technology:

Dear guests, comrades and friends:

Beijing boasts autumn clear sky and fresh air in this fruitful season of October. Today, we hold the 2017 award ceremony of HLHL Foundation at the Diaoyutai State Guesthouse in Beijing. This ceremony is held at a jubilant time when the 19th National Congress of the CPC is concluded, when it is time to celebrate the 20th anniversary of the returning of Hong Kong to the motherland, and when the construction of the socialism with Chinese characteristics enters a new age. This ceremony will grant prizes of HLHL Foundation to 52 outstanding science and technology workers, which is of important significance. Vice premier Liu Yandong sent a letter to warmly congratulate the opening of this award–granting ceremony. The letter extends warm congratulations to the prize–winning scientists on behalf of the State Council, expresses the lofty respect for the representatives of donors, and extends sincere greetings to the broad masses of science and technology workers. Mr. Zhang Baowen, vice chairman of the Standing Committee of the National People's Congress and Mr. Wan Gang, vice chairman of the Chinese Political Consultative Conference and Minister of Science and Technology come to this meeting to give their guidance. Their arrival gives considerable encouragement to us. On behalf of all my colleagues at HLHL Foundation, I would express my heartfelt thanks to the leaders of the CPC and the state for their care and guidance, and extend my warm welcome to the representatives of donors, and the distinguished guests from the education circle, science and technology circle and all other walks of life on the mainland and Hong Kong for their presence at this ceremony.

Next, I will deliver the work report on behalf of the Selection Board.

I. About the Selection Work of HLHL Foundation in 2017

On June 6, 2017, the Trust Board of HLHL Foundation held the plenary meeting at Bank of China (Hong Kong). It deliberated and approved the report made by the Investment Board on the investment of last year, and deliberated and approved the 2016 work report of the Selection Board and the 2017 work plan. In 2016, despite unclear global economic situation and fragile global economic recovery, the HLHL Foundation maintained stable financial conditions on the whole. By the end of March 2017, the market value of the investment made by HLHL Foundation reached 683 million HK dollars. Compared with the initial market value of the investment, which stood at 390 million HK dollars when HLHL Foundation was established in March 1994, the current market value of the investment of HLHL Foundation has registered a 75 percent total increase and a 3.27 percent of annual increase in its capitals, under the precondition that the annual award-granting activities are normally held. Impacted by global economic environment, it is hard to expect that there will be a big increase in the revenues of the Foundation in a short period of time. However, we are fully confident that under the prudent management of and wise response from the Investment Board, we can ensure the normal operation of award-granting activities by maintaining a certain level of investment benefits.

Based on comprehensive economic prediction, the Trust Board decided the budget for the total amount of the prize money to be granted this year would be 12 million HK dollars, which is slightly higher than the amount of last year. The sum of money does not come by easily. We would like to express our thanks to the Investment Board for the precious contributions they made under hard conditions.

Early this year, the office of the Selection Board sent more than 2200 nomination forms to effective proposers at both home and abroad. Within the prescribed period of time, the Board received 683 recommendation materials. There were 627 effective nominees, hitting a new record. In particular, the recommendation materials and the effective nominees for the Prize for Scientific and Technological Innovation both exceeded 200, setting new records. Such new records reflect from a certain perspective the enhancement in the prestige and influences of HLHL scientific and technological awards in the eyes of science and technology workers. These new records also pose a new challenge to our efforts to do a good job in evaluation.

On July 3–7 this year, the special review meeting of HLHL Foundation was held at Beijing Railway Hotel. A total of 72 candidates for the Prize of Scientific and Technological Progress and 28 candidates for the Prize of Scientific and Technological Innovation were determined after the preliminary expert evaluation. The Prize for Scientific and Technological Achievements is the top prize of HLHL Foundation. As it is of the highest rank, the selection of the winners of the Prize for Scientific and Technological Achievements is the most important task in the selection work. In accordance with the relevant stipulations in the Selection Regulation, the preliminary review team was established. It was composed of some members of the specialized review committees and members of the Selection Board from the mainland of China under the leadership of the general secretary Duan Ruichun. The members of the preliminary review team conducted the field investigation and hearing. After making comprehensive appraisal, they selected two candidates for the Prize for Scientific and Technological Achievements. The list of all the above-mentioned candidates was submitted to the plenary meeting of the Selection Board for deliberation and approval.

On August 29, the Selection Board of HLHL Foundation held a plenary meeting at Beijing Friendship Hotel. Based on scientific evaluation following the principle of "selecting the top from among the excellent candidates" and voting by ballot, the Board selected two winners of the "Prize for Scientific and Technological Achievements", 34 winners of the "Prize for Scientific and Technological Progress", and 16 winners of the "Prize for Scientific and Technological Innovation", satisfactorily completing the work of selecting the prize winners this year.

II. General Information about the Prize-winning Scientists This Year

The year of 2017 marks the 90th anniversary of the founding of the People's Liberation Army of China. The top prize of HLHL Foundation– "Prize for Scientific and Technological Achievements" would be granted to two eminent scientists who have devoted their lives to the construction of nuclear-powered submarine and nuclear power plant—the two pieces of treasure symbolic of a major country. One of them is a renowned expert on nuclear power who was the first chief designer of China's nuclear submarine and a leading figure in introducing, transforming, independent designing and innovation of nuclear power plant. The other winner is a renowned expert on the overall design of nuclear submarine, who has served as the chief designer of China's nuclear submarine for many years and has contributed greatly to the creation and upgrading of the first-generation nuclear submarine, the designing of the second-generation nuclear submarine that caught up with and surpassed the world advanced level, and the leapfrogging development of the third-generation nuclear submarine. Under extremely hard conditions, they have lived in incognito for decades. They have devoted their lives to developing science and technology of national defense with neither complaints nor regret, and accomplished incredible deeds. With their outstanding achievements and lofty virtues, they will always be remembered in the history of the scientific and technological development and innovation in the People's Republic of China.

Overall speaking, under the guidance of the strategy of innovation-driven development, 50 people have won "Prize for Scientific and Technological Progress" and "Prize for Scientific and Technological Innovation" in the wave of mass entrepreneurship and innovation. They have all made fruitful achievements and performed satisfactorily in their efforts to make innovations. With their remarkable success, they have become the epitome of the excellent technology talents, talents in the field of strategic science and technology, leading technological talents, and young technological talents. Compared with the winners of the previous years, the winners of 2017 and their achievements have the following characteristics:

First, the significant achievements in the field of national defense science and technology demonstrate the strength of a major country. The technological research results in independently developed unmanned underwater vehicle represent the leapfrogging development of SLLM in China. The successful launching of Long March 7 Carrier Rocket lays a solid foundation for the construction of China's space station. The successful development of J-20 fighter realizes the historical breakthrough in

China's capability of making innovations in aviation weapon and equipment, and enables China to have the command of the air in real sense.

Second, outstanding original achievements in basic research have been scored. For example, the development of Sp hybridized 2D graphdiyne opens a new direction for the international development of 2D carbon materials. The development of 2D black phosphorus field-effect transistors makes it possible to observe the phenomenon of quantum oscillation and integer quantum Hall effect in a small amount of black phosphorous crystals. Thus phosphorene becomes another 2D quantum crystal material system following graphene.

Third, the collaboration between enterprises, universities and research institutes kindles the enthusiasm for making innovations and starting business. For example, the breakthrough in the key technology of environmentally-friendly flame-retardant thermal plastic resin fundamentally puts an end to the monopoly of the relevant foreign products. Stream beam-forming wireless transmission technology has become the symbolic core technology of the international standard of TD-LTE 4G, which greatly contributes to making mobile telecommunication one of the internationally competitive hi-tech fields.

Fourth, outstanding benefits have been obtained through commercialization of scientific and technological achievements. For example, the research and development of volatile memory in the integrated circuit changes the passive situation where China had to depend on foreign technologies in its development of high-end integrated circuit products. The theoretical research and the research on environmental engineering technology on the prevention and control of specially polluted water and the life support in confined space constitute a system for controlling the environmental pollution in special area, and make important contributions to the prevention and treatment of special pollution in China.

Fifth, regional innovations serve the regional development in a comprehensive way. For example, an excellent science and technology worker never forgets his original intention, and has worked in the north-western border area for 28 years. He has made contributions to establishing a national ecological protective screen to change the harsh environment, and his efforts have created considerable ecological and economic benefits.

Sixth, there is fierce competition between excellent talents in the fields of medicine and pharmacy. Eight winners selected from more than 100 nominees are all leading scientists in the fields of medicine, pharmacy and life science in China. Of these scientists, there are women scientists who have successfully developed the genotype−based new "recombinant Ebola vaccine", and have realized significant breakthrough in the cutting−edge field of the prevention and control of biological hazard. There are also excellent talents who have made considerable accomplishments in the "minor" subjects of ophthalmology, oral medicine, genetic diagnosis and trauma repair.

Seventh, outstanding Hong Kong talents have come to the fore, and the results of the collaboration between the mainland of China and Hong Kong are gratifying. A series of original and leading research results obtained in the cutting edge area of aggregation−induced emission (AIE) opens an entirely new research field in which Hong Kong scientists take the lead and are followed by scientists from various countries. In addition, the Leung Kao Kui Center for Brain Science Research established by a representative of the donors to HLHL Foundation is engaged in cultivating the high−end talents in the field of neuroanatomy, and conducting the research in the neural mechanism of pain and alleviation of pain. The Center has also obtained a number of original research results.

Eighth, middle−aged and young talents and the talents returning from abroad have become the main force of making innovations. This year, the oldest winner is 92 years old, while the youngest winner is only 40 years old. The average age of winners is 56 years. The winners aged below 50 account for about 13.5 percent of all the winners; those aged between 50 and 60 account for about 71.2 percent; and those aged above 60 account for about 15.3 percent. The age distribution and structure of the winners is more improved. The winners who returned from abroad account for 69.2 percent of all the winners. Middle−aged and young talents and the talents returning from abroad have become the main force of making innovations. They have contributed to making innovations through the collaboration between enterprises, universities and research institutes, making innovations through deepened civil−military integration, commercialization of scientific achievements, and promoting the industrial transformation and upgrading. Their contributions have been highly recognized by science and technology circle, education circle, and people from all other walks of life.

It is noteworthy that prize-winning scientists this year have shown excellent performances in terms of their academic papers, inventions and patents. The 34 winners of "Prize for Scientific and Technological Progress" have published 5804 academic papers, or 170.7 papers for each person. The 16 winners of "Prize for Scientific and Technological Innovation" have published 784 academic papers, or 49 papers for each person, almost the same as that of the last year. In terms of the authorized inventions and patents, the 52 prize-winning scientists this year have possessed 1653 patents, or 31.8 patents for each person, with a 13.1 percent increase in the per capita number of patents.

Each year I would like to tell you something from the bottom of my heart when I come to this part of the work report. In recent years, the annual number of candidates increased from 400 to 500, and such a number exceeded 600 last year and reaches 627 this year. The scientific and technological prizes of HLHL Foundation have great influences, enjoy much popularity, and carry great weight. That's why there are so many nominees each year. This is a good thing. However, due to the sluggish global economy, the total prize money which is drawn from the surplus generated from the capital operation is only 12 million HK dollars, albeit a slight increase than that of last year. To resolve the contradiction between an increasing number of nominees and the limited total amount of prize money, the Selection Board could do nothing but observe the principle of selecting the best from among the excellent candidates. Based on full discussions, the members of the Selection Board made their independent judgment and made the final decision as to prize winners by casting ballots. This year, the candidates in the preliminary selection were put up in accordance with the proportion of one candidate from six nominees, and the candidates in the final selection were put up in accordance with the proportion of one candidate from two nominees. So for each 12 or 13 candidates, there is only one prize winner. There must have been regrets, to be sure. It is indeed unfortunate for some excellent science and technology workers to fail to be selected as prize winners. However, I would like to say that first, we welcome the participation in nomination and selection, because this represents a bold move to challenge oneself and a support for HLHL Foundation; second, we hope all nominees can accept readily two possible outcomes: they will either feel happy when they are selected or remain calm when they fail to be selected; in sum, they should prepare themselves for any outcome; third, as the prizes of HLHL Foundation are selected and granted each year, science and technology workers can participate in the selection each year and they stand chance of winning the prizes each year. The gate of the scientific and technological prizes of HLHL Foundation is always open to the outstanding science and technology talents engaged in scientific and technological undertaking of China.

Comrades and Friends!

Patriotic Hong Kong financers Ho Sin-hang, Leung Kau-Kui, Ho Tim and Lee Quo-Wei registered and established Ho Leung Ho Lee Foundation with a donation of 400 million HK dollars in the spring of 1994, on the eve of Hong Kong's return to the motherland. In the blink of eyes, more than 20 years have passed. Four founders of HLHL Foundation have all passed away successively in their nineties. We will always cherish the memory of them. It is gratifying that the family members of these four financers including their children continue to fulfill the aspirations of these founders by further promoting this lofty undertaking despite hardships. For more than 20 years, the Trust Board, Selection Board and Investment Board and colleagues from both China and abroad never forget their original intentions, bear in mind the mission of HLHL Foundation, work together with one heart, make pioneering efforts, observe the principle of "fairness, justice and openness" in selection of prize-winners, and work hard to make the HLHL awards a prestigious and trustworthy awarding brand with Chinese characteristics. Thanks to their constant and unremitting efforts, HLHL Foundation has become an outstanding representative and successful example of the science and technology awards established by private sectors in China. HLHL Foundation has received wide attention from all walks of life and has been praised extensively. This is the result of the concerted efforts made by the science and technology circle, education circle and all other walks of life in China. In the future,

· 32 ·

the colleagues of HLHL Foundation will bear in mind the sincere expectations and important instructions of vice premier Liu Yandong and all other leaders, live up to people's expectations, bring the mission of HLHL Foundation to success, carry forward the undertaking pioneered by predecessors and forge ahead into the future. They will work hard to make HLHL Foundation a world-class science and technology award, and make new contributions to making China an innovative country.

Dear guests, comrades and friends, the 19th National Congress of the CPC has been successfully concluded, and China has embarked on the voyage of building a socialist country with Chinese characteristics. It is pointed out in the report delivered to the 19th National Congress of the CPC that "Innovation is the primary driving force for development; it is the strategic underpinning for building a modernized economy." Let's rally closely around the Central Committee of the CPC with comrade Xi Jinping at its core, earnestly study and implement the principles of the 19th National Congress of the CPC, and make still more contributions to promoting the implementation of the innovation-driven strategy, secure a decisive victory in building a moderately prosperous society in all respects, and to fulfill the Chinese Dream of the great rejuvenation of the Chinese nation.

Thank you!

目　录

何梁何利基金科学与技术创新奖获得者传略

附　录

CONTENTS

PROFILES OF THE AWARDEES OF PRIZE FOR SCIENTIFIC AND
TECHNOLOGICAL INNOVATION OF HO LEUNG HO LEE FOUNDATION

APPENDICES

何梁何利基金科学与技术成就奖获得者传略

PROFILES OF THE AWARDEES OF PRIZE FOR
SCIENTIFIC AND TECHNOLOGICAL ACHIEVEMENTS OF
HO LEUNG HO LEE FOUNDATION

彭 士 禄

彭士禄，1925 年出生于广东省海丰县，1956 年毕业于莫斯科化工机械学院，1958 年修毕于莫斯科动力学院核动力专业。历任中国原子能科学研究院核动力研究室副主任、核动力研究所副总工程师、核潜艇研究所副总工程师、中国舰船研究院副院长、造船工业部副部长兼总工程师、核潜艇总设计师、水电部副部长兼总工程师、大亚湾核电站董事长兼总经理、核工业部总工程师、秦山核电二期工程董事长，中国核学会名誉理事长。1994 年，选聘为中国工程院首批院士。

彭士禄一直从事核动力事业的开拓与发展，为我国核潜艇、核电站的持续发展做出了突出贡献。

一、担任核潜艇第一任总设计师，实现我国核潜艇从无到有的历史性突破

1. 主持第一座核潜艇陆上模式堆的设计建造及运行

（1）结合我国需求和工业基础，确定第一艘核潜艇采用分散布置压水堆的技术路线，确保了研制进程。

（2）主持开展各种气候条件下扩散试验等工作，以科学数据力排众议，确定厂址为西南某地。

（3）开创性研发反应堆一维燃耗计算程序，建立一代核动力反应堆物理设计方法。

（4）针对当时主泵输送能力及反应堆尺寸受限，巧妙提出了采用圆形燃料元件盒、同心圆布置的双流程堆芯技术方案。

（5）突破性提出采用一个驱动机构带动多根控制棒的组合传动控制技术。

（6）首次建立了核动力装置稳态和瞬态主参数计算方法，确定核动力总体技术参数，后期运行表明参数选取合理安全。

（7）发挥全国大协作精神，组织完成主泵、压力容器等多台（套）关键设备的首次自主研制，达到当时世界先进水平。

第一座陆上模式堆历经 5 年，于 1970 年反应堆顺利达到临界和满功率，实现了我国大陆第一次原子能发电。

2. 主持我国第一艘核潜艇的设计建造

作为第一任总设计师，负责核动力装置的设计研制，坚持模式堆和核潜艇基本同步开展，创新性提出并完成核动力装置进舱安装模型，有效释放技术风险，创造了首艇核动力装置不足 5 个月完成安装的奇迹；在首艇试航过程中，解决了核动力装置冷启动等多个关键技术问题。

我国第一艘核潜艇在陆上模式堆临界一年后成功下水，使我国成为世界上第五个拥有核潜艇的国家。

3. 指导我国军用核动力技术持续发展

卸任总师后，彭士禄仍担任国防科工委核潜艇技术顾问。长期参与第一代潜艇核动力的改进和升级工作；指导后续潜艇核动力的技术论证预研，为反应堆主参数、堆芯布置等性能提升做出了贡献；指导新型潜艇核动力技术方向和总体技术方案，提升核动力装置安全性、可靠性；指导大型水面舰船核动力技术战略发展，逐步明晰总体技术性能目标图像。

二、开创我国核电站自主设计与建设，促进我国核电持续发展

1. 力推我国第一座核电站采用压水堆路线

1974 年，在我国第一座核电站——秦山一期反应堆选型论证过程中，彭士禄根据核潜艇的成功经验和当时国家技术水平，力推采用压水堆路线、功率为 30 万千瓦的技术方案，为采用压水堆路线做出贡献。

2.组织引进我国第一座百万千瓦级核电站——大亚湾核电站

1983年，彭士禄被任命为大亚湾核电厂建设总指挥、水利部副部长、国务院核电领导小组成员，负责大亚湾核电站的引进、总体设计和前期工作。在选址过程中，组织完成水温、气象、地震等具体工作；及时决策，组织现场高效率、超常规完成了核电站前期的"四通一平"工作；参与法国M310核电技术和管理方法的引进工作，亲自验算部分反应堆主参数；提出核电工程的进度、投资、质量三大控制管理方法。

3.组织建造第一座商用大型核电站——秦山二期核电站

1986年，彭士禄被任命为核工业部总工程师，后担任秦山联营公司董事长，作为技术型的负责人，组织了秦山二期核电站的设计与建造工作。

（1）根据当时电力市场和工业基础，组织确定了自主设计60万千瓦压水堆的技术方案。亲自参与计算主参数，指挥完成法国M310三环路改两环路的自主设计工作，组织完成两环路的所有设计数据重新计算和试验验证，并实现工程应用。具备了自主产权的30万千瓦/环路百万千瓦级压水堆的国际标准设计能力。

（2）坚持设备国产化。借助全国大协作精神，亲自带队到主要设备厂进行调研，确定重点设备的采购和厂商合作方案，为55项重点设备中压力容器、主泵、汽轮发电机等47项实现国产化发挥了关键作用。

（3）重视管理机制创新。提出"业主负责制、招投标制、工程监理制"，确保工程顺利实施，有效控制建设成本，其投资是国内已建成核电站中最低的，低于发达国家平均造价。

秦山二期核电站安全运行已进入世界核电运营者协会（WANO）的先进行列。培养的设计人才队伍和形成的设备自主研制能力，结合后续技术发展，推动我国自助设计的三代核电技术与美、法、俄等比肩。同时，秦山二期核电的设计标准、计算程序、研制能力等成功经验为我国后续潜艇核动力研发做出了贡献，是军民融合的又一典范。

4.建言献策，指导我国核电技术持续发展

多次为我国核电发展规划建言献策。策划召开了"合作共赢，促进核电和谐发展"大型年会并作主题报告，有力地推动了我国核电产业的健康发展。多次现场考察指导秦山核电二期3/4号机组扩建、三门核电、海南昌江核电等核电站建设，并对我国快堆建设、空间堆试验等进行指导。

三、获奖情况

彭士禄既是组织领导者、重大技术问题的决策者，又是研究设计的直接参与者、带头人。1978年荣获全国科学大会奖；1983年，"196反应堆总体设计"获国防科技进步奖一等奖（第一完成人）；1985年，"核潜艇的研究设计"获国家科学技术进步奖特等奖（第一完成人）；1988年获国防科工委为表彰全军各兵种优秀总设计师而颁发的"为国防科技事业做出了突出贡献"的荣誉奖；1996年获何梁何利基金科学与技术进步奖。

四、著作情况

1983 年，《关于广东核电站经济效益的汇报提纲》

1985 年，《核能在我国能源中的地位》，核动力工程

1985 年，《我国核能的展望》，工业设备与原料

1987 年，《中国核电发展的现状与展望》，Proceedings of the SixthP13NC

1989 年，《中国核能的现状和展望》，核科学与工程

1989 年，《为促进我国核电事业的发展而努力》，核动力工程

1993 年，《2×600MW 压水堆核电厂的上网电价计算与分析》，核动力工程

1995 年，《核能工业经济分析与评价基础》，原子能出版社

1996 年，《我国沿海地区急需加快发展核电》，核经济研究

1997 年，《核能是能源可持续发展的希望》，世界科技研究与发展

1997 年，《中国"巨鲸"人民智慧的结晶》，现代舰船

1998 年，《核能——高科技产业的前景》（上、下），科学学与科学技术管理

Profile of Peng Shilu

Peng Shilu was born in Haifeng County of Guangdong Province in 1925, graduated from Moscow Chemical Machinery University in 1956 and National Research University Moscow Nuclear Power Engineering Institute in 1958. Chief engineer and chief designer of nuclear submarine of the Ship-Building Ministry, vice minister and chief engineer of the Ministry of Water Resources, president and general manager of the Daya Bay Nuclear Power Station, chief engineer of CNNC, president of the Qinshan Phase II, as well as honorary president of CNS. He was elected as one of the first group of academicians of the Chinese Academy of Engineering in 1994.

Peng Shilu devotes himself to exploration and development of nuclear power industry in China, making prominent contributions to the sustainable development of China's nuclear submarines and nuclear power plants.

1. As the first chief designer of nuclear submarine, historic breakthrough from scratch has been achieved in China's nuclear submarine technology, realized atomic power generation for the first time in mainland China

（1）Peng presided over the design, construction and operation of the first land-based prototype nuclear submarine reactor in China. He selected the dispersed arrangement of PWR for China's first nuclear submarine, initiated the one-dimensional burn-up calculation code physical design method, proposed smart application of the circular fuel element case and concentric circle arrangement of the double-pass core technology scheme, proposed the combined drive control technology, established the calculation method for the main parameters, led independent development of much key equipment for the first time in China.

（2）As the first chief designer of nuclear submarine in China, he took charge of the design and development of nuclear power facilities. The first nuclear submarine after land-based prototype reaching the critical for one year made China the fifth owner of nuclear submarine in the world.

（3）After leaving his post as chief designer of nuclear submarine, Peng is still engaged as the national technical consultant. Peng guided the successive development of military nuclear power technology in China.

2. Peng initiated independent design and construction of nuclear power plants, which promoted continuous growth of China's nuclear power industry

（1）The first domestic nuclear power plant of China, Peng Shilu strongly proposed to adopt the 300MW PWR scheme based on experiences gained from development of nuclear submarine and technologies owned by China at that time.

（2）Peng organized the introduction of the first 1000MW nuclear power plant to China—Daya Bay Nuclear Power Station. He directed the import, general design and preparatory work related to the first 1000MW nuclear power plant in China.

（3）Peng organized construction of Qinshan Phase II, the first large commercial nuclear power plant of China. China independent gained the capability of international level to design 300MW/loop type 1000MW PWR. He insisted on the localization of equipment manufacturing. The specific investment is the lowest in domestic nuclear power plants and is even lower than the average cost in developed countries. Qinshan Phase II project has been listed on WANO for its safety on operation. HPR1000 rank the international advanced level, and compete with that of countries such as the United States, France, and Russia.

（4）Peng provided advices on the continuous development of nuclear power technology in China. He conducted field visits to direct construction of nuclear power plants.

Peng has been awarded many national prizes, including the National Scientific Conference Award in 1978, the first prize in National Defense Science and Technology Progress Award as the leading participant in 1983, the special prize in The State Scientific and Technological Progress Award for "the research and design of nuclear submarines" as the leading participant in 1985, the honorary award of "outstanding contributions to national defense science and technology" in 1988, the Prize for Scientific & Technological Progress of the Ho Leung Ho Lee Foundation in 1996.

黄 旭 华

  黄旭华，1926 年出生于广东省汕尾市。1949 年毕业于上海交通大学造船专业，获学士学位。1951—1958 年任职于上海船舶工业管理局，1958—1961 年任北京海军造船技术研究室工程师、副总工程师，1961—1965 年任国防部第七研究院〇九研究室、十五研究所副总工程师。1965 年至今，历任中国船舶重工集团公司第七一九研究所副总工程师、所长、名誉所长，是我国核潜艇工程第一代副总设计师、总设计师。1994 年，选聘为中国工程院首批院士。

  黄旭华自 1958 年起一直致力于我国核潜艇事业的开拓与发展，是我国研制核潜艇的先驱者之一，在核潜艇总体设计、快速性和操纵性研究、大直径艇体结构设计计算、重大试验等方面做了一系列开创性研究工作，为我国第一代核潜艇的从无到有、第二代核潜艇的跨越发展和第三代核潜艇的探索赶超做出了卓越贡献。

一、先后担任核潜艇工程副总设计师和总设计师，主持我国第一代核潜艇的研制，实现了我国核潜艇从无到有的历史性突破

核潜艇的研制是一项技术非常复杂、综合性强、要求高、协作面广、研制周期长、成本高的国防尖端高新工程，就像一座现代化的水中城市，在有限空间内集现代潜艇技术、水下核能技术、水下导弹技术和核弹技术以及水下导弹机动发射技术于一身，是一个国家科学技术水平与工业生产能力的缩影。

我国第一代核潜艇的研制工作是在极其艰苦的条件下起步的。面对各国严密的技术封锁，黄旭华从情报调查研究工作入手，摸清了国外的研制情况和发展趋势，深入了解了国内科研和生产水平，合理地制定了我国第一代核潜艇艇体总体和全艇主要设备配置方案，解决了核潜艇总体设计难题，实现了我国第一代核潜艇总体设计的"化繁为简、总体集成、完全自主、100%国产"。在我国第一艘核潜艇的线型选择上，他大胆提出并决策直接采用水滴线型，出色地解决了水滴型核潜艇高、低速下的稳定性和操纵性难题，实现了我国"核动力水滴型"的一步到位。作为艇体结构研究设计的带头人，他论证了导弹舱的多种结构方案，推导了导弹舱大型复杂耐压结构新的设计计算方法，攻克了大直径艇体结构设计与建造重大技术难题。作为技术总负责人之一，他组织、指挥了核潜艇系泊航行试验、水下发射运载火箭、深潜试验等一系列重大试验，及时解决了试验中发现的技术问题，从技术上保证了试验任务的圆满成功。尤其是最危险的极限深潜试验，他作为总师亲自参加并及时分析试验采集的数据，成为世界上核潜艇总设计师亲自下水做深潜试验的第一人。

在他的带领下，先后突破了水滴形艇型、大直径艇体结构、艇用核动力装置、远程水声系统、惯性导航系统、鱼雷指控设备、综合空调系统七项最为关键、最为重大的核潜艇技术（被誉为"七朵金花"），解决了我国核潜艇的有无问题，实现了毛主席"核潜艇，一万年也要搞出来"的伟大誓言，使我国拥有了海上核威慑和核反击能力。

二、主持第一代核潜艇的现代化改装，大幅提升在役核潜艇的综合作战、反潜隐身等技术水平

在一代艇的现代化改装中，他主持了总体方案设计研究，开展了新技术应用于核潜艇的可行性和适应性分析，解决了新设备与艇总体的协调匹配性、电磁兼容性和可靠性设计等问题，提出了现代化改换装的总体方案；提出采用新型螺旋桨等新技术，显著降低了第一代核潜艇的水下噪声，提高了艇的隐蔽性；综合集成了当时最先进的鱼雷武器、水声对抗武器和综合声呐系统，大幅提升了一代艇的综合作战能力；提出了核潜艇延寿论断和经济、安全的退役处理总体方案，使一代艇的服役期增加1/3以上，满足了当时形势下海军的作战需求。

三、主持第二代核潜艇预先研究工作，为核潜艇的跨越式发展奠定重要基础

在第二代核潜艇立项之前，他提出了二代艇的概念图像，梳理了关键技术并开展预先研究工作。他梳理了战略导弹新的发射方式面临的主要困难，应用系统工程方法分析了总体、水动力、结构、武备和操艇等多专业间的复杂耦合关系，并组织力量论证了解决方法，为二代艇实现战略核威慑能力的跨越提供了技术储备。基于预研工作，我国第二代核潜艇的研制取得了巨大成功，在国际上产生了重大反响。

四、指导未来核潜艇的发展，引领核潜艇技术创新超越

作为我国核潜艇领域的战略科学家，黄旭华始终关注世界科技前沿和国际军事变革，指导开展了我国未来核潜艇的发展型谱规划；指导探索了新一代隐身多用途核潜艇等多个创新概念；指导论证了水下作战体系的技术发展路线图，为我国未来核潜艇发展战略目标的制定提出了建设性意见和建议。

鉴于在我国核潜艇研制事业中所做出的突出成绩和贡献，黄旭华于 1978 年获全国科学大会奖（排名第一），1985 年获国家科技进步奖特等奖（排名第二），1985 年和 1993 年两次获中国船舶工业总公司科技进步奖特等奖（均排名第一），1995 年获何梁何利基金科学与技术进步奖，1996 年获国家科技进步奖特等奖（排名第一）。1986 年获中国船舶工业总公司授予的"劳动模范"称号，1988 年荣立中国船舶工业总公司一等功，1989 年被国务院授予"全国先进工作者"称号；1989 年起获国家政府特殊津贴，1994 年选聘为中国工程院首批院士；2009 年在国家海洋局、中央人民广播电台联合举办的新中国成立 60 周年海洋成就奖评选活动中，被评为"十大海洋人物"；2014 年荣获"感动中国十大人物"称号。

在为核潜艇的研制、突破一系列重大关键技术呕心沥血的同时，他时刻不忘自己肩负的另一个重要使命——为核潜艇研制事业培养新人。多年来，通过重点型号研制这一创新平台，他培养锻炼了一大批优秀的科技人才，其中中国工程院院士 1 位、船舶设计大师 3 位、中国船舶重工集团公司首席技术专家 2 位、核潜艇工程总设计师 1 位、型号总设计师 7 位、型号副总设计师 30 余位。

自 1958 年从事核潜艇研制工作开始，他坚守组织要求，不透露工作单位、工作性质，隐姓埋名 30 年，他的家人不知道他在做什么，他也没有回过一次老家探望双亲，他的父亲直至去世都没有见到他。1988 年南海深潜试验，黄旭华顺道探视母亲，95 岁的母亲与儿子对视却无语凝噎，30 年后再相见，62 岁的他也已双鬓斑白。

黄旭华为我国核潜艇事业奉献了毕生的精力，为海基核力量建设做出了卓越贡献，在他的身上充分体现了"自力更生、艰苦奋斗、大力协同、无私奉献"的核潜艇精神。对他而言，选择了核潜艇事业也就是选择了奉献，虽穷此一生，也无怨无悔。如今，年过九旬的他仍在为国防武器装备现代化建设殚精竭虑、献智献策，期盼中国核潜艇更上一层楼。

Profile of Huang Xuhua

Huang Xuhua was born in Shanwei City of Guangdong Province in 1926. He graduated from the major in Shipbuilding of Shanghai Jiao Tong University for his bachelor's degree in 1949. He was elected as one of the first group of academicians of the Chinese Academy of Engineering in 1994.

Huang Xuhua has been devoting himself to the initiation and development of Chinese nuclear submarines since 1958. As the first generation of deputy chief designer and then chief designer of Chinese nuclear submarine project, he led the research of Chinese first generation of torpedo attack nuclear submarines and strategic missile nuclear submarines, realizing a historic breakthrough for China. Huang Xuhua formulated the overall scheme and main equipment arrangement scheme of the first generation of nuclear submarines. He proposed and decided to adopt the droplet hull, realizing the "nuclear power droplet" goal directly. He deduced a new design calculation method of missile cabin large scale complicated pressure structure. He organized and led a series of significant experiment such as the nuclear submarine mooring sailing trial, lauch vehicle underwater launching test, and deep diving test.

And then, Huang Xuhua was in charge of the first generation of nuclear submarines modernization, enhancing the comprehensive fighting level of inservice nuclear submarines. He took charge of the advanced research of second generation of nuclear submarines and guided the future nuclear submarines development exploration work.

Huang Xuhua received various science and technology awards and honor. Such as the National Science Conference Award (ranking No.1) in 1978, the top award of National Science and Technology Progress Award (ranking No.2) in 1985 and the top award of National Science and Technology Progress Award (ranking No.1) in 1996. In 2014, he was elected as one of "The top 10 people moving China".

Huang Xuhua has lived incognito for 30 years and dedicated himself to Chinese nuclear submarine career. Now, over ninety years old, he still exhausts his thoughts and ingenuity and offers his wisdom and advice for the modernization of national defense weapons and equipment, looking forward to achieve greater progress of Chinese nuclear submarines.

何梁何利基金科学与技术进步奖获得者传略

PROFILES OF THE AWARDEES OF PRIZE FOR
SCIENTIFIC AND TECHNOLOGICAL PROGRESS OF
HO LEUNG HO LEE FOUNDATION

数学力学奖获得者

唐 志 共

唐志共，1965 年 5 月出生于广西壮族自治区全州县。1984 年毕业于国防科技大学空气动力学专业，1999 年取得南京航空航天大学硕士学位，2010 年取得西北工业大学博士学位。2000 年 8—12 月在澳大利亚国立大学做访问学者。1984 年起在中国空气动力研究与发展中心超高速空气动力研究所工作，历任助理工程师、工程师、高级工程师、副总工程师、副所长，2001—2011 年担任中国空气动力研究与发展中心副总工程师、研究员，2011 年 8 月至今担任中国空气动力研究与发展中心总工程师、研究员、博士生导师。唐志共是新世纪百千万人才工程国家级人选，"973" 项目技术首席专家，国家 "863" 计划重大项目责任专家；先后担任中国空气动力学会第六、第七届理事会副理事长，核心期刊《空气动力学学报》主编、《实验流体力学》副主编，国防科技大学、电子科技大学兼职教授。

唐志共长期从事空气动力学研究与应用，在高超声速风洞设备体系构建、试验理论和试验技术发展、新型飞行器气动设计等方面取得了系统性和创造性成果，在解决新型飞行器研制中的关键气动问题方面做出突出成绩，为我国空气动力学学科发展和空天飞行器研制做出了重大贡献。

一、规划并建立整体试验能力达到世界领先水平的高超声速风洞设备体系

临近空间高超声速飞行空域大、速域宽、跨流域，对其进行风洞试验模拟是世界难题，建立尺寸配套、参数衔接的试验研究体系是支撑高超飞行器研制的迫切需求。针对我国临近空间跨流域高超声速飞行器的发展需求，他提出了高超声速空气动力学地面试验设备体系规划，组织建成基本覆盖高超声速飞行环境的试验设备体系，整体性能世界领先。他负责研制 Φ1 米高超声速风洞，带领团队攻克电预热金属板蓄热式加热器、高温高压气流快速精确调节等关键技术，该风洞性能超美国同类设备；突破大功率气流加热、大流量气流快速换向等技术，实现风洞宽参数高精度控制，成功研制了 Φ2 米高超声速风洞，设备规模世界第一；主持研制 Φ1 米低密度风洞，创造性采用混合冷气消旋、双凹槽稳弧、旋转气流保护电极端面等设计思想，解决了电弧波动大、流场稳定性差、参数重复性低的技术难题。主持改造 Φ0.3 米低密度风洞，研制大功率石墨电阻和储热式电阻加热器，实现模拟高度从 80～94 千米下延至 27～94 千米。这些设备已成为我国空气动力学试验主力设备，支撑了我国近年来所有高超声速飞行器研制，在工程中发挥了重要作用。

二、研究发展高超声速试验模拟理论和试验技术，使我国高超声速飞行器气动特性预测能力达世界先进水平

大气层内的高超声速飞行仍有许多认识不清的领域，风洞试验理论与技术是准确预测高超声速气动力热特性的基础与关键。针对地面试验能力难以覆盖临近空间全程飞行的现状，唐志共系统研究了气动力／热、热结构／热匹配以及力／热联合模拟试验理论，提出一种新的基于黏性干扰关联参数的试验模拟准则，建立工程适用的试验数据外推和数据质量评估方法，解决了高超声速飞行器地面准确模拟、试验数据使用等问题，为飞行器地面试验提供了理论指导，为工程设计提供了重要依据。同时，提出飞行器内外流模拟试验方法和通气模型设计准则，建立了内外流一体化试验技术，解决了内外流相互干扰下气动力高精度测量难题，并系统研究飞行器进气道唇口流场结构与启动特性的关联规律，为某飞行器气动设计、进气道宽参数启动提供了解决方案。他创新融合 CTS、网格测力风洞试验和大规模并行多体分离数值模拟方法等手段，建立了高动压、大翼面、轻质体分离投放综合预测技术，地面预测结果与飞行试验一致。

三、开展高超声速飞行器气动关键技术攻关，攻克力热耦合、多学科优化设计等气动难题，完成多型飞行器气动设计

高超声速飞行器是当今世界空天领域的研究热点，在该领域取得新的科学认知、提出新的设计理念是引领高超飞行器创新发展的迫切需求。唐志共完成了国家高技术重大项目二型飞行器试验样机气动布局设计，提出"钝头体机身＋边条厚三角翼＋立尾"布局构型，攻克了气动力／热相容性、厚翼力矩强非线性、高速航向不安定性、垂直发射和低速水平降落等技术难题，发展了表面摩阻数据修正方法，准确获得了带防热瓦／毡的全机阻力系数，为飞行器成功实现无动力能量管理、进场着陆提供了保障。针对某新型飞行器挂飞投放、助推爬升、助推分离、高速巡航和高低速兼顾研制需求，他提出"尖头体身＋大三角翼＋翼尖垂尾"布局构型，解决了飞行器高空高速巡航、安全分离边界评估、能量管理自主返回等问题。同时完成临近空间某飞行器验证机气动设计，针对级间分离、头罩分离、进气道启动等研制需求，提出"轴对称弹身＋尾裙＋尾翼"布局构型，解决了进气道通流特性、舵轴／缝隙防热设计等难题，提出了基本模型加组合舵偏修正的混合模型气动力建模方法，建模精度比传统方法提高 1 倍以上。参与研制的飞行器飞行试验

均取得圆满成功。

唐志共获国家科技进步奖二等奖 5 项，部委级科技进步一等奖 7 项、二等奖 9 项、国家发明专利 5 项；曾获得中国青年科技奖、中国科协"求是奖"，被评为全国优秀科技工作者，今年获得首届全国创新争先奖。出版著作 2 部，分别是《高超声速气动力试验》《空气动力试验指挥概论》；出版译著 2 部，分别是《高超声速飞行器气动热力学设计问题精选》《航天飞行器空气动力学数据集》；在国内外学术期刊发表论文和撰写科技报告 120 余篇。指导 20 多名流体力学、航空宇航科学与技术专业硕士、博士研究生，带出一支在国内空气动力学界有较大影响的高超声速空气动力研究团队。

Awardee of Mathematics and Mechanics Prize, Tang Zhigong

Tang Zhigong was born in Quanzhou County of Guangxi Zhuang Autonomous Region in May 1965. He graduated from National University of Defense Technology（NUDT）in 1984, major in aerodynamics, and obtained PhD degree in 2010. Started the career in Hypervelocity Aerodynamics Institute of China Aerodynamics Research and Development Center（CARDC）in 1984. Visiting scholar in Australian National University（ANU）in 2000. From 2001 to 2011, served as Deputy Chief Engineer and Research Fellow of CARDC. And has been holding the position of Chief Engineer, Research Fellow and PhD Supervisor since August 2011. One of the state class persons of New Century National Talents Project, technical project chief of "Program 973", responsible project expert of "Program 863". Deputy Director of the sixth and seventh board of China Aerodynamics Research Society. Chief Editor of "ACTA Aerodynamica Sinica", Deputy Chief Editor of "Journal of Experiments of Fluid Mechanics", adjunct professor of NUDT and University of Electronic Science and Technology of China（UESTC）. Owns 5 Second-class National Prize for Progress in Science and Technology and 5 licenses of National Invention Patent. Winner of the First National Innovation Award, the Science and Technology Award for Chinese Youth.

Tang Zhigong has been long engaged in aerodynamics research and application, and has achieved systematic and creative goals in hypersonic wind tunnel's construction, test theory and test technology development, aerodynamic design of new flight vehicle, and other fields, achieving outstanding results in solving key aerodynamic problems of new flight vehicle development, and making great contributions to the development of Chinese aerodynamic discipline and aerospace vehicle. He planned and established the hypersonic wind tunnel system with test capability of world-wide leading level, supporting nearly all the Chinese hypersonic flight vehicles development. He improved the hypersonic test simulation theories and test technologies, and created the methods of data extrapolation and quality evaluation for wind tunnel test, solving the problem of accurate ground simulation and data use. He tackled the problems on thermo-mechanical coupling and multidisciplinary optimization design, completed the aerodynamic design of a series of flight vehicles, leading and promoting the development of Chinese hypersonic vehicle.

物理学奖获得者

陈 仙 辉

陈仙辉，1963 年 3 月出生于湖南省湘潭县。1992 年毕业于中国科学技术大学物理系，获理学博士学位，后留校工作至今。现为中国科学技术大学教授、中国科学院强耦合量子材料物理重点实验室主任。曾先后在德国卡尔斯鲁厄研究中心和斯图加特马普固体物理研究所、日本高等研究院（北陆）、美国休斯敦大学得克萨斯超导研究中心以及新加坡国立大学作为洪堡学者和访问教授进行学术交流。1998 年获国家自然科学基金委杰出青年基金，2002 年获聘教育部"长江学者"特聘教授，2015 年荣获国际超导材料领域最高奖马蒂亚斯奖，2015 年当选为中国科学院院士。

陈仙辉主要从事超导和量子材料的探索及其物理研究，取得了一系列重要创新成果。因在铁基超导体研究中突破麦克米兰极限，荣获 2013 年国家自然科学奖一等奖；发展了一种新超导体合成方法，并首次获得零电阻温度 43K 的新型铁硒类超导体——锂铁氢氧铁硒；首次使用锂离子导电玻璃陶瓷作为场效应管栅介质，在 FeSe 薄层中实现大范围的载流子浓度调控，获得 46K 的高温超导相，进一步观察到超导—绝缘态转变，开辟了利用固态离子导体门电压技术探索超导电性的研究方向；与合作者成功实现黑磷晶体场效应管，开辟了继石墨烯之后又一个量子功能材料领域。

一、突破常规超导体的麦克米兰温度极限

自 1986 年高温超导体第一次被发现以来，人们一直在努力寻找更多的高温超导体材料，希望能帮助人们进一步理解高温超导现象背后的物理机制以及实现室温下的超导电性。然而截至 2008 年，高温超导电性只在特定结构的铜氧化合物材料中被发现，如何突破这一材料瓶颈成了高温超导研究领域的核心问题。2008 年年初，日本科学家报道了一个 26K 的镧氧氟铁砷超导体，这一发现引起了超导科学界的关注。此前，具有二十几开超导转变温度的超导体也发现过几个，但后来证明并不都是具有非常规超导机制的高

温超导体，大家迫切关注的一个焦点问题就是铁基超导体是否是新的一类非常规高温超导体？

陈仙辉领导的实验小组对这一问题率先给出了答案。他首次在（常压下）铁基超导体中突破常规超导体的麦克米兰温度极限，证实了铁基超导体是除铜基高温超导体之外的又一类非常规高温超导体。该研究结果在 *Nature* 发表后，立刻引起了学术界的强烈关注，*Science*、*Nature*、*Physics Today* 等知名刊物对该工作均做了专门评述或亮点跟踪报道。《亚洲材料》亮点介绍中评述："陈仙辉和他的合作者把非磁性 La 用磁性的 Sm 替换后发现 $SmO_{1-x}F_xFeAs$ 的超导转变温度比日本小组报道的材料高将近 20K……这个发现具有非常重要的意义。由这个中国小组报道的超导转变温度比描述电声子相互作用导致超导的 BCS 理论的极限还要高。这些结果和后来由同一个组发现的更高的超导转变温度表明铁基超导体不能用传统的 BCS 理论解释。"该工作作为代表性成果之一，被美国 *Science* 杂志、美国物理学会和欧洲物理学会分别评为 2008 年度十大科技进展。*Physics Today* 2010 年 3 月发表了《物理在中国》特稿介绍中国物理，文章一开始就以陈仙辉团队的工作作为标志成果之一介绍："汤森路透社宣布了一篇中国人的论文是本年度最热门论文之一。这篇出自中国科技大学陈仙辉与合作者的论文报道了在新发现的铁基材料中 43K 温度的超导电性，当年即被引用 100 次。"2008 年 4 月，*Science* 发表了题为《新超导体将中国物理学家推到最前沿》的专题评述。文中报道："2008 年 3 月 25 日，中国科技大学陈仙辉首次把钐氧氟铁砷超导体的临界温度提升到 43K"，这标志着中国在铁基高温超导方面的研究处在世界前列。目前，该工作已被引用 1380 余次，为铁基超导研究奠基工作之一，推动了铁基超导体的研究并引发了世界范围的研究热潮。该工作之后，陈仙辉在机理研究方面也取得突出成就——发现反铁磁与超导电性竞争和共存的直接证据及相图和大的铁同位素效应；发现反铁磁相变温度之上磁化率线性温度依赖关系的普适行为。以上铁基超导体相关成果荣获 2013 年国家自然科学奖一等奖（排名第二）。

2014 年以来，陈仙辉在铁硒类超导体研究中又取得系列成果：①发展了一种新超导体合成的方法，并借此方法合成和发现零电阻温度为 43K 的新型铁硒类超导体，该新超导体具有与其他铁基超导体不同的全新晶体结构，具有很好的稳定性和单相性，克服了已知铁硒类超导体相分离或不稳定的问题，促进了铁砷和铁硒两类超导体物理图像的统一；②利用液态门电压法，将 FeSe 块材的超导温度从 10K 以下成功提升到 48K，这一结果将帮助人们更好地理解在 FeSe 薄膜材料中观察到的 65K 高温超导现象的物理机理。由于在超导材料方面的长期杰出贡献，2015 年陈仙辉荣获国际超导材料领域最高奖马蒂亚斯奖，这是中国科学家首次获此殊荣。

二、实现二维黑磷晶体的场效应晶体管

2014 年，陈仙辉与其合作者成功制备出了基于具有能隙的二维黑磷单晶的场效应晶体管。单层原子厚度的石墨烯的发现，标志着二维晶体成为一类可能影响人类未来电子技术的材料。然而二维石墨烯的电子结构中不具备能隙，从而在电子学应用中不能实现电流的"开"和"关"，弱化了其取代计算机电路中半导体开关的用途。2013年，陈仙辉基于黑磷具有与石墨类似的二维结构且有能隙，提出开展对其研究的思想。随后，利用高温高压技术生长出高质量黑磷单晶，并与张远波等小组合作在2014年成功地在二维黑磷薄层晶体实现了场效应晶体管。二维黑磷单晶场效应晶体管的出现，弥补了石墨烯不具备能隙的这一缺陷。随后的实验表明，该效应晶体管具有极高的应用潜力，可以成为未来纳米电子和光电应用中的一个重要材料基础。同时，相关工作得到国际学术界的广泛关注，《自然·纳米技术》杂志发表了题为 *Phosphorus Joins the Family* 的评论文章，对此工作进行了专题评论："陈仙辉、张远波以及他们的同事把黑磷——一种已经发现100年的稳定元素磷形式——带回到人们的焦点。" *Nature* 也发表了题为 *Phosphorene Excites Materials Scientists* 的评论文章，对包括此工作在内的两篇有关二维黑磷场效应晶体管工作的报道进行了亮点介绍："来自美国和中国的研究小组报道了一个可以拥有类似石墨烯性质且具有能隙的候选材料——磷烯，一种只有原子级厚度的元素磷的层状结构，它具有天然的能隙。"论文发表三年来已被引用1600余次。之后，陈仙辉与其合作者又成功提高了黑磷二维薄膜材料的迁移率，从而观察到量子振荡现象以及整数量子霍尔效应，并在黑磷块体材料中观察到压力诱导的电子结构的拓扑转变，为实现黑磷二维材料的后续应用奠定了坚实的基础。

Awardee of Physics Prize, Chen Xianhui

Chen Xianhui was born in Xiangtan County of Hunan Province in March 1963. He obtained his doctorate degree from University of Science and Technology of China（USTC）in 1992. Now he is a professor at USTC，and the director of the Key Laboratory of Strongly Coupled Quantum Materials of CAS. He has been a Humboldt Scholar at the Karlsruhe Research Center in Germany and the Max Planck Institute for Solid State Physics in Stuttgart，a visiting professor at the Japanese National Institute of Advanced Studies（Hokuriku），Texas Superconductivity Research Center at the University of Houston，and the National University of Singapore. He won the National Outstanding Youth Fund in 1998 and been appointed as a "Yangtze River Scholar" Distinguished Professor by the Ministry of Education of China in 2002. He was elected as a member of the Chinese Academy of Sciences in 2015.

Chen Xianhui mainly focused on exploration of novel superconducting materials and strongly-correlated electronic materials，and experimentally studying their underlying physics.

1. Breaking the McMillan limit of BCS superconductors

By substitution of La with magnetic rare earth element Sm，superconductivity above 40K was found in $SmFeAsO_{1-x}F_x$ under ambient pressure by Chen and his colleagues，which breaks the

McMillan limit of BCS superconductors in the iron−based superconductors. It proves that iron−based superconductors are the second family of high−temperature superconductors besides high−Tc cuprates superconductors. Chen got outstanding achievements in the research of superconducting mechanism of iron−based superconductors as well: he mapped out the phase diagrams of series of systems, and discovered the evidence of the competition and coexistence between antiferromagnetism and superconductivity, large iron isotopic effect, the linearly temperature−dependent magnetic susceptibility above antiferromagnetic transition temperature and etc. Due to the breakthrough in the study of iron−based superconductors, he and his colleagues won the First Prize of State Natural Science Award in 2013.

Since 2014, Chen Xianhui made further progress in the exploration of FeSe−based superconductors. By using hydrothermal method, Chen and his colleagues synthesized a novel air−stable FeSe−based superconductor ($Li_{0.8}Fe_{0.2}$) OHFeSe, which shows T_c as high as 43K. By using liquid gating technique, the superconducting temperature of FeSe bulk is promoted from less than 10K to 48K. In 2015, Chen was awarded the supreme prize in the field of superconducting materials—the Bernd T. Matthias Prize, for his long−standing contribution to superconducting studies.

2. Realization of field effect transistors based on two−dimensional black phosphorus crystal

In 2014, Chen and his collaborators were the first to fabricate field effect transistors (FET) based on few−layer black phosphorus (BP), which established a new field on quantum functional materials after graphene. The few−layer BP based FET has great potential and will become a kind of fundamental material in nano−electronics and optoelectronics applications. Chen and his collaborators also observed quantum oscillations and integral quantum Hall effect in BP thin flakes with higher mobility, and a pressure induced Lifshitz transition was observed in bulk BP. All of the above pave the way to realize the practical application of two dimensional BP materials.

化学奖获得者

李 玉 良

李玉良，1949 年 10 月出生于山东省青岛市。1975 年毕业于北京化工学院基本有机合成专业。作为访问学者和访问教授，先后在荷兰阿姆斯特丹大学有机化学实验室、香港大学化学系、美国圣母大学放射化学实验室和美国佐治亚理工学院材料学院进行合作研究。1975 年至今在中国科学院化学研究所工作，任有机固体院重点实验室研究员。2004 年 1 月—2015 年 12 月任中国科学院化学研究所有机固体院重点实验室副主任。先后担任中国科学院大学教授，哈尔滨工业大学和苏州大学等校兼职教授和名誉教授。作为首席科学家，两次主持了科技部国家重大科学研究计划项目（2007—2015 年），是国家自然科学基金委员会重大研究计划项目指导专家组成员（2008 年至今），中国科学院院士。2002 年、2005 年和 2014 年三次获得国家自然科学奖二等奖（第一、第二和第四完成人各 1 项），两次获北京市科学技术奖（自然科学）（2010 年和 2015 年）一等奖和中国科学院自然科学二等奖一次，是 2017 年全国创新争先奖获得者，是 1978 年全国科学大会奖集体奖成员之一，2006 年获得中国科学院和中国科学院研究生院优秀导师奖。在 *Nat. Commun.*、*Acc. Chem. Res.*、*Chem. Soc. Rev.*、*J. Am. Chem. Soc.*、*Angew. Chem. Int. Ed.* 和 *Adv. Mater.* 等刊物发表论文 600 余篇，文章共被他人引用 16000 余次，论文被 *C& EN News* 和 *Material Today* 等多次作为专题评述。获授权发明专利 14 项。应邀在国际会议作 30 余次大会报告或邀请报告，担任环太平洋化学大会的分会主席等。培养了 80 多名博士和硕士研究生，其中多人获得国家自然科学基金委杰出青年基金、优秀青年基金、国家青年千人和中科院"百人计划"等人才项目资助。

李玉良长期从事以无机化学为基础的交叉科学研究，致力于碳及富碳分子设计、聚集态结构和性能研究。在碳的新同素异形体的合成与性质、无机 / 有机异质结构和材料以及异质结构分子固态界面表面效应等方面做出了系列原创性的研究工作。

一、建立了碳材料化学合成系统方法，发现了碳的新同素异形体石墨炔

（1）碳具有 sp^3、sp^2 和 sp 三种杂化态，通过不同杂化态可以形成多种碳的同素异形体。合成、分离新的不同维数碳同素异形体是过去二三十年研究的焦点，科学家们先后发现了三维富勒烯、一维碳纳米管和二维石墨烯等新的碳同素异形体，这激起了科学家们探索新碳同素异形体的研究热忱和兴趣，并成为国际学术研究的前沿和热点。石墨炔是以 sp 和 sp^2 两种杂化态形成的新的碳同素异形体，是由 1，3-二炔键将苯环共轭连接形成二维平面网络结构，具有丰富的碳化学键、大的共轭体系、宽面间距、优良的化学稳定性和半导体性能，被预测为非天然碳的同素异形体中最稳定的、最有可能通过合成化学方法获得的全碳材料。石墨炔特殊的电子结构和孔洞结构使其在光、电、信息技术、电子、能源、催化以及光电转换等领域具有潜在的、重大的应用前景。

2010 年，李玉良和他的研究团队首次发现了带隙为 0.46 eV 的二维碳的新同素异形体——石墨炔，使得受国际科学界高度重视的碳材料家族又诞生了一个新成员。石墨炔是具有我国自主知识产权的碳材料，它的成功合成开辟了人工合成碳新同素异形体的先例，是国际上第一个在常压、低温下通过人工合成化学获得的全碳材料，被认为是"碳化学的一个令人瞩目的进展，是真正的重大发现""开辟了人工合成碳新同素异形体的先例"。*Materials Today* 专题评述指出："合成、分离新的碳同素异形体是过去二三十年研究的焦点，中国科学家首次合成了新的碳同素异形体——石墨炔；化学家通过碳原子制备独特的分子，然而化学合成仅含碳的材料更具挑战性，中国科学家用一种直接的方法合成了 $3.6cm^2$ 的石墨炔薄膜。中国科学家的研究表明，石墨炔优良的性能可与硅媲美，有可能成为未来电子器件的关键材料……。"*Nature China* 报道："中科院李玉良首次合成二维结构石墨炔，石墨炔具有和已知碳同素异形体不同的结构和性质，最有可能成为电子器件领域最重要的材料。"著名杂志 *NanoTech* 2012 和 2015 年发布年度报告，两次将石墨炔列为专题进行评述，指出石墨炔的发现提升了科学家对碳材料研究的强烈兴趣，欧盟已将石墨炔等研究列入下一个框架计划，美、英等国也将其列入政府计划，并在电子、能源、航空航天、电信、医疗以及催化领域的重要潜在应用价值。近年来，石墨炔基础和应用研究在中国科学家的引领下形成了一个新领域，目前包括美国、德国、法国、英国和日本等发达国家在内的 20 多个国家（包括哈佛大学、MIT、东京大学等）都开展了相关研究工作。这是中国科学家在国际材料领域为数不多的具有引领性国际研究的范例。

（2）他率先提出了 C_{60} 聚集态结构的研究，在国际上首先建立了系列低维 C_{60} 晶态结构和材料生长新方法，发现了 C_{60} 半导体本征特性，揭示了 C_{60} 固态结构本征性质，开辟了富勒烯研究的新途径。

二、建立了无机和富碳分子异质结构共生长方法学

无机 / 有机异质结构是化学领域最具挑战性的研究之一，如何实现界面的高效连接是

研究异质结本征性质的基础。

（1）依据无机和富碳分子的电子结构，提出了结构和能量匹配的原则，首次建立了异质结构的共生长方法学，突破了异质结构相容生长瓶颈，发现了异质结界面和结效应导致的可控半导体特征。被美国著名杂志 *C & EN News* 专题报道，认为"这将导致新型微型电路的产生和应用的新材料"；*NPG Asia Mater* 则认为"无机和有机材料组装形成单一纳米结构之后产生不同于独立材料的新性质，开辟了新的路线，获得了异质结纳米线，真正实现了 1+1 大于 2 的效果。"

（2）提出了气—固相生长结合固体表面反应的新方法和能级及带隙可调的固态超分子结构调控原则，发现了大面积金属／富碳分子异质结阵列的可控生长的一般规律，将电荷转移盐从体材料引入到小尺度研究并发现光学和电学尺度效应。实现了无机／有机固态界面可控构筑，高选择性地在无机固态表面可控生长不同功能的异质结界面，导致了可调的光学和电学性质。

三、建立了大面积、高有序富碳分子聚集态阵列生长的系列新方法

（1）大面积、高有序自组装是迫切需要解决的重要科学问题，李玉良提出了自然生长结合表面和界面作用驱动等策略，实现了富碳分子高有序大面积聚集态阵列的调控，阐明了从无序到有序自组装机理，揭示了性能对有序结构的强烈依赖性，构建了系列原理器件，第一次实现了分子水平上的物质输运。

（2）提出了表面和界面调控机制，实现了在无机材料表面合成大面积、高有序富碳体系纳米阵列，解决了材料可控大面积生长的瓶颈，发现了光学依赖维数效应。

Awardee of Chemistry Prize, Li Yuliang

Li Yuliang was born in Qingdao City of Shandong Province in October 1949. He graduated from the Beijing Institute of Chemical Technology in 1975, and received Bachelor's degree of Science. He worked as a visiting scholar or visiting professor in the University of Amsterdam in the Netherlands, the University of Hong Kong, the University of Notre Dame and Georgia Institute of Technology（1998—2000）. He has been working as a professor in the Institute of Chemistry, Chinese Academy of Sciences（CAS）in 1996. He was the deputy director of Key Laboratory of Organic Solid, Chinese Academy of Sciences（2004—2015）. He has served as the professor of the University of Chinese Academy of Sciences, the guest professor of Harbin Institute of Technology and Suzhou University et al. He was the chief scientist of National Science Research Program "973" project of Ministry of Science and Technology（2007—2015）. Currently he is the member of the expert group for the Major Research Plan of the National Natural Science Foundation of China (2008—present). He is the academician of the Chinese Academy of Sciences. Prof. Yuliang Li has received several awards, including the second prize in National Natural Science Award in 2002, 2005 and 2014, respectively, twice of the first prize in the Beijing Municipal Science and Technology Awards (2010 and 2014), the second prize in Natural Science Award of CAS in 1999, National Innovation Award of 2017, the Collective Award of the National Science Conference in 1978, the Excellent Tutor Award from CAS and the Graduate School of CAS in 2006. He has published more than 600 peer reviewed scientific articles, 14 items of authorized patents and invited reviews in the journals, such as *Nat. Commun.*, *Acc. Chem. Res.*, *Chem. Soc. Rev.*, *J. Am. Chem. Soc.*, *Angew. Chem. Int. Ed.*, *PNAS* and *Adv. Mater. et al.*. These papers were cited by others for more than 16000 times. His research works have obtained highly commended and attention by international scientists and several highlights by academic journals such as *C & EN News* and *Materials Today et al.*. He was invited to do more than 30 times of plenary and Keynote reports in the International Conference, served as the branch chairman of Central Pacific Chemical Conference. Trained more than 80 doctoral and master's degree graduate students, many of whom won the National Science Fund for Distinguished Young Scholars, Excellent Young Scholars, Thousand Youth Talents Plan Project of Thousand Youth Talents and CAS "Hundred Talents Program" and other personnel projects funded.

Li Yuliang has long been engaged in interdisciplinary research based on inorganic chemistry, and worked on the design, aggregation structure and properties of carbon and carbon-rich molecules. He has made a series of original research work on new allotrope of carbon, inorganic/organic heterostructures and materials and the heterogeneous structure of molecular solid interface and surface effect.

化学奖获得者

唐 本 忠

　　唐本忠，1957 年 2 月出生于湖北省潜江市。1982 年于华南理工大学获得学士学位，1985 年和 1988 年先后获日本京都大学硕士和博士学位。曾在日本 NEOS 公司中央研究所任高级研究员，在多伦多大学化学系和药学院从事博士后研究。1994 年 7 月入职香港科技大学化学系，历任助理教授、副教授、教授、讲座教授和张鉴泉（Stephen K. C. Cheong）理学教授。2015 年起担任国家人体组织功能重建工程技术研究中心香港分中心主任。唐本忠长期从事高分子合成方法论的探索以及聚集诱导发光（aggregation-induced emission，AIE）现象、材料及其应用研究，发表学术论文 1000 余篇。2009 年当选中国科学院院士，2013 年入选英国皇家化学会（RSC）会士。现为华南理工大学发光材料与器件国家重点实验室学术委员会主任、华南理工大学 – 香港科技大学联合研究院院长、中国化学会和 RSC 联合期刊 *Materials Chemistry Frontiers* 主编以及 *RSC Polymer Chemistry Series* 主编。2014—2016 年连续入选材料科学和化学双领域全球高被引科学家。唐本忠于 2014 年获第 27 届夸瑞兹密国际科学奖，2012 年获美国化学会高分子学术报告奖，2007 年获裘槎高级研究成就奖和国家自然科学奖二等奖。

　　唐本忠是 AIE 概念的提出者和 AIE 研究领域的引领者。AIE 是指一类在溶液中发光微弱或者不发光的分子在聚集态或者固态高效发光的现象。AIE 与聚集导致发光猝灭（aggregation-caused quenching，ACQ）这一教科书常识完全相反，为固态发光材料的设计开辟了一条新径。唐本忠在 AIE 分子的设计、发光机制和应用开发等方面做出了原创性和引领性的工作。

一、新概念的提出——突破传统，创造机遇

　　传统有机发光分子在稀溶液中发光很强，但在浓溶液中或聚集态下荧光变弱甚至完全消失。研究人员试图用化学、物理或工程的方法来减弱或消除 ACQ 效应，但收效甚微。

2001 年，唐本忠团队观察到一些噻咯衍生物在溶液中不发光但聚集后高效发光。他敏锐地意识到这一现象的重要性，并创造性地提出了 AIE 这一光物理领域的新概念。AIE 从根本上解决了有机发光分子的 ACQ 问题，革新了人们设计发光材料的思想，开启了人们重新思考和认识经典光物理过程的新篇章。

二、新模型的建立——追本溯源，揭示真相

深入理解 AIE 现象背后的物理机制是 AIE 能否从一个科学概念发展成为一个研究领域的关键。唐本忠团队基于实验数据和理论模拟手段，提出了分子内运动受限（restriction of intramolecular motion，RIM）的 AIE 工作机制。RIM 模型通俗易懂，对 AIE 分子结构设计具有很强的指导意义，极大地促进了 AIE 研究领域的发展。目前，全世界 60 余个国家 / 地区的 1100 多个单位的科学家在从事 AIE 相关的研究工作。AIE 在中科院文献情报中心和汤森路透联合发布的《2015 年研究前沿》荣列排名第二的重点热点前沿。

以 RIM 机理为基础，唐本忠团队提出了用 AIE 基元改造传统 ACQ 分子的策略，极大地丰富了固态高效发光材料的种类。随着研究的深入，还提出了"结晶诱导发光（CIE）"的 AIE 衍生概念，并发展了结晶诱导的纯有机高效室温磷光体系。在对不含芳香环的非共轭 AIE 大分子体系的研究基础上，提出了"簇发光（Clusteroluminescence）"的新概念和机理。这些成果丰富了光物理学的基础理论。

三、新材料的发展与新应用的开发——开疆拓土，魅力驰骋

唐本忠始终坚信："好的研究应该能够切实地为国家的发展和社会的进步做出贡献，而非仅仅是在实验室满足好奇心，更不能只是一个自娱自乐的学术游戏。"而实现这一目标的载体则是新材料和新应用的开发。

相对于传统发光材料，AIE 材料的高固态发光效率使其在光电领域有着巨大的应用潜力。例如，基于有机发光材料的有机发光二极管（OLED）正在引发柔性显示和照明的技术变革浪潮，也是我国最有希望实现弯道超车的高新领域之一，AIE 材料在此领域大有用武之地。除了在光电领域的应用之外，AIE 材料在传感和成像等领域也有着广泛的应用前景。例如，对外界刺激具有响应的智能或聪明材料，可调谐折射率的液晶或偏振光材料与光波导材料，特异性和高灵敏度的化学传感材料以及可针对细胞器、微生物和活体的荧光成像材料等。AIE 材料在上述领域显示了其优于传统发光材料的特征，甚至可实现传统材料无法实现的新功能。

2008 年和 2014 年的诺贝尔化学奖分别授予了绿色荧光蛋白和超分辨荧光显微技术，足以凸显荧光成像材料及技术的重要性。但目前使用的商用荧光探针主要是荧光蛋白或 ACQ 型染料，其化学结构复杂、成本较高；此外，这些染料光稳定性较差，在光学扫描时易被光漂白，导致荧光信号消失，因此很难满足基础科研和临床诊疗的需要。AIE 材料制备成本低、操作简单（如免洗）且光稳定性好，有望成为人们观测微观生物世界的有

力工具。

综上所述，在唐本忠的带领下，AIE 研究在概念创新、模型建立、材料发展和技术开发等领域都得到了飞速发展。AIE 研究还造就了一支具有原始创新意识和国际影响力的青年学者队伍。唐本忠至今已培养了 530 余名研究生、博士后、研究员和访问学者，其中 60 余人在国内外担任教职，包括 8 名国家杰出青年基金获得者、5 名国家自然科学基金优秀青年基金获得者和 3 名中组部青年千人计划入选者。但是，唐本忠时刻警醒自己的队伍，必须保持头脑清醒，以迎接和应对滚滚大浪中的机遇与挑战。

"侠之大者，为国为民"，AIE 诞生在这片沃土，也应该造福于这一方人民。如何维持我们在原始创新领域的头羊地位，把 AIE 这块中国品牌擦得更亮，从而不断革新我们自己的思想和理念；如何推进 AIE 从基础研究向实际应用的转化，将具有中国自主知识产权的 AIE 材料和技术产业化和市场化，切实地为人民生活质量的提高和医疗条件的改善贡献力量——这正是唐本忠团队当下思考的问题和奋斗的目标。

唐本忠坚信："United we stand, together we shine（团结力量大，聚集发光强）"。让我们伸开双臂，拥抱新的机遇，撸起袖子加油干，让 AIE 之光照亮未来！

Awardee of Chemistry Prize, Tang Benzhong

Tang Benzhong was born in Qianjiang City of Hubei Province in February 1957. He received his BS and PhD degrees from South China University of Technology（SCUT）and Kyoto University in 1982 and 1988，respectively. He then worked as a senior research scientist in the Central Research Laboratory of Neos Co. Ltd. and as a postdoctoral fellow at University of Toronto. In 1994，he joined the Department of Chemistry of the Hong Kong University of Science & Technology（HKUST）. Currently，he is Chair Professor of Chemistry and Stephen K. C. Cheong Professor of Science of HKUST. Tang was elected to the membership of the Chinese Academy of Sciences in 2009 and the fellowship of the Royal Society of Chemistry in 2013. He is now serving as Editor-in-Chief of *Materials Chemistry Frontiers* and *RSC Polymer Chemistry Series*. He has received many awards including National Natural Science Award, Khwarizmi International Award, Macro Lecture Award, and Croucher Senior Research Fellowship Award. Tang has published >1000 peer-reviewed papers that have been cited >50000 times, with a high h-index of 110. He was listed as one of the Highly Cited Researchers from 2014 to 2016 in the fields of *Chemistry* and *Materials Science* by Thomson Reuters.

Tang is interested in the development of new polymerization methodology and the study of aggregation-induced emission（AIE）. Particularly，he coined the novel concept of AIE which refers to an "abnormal phenomenon" that certain kind of molecules are weakly or non-emissive in solution but emit strongly in the aggregate or solid state. Currently，AIE materials have been widely applied in optoelectronic, chemosensing and bioimaging fields. Scientists from >1100 institutes in over 60 countries/regions are now conducting AIE research. In 2015, AIE was ranked #2 research front in the fields of *Chemistry* and *Materials Science* by Thomson Reuters.

During the course of AIE study, Tang further coined new concepts of crystallization—induced emission and clusteroluminescence and developed efficient phosphorescence systems at room temperature from pure organic molecules. These contributions have enriched our understanding of photophysical processes.

"The research of AIE should not be confined to satisfying curiosity but making great contributions to societal development and economic growth", said Tang. Hence, how to promote industrialization and commercialization of AIE materials and technologies to improve the quality of people's lives are the future pursuit of Tang's team.

Tang believes: "United we stand, together we shine!" Let's open our arms to embrace new opportunities! Let's "roll up our sleeves to work harder" to make AIE an even brighter star in the research community!

化学奖获得者

谢　毅

谢毅，女，1967年7月出生于安徽省阜阳市。1988年毕业于厦门大学化学系获学士学位，1996年毕业于中国科学技术大学获博士学位后留校任教。1998年获国家杰出青年基金后晋升为正教授，2000年入选长江特聘教授；2004—2009年作为学术带头人主持基金委创新群体基金，2009—2013年作为首席科学家主持科技部重大研究计划项目。

谢毅一直从事无机固体化学研究，在纳米尺度下的固体化学，特别是在基于电、声调制的无机功能固体设计与合成这一重要前沿交叉领域做出了深入系统的工作。

谢毅于1995年读博期间将溶剂热合成技术发展成制备III–V族非氧化物的普适性方法，该工作于1996年发表在 Science 上，这一系列工作不仅入选了无机专业教科书，还获得2001年国家自然科学奖二等奖（排名第二）。在相关工作基础上，溶剂热合成现已发展成为重要的固体合成方法。

1998年获得国家杰出青年基金后，谢毅开始开拓独立的研究方向。针对当时对无机功能材料结构构筑的探索往往很难建立在清晰的原子分子层次上，她的小组另辟蹊径，注重从固体化学的基本原理出发，从物质的内在特征结构为导向来控制它们的生长，同时建立和发展了系列结合特征晶体结构和特征模板导向的二元协同策略来构筑三维组装结构。这些工作得到国际相关领域最有影响力的一些课题组的肯定，并以第一完成人获2012年国家自然科学奖二等奖。同时还获得中国青年科学家奖（2002）及中国青年女科学家奖（2006）等重要个人奖项。

2008年以来，她试图从更本质的电子、声子结构的调控来实现对无机固体的性能优化。她利用纳米尺度下调制电、声输运性质的思想，发展了系列高效热电转换新体系。相关工作被誉为化学化工领域风向标的美国化学会《化学与工程新闻》做了长篇专题评述。2016年《自然·材料》刊登特征论文，将其在热电领域的工作列为中国热电研究领域的重要进展之一。

2011 年以来，谢毅进一步丰富和发展了纳米固体化学，阐明了纳米固体化学的内涵，提出原子级厚二维超薄结构是原子层次上建立清晰的构效关系的理想模型体系；建立了制备二维超薄材料的普适方法，解决了其精细结构和缺陷结构表征上的困难，并探究其特殊电子态及在光 / 电催化及热电效率关系的基本规律。相关成果入选"2016 中国科学十大进展"，并两次入选《中国科学院重大科技基础设施重大成果》。2013 年，谢毅被国际理论与应用化学联合会授予化学化工杰出女性奖，以"表彰她在全球化学领域的科学贡献"，成为该奖项首位华人获奖者。2014 年，被发展中国家科学院授予化学奖，以"表彰她在纳米尺度的无机固体化学特别是在基于电子和声子结构调制的无机功能固体领域的突出贡献"；该奖每年在发展中国家中授予一项，谢毅为 2014 年该奖唯一的获奖者。2015 年，被联合国教科文组织授予世界杰出女科学家成就奖，以"表彰她在创造超薄二维固体及其在热或者太阳光到电能转化方面的有前景应用的突出贡献"；该奖每两年在全部自然科学领域遴选 5 人，五大洲各 1 人，谢毅为 2015 年度亚洲太平洋地区的唯一获奖者。2017 年获得 Nano Research Award，该奖每年在全世界纳米研究领域遴选 1 位杰出科学家，谢毅为该奖设立以来首位美国以外的获奖者，获奖理由是"认可她在纳米科学与技术方面的突出贡献"。

迄今为止，谢毅围绕相关工作以通讯作者身份在《自然》及子刊以及化学顶级三大刊《美国化学会志》《德国应用化学》和《先进材料》上共发表 SCI 论文 320 多篇；另以第一作者在《科学》发表论文 1 篇。受邀在美国化学会《化学研究述评》、英国皇家化学会《化学会评论》等重要综述刊物上发表综述和展望 15 篇及 5 部英文专章；29 篇论文入选 ISI 十年间前 1% 高引用论文。30 余篇次被美国化学会《化学与工程新闻》、英国皇家化学会《化学世界》等专题评述、获最受关注或热点论文。她本人连续入选 Elsevier 中国高被引学者榜单，已被 SCI 引用超过 20000 次，个人 H 因子 82。相关工作在国际上产生重要影响，2015 年元旦前夕，《自然》邀请全球 9 位科学引领者撰写 2015 年的新年展望，谢毅作为唯一的化学家应邀撰写了题为"更高能效，学科交叉"的新年展望评论。

谢毅现任中国化学会无机化学学科委员会副主任、中国化学会女化学工作者委员会副主任；曾任英国皇家化学会 – 中国化学会合办《无机化学前沿》创刊副主编四年，现任化学顶级期刊《美国化学会志》《德国应用化学》以及美国化学会《ACS 中心科学》和英国皇家化学会《材料地平线》的国际编委。在培养人才方面，谢毅成绩卓然，目前其课题组已培养国家优青获得者 4 名、青年千人获得者 4 名。由于在教书育人方面的突出成绩，她先后十余次获得中国科学院优秀研究生导师奖和朱李月华优秀导师奖。

Awardee of Chemistry Prize, Xie Yi

Xie Yi, female, was born in Fuyang City of Anhui Province in July 1967. She obtained her BS degree from Xiamen University (1988) and a Ph.D. from the University of Science and Technology of China (USTC, 1996). She is currently a Principal Investigator of Hefei National Laboratory for Physical Sciences at the Microscale and a full professor of the Department of Chemistry, USTC. She was nominated as the Cheung Kong Scholar Professor of inorganic chemistry in 2000 and elected as a member of the Chinese Academy of Sciences in 2013.

Xie Yi has been active in the research of inorganic solid–state chemistry at the nanoscale, and has particularly performed the research in the interdisciplinary frontier field for the design and synthesis of inorganic functional solids with efforts to modulate their electron and phonon structures.

Since 2008, her research has more fundamentally focused on the modulation of electronic and phononic structures towards the performance optimization of inorganic solids. She proposed the strategy for modulating the electron and phonon transport properties at the nanoscale, and developed new high–efficiency thermoelectric materials. The related works have been highlighted by ACS *Chemical & Engineering News* in large space, and highlighted as one of the important China thermoelectric research progresses in a Feature Article of *Nature Materials* in 2016. Specifically she developed the generic methodology for synthesizing ultrathin two–dimensional materials, and addressed the challenges in the characterizations of fine structures and defect structures. As a result, she has been able to explore the principles in the relationship between unique electronic states and photocatalytic/electrocatalytic/thermoelectric efficiencies. The related works have been selected to the "Top 10 Progresses in China Science in 2016" and the "Major Achievements on Huge Basic Infrastructure of Science and Technology" by the Chinese Academy of Sciences (CAS) twice. In 2013, she was granted the "IUPAC Distinguished Women in Chemistry/Chemical Engineering Award" by the International Union of Pure and Applied Chemistry (IUPAC) as the first Chinese awardee for her scientific contribution to global chemistry community. In 2014, she won the Third World Academy of Sciences (TWAS) Prize in Chemistry for her outstanding contribution to inorganic solid state chemistry at the nanoscale, especially in inorganic functional solids with modulated electron and phonon structures. In 2015, she was conferred on the L'oreal–UNESCO for Women in Science Award for her significant contributions to creating new materials a few atoms thick with promising applications in conversion of heat or sunlight into electricity. Xie Yi has published more than 320 scientific papers in international journals as the corresponding author, including 8 in *Nature* and sister journals as well as 65 in *J. Am. Chem. Soc.*, *Angew. Chem. Int. Ed.* and *Adv. Mater.*, and 1 in *Science* as the first author. She has been invited to contribute 15 review or perspective articles for *Acc. Chem. Res.* and *Chem. Soc. Rev.* etc., and 5 monographs for 4 books. Her publications have been extensively cited by more than 20000 times by the international research community with an H index of 82.

地球科学奖获得者

傅 伯 杰

傅伯杰，1958年1月出生于陕西省咸阳市。中国科学院院士、英国爱丁堡皇家学会外籍院士和发展中国家科学院院士。1982年毕业于陕西师范大学地理系，1989年毕业于北京大学地理系获理学博士学位。1992—1994年在比利时LEUVEN大学土地和水管理研究所进行博士后研究。1994年回国至今在中国科学院生态环境研究中心工作，任城市与区域生态国家重点实验室研究员、学术委员会主任。1996年9月—2001年1月任中国科学院生态环境研究中心副主任，2001年2月—2008年11月任中国科学院资源环境科学与技术局局长。现任中国地理学会理事长、国际生态学会副主席、国家生态保护与建设专家咨询委员会副主任，兼任中国科学院地学部主任、国家自然科学基金委员会地球科学部主任。

傅伯杰长期致力于自然地理学和景观生态学研究，取得了系统性和创新性的学术成就，推动了我国景观生态学的发展。

（1）开创了景观格局与生态过程耦合研究的新方向，系统揭示了土地利用格局与水土过程的相互作用机理。开展了多尺度的观测、实验和模型模拟研究，率先将尺度—格局—过程有机结合，系统揭示了黄土丘陵沟壑区土地利用格局对土壤水分、养分和土壤侵蚀的影响机理；建立了黄土丘陵坡地土壤水分空间分布模型，提出了黄土丘陵坡地和小流域合理的土地利用结构。为黄土高原植被恢复提供了科学依据，将综合自然地理的格局和分类研究深化到了过程研究，其研究成果获国家自然科学二等奖。

（2）发展了生态系统服务权衡分析方法与区域集成模型，揭示了不同尺度生态系统服务演变机理，在生态系统服务理论和方法方面取得了重要突破。建立了定量分析生态系统服务协同与权衡方法，实现了生态系统服务权衡与协同的空间表达；研发了具有生态系统服务定量评估、情景分析与模拟、土地利用优化、决策支持等功能的区域生态系统服务综合评估与优化模型系统；定量评估了水源涵养、土壤保持、碳固定、粮食生产等生态系统服务的演变规律，揭示了土地覆被变化的生态环境效应。研究成果发表在 *Nature Geoscience*、*Nature Climate Change* 等高水平刊物上，获 2016 年中国科学院杰出科技成就奖。

（3）首次编制完成了中国生态区划，为国家构建生态安全格局提供了科学依据。他主持开展了中国生态区划研究，综合了生态系统的地域差异、生态系统功能和人类活动特征，该区划方案已被国家环保部和国家发改委应用。同时，傅伯杰还应 *Science* 杂志邀请就中国的生态环境问题撰写了述评。研究成果获国家科技进步奖二等奖和国际景观生态学会杰出贡献奖。

傅伯杰发表学术论文 400 余篇，其中 SCI 收录论文 230 余篇，SCI 引用 5600 余次，入选高引用作者，国内引用 33000 余次；获国家和省部级科技奖 7 项，出版著作 10 余部。主持了国家自然科学基金委员会"十三五"地球科学发展战略研究和国家科技部"十三五"生态保护与恢复领域战略研究，为我国地球科学的发展做出了重要贡献。

Awardee of Earth Sciences Prize, Fu Bojie

Fu Bojie was born in Xianyang City of Shanxi Province in January 1958. He is a professor of physical geography and landscape ecology at the State key Lab. of Urban and Regional Ecology, Research Centre for Eco-Environmental Sciences, Chinese Academy of Sciences. He got his PhD degree in Physical Geography from Peking University in 1989. He is member of Chinese Academy of Sciences, Fellow of the Academy of Sciences for Developing World (TWAS) and Corresponding Fellow of the Royal Society Edinburgh UK. He is President of the Geographical Society of China, Director-General of Department of Earth Sciences, National Natural Science Foundation of China. His research areas are land use and land cover change, landscape pattern and ecological processes, ecosystem services and management. He has done pioneering work on how ecological processes lead to ecosystem restoration and ecosystem services provision, as well as on integrated ecosystem management in China. His achievements have resulted in significant international distinction and recognition, and promoted the development of landscape ecology and ecosystem services study not only in China but also in the world.

1. Discovery of the mechanisms of land use patterns impacting ecological processes

The interactions of landscape pattern and ecological processes are the frontiers of landscape ecology research. Prof Fu is a leading scientist in the world to study the relationship between land use pattern and ecological processes at various spatial scales including specific ecotope, hill slope, watershed, and regional level. Based on long term field monitoring and observations, he and his team have discovered the mechanism of how land use pattern and dynamics affect soil moisture, soil nutrient and soil erosion, and subsequently developed the suitable ecological restoration models and best practices. These findings are particularly valuable for ecological restoration and land use optimization in the semi–arid land.

2. Coupling the ecosystem processes and ecosystem services

Prof. Fu's work in linking ecosystem processes with ecosystem services has revealed the relationships between ecosystem structure, land use structure, vegetation functional traits, vegetation biomass, ecological processes (e.g. hydrological processes, nutrient cycling) and ecosystem services. He developed analysis methods for ecosystem service trade–off at multiple scales, which results provide a solid scientific base for wide application of "Grain for Green" programme and regional ecosystem services improvement in semi–arid and semi–humid regions. Based on the understanding of the relationships between ecosystem processes and services at multiple scales, he led his team in developing a spatially explicit assessment and optimization tool for regional ecosystem services (SAORES), including database compilation, ecosystem services assessment, scenario analysis, tradeoff analysis and integrated optimization. He also revealed the spatial–temporal dynamic features of ecosystem services, including water and soil retention, carbon sequestration and food production in the Loess Plateau. The above results have provided a scientific basis for the optimization of ecosystem services in the Loess Plateau and the identification of governance strategies in the Yellow River basin.

3. Opening up a new research direction of ecosystem services and regional ecological security

He conducted ecological regionalization and ecosystem service regionalization of China for the first time. He and his colleagues established the theory and methodology of ecological regionalization and ecosystem service regionalization, which have been applied by Ministry of Environmental Protection of China and provided an important basis for ecological protection and identification of ecological security patterns in China.

Prof. Fu has published 480 scientific papers and 12 books, of which more than 230 published in the international journals including *Science*, *Nature Climate Change*, *and Nature Geoscience*. He has attained the highest international standards in the fields of physical geography, landscape ecology, ecosystem services and ecological restoration. His scientific achievements have been widely recognized by international scientific communities. His research findings have been widely applied in vegetation and ecological restoration in the Loess Plateau of China. In summary, he has opened the science of ecological processes, ecosystem services, ecosystem restoration and ecosystem management and moved it into a real–world practice at different spatial scales.

地球科学奖获得者

万卫星

万卫星，1958年7月出生于湖北省天门市。1982年本科毕业于武汉大学空间物理系，并于1984年和1990年在中科院武汉物理研究所获空间物理硕士、博士学位。1984—2004年在武汉物理所（后扩充为武汉物理与数学研究所）从事空间物理研究，1994年任该所研究员及电离层物理研究室主任。其间赴美国Lowell大学大气研究中心访问一年，并分别短期赴日本邮政省综合通信研究所和澳大利亚La Trobe大学进行合作研究。2004年起任中科院地质与地球物理研究所研究员和该所地磁与空间物理研究室主任，2012—2014年任中科院电离层空间环境重点实验室主任，2014年起任中科院地球与行星物理重点实验室主任。2016年出任我国首次火星探测任务首席科学家。2011年当选为中国科学院院士。

万卫星长期从事电离层物理、电离层电波传播、高层大气物理等领域的理论、观测和应用研究，带领科学团队取得了丰硕的学术成果，研究成果获得国内外同行的好评，获得国家自然科学成果二等奖等多项奖励。至今已正式发表SCI学术论文307篇，学术论文被SCI引用4084余次；2000年以来，在全世界以"电离层"为主题的SCI论文（共21519篇）单篇引用排名检索中，有4篇论文进入前1%、17篇论文进入前5%。

一、我国电离层结构与扰动地域特性研究

坚持进行实验观测，从长期观测数据中分析发现我国中部地区电离层重力波扰动主要有东北、东南两种优势传播方向；改进重力波射线跟踪技术，分析得出上述两种优势重力波的激发源分别位于青藏高原的东南缘和东北缘的地形突变处；发现重力波扰动源出现率与相同地区的低涡天气事件出现率有非常一致的地理分布及季节变化。这一系列工作以第一手观测资料揭示出我国电离层扰动的地域特性，为我国电离层研究与预报提供了重要观测基础；并且将电离层扰动与相关气象活动及青藏高原地形隆起的地形地貌

联系起来，不仅解释了我国电离层扰动起源的问题，还为电离层与其他地球学科的交叉研究提供了一条创新思路。上述成果发表后，受到了国内外同行的好评与引用；在两篇重要综述文章中，大篇幅介绍了万卫星等得出的"中国电离层的扰动源自青藏高原背风坡"的结果，并强调了万卫星等人得出的"对流层低涡是电离层扰动源"的结论。

二、低纬电离层"四波"经度结构研究

首先利用全球地基 GPS-TEC 观测资料，分析发现电离层总电子含量等参量的经度"四波"结构，并首次得到电离层"四波"的日变化特性和年变化、年际变化等气候学特征；在此基础上，与高层大气的卫星观测数据进行比较分析，揭示出电离层经度结构与大气层潮汐具有高度相关的关系，从而给出了"电离层—大气层耦合"的直接证据；此外，还采用控制模拟方法揭示出两种"电离层—大气层潮汐耦合"的机理及对称与反对称两种不同潮汐模式的耦合效率，并据此提出了"潮汐耦合"物理模型。低纬电离层"四波"经度结构是当今电离层物理研究中广受关注的前沿科学问题，上述研究成果一方面从观测上系统揭示了"四波"结构的变化特性，另一方面提出了"四波"结构形成的物理机制。有关结果被同行大量引用和评价，包括两本专著与 3 篇综述文章的大篇幅介绍和对原图的直接引用。

三、太阳风 – 磁层 – 电离层电动力学耦合研究

在这一传统研究热点上，万卫星从新视角着手，大胆创新研究方法，取得了国际学界认同的结果。影响较大的工作有：利用卫星数据及地基电离层观测资料，发现了太阳风磁场通过极区电离层电场的耦合对电离层偶发 E 层形成的控制作用，并提出电场随机性在偶发 E 层的形成过程中具有决定关键作用。这些发现揭示了太阳风对极区电离层的一种新的耦合作用，研究结果在国际同行中引起广泛兴趣，得到一些学者的引用和跟进研究。例如，有国际团队将万卫星等人对南极地区电离层偶发 E 层形成的研究思路和方法成功用于北极地区的相关研究。

四、若干电离层物理中的基本论点的检验

针对若干长期争论或悬而未决的问题，万卫星使用新观测与新分析方法对现有电离层物理中的基本论点进行检验，修正或者推翻了某些长期广泛接受的不正确观点。代表性的工作有：从理论上导出了太阳耀斑爆发期间电离层总电子含量突然增强与太阳天顶角的 Chapman 函数成反比的新结论，并在全球 GPS-TEC 观测实验中得到了证实。该结果纠正了 80 年代关于总电子含量突然增强与太阳天顶角无明显关系的错误看法，是近年来日地关系研究中的一个重要进展。此外，利用全球电离层综合观测资料，指导学生分析研究了超级磁暴引起的中低纬电离层扰动，通过理论分析提出超级磁暴期间磁层的阿尔芬屏蔽效应消失的新机理，对观测到的磁暴时赤道电离层抬升等现象进行了完满解释。

五、电离层实验观测与分析方法研究

万卫星十分重视实验观测等基础性工作，在前辈工作基础上，通过参加国家"子午工程"及中科院"日地空间环境网络"建设，组织对现有设备的改造升级和新设备的研制引进，将原来单一的电离层观测发展成具有多种手段的地球空间环境综合观测，并通过与地磁台链整合，建成了由漠河、北京、武汉、三亚等台站组成的观测台链，拥有数字测高仪、全天空流星雷达、超高频相干散射雷达等众多先进设备，目前正在建设国际上最先进的相控阵三亚非相干散射雷达等，探测高度可覆盖整个电离层与中高层大气，探测参量包含电离层结构与运动、高层大气温度与风场等，为空间物理基础研究和空间天气应用服务积累了丰富的观测数据，提供了一个具有当今国际先进水平的观测研究基地。

六、电离层观测数据分析方法研究

万卫星提出了电离层扰动剖面的广义射线反演原理等分析方法，在世界上首次解决了数字测高仪新模式观测数据的分析问题，极大发挥了台站观测设备的潜力。发展了非单一电离层重力波扰动场的分析方法，解决了台站多普勒观测阵的数据分析，为利用自主观测数据揭示我国电离层扰动地域特性奠定了基础。此外，他还大力开发新的电离层观测模式，如采用统计本征模技术，基于台链实时观测建成了我国首个电离层 TEC 现报系统，在互联网上实时发布覆盖我国全境的电离层总电子含量参量。该系统至今已稳定运行 10 余年，其时实性、分辨率、精度等均达到国际同类系统的最好水平。这一系统的成功研制与运行受到有关用户的好评，相关技术已被移植应用到国内多家业务应用部门。

Awardee of Earth Sciences Prize, Wan Weixing

Wan Weixing was born in Tianmen City of Hubei Province in July 1958. He graduated from Wuhan University in 1982, and then began his graduate study in Chinese Academy of Sciences (CAS). In 1989, he received his doctorate from Wuhan Institute of Physics and Mathematics (WIPM, CAS). Five years later, he became a professor of space physics in WIPM and severed as the director of Wuhan Ionospheric Observatory (WIO). In 2004, the observatory joined Institute of Geology and Geophysics, CAS (IGGCAS), and he continued to serve as the director of Laboratory of Geomagnetism and Space physics. He reformed the laboratory to Key Laboratory of Ionospheric Environment, CAS in 2012, and then upgraded it to Key Laboratory of Earth and Planetary Physics, CAS (EPPCAS) in 2014, extending to the research field of comparative planetology. In 2016, he served as the chief scientist of China Mars Exploration Project. He was elected as an academician of Chinese Academy of Sciences in 2011.

As a scientist in space physics, Professor Wan has published more than 300 scientific publications which were cited by SCI papers more than 4000 times. He also won the National Natural Science Award second prize in 2015. He reached his international reputation in a number of topics including ionospheric physics, ionospheric radio propagation and upper atmospheric physics. His main contribution is as follows.

(1) He found the regional properties of the ionospheric disturbances from observations at Central China, and explains the observed results as the meteorological vortices around the Qinghai–Tibet Plateau, which in turn are produced by the topography of the plateau.

(2) He studied systematically the variability of the longitudinal 'wave four'structure of the low–latitude ionosphere, and revealed the correlation between the 'wave four' and the atmospheric tide. He also proposed a new physical mode describing the tidal coupling between the atmosphere and ionosphere.

(3) He also found the control of solar wind on the formation of sporadic E layer at high–latitudes and polar region, and pointed out that the randomness of the ionospheric electric field play a key role in the strength of sporadic E.

(4) He derived a formula describing the relationship between the solar zenith angle and the sudden increment of the total electron content produced by a solar flare. This new formula, which is different with the previous results, is confirmed by the later observation of the worldwide GPS observation.

(5) Together with his team, he established a meridian chain observation with various measurements of the ionosphere, upper atmosphere and geomagnetic field at four stations around 120°E. He also proposed an inversion algorithm for the data analysis of the new mode of the ionospheric observation.

(6) He developed an ionospheric model of total electron content (TEC) based on the empirical orthogonal function (EOF) analysis, then set up a nowcasting system by assimilate the TEC data from the meridian chain observation to the EOF model.

生命科学奖获得者

徐 国 良

徐国良，1965 年 2 月出生于浙江省诸暨市。1985 年毕业于浙江大学（原杭州大学）生物系。1993 年获德国马普分子遗传研究所暨柏林技术大学博士学位，之后在美国哥伦比亚大学完成博士后研究，2001 年回到中科院上海生命科学研究院生物化学与细胞生物学研究所工作，并担任中科院与德国马普学会合作项目青年科学家小组组长。2015 年当选中国科学院院士。作为中科院生物化学与细胞生物学研究所表观遗传学和发育生物学领域的学科带头人之一，徐国良在 DNA 甲基化与去甲基化的分子机制以及重编程过程中的表观遗传调控机制研究领域做出了一系列国际前沿和领先的成果。曾获国家杰出青年科学基金、2014 年度陈嘉庚生物科学奖和 2016 年度上海市自然科学一等奖，并担任 *Development* 编辑顾问和 *National Science Review* 编委。

徐国良长期致力于探索 DNA 甲基化谱式在哺乳动物胚胎发育中如何建立、DNA 上是否还存在着与甲基化胞嘧啶相关的未知修饰、DNA 去甲基化如何发生及其生物学意义等重大科学问题，他的研究工作为这些问题提供了答案。

一、发现 5- 甲基胞嘧啶的酶促氧化介导 DNA 去甲基化

细胞内 DNA 甲基化能引起染色质的压缩和基因沉默，因此，DNA 甲基化的去除对于沉默基因的重新激活起着重要作用。DNA 去甲基化如何发生是长期被关注的科学问题。由于几十年探索都未能找到哺乳动物去甲基化酶或任何去甲基化的分子途径，因而学术界对哺乳动物中是否发生去甲基化一直争论不休。

徐国良研究团队发现 DNA 中的 5- 甲基胞嘧啶（5mC）可以被干细胞核抽提物转变为 5- 羧基胞嘧啶（5caC），后者的产生是由双加氧酶 TET（Ten-Eleven-Translocation）催化完成的，而 TDG（Thymine DNA Glycosylase）糖苷酶能够特异性地识别这一新的修饰碱基并将其从基因组中切除，随后通过 DNA 碱基修复途径替换进不含修饰的胞嘧啶完成去甲

基化。该研究成果勾画出了 DNA 去甲基化的分子通路，为研究 DNA 甲基化谱式的动态变化及其生理功能提供了理论框架。同期 *Science* 杂志发表专评指出，徐国良等的发现解决了困扰科学界多年的 DNA 去甲基化难题。

二、发现 DNA 氧化去甲基化在早期胚胎发育中的生物学功能

哺乳动物中最剧烈的细胞重编程发生在雌雄生殖细胞向具有发育全能性的合子（受精卵）的转变过程中。精子和卵细胞具有各自配子特异性的表观遗传谱式。因此，为了形成一个具有全能性的早期胚胎，合子会经历一系列的重编程，其中最显著的就是 DNA 的去甲基化。

徐国良研究团队发现来自卵子的 Tet3 双加氧酶在合子中负责父本基因组 DNA 中 5mC 的氧化，这一改变启动 DNA 去甲基化，以激活早先在精子中被甲基化的 *Oct4* 和 *Nanog* 等全能性基因的表达。如果受精卵中 Tet3 被去除，很多胚胎会在着床后发生退化，而全身性敲除小鼠出生后全部死亡。这些结果首次证明了 Tet 双加氧酶介导的 DNA 酶促氧化在生物体内的功能。此外，卵源 Tet3 在体细胞核移植时对供体 DNA 进行氧化去甲基化。上述发现深化了对动物克隆原理的认识，也为不孕不育症提供了新的科学认知。最近，其课题组又发现母本基因组也发生 Tet3 介导的氧化去甲基化，这一发现打破了母本基因组仅伴随卵裂而发生被动去甲基化的传统观念，使人们对胚胎发育早期的重编程过程有了崭新的认识。关于"揭示 Tet 双加氧酶在哺乳动物胚胎发育表观遗传调控中的重要作用"研究被评为 2011 年度"中国十大科学进展"。

三、发现 DNA 氧化去甲基化在小鼠神经发生及认知方面的功能

在发现大脑细胞 DNA 含有氧化修饰碱基（包括 5caC）之后，人们对 DNA 氧化修饰在神经生物学方面的功能产生了巨大好奇。徐国良团队的研究工作表明，Tet1 蛋白能够调控成年小鼠大脑海马内神经前体细胞的增殖。Tet1 缺失后，成年小鼠神经前体细胞增殖能力明显降低，神经发生过程受损，并伴随有空间学习和记忆能力的下降。*Cell Stem Cell* 同期专评指出，该研究揭示了 Tet 酶介导的 DNA 氧化修饰对小鼠神经系统的表观遗传调控作用。

四、发现 DNA 氧化去甲基化为体细胞重编程所必需

Tet 与 TDG 介导 DNA 去甲基化的理论得到了广泛关注和认可，然而这一分子通路在细胞命运转变过程中的功能却不清楚。徐国良研究团队利用体细胞重编程研究体系，证明三个 *Tet* 基因全部敲除或 TDG 缺失的小鼠成纤维细胞由于不能发生间充质向上皮细胞的转化（MET）而不能进行重编程。原因是 Tet 或 TDG 的缺失至少导致了 MET 发生过程中关键的 *miRNA* 基因不能被去甲基化而保持了沉默状态。这些发现揭示了 DNA 甲基化这一表观遗传屏障在细胞命运决定与转换中的作用，为认识细胞可塑性本质提供了崭新视角。

五、发现 DNA 去甲基化与甲基化共同作用控制小鼠胚胎原肠运动

虽然 DNA 甲基化在哺乳动物基因组印记和 X 染色体失活等过程中具有非常重要的作用，但是对 DNA 甲基化及其进一步氧化修饰在小鼠胚胎发育过程中的功能意义还知之甚少。徐国良研究团队研究发现，Tet 双加氧酶介导的 DNA 去甲基化与 DNMT 甲基转移酶介导的 DNA 甲基化共同作用，通过调控 Lefty-Nodal 信号通路控制小鼠胚胎原肠运动。该研究首次在体内证明了 DNA 甲基化及其氧化修饰在小鼠胚胎发育过程中具有重要功能，揭示了胚胎发育过程中关键信号通路的表观遗传调控机理，为发育生物学提供了新的认识。关于"揭示胚胎发育过程中关键信号通路的表观遗传调控机理"的研究被评为 2016 年度"中国十大科学进展"。

Awardee of Life Sciences Prize, Xu Guoliang

Xu Guoliang was born in Zhuji City of Zhejiang Province in February 1965. He received his B.S. degree from Zhejiang University in 1985 and his doctorate in Genetics from the Max-Planck Institute for Molecular Genetics in Germany in 1993. His postdoctoral work was conducted in the Department of Genetics and Development of Columbia University, New York. After returned to China in 2001, Dr. Xu is currently a Principal Investigator at the Institute of Biochemistry and Cell Biology, Chinese Academy of Sciences. He is interested in the epigenetic regulation of mammalian development and the research of his team has provided insights into DNA methylation and oxidation during embryonic development. He has won several prestigious scientific awards, including Distinguished Young Investigator Research Fund from China NSF（2002）, Tan Jia Zhen Life Sciences Innovation Award（2012）, TWAS Prize in Biology（2013）, Tan Kah Kee Science Award（2014）.

1. Elucidated the mechanism of DNA demethylation

Dr. Xu's lab discovered that the Ten-eleven-translocation（Tet）dioxygenases oxidize the 5-methylcytosine（5mC）into 5-carboxylcytosine（5caC）in mammals and this oxidized base is recognized and excised by a DNA glycosylase. These findings indicate that the oxidation of 5mC by Tet followed by TDG-mediated base excision of 5caC constitutes a pathway for active DNA demethylation.

2. Revealed the role of Tet dioxygenase in epigenetic reprogramming in zygotes

Dr. Xu's lab proved that Tet3-mediated DNA hydroxylation is involved in epigenetic reprogramming of the zygotic paternal DNA and also contributes to somatic cell nuclear reprogramming during animal cloning. In 2014, their further work showed that both maternal and paternal genomes in zygotes undergo widespread active and passive demethylation before the first mitotic division.

3. Provided evidence on the importance of DNA hydroxymethylation in adult hippocampal neurogenesis and cognition

DNA hydroxylation catalyzed by Tet dioxygenases occurs abundantly in neurons. However, its biological function *in vivo* is largely unknown. Dr. Xu's lab demonstrated that Tet1 plays an important role in regulating neural progenitor cell proliferation in adult mouse brain.

4. Provided mechanistic insight into the essential role of TET–TDG mediated DNA demethylation during cell reprogramming

Dr. Xu's lab showed that *Tet*–deficient and *TDG*–deficient MEFs cannot be reprogrammed because of a block in the mesenchymal–to–epithelial transition (MET) step. The block in reprogramming is caused at least in part by defective activation of key miRNAs, which depend on oxidative demethylation promoted by Tet and TDG for demethylation.

5. Revealed the roles of TET and DNMT3 enzymes in the Lefty–Nodal feedback loops in embryonic development

Dr. Xu's lab showed that inactivation of all three *Tet* genes in mice leads to gastrulation defects and TET mediated oxidation of 5mC modulates Lefty–Nodal signalling by promoting demethylation in opposition to methylation by DNMT3 methyltransferases. These findings reveal a fundamental epigenetic mechanism featuring dynamic DNA methylation and demethylation crucial to the regulation of key signalling pathways in early body plan formation.

农学奖获得者

张 福 锁

张福锁，1960年10月出生于陕西省凤翔县。1985年于北京农业大学硕士毕业后留校任助教，1989年获得德国霍恩海姆大学植物营养博士学位，1990—1991年任北京农业大学土壤与植物营养系讲师，1991—1993年任北京农业大学土壤与植物营养系副教授。1993年至今任北京农业大学（1995年改名为中国农业大学）资源与环境学院植物营养系教授。1996—2011年任农业部植物营养学重点实验室主任，2001年起任教育部长江学者特聘教授，2002年至今任教育部植物—土壤相互作用重点实验室主任。2004年起任中国植物营养与肥料学会第六、第七届副理事长，中国土壤学会第十、第十一届副理事长，中国自然资源学会第五、第六届副理事长；2005年至今担任农业部测土配方施肥技术专家组组长；2008年至今任第八、第九届农业部科技委委员；2009年至今任第六、第七届教育部科技委农林学部副主任、委员。2003年至今任国际植物营养委员会委员、第十五届主席，2008年和2014年分别任丹麦哥本哈根大学和青岛农业大学名誉教授，2008年起任联合国全球养分管理协作委员会委员，2012年至今任国际根系研究学会常务理事，2013年起任联合国农业与食物系统可持续发展专家组成员，2014年入选欧亚科学院院士。

张福锁一直从事植物营养科研与教学工作，在植物营养理论研究、技术创新与应用等方面做出了突出贡献。

一、系统揭示了化肥的增产效应和环境影响，提出了协调高产与环保的新思路和可行途径

研究发现我国主要农田土壤 pH 值下降 0.5 个单位，出现显著酸化现象，氮肥过量施用是其主要成因，土壤酸化严重威胁农业生产和生态环境；发现近 30 年来我国陆地生态系统大气氮沉降增加了 60%，2/3 来自化肥等农业源；发现我国氮肥生产和施用过程中温室气体的排放占全国总量的 7%，通过技术优化和政策调控可减排近 50%；发现根层调控能增强养分活化利用，实现减肥增效。该系列成果分别在国际顶级期刊 *PNAS*（2009、2011）和 *Nature*（2014）上发表，并于 2005 年获国家自然科学二等奖。其中 *Nature* 文章入选 2014 年度"中国十大科学进展"。

二、创建了养分管理新技术，突破高产与环保难以协同的技术瓶颈

通过定位试验，全面定量了根层养分来源、去向及其转化过程，阐明了根层氮素供应与作物需求匹配规律，创建根层氮素实时监控技术。在全国开展的 5147 个试验示范中，该技术平均增产 12%、节氮 24%、减少损失 40%；利用全国 23 个长期定位试验，揭示了根层磷钾活化利用规律，创建根层磷钾恒量监控技术，比常规技术节肥 20% 以上，降低测土频次 60% ~ 80%，避免了过量施用和过多残留；依据中微量元素营养从缺到过量范围狭窄的特点，建立了"因缺补缺、矫正施用"的养分管理技术，更新了不同作物的中微量元素诊断指标与养分管理技术体系；针对不同生态区作物增产增效关键限制因子，综合集成养分管理、高产栽培和水分管理等技术，建立了我国 12 种主要作物养分管理技术体系，先后在全国累计推广 6815 万亩，平均增产 8%、节氮 26%、节磷 20%、增粮 193.6 万吨、增收节支 34.9 亿元，实现了高产与环保的协同。成果获得 2008 年度国家科技进步奖二等奖。

三、建立以"科技小院"为核心的区域技术应用新模式，大面积推广高产环保技术，推动我国农业转型发展

针对小农户技术推广难的问题，创建了在生产一线开展科技创新、社会服务和人才培养三位一体的"科技小院"新模式——师生长期扎根农村，零距离、零时差、零门槛、零费用为农民服务——解决了科技人员与农民脱节的问题，提高了技术到位率，取得了作物增产、农民增收、农业增效的好效果，得到了政府、企业和农民的认可。"科技小院"师生在生产中发现问题，在农民地里做试验、创新技术、集成模式，把研究成果直接应用到农民地里，走出了一条研究与生产相结合的科研之路。河北曲周"科技小院"的研究结果于 2016 年发表在 *Nature* 上，成为"国际小农户增产增效的范例"。"科技小院"研究生在农村、在生产一线得到培养，他们既是研究生，又是农民、农技员、培训师、挂职干部，理论与实践结合、研究与生产结合，科研能力、实践技能、综合素质和三农情怀得到全面提升，解决了人才培养与社会需求脱节的问题。"科技小院"人才培养模式于 2014 年获国家教学成果二等奖。目前已在全国 23 个省市区建立了 81 个"科技小院"，既有粮食作物，也有经济作物；既有小农户，也有大农场；先后研究了 96 项技术、集成了 44 个技术模式；服务 200 多个村庄、培训 50 多万农民；指导 60 多个合作社、8 家企业，推广技术 1000 多万亩。荣获 2016 年中国三农创新榜第一名。

近年来，为解决技术大面积应用难题，创建了"总量控制、分期调控"的区域施肥技术，解决了与政府行动结合难的问题；建立了"大配方、小调整"的区域配肥技术，解决了与企业结合难的问题；为全国制定了小麦、玉米、水稻大配方 33 个，以农业部文件发布，推动了企业配方肥生产和大面积应用。研发的配方肥产品近五年直接应用 364.2 万吨，覆盖 9105 万亩。针对未来需要持续高产与环境保护的尖锐矛盾，通过高产群体设计和根层养分供应与高产群体养分需求匹配规律的研究，定量阐明了高产体系大幅度降低养分环境排放的潜力与途径，于 2011 年在 66 个玉米试验中创造了产量和效率同时翻番的记录，并于 2014 年在三大粮食作物突破高产高效和环保的技术难题，为全球可持续集约化现代农业发展提供了范例。2013 年，应 *Nature* 邀请，张福锁撰文阐述了 21 世纪以来我国农业在协调作物高产与环境保护科学研究和技术应用方面取得的重要进展与成就，提出"中国为世界农业科技发展提供了重要的借鉴""值得其他发展中国家学习，发达国家也应广泛借鉴"。这些进展有力地支撑了全国测土配方施肥和化肥零增长等国家行动。

张福锁在植物营养理论和技术研究及其大面积应用方面取得的成果得到了国内外同行的认可，先后获国家自然科学二等奖 1 项、国家科技进步奖二等奖 1 项和省部级科技奖励 8 项；先后 65 次应邀在国际会议上作学术报告，获德国霍恩海姆大学杰出成就奖（2005）、丹麦哥本哈根大学荣誉教授称号（2008）和发展中国家科学院农业科学奖（2014）。二十多年来，他坚持教书育人，培养了一大批硕士生和博士生，培养建立了一支优秀的学术团队，连续三届入选国家自然科学基金创新群体。张福锁积极推动国内外多学科合作，通过主持"973"、行业专项等，组建了土肥、栽培、环境等多学科结合的全国养分管理协作网，搭建了科学研究和技术应用的创新平台；通过中德、中英等实质性项目合作，建立了养分管理国际协作网，参与制定联合国 2020 年养分管理计划和全球农业可持续发展规划。发表 SCI 论文 300 余篇，包括 *Science* 和 *Nature* 5 篇、*PNAS* 4 篇，H 因子 69。

Awardee of Agronomy Prize, Zhang Fusuo

Zhang Fusuo was born in Fengxiang County of Shaanxi Province in October 1960. He graduated from Beijing Agricultural University（BAU）in 1985 as a master student, and became an assistant Professor in BAU afterwards. He got his Ph.D. degree in Plant Nutrition at Hohenheim University, Germany, in 1989. He was a lecturer, associate Professor and Professor in Department of Plant Nutrition, BAU（renamed China Agricultural University since 1995）during 1990—1991, 1991—1993, and after 1993, respectively. He served as a director of Key Laboratory of Plant Nutrition of Chinese Ministry of Agriculture during 1996—2011, was authorized the position of professor fellowship of Changjiang Scholar Program in 2001, and a director of Key Laboratory of Plant-Soil Interactions of Chinese Ministry of Education since 2002. He was elected as the 6th and 7th vice president of Plant Nutrition and Fertilizer Society of China, the 10th and

11th vice president of China Society of Soil Sciences, the 5th and 6th vice president of China Society of Natural Resources. He served as the expert team leader of Soil Testing and Fertilization Recommendation in the Chinese Ministry of Agriculture since 2005, the 8th and 9th member of the Science and Technology Committee of the Chinese Ministry of Agriculture since 2008, and member of the 6th and 7th Agriculture and Forestry Division of Science and Technology Commission in Ministry of Education since 2009. He was appointed as honorary professors at University of Copenhagen, Denmark and Qingdao Agricultural University in China in 2008 and 2014, respectively. He was a member of the UN Global Nutrient Management Partnership Committee since 2008, a member of the United Nations Expert Group on Sustainable Development of Agriculture and Food System since 2013. He was a member of the International Committee on Plant Nutrition after 2003 and the 15th president of the Committee (2005—2009). He served as executive director of the International Society for Root Research in 2012 and was elected as the Fellow of the Eurasian Academy of Sciences in 2014.

农学奖获得者

邹学校

邹学校，1963 年 7 月出生于湖南省衡阳县。1986 年于湖南农学院农学系获农学硕士学位后进入湖南省农业科学院工作至今，1998 年 8 月晋升研究员。1996 年 3 月—2000 年 8 月任湖南省蔬菜研究所所长，湖南湘研种苗中心总经理，湖南湘研集团有限公司总经理，袁隆平农业高科技股份有限公司董事、副总裁；2000 年 9 月—2005 年 2 月任湖南省农业科学院副院长，2005 年 3 月起任湖南省农业科学院院长；2017 年 3 月任国家特色蔬菜产业技术体系首席专家、国家特色蔬菜产业技术研发中心主任。2002 年 12 月获华中科技大学管理学博士学位，2005 年 7 月获南京农业大学农学博士学位。先后任中国园艺学会副理事长、辣椒分会会长，湖南省园艺学会理事长，湖南省农学会常务副会长，湖南省作物学会副理事长，湖南省科学学与科技管理研究会副会长，湖南省农作物品种审定委员会副主任委员；《长江蔬菜》《湖南农业科学》《辣椒杂志》主编，《中国农业科学》《园艺学报》《中国蔬菜》《农学学报》等刊物编委；中南大学、湖南大学、湖南农业大学博士生导师；农业部科学技术委员会委员，中国农业科学院学术委员会委员。2016 年入选国家"万人计划"领军人才。

邹学校从事辣椒遗传育种研究，在辣椒优异种质资源创制、育种技术创新、新品种培育等方面取得了系列创新性成果。获国家科技进步奖二等奖 4 项，其中排名第一 3 项、排名第四 1 项；作为第一完成人，获湖南省科技进步一等奖 2 项。先后出版著作 12 部，发表学术论文 112 篇，其中 SCI 论文 16 篇。培养博士、硕士研究生 39 名。为提高我国第一大蔬菜作物辣椒的育种科技水平、促进蔬菜产业发展做出了突出贡献。

一、全面提升我国辣椒品种早熟、丰产、抗病、耐贮运、加工、机械化采收水平，引领辣椒育种方向

辣椒是我国第一大蔬菜作物，面积和产量均居世界第一，但存在品种不能满足产业需求的问题。为此，邹学校带领团队育成辣椒新品种 53 个，累计推广 6780.5 万亩，是世界上种植面积最大的系列辣椒品种。

20 世纪 80 年代，针对我国当时辣椒地方品种产量低、上市晚等问题，邹学校作为主要参加人，突破了辣椒杂种优势育种技术，育成了早熟、高产系列辣椒杂交品种湘研 1-6 号，提早上市 33～36 天，平均增产 28.7%，是八九十年代我国种植面积最大的辣椒品种。

90 年代初，针对当时辣椒连年连片种植导致病害严重、品种抗性差等问题，邹学校主持突破了辣椒多抗性人工接种鉴定技术，选育出抗病毒病、疮痂病、疫病和日灼病等多种病害的辣椒品种湘研 7-10 号 4 个品种，田间病害损失减少 58.9%、平均增产 18.7%，是 90 年代中后期我国种植面积最大的辣椒品种。

90 年代后期，针对辣椒规模化基地生产的需求，他利用辣椒雄性不育育种技术育成了高产、抗病、商品性好、耐贮藏运输的系列辣椒品种湘研 11-20 号、湘辣 1-4 号共计 14 个品种，平均增产 14.6%，长途运输损耗降低 76.7%，是 21 世纪初我国种植面积最大的辣椒品种。

21 世纪初，针对我国辣椒加工业的快速发展，邹学校利用分子标记辅助选择技术突破了辣椒高产就难以高辣椒素的技术瓶颈，育成了加工专用品种 13 个，鲜食、加工兼用品种 10 个，平均增产 11.9%，原料利用率提高 20.9%，是目前我国种植面积最大的加工辣椒品种。

近年来，针对劳动力成本高的问题，他又育成了坐果集中、适合高密度种植、便于机械化采收的博辣红牛等 6 个辣椒新品种，平均增产 8.6%，每亩节约采收成本 700 元左右。

二、建成我国保存份数最多的辣椒种质资源库，创制出育成品种最多、应用最广的辣椒骨干亲本

20 世纪 80 年代，邹学校率先系统开展了辣椒种质资源研究，到 2016 年已建成保存国内外辣椒种质资源 3219 份的辣椒种质资源库。经系统评价，筛选出抗病抗逆性强、品质优、丰产性好的优异种质资源 426 份，创制重要育种材料 20 份。上述优良种质被国内 80% 的育种单位广泛应用。首创辣椒基因表达数据库，明确了辣椒根、茎、叶、花、果实特定发育时期及非生物胁迫和激素处理下的基因表达模式。

创制了 3 个辣椒骨干亲本。利用优异资源"伏地尖"经 5 年 8 代系统选择，育成抗性强、耐低温弱光、早期挂果能力强的早熟骨干亲本 5901；再利用 5901 与抗病性强、耐贮运的矮秆早杂交，经 5 年 10 代自交和定向选择育成优良亲本 9001，提高了抗病性和耐贮运性。国内育种单位利用 5901 及其衍生系 9001 育成辣椒优良品种 46 个。

利用优异资源"河西牛角椒"经 6 年 8 代系统选择，育成抗 4 种病害、耐热、耐旱、高温下坐果能力强的中熟骨干亲本 6421；并在 6421 中发现天然不育株，经 6 年 10 代选育出我国首个易恢复、配合力强的辣椒胞质雄性不育系 9704A。国内育种单位利用 6421 及其衍生系 9704A 育成优良品种 63 个。

利用优异资源"湘潭迟班椒"经 5 年 7 代单株定向选择，育成抗 5 种病害、耐热、耐湿、耐贮运的晚熟骨干亲本 8214。利用 8214 与潘家大辣椒杂交、再与长沙光皮椒杂交，经 7 年 10 代自交和定向选择育成优良衍生系 9003，提高了抗病性和商品品质。利用 8214 与永丰线椒杂交、再与台湾美香分离自交系杂交，经 10 年自交和定向选择育成优良衍生系 J01-227，提高了加工成品率，改善了风味。国内育种单位利用 8214 及其衍生系 9003、J01-227 等育成优良品种 72 个。

全国育种单位利用上述 3 个骨干亲本及其衍生系育成优良品种 165 个，占全国同期审定辣椒新品种的 23.34%；在 20 多个省大面积应用，累计推广面积达 1.3 亿亩，占同期新品种推广面积的 42.07%。5901、6421 和 8214 是我国育成品种数量最多、育成品种种植面积最大的辣椒骨干亲本。

三、创新辣椒育种技术，促进我国辣椒科技发展

突破了辣椒杂种优势育种技术。率先系统开展辣椒杂种优势利用研究，突破了辣椒人工制种杂种优势利用技术，使我国辣椒生产于 20 世纪末就完成了由地方品种向杂交品种的更新换代。

突破了辣椒雄性不育育种技术。在骨干亲本 6421 中发现了抗病抗逆性强、商品品质好、耐贮运、综合性状优良、易恢复、配合力强的新型辣椒胞质雄性不育源 9704A，探明了 9704A 的不育机理，建立了配套的雄性不育育种技术体系，已被国内 50% 的育种单位应用于实际育种。9704A 是目前我国大面积种植的辣椒雄性不育杂交品种的主要不育源。

为此，邹学校先后获中国青年科技奖、全国优秀科技工作者、光华工程科技奖、中华农业英才奖、全国"五一劳动奖章"等名誉称号。团队入选农业部"农业科研杰出人才及创新团队"。

Awardee of Agronomy Prize, Zou Xuexiao

Zou Xuexiao was born in Hengyang County of Hunan Province in July 1963. He obtained his master degree in agriculture science from Hunan agricultural college in 1986. After that, he began to work at Hunan academy of agriculture science, where he was promoted to be a researcher professor in August 1998. He gained his Ph.D. degree in agriculture science from Nanjing Agricultural University in July 2005.

In his academic career, Zou is the chief expert of National Characteristic Vegetables Industry Technology System and the director of National Characteristic Vegetables Industry Technology R&D Center since March 2017, and he successively served as the vice president of Chinese Society for Horticultural Science（CSHS）, the director of Pepper Branch of CSHS, the chief editor of

Journal of Changjiang Vegetables, Hunan Agricultural Sciences and Journal of China Capsicum, and as the editorial board member of Scientia Agricultura Sinica, Acta Horticulturae Sinica, and China vegetables, etc. In 2016, Zou has been selected as the leading academic of "Ten Thousand Talent Program" in China.

In Zou's research, he focuses on genetic breeding of pepper and has achieved a series of innovative achievements. Notably, he has obtained the second prize of State Science and Technology Progress Award for four times, of which he ranked the first name for three times and ranked the fourth name for once. As the most important contributor, he awarded the first prize of Hunan Provincial Science and Technology Progress Award for two times, and has published 12 professional books and 112 academic papers (16 SCI papers). All of these indicate that Zou Xuexiao has made an outstanding contribution to the improvement of pepper's breeding technology and the development of vegetable industry in China.

Zou's research benefits the comprehensive enhancement of pepper varieties in precocity, high yield, disease resistance, storage and transportation, process, and mechanized harvest level traits, which has become the leading direction in pepper breeding.

Zou's group has built the largest library of pepper germplasm resources in China, and has created the backbone parents which were cultivated the maximum varieties, and which were the most widely applied in China.

Zou had broken through the problems of hybrid and male sterility breeding technology of the pepper, and promoted the development of China's pepper investigation.

Owing to Zou's creative research, he successively awarded the prize of China Youth Science and Technology, National Excellent Science and Technology Workers, Guanghua Engineering Science, Chinese Agricultural Talents, and the titles of national "May Day" labor medal, etc. His team has been selected into Agricultural Research Outstanding Talent and Innovative Team of agricultural department.

农学奖获得者

周 雪 平

周雪平，1965 年 7 月出生于江苏省吴县。1992 年毕业于南京农业大学植物病理专业获农学博士学位。1992—1994 年在浙江农业大学博士后流动站工作，出站后留校任教，历任浙江农业大学生物研究所副所长，浙江大学农业与生物技术学院书记、副院长、院长。2013 年 5 月任中国农业科学院植物保护研究所所长。担任国际植物保护科学协会执委，国际植物病理学会理事，国际病毒分类委员会委员，植物病虫害生物学国家重点实验室主任，农业部第九届科学技术委员会委员，第七届国家自然科学基金委生命科学部专家咨询委员会委员，*Annual Review of Phytopathology*、*Journal of General Virology* 和 *Virology* 等杂志编委。

由植物病毒引起的作物病毒病素有"作物癌症"之称，是制约作物生产的重要因素。周雪平长期从事植物病毒病害研究。针对我国安全、高效防控作物病毒病的重大需求，他率领团队系统性地开展了多种重要作物病毒的生物学、致病机理、流行学、预警监控和防控技术研究，取得了突出成绩。

一、在双生病毒种类鉴定、分子变异和致病机理研究方面取得重要进展

双生病毒是植物病毒中数量最多的一个类群，约占植物病毒的 1/3，并在多种作物上造成毁灭性危害。周雪平对双生病毒开展了系统研究，建立了双生病毒快速诊断检测技术，系统调查了双生病毒在我国的发生分布，分离鉴定 41 种双生病毒，其中 31 种为新种，发现的新双生病毒数量居国际首位；构建了 17 种双生病毒及 8 种卫星 DNA 的侵染性克隆，明确了双生病毒及卫星 DNA 在致病中的作用，并建立了作物抗双生病毒的快速筛选技术，被全国多家单位用于抗病育种，已筛选出一批抗病品系及品种；发现双生病毒不能通过种子传播，其侵染循环主要通过烟粉虱在作物与作物之间以及杂草与作物之间传播，因此提出了以"切断病毒初侵染源、控制苗期侵染"为核心的作物双生病毒病

综合防控技术，在浙江、广西和云南等地区示范推广。RNA 沉默是植物抵御病毒侵染的重要防卫机制，周雪平通过深入研究发现双生病毒卫星 DNA 编码的 βC1 是重要致病因子和 RNA 沉默抑制子，阐明了 βC1 抑制转录水平基因沉默（TGS）的机制，*Nature Reviews Microbiology* 两篇综述论文都对此发现进行了介绍。同时发现 βC1 通过上调植物钙调素类似蛋白 rgs-CaM 表达并抑制植物 RNA 沉默通路中重要组分 RNA 依赖的 RNA 聚合酶 6 的功能；此外，Nbrgs-CaM 还能与双链 RNA 结合蛋白 SGS3 互作，并通过细胞自噬途径介导 SGS3 的分解，从而破坏转录后基因沉默（PTGS）。为了对抗毒蛋白 βC1，植物激酶蛋白 SlSnRK1 通过与 βC1 互作并磷酸化 βC1 降低其抑制 TGS 和 PTGS 的能力；而植物 E3 连接酶蛋白 NtRFP1 通过介导 βC1 泛素化并利用 26S 蛋白酶体分解 βC1，从而减弱毒蛋白 βC1 对植物的毒害，这些发现为该类病害的防治策略提供了新的思路和靶标。

周雪平发现双生病毒遗传结构是异质种群，病毒种群具有准种特征，具有与 RNA 病毒相似的突变率，*Nature Reviews Genetics* 认为这是病毒进化方面的重要发现之一。他发现双生病毒基因组重组可产生新的双生病毒，*New Scientist* 以"致命的杂合体使丰收无望"为标题介绍了该发现，植物病毒专著 *Matthews' Plant Virology* 第四版也对该发现做了详细介绍。

通过与昆虫学家合作，周雪平明确了近年入侵我国 B 型烟粉虱与其所传播的双生病毒之间存在互利关系，双生病毒卫星 DNA 降低了植物中茉莉酸的滴度，从而提高了烟粉虱的存活力和生殖力，纽约的《科学现场》称"这是国际科学界首次发现一种入侵昆虫与其所传播的病毒之间存在互利共生关系"。

相关研究发表 SCI 论文 115 篇，授权发明专利 10 项，获全国百篇优秀博士学位论文 1 篇、提名论文 2 篇，并获 2014 年度国家自然科学二等奖。周雪平因在双生病毒研究领域的突出贡献，应邀为植物病理学领域中最有影响的 *Annual Review of Phytopathology* 撰写了关于双生病毒卫星分子的综述文章。

二、建立了水稻主要病毒病的监测预警技术，为病害绿色防控提供技术支撑

作为水稻产业体系的岗位科学家，周雪平负责我国水稻病毒病防控技术研究。研制了针对水稻条纹病毒、南方水稻黑条矮缩病毒、水稻黑条矮缩病毒、水稻齿矮病毒和水稻矮缩病毒等病毒的特异性单克隆抗体，开发了检测水稻和介体中病毒的免疫学快速检测试剂盒，对介体带毒检测周期缩短至 3 小时、灵敏度达到 1∶1600、准确率提升为 99%，普及应用至县级农技部门，使实验室技术应用到了田间地头。依据介体带毒率和数量，构建了病害中长期预测模型，实现了水稻病毒病的早期预警和实时预报。上述技术被全国农技推广服务中心在我国稻区普遍推广，有效预测了病毒病的发生动态，提高了病害防治的有效性，为病害防控的绿色治理提供了重要支撑。此外，他还对水稻条纹病毒基因功能开展研究，发现 RNA4 编码的 NSvc4 为病毒的运动蛋白，这是在纤细病毒属中首次鉴定出病毒运动蛋白，被 *Nature China* 作为突出科学研究成果刊登；明确了 RNA4

编码的 SP 蛋白通过与寄主 PsbP 蛋白互作减少其在叶绿体中的积累量从而破坏寄主光合作用，引起条纹症状。发现 RNA3 编码的 NS3 能抑制植物抵御病毒侵染的防卫系统——RNA 沉默，而在介体昆虫体内，NS3 通过与灰飞虱的 RPN3 互作而破坏灰飞虱泛素化蛋白降解途径对病毒蛋白的降解能力，从而有利于病毒传播。

相关研究发表 SCI 论文 12 篇，授权发明专利 5 项，获全国百篇优秀博士学位提名论文 1 篇，并获 2016 年国家科学技术进步奖二等奖。

三、制备了 40 多种重要作物病毒的单克隆抗体，建立了病毒病监测预警技术

植物病毒缺乏有效治疗作用的抗病毒剂，国际上均采用早期监测与防控的方法（如应用无病毒种子种苗）减轻病毒病的危害，而早期监测与防控的核心就是病毒检测技术。针对我国缺乏作物病毒有效检测技术之现状，周雪平通过提纯病毒粒子或表达病毒外壳蛋白基因获得高纯度抗原，并免疫小鼠，制备了大麦黄矮病毒等 40 多种侵染小麦、玉米及经济作物的重要作物病毒的单克隆抗体；并利用制备的检测特异性好、灵敏度高的单克隆抗体创制了病毒快速检测术及检测试剂盒，试剂盒已广泛应用于我国作物病毒病的早期诊断、监测预警与防控，为健康种苗生产、病毒病预测预报和科学使用农药提供了关键技术。相关研究发表 SCI 论文 25 篇，授权发明专利 8 项。

周雪平注重学生教育培养与学科建设，他共指导博士后 15 名、博士生 75 名、硕士生 38 名，其中 1 人获长江特聘教授、1 人获国家杰出青年基金、1 人入选中组部青年拔尖人才支持计划、3 人获国家优秀青年基金、1 人获全国优秀博士学位论文、3 人获全国优秀博士学位论文提名，为植物保护学科培养了一批学术骨干。他注重学科建设，共同主编的英文专著 *Current Research Topics in Plant Virology* 由 Springer 出版社出版；同时作为副主编，协助主编谢联辉院士出版普通高等教育"十一五"规划教材《植物病毒学（第三版）》和国家精品课程配套教材《普通植物病理学》，并作为共同主编出版普通高等教育"十二五"规划教材《植物病理学》。

Awardee of Agronomy Prize, Zhou Xueping

Zhou Xueping was born in Wu County of Jiangsu Province in July 1965. He completed his PhD degree in 1992 in Nanjing Agricultural University. Then, he accepted a postdoctoral fellowship at Zhejiang Agricultural University. He was promoted to full professor in 1997, and after 1998, held successive appointments in Zhejiang University as Vice Dean and Dean of the College of Agriculture and Biotechnology. In 2013, he accepted his current position as Director of the Institute of Plant Protection, Chinese Academy of Agricultural Sciences.

Zhou Xueping has made significant contributions for detection of plant viruses and understanding of virus pathogenesis. In applied research, he raised monoclonal antibodies against more than 40 plant viruses and used them to design sensitive serological methods for virus detection in crops and transmission vectors, and to implement disease control measures. For example, he provided leadership that reduced rice stripe virus (RSV) disease to low levels by using virus detection and control methods. Zhou Xueping's extensive fundamental research has focused on identification and elucidation of molecular functions of geminiviruses and their associated DNA satellites. He has identified 41 geminiviruses, 31 of which are distinct species, and demonstrated that 17 geminiviruses are associated with DNA satellite. Zhou Xueping has analyzed functions of satellite βC1 encoded protein against host gene silencing. These findings show that the βC1 interacts with a host methyltransferase cofactor to suppress methylation activities that interfere with epigenetic modifications of the viral genome. He demonstrated that a tobacco calmodulin-like protein is up-regulated by βC1 to affect gene silencing by repression of an RNA-dependent RNA-polymerase and degrading SGS3 via the autophagy pathway in the RNA silencing pathway. He has also identified host defense responses in which a tobacco E3 ligase interacts with βC1 to mediate βC1 degradation. In addition, he discovered that a tomato phosphokinase can phosphorylate βC1 to interfere with its gene silencing suppression ability. Furthermore, he has shown that βC1 also suppresses jasmonic acid responses to permit increased whitefly multiplication and population dynamics that facilitate geminivirus spread.

Zhou Xueping also has made contributions to the plant pathology community include service as a Governing Board Member of the International Association for the Plant Protection Sciences and the International Committee on Taxonomy of Viruses, and Councilor of the International Society for Plant Pathology. He has served as an editorial board member for more than 15 journals, including Annual Review of Phytopathology. Since 2010, he has hosted visits of more than 50 scientists from the USA, Europe and Asia. These visits have resulted several collaborations in the USA, and the development of integrated pest management programs in East Asia.

医学药学奖获得者

陈　薇

陈薇，女，1966年2月出生于浙江省兰溪市。1988年浙江大学本科毕业，1991年清华大学硕士毕业，同年4月特招入伍。1998年军事医学科学院博士毕业，获医学博士学位，2002年晋升研究员并遴选为博士生导师，2015年晋升专业技术少将。现任军事医学科学院生物工程研究所所长、研究员，全国人大代表，全国妇联执委，全军生物武器损伤防治药物重点实验室主任，国家生物安全专家委员会委员，全军生物技术专业委员会主任委员，中华预防医学会生物安全分会主任委员，中华医学会微生物与免疫学分会候任主任委员，国家药典委生物技术专业委员会副主任委员。

陈薇长期从事生物防御和生物高技术研究，领衔"生物危害防控"国家重点领域创新团队，创立生防特需疫苗和药物研究新技术体系，为SARS、炭疽、埃博拉等重大疫情防控做出了突出贡献。

（1）成功研制我军首个病毒防治生物新药——重组人干扰素ω。抗击"非典"期间，完成小汤山医院等6省市31家SARS定点医院14061例临床研究，结果表明使用该药物对防范一线医护人员感染起到重要作用。全国20余万高危人群使用，实现使用人群"零"感染。获1类新药证书和生产文号，先后应用于H5N1、H1N1、H7N9、腺病毒等突发疫情的应急防控以及"神五"发射、"9.3"阅兵、援非抗埃等重大活动卫勤保障。2016年获国家技术发明奖二等奖（排名第一）。

（2）应对A类生物战剂炭疽芽孢的威胁，成功研发基因工程炭疽疫苗，2012年获1类新药证书和生产文号，是首个纳入国家战略储备的重组疫苗，并应用于我国近年多起炭疽疫情防控，标志着我国对炭疽芽孢"白色粉末"的生物防御能力达到世界领先水平。部分成果于2006年获军队科技进步一等奖（排名第一）。

（3）成功研发全球首个2014基因型重组埃博拉疫苗，带领团队在疫情最严重的西非国家塞拉利昂完成了疫苗接种，临床研究结果于2015年3月、2017年2月两次以通讯作者发表于国际权威医学杂志《柳叶刀》，是我国首个在境外完成临床试验的创新疫苗。

（4）先后牵头承担国家"863"计划重大项目、国家新药创制重大专项、国家杰出青年科学基金、国家传染病防治重大专项和国家科技部科技改革与发展专项等课题，建成全军生物武器损伤防治药物重点实验室和全军唯一的特需生物药品中试基地，形成完整的特种生物药物研发技术体系。

2008 年汶川地震期间，担任国家减灾委—科技部抗震救灾专家委员会卫生防疫组长并赴灾区一线，为"大灾之后无大疫"做出重要贡献；北京奥运会期间，作为奥运安保军队指挥小组专家组成员，带队负责国家体育场等 20 个场馆的现场安保任务，成功处置数十起核生化疑似事件，被表彰为总后勤部"援奥工作先进个人"。

荣立个人二等功 2 次、三等功 2 次；培养毕业研究生 76 名；以通讯作者在 The Lancet、Nature Nanotechnology 等杂志发表论文 195 篇；以第 1 发明人获国家发明专利授权 20 项、1 类新药证书 2 项、生产批件 2 项、临床批件 10 项；以第 1 完成人获国家技术发明奖二等奖、军队科技进步一等奖，并荣获中国十大杰出青年、"求是"杰出青年奖、中国青年女科学家奖等，入选国家百千万人才工程、"万人计划"领军人才。

Awardee of Medical Sciences and Materia Medica Prize, Chen Wei

Chen Wei, female, was born in Lanxi City of Zhejiang Province in February 1966. She obtained her BSc from Zhejiang University, MSc from Tsinghua University, and MD from AMMS. Dr. Chen was promoted to Principal Investigator and PhD student advisor in 2002. She currently holds a position as director and principal investigator of Beijing Bioengineering Institute. In addition, Dr. Chen also serves as a representative in the National People's Congress, Chairperson of the Biosafety committee of the Chinese Preventive Medicine Association and Chairperson elect of the Microbiology and Immunology chapter of the Chinese Medical Association.

Dr. Chen has led a national biological hazard prevention research and development team and established new technology platforms for innovative vaccines and drugs. She has made significant contributions to control and prevention of SARS, anthrax and Ebola, by the development of medicines such as the broad-spectrum antiviral recombinant human interferon ω, and the world's first Ebola vaccine based on a 2014 genotype. As an accomplished researcher, she has published her scientific findings as a corresponding author in numerous outstanding scientific journals such as The Lancet, Nature Nanotechnology, etc. She has also obtained various awards for her achievements, including second prize of National Technology Invention Award as first inventor,

China's Top Ten Outstanding Youth, CAST Qiu Shi Outstanding Young Researcher Award, L'Oréal–UNESCO for Women in Science China fellowship, national candidate of "Millions of Talent Projects" and leading academic of "Ten Thousand Talent Program".

医学药学奖获得者

果 德 安

果德安，1962 年 4 月出生于山东省郓城县。1990 年取得北京医科大学药学院博士学位，1993—1996 年在美国得州理工大学化学系从事博士后研究，1996—2005 年分别担任北京医科大学药学院副教授及北京大学药学院教授。现任中国科学院上海药物研究所研究员、中药标准化技术国家工程实验室主任、上海中药现代化研究中心主任。

果德安长期致力于中药分析与质量标准研究，在中药标准基础和应用研究及推动中药国际化方面取得了突破和创新性成果。

一、提出"深入研究，浅出标准"中药质量研究的指导思想和"整体—组分—成分"整合分析的研究策略，创建了中药"化学分析—代谢分析—生物分析"三位一体的系统分析方法，解决了制约制定中药标准的关键基础科学问题，为构建科学可行的中药质量标准奠定了坚实基础

中药为多成分复杂体系，但由于缺乏系统分析方法，导致其成分不清、有效成分不明，成为制约中药产业健康发展和中药走向国际的关键瓶颈。据此，果德安创新性地提出了适合中药复杂体系特点的"深入研究，浅出标准"的指导思想，制定了"整体—组分—成分"整合分析策略，构建了"化学分析—代谢分析—生物分析"三位一体的系统分析方法，解决了前人单靠化学分析或生物分析而无法明晰中药活性成分的关键科学问题。

率先发展了中药多维色谱–质谱联用分析、代谢指纹图谱分析、超高效液相体内外定量、中药蛋白质组学等系列新技术方法，大幅提升了中药活性成分分析鉴定的能力和水平，从丹参、三七、人参等中药材和复方中分析鉴定 5000 余个成分，结合体内分析和生物分析明晰活性成分 200 余个；以丹参为例开展了中药系统分析示范研究，从中分析鉴定 190 多个成分，阐明了丹酚酸和丹参酮类成分的体内代谢过程及药效作用机制与调控网络，为确定这两类成分为丹参治疗心血管疾病的有效成分提供了充分的科学证据

（发表 SCI 论文 45 篇，他引 1068 次），成为中药活性成分系统分析的典范。受邀在药物分析、药物代谢和药理学权威期刊发表特邀综述。在对丹参和三七深入研究的基础上，开发出成分清晰、质量可控的现代创新中药"丹七通脉片"，2009 年获临床批文，现开展 Ⅱ b 期临床研究。

该成果获 2012 年国家自然科学奖二等奖（排名第一）。

二、创建了中药整体质量标准体系，应用于中国药典、美国药典、欧洲药典和中药产品标准中，实现了中国学者制定美国药典和欧洲药典中药标准零的突破，为推动国家中药标准体系建设、中药标准国际化和中药产业标准化发展做出了突出贡献

"中药标准主导国际标准制定"是国家战略目标，标准是确保中药疗效与安全的核心要素，中药国际化需标准引领。现行的单一成分质控模式难以甄别中药的真伪和优劣，据此，在上述"深入研究"的基础上，果德安对丹参、三七等中药材和肾康注射液等中成药开展了标准制定的示范性研究，创建了以指纹图谱结合多成分定量为核心的整体质量标准体系。

他致力于中药标准的国际化研究，带领团队经过长期不懈地探索，发展了国际认同的中药质量标准框架和核心技术，制定了诸如《薄层色谱鉴别国际通用技术要求》等具有普遍指导意义的指导原则。构建的丹参、三七等 7 个中药 26 个标准首次载入美国药典，实现了中药标准被 140 多个国家使用的《美国药典》收载的突破，美国药典会评价"果德安领导的团队所制订的相关标准质量极高，是美国药典所收到的植物药相关标准中最好的。"建立的钩藤等 4 个中药标准被 39 个欧盟国家使用的《欧洲药典》采纳，是第一个制定欧洲药典中药标准的中国学者，欧洲药典会评价"果德安团队极高质量的标准工作大大加快了欧洲药典质量标准的研究步伐，我们受益巨大。"

他将所建立的中药整体质量标准体系成功用于肾康注射液、丹参多酚酸盐、血栓通等多个中成药大品种的标准提升中，显著提高了这些产品的质量可控性，产品销售额大幅提升（近三年新增销售额 116 亿元），推动了中药产业的标准化和规范化发展。

该成果获 2016 年国家科技进步奖二等奖（排名第一）。

三、搭建了国际一流的中药标准研究国家与国际合作平台，在中药现代化研究与中药标准制定方面建立了广泛的合作关系，为开展高水平的中药标准研究、制定与产业服务提供了重要的支撑平台

果德安重视平台建设，于 2005 年成功组建上海中药现代化研究中心，2008 年获国家发改委首批工程实验室建设项目，2012 年通过验收建成我国第一个"中药标准化技术国家工程实验室"，于 2016 年又获准建设发改委"国家中药质量检测中心"平台，形成了从中药标准基础研究、中药标准体系建设、中药标准国际化到中药质量检测服务一体化的具有重要国际影响力的中药标准研究平台，为推动我国中药标准化研究与发展提供了保障、发挥了引领和示范作用。

基于长期的国际科研合作，建成了设备与技术一流的国际合作平台，与美国国家天然产物研究中心成立"中美中药研究中心"；与奥地利格拉茨大学成立"上海药物所－格拉茨大学中药合作中心"；与安捷伦科技成立"上海药物所－安捷伦中药中心"，成为沃特世公司在中国大陆唯一的全球创新中心；成为开展中药新分析方法研究、中药国际标准制定等一系列引领性研究工作的重要支撑平台。他还发起和连续主办9届"上海中医药与天然药物国际大会"和7届"中药分析国际大会"，有力促进了中药的国际交流与合作，显著提升了中药的国际影响。鉴于其取得的突出成绩和国际影响力，果德安曾获得香港张安德中医药国际贡献奖、国际植物药科学大会（美国）首届杰出贡献奖、美国植物药委员会 Norman Farnsworth 卓越研究奖、美国生药学会 Varo Tyler 奖、吴阶平医药创新奖等知名个人奖项。

Awardee of Medical Sciences and Materia Medica Prize, Guo Dean

Guo Dean was born in Yuncheng County of Shandong Province in April 1962. He received Ph.D of Pharmacognosy in Beijing Medical University in 1990, now working as a chair professor in Shanghai Institute of Materia Medica, Chinese Academy of Sciences, director of National Engineering Laboratory for TCM Standardization Technology, director of Shanghai Research Center for TCM Modernization. He focused his research on the modernization of traditional Chinese medicine for more than 30 years. He has developed a model for TCM holistic quality control and developed holistic quality control system of TCM, which has been successfully applied in Chinese Pharmacopoeia, United States Pharmacopoeia and Europe Pharmacopoeia for the herbal standards. These achievements were considered to have a great global impact. He got National Outstanding Youth Foundation for the Talents, NSF of China in 1999, received the Second prize in National Natural Sciences Award in 2012, got American Botanical Council Norman R. Farnsworth Excellence in Botanical Research Award. He received Outstanding Contribution Award in International Conference on the Science of Botanicals, received Wujieping Medicine Innovation Award in 2013, won Cheung On Tak International Award For Outstanding Contribution to Chinese Medicine in 2015, and awarded The American Society of Pharmacognosy Varo Tyler Prize and the Second Prize of The State Scientific and Technological Progress Award in 2016. He is the first Chinese scientist to elaborate TCM standards for USP and EP. He published over 418 SCI papers and 25 authorized patents. His concurrent academic posts include Executive Committee member of Chinese Pharmacopoeia; Vice Chair of Botanical Dietary Supplement and Herbal Medicine Expert Committee of United States Pharmacopoeia, Expert Member of European Pharmacopoeia; Chairman of The Specialty Committee Of TCM

Pharmaceutical Analysis Of WFCMS; Editor in Chief, Associate editor or editorial board members of 18 international journals, such as Journal of Ethnopharmacology, Phytomedicines, etc. He has delivered more than 40 plenary lectures in the major international conferences. He initiated and organized Shanghai International Conference on Traditional Chinese Medicine and Nature Medicine meeting series, which has successfully held for 9 times and becomes an international well-known event. As the president, he also held 8 consecutive meetings of International Conference on TCM Pharmaceutical Analysis.

医学药学奖获得者

刘奕志

刘奕志，1962 年 7 月出生于广东省广州市。1984 年毕业于中山医科大学临床医学系，1991 年获博士学位，在中山眼科中心工作至今。现为国家"973 计划"首席科学家，眼科学国家重点实验室主任，中山大学中山中心主任、眼科医院院长。

刘奕志从事重大致盲眼病的临床及基础研究工作 33 年，是我国微创白内障手术的开拓者之一，亲手实施白内障手术 20 万例，以通讯/共同通讯作者发表 SCI 论文 82 篇（包括 *Nature* 3 篇、*Nature Biomedical Engineering* 1 篇），在建立新型白内障防治体系及眼再生医学领域做出了一系列开创性工作。

一、创建新型白内障防治体系，提升了全球白内障诊治水平

1. 创建白内障扭动粉碎技术

微创白内障手术的关键是将白内障核粉碎并避免组织损伤。传统白内障超声乳化探头单向"振动"的能量利用效率仅 50%，并发症多。为此，刘奕志开展大样本临床随机对照研究，首次验证了"扭动"碎核技术优于传统的"振动"碎核，效能提高 30%，眼内组织损伤减轻 20%，并在 *J Cataract Refract Surg* 发表了全球首篇扭动技术论文，被编入美国、英国、德国等 8 部国际白内障专著，在全世界推广应用，"扭动"技术已成为目前国际先进白内障手术的主流技术；受 *Ocular Surgery News* 特邀撰写了关于扭动技术的专题述评；同时，还建立了涵盖基层、大中型医院和国际高端的白内障手术技术及推广体系，推动了我国白内障手术治疗整体水平的提升，获国家科学技术进步奖二等奖（第一完成人，2014）和中国医师奖（2016）。

刘奕志还基于白内障微创手术安全性的提高，倡导和推行眼科日间手术模式，改变了眼科手术必须住院的现状，提高了医疗效率并降低了成本。他注重人才培养，尤其注重年轻医生的培养，提出年轻手术医生的培养方略。目前已培养 1 名杰青、1 名新世纪人

才、100 多名研究生和数十名研究生导师及学科带头人，为白内障手术提供了高质量的技术保障，推动了我国白内障手术率和复明率的大幅提升，为高效、低成本解决白内障这一全球性重大公共卫生问题发挥了重要作用。

2. 创新白内障诊断方法

创建了全球第一个临床应用的人工智能眼病筛查—诊断—随访系统。利用人工智能对先天性白内障临床图片进行分析和深度学习，开发了一个人工智能诊断云平台。基层医生或患者上传图片至云平台，即可获得诊断和治疗方案，已应用于临床，突破了传统的医疗模式，拓展了优质医疗资源的辐射面。此外，借助移动通信还可进行患者跟踪随访，制定全球应用的检眼镜诊断白内障技术规范。利用简单的检眼镜红光反射，全科医生在例行的健康体检中就能发现白内障患者，使患者能够得到及时的诊治。建立全球首个疑难白内障研究及诊治共享平台。研究者相互开放、共同使用标准化的临床信息和生物样品数据，将零散的临床病例整合成数据标准的大样本，有利于开展对照研究和治疗。

3. 发现治疗白内障的药物新靶点

刘奕志多年来开展了系列白内障致病基因研究，探索其发病机理。近年来，通过研究突变位点功能，发现羊毛甾醇合成酶（LSS）基因突变可导致 LSS 活性下调、羊毛甾醇水平下降以及晶状体蛋白异常聚集；体外补充羊毛甾醇可逆转晶状体蛋白异常聚集，使狗眼白内障恢复透明；确定了羊毛甾醇 Lanosterol 是防止晶状体蛋白质聚集的关键分子，为预防与治疗白内障提供了新的策略。*Nature* 同期和 *Nature Review Drug Discovery* 杂志将其列为热点文章；*Science* 杂志评论"这是近十年来在该领域中最全面和有说服力的文章""为白内障的药物治疗带来了新曙光"。

二、在眼再生医学领域取得重大突破

1. 首次实现人晶状体再生并用于临床治疗白内障

刘奕志带领团队经过 18 年的不懈努力，利用人内源性晶状体干细胞实现了晶状体原位再生用于临床治疗先天性白内障。发现晶状体内源性干细胞及其关键调控因子，进一步确定了 Bmi1 和 Pax6 是调控晶状体上皮干细胞自我更新和分化的关键因子，可促进细胞分化并形成晶状体；创建了一种内微创白内障新术式，既能清除病变组织，又能保留组织的干细胞，利用人体自身的晶状体干细胞再生出有功能的晶状体，并已成功用于白内障患儿的临床治疗，解决了尚在发育阶段的婴幼儿因白内障术后不能植入人工晶状体进而严重影响视觉发育的世界性难题，为白内障提供了新的治疗方法，也为组织器官再生及内源性干细胞的应用提供了范例。*Nature* 同期评价这种方法为"远见卓识的干细胞疗法"，BBC 新闻报道国际同行评价"是再生医学最好的成就之一"。这一利用自体细胞介导组织修复的治疗方法被 *Nature Medicine* 杂志列为"2016 年度全球生命科学七大领域（基因治疗、免疫疗法、传染病、癌症、再生医学、自身免疫疾病、神经生物学）八大突破性进展"，被中国科协评选为"2016 年度中国生命科学领域十大进展"。

2. 首次成功将自体皮肤上皮细胞直接转化为角膜上皮，治疗角膜缘上皮干细胞衰竭

刘奕志与他的团队发现 Wnt7a/Pax6 是决定角膜上皮干细胞更新、分化的关键因子，其缺失将导致角膜缘干细胞形成"皮肤样"上皮细胞；并将 Pax6 转导入皮肤上皮干细胞使之转化为类角膜缘干细胞，进而移植到兔眼角膜损伤模型中，成功修复受损组织，形成透明的角膜上皮层，可望解决角膜供体来源匮乏的问题。国际同行在 *Cell Stem Cell* 杂志撰文评价"该项工作对双眼角膜干细胞衰竭患者具有重要意义"。

刘奕志担任亚太眼科学会理事、中华医学会眼科学分会副主委、广东省医学会眼科学分会主任委员以及国际杂志 *Mol Vision* 共同主编、*Current Molecular Medicine* 副主编。自他担任中山眼科中心主任以来，中山眼科中心专科声誉及科研排行均位居国内第一，推动了我国白内障学科发展和参与国际竞争。鉴于刘奕志在眼科领域创新及教育等方面的成绩，他曾获得 APACRS Gold Medal、亚太眼科年度 Arthur Lim 奖、广东省"五一劳动奖章"、中国青年科技奖、中国百名优秀青年志愿者等荣誉。

Awardee of Medical Sciences and
Materia Medica Prize, Liu Yizhi

Liu Yizhi was born in Guangzhou City of Guangdong Province in July 1962. He is now not only one of the chief scientists in charge of 973 program, but also serves as Director of both State Key Laboratory of Ophthalmology and Zhongshan Ophthalmic Center.

In addition, he is widely acknowledged as one of the pioneers and reformers of minimally invasive cataract surgeries in China. He has engaged in enormous clinical and basic research studies, accomplished a series of innovative and groundbreaking work in the field of cataract prevention and treatment, applied regenerative medicine in ophthalmology.

With regards to the reforms in traditional surgeries, Liu Yizhi with his team conducted the first randomized study confirming the safety and efficacy of the torsional mode, an emerging phacoemulsification technology. This Surgical technique has been widely propagated through China, leading to tremendous progress of surgical management of cataracts on the whole-scale. And he was granted "The State Scientific and Technological Progress Award" and "Chinese Physician Prize" for his contribution in this field in 2014 and 2016, respectively. Apart from that, he is also the first person advocating the idea that the ophthalmological surgeries can be performed for patients as outpatients.

Moreover, the very first artificial intelligence (AI) platform was established in ZOC and applied to clinical screening, diagnosis and follow-up. Furthery, follow-up with these patients is feasible with the development of modern mobile communications. Consequently, the first shared and open platform for advanced and complicated cataracts was founded in China.

Apart from that, he also believes that breakthrough in scientific research is the key to tackle those clinical questions faced by doctors every day, i.e. "from bench to bedside". Liu Yizhi with his team identified that Lanosterol was a key molecule in preventing the aggregation of crystallins and provided a new strategy for the prevention and treatment of cataracts. They also found that transduction of PAX6 in skin epithelial stem cells could convert them to limbal stem cells (LSCs) like cells, and these reprogrammed cells were able to replenish cornea epithelial cells (CECs) and repair damaged corneal surface, which was expected to solve the problem of lack of corneal donor source.

Also, he has been showing great interests in regenerative medicine. The team has also provided a novel approach to lens regeneration using endogenous stem cells. They have created a new minimally invasive cataract surgery, which could preserve the integrity of lens epithelial stem cells (LECs), facilitating functional lens regeneration. Notably, this study was rated as one of the top 8 notable advances in the field of life sciences 2016 by *Nature Medicine*.

Last but not least, as a supervisor for over 100 Master and PhD students, professor Liu Yizhi has been paying great attention to cultivating and guiding young doctors, proposing the modified residency and fellowship training programs for medical graduates in China.

医学药学奖获得者

李 云 庆

李云庆，1961 年 8 月出生于新疆维吾尔自治区乌鲁木齐市。1984 年毕业于第四军医大学获学士学位，1990 年和 1993 年分别在第四军医大学和日本京都大学获博士学位。1993 年回国后任第四军医大学人体解剖学教研室副主任、副教授，1996 年任该室主任并兼任梁铽琚脑研究中心副主任、教授和博士生导师，2005 年任梁铽琚脑研究中心主任。先后担任日本京都大学、日本国立生理研究所、华中科技大学、中山大学、暨南大学、郑州大学等校兼职教授，四川大学华西医学中心、福建医科大学、广西医科大学等校兼职研究生导师。曾任中国解剖学会第 31 届、第 32 届理事长，现任国际解剖学工作者协会联盟（IFAA）第 18 届执委会副主席、国际形态科学大会（ISMS）第 25 届委员会副主席、亚太地区解剖学会（APICA）第 8 届执委会执委、中国解剖学会第 33 届副理事长、中国神经科学学会第 5 届和第 6 届常务理事、《神经解剖学杂志》主编、*Frontiers in Neuroanatomy* 副主编等职务。

李云庆从事人体解剖学教学和痛与镇痛机制研究，是我国人体解剖学和神经生物学界的优秀学者，也是有国际影响力的学科和学术带头人。神经系统有传递痛信息和抑制痛信息传递（镇痛）的两个系统。痛与镇痛机制是困扰医学界的难题，也是他的研究重点。

一、科研攻关克难，研究成果造福病患

他长期在神经环路、细胞、分子等水平对痛与镇痛的机制进行研究，在中枢镇痛系统结构和功能、阿片镇痛与副作用机理、内脏痛信息调控等方面取得了有国际影响并对临床有指导作用的成绩。

（1）揭示了具有镇痛作用的下行抑制系统的起源、构成及其递质，特别是发现该系统在脊髓构成的三种环路，解决了其镇痛的关键难题，阐明了该系统的镇痛机理。提出该系统起源于中枢的多个核团，它们构成功能复合体，同时参与镇痛，具有强化和维持镇痛效应的新观点。这些结果分别被国际疼痛权威专著 *Textbook of Pain* 和 *Science of Pain* 收录，他本人也应约在国际著名神经科学期刊 *Progress in Neurobiology* 上发表综述。

李云庆积极将这些成果向临床推广，如指导医生在进行深部脑刺激（DBS）等治疗时，将刺激电极准确埋置在该系统的起源部位或投射径路上治疗顽固性疼痛等疾病，不仅显著减少了止痛药的用量，而且使绝大部分患者获得了满意的疗效。

（2）以往对内脏信息的传递尤其是盆腔脏器（如膀胱、直肠）痛信息的传递途径并不清楚。针灸、推拿等疗法能够治疗内脏疾病是不争的事实，但其机理不明且易引起质疑。李云庆在本科室前辈们工作的基础上，发现来自躯体感觉的非痛信息与来自内脏感觉的痛信息汇聚到骶髓后连合核内的同一个投射神经元，且前者能调控后者的活动。上述结果阐明了盆腔内脏感觉信息的传递和调控机制，为内脏痛的治疗提供了新线索，还为体表与内脏相关、内病外治的理论和疗法提供了科学依据，有助于祖国传统医学的现代化和发扬光大。这些结果已经写入医学本科生教材。

二、勤奋钻研创新，军旅学子成果丰硕

李云庆在本科毕业当年就考上了母校人体解剖学专业的硕士研究生，后因学习和科研成绩优秀，经过严格考核和考试，提前进入攻读博士学位的学习，并提前通过毕业答辩获得博士学位，毕业后留校在人体解剖学教研室任讲师。1991 年他获得日本政府文部省奖学金资助，赴京都大学深造，1993 年获得京都大学博士学位。在出国留学期间的 1992 年，他被提前晋升为副教授，1994 年又提前晋升为教授，成为学校当时最年轻的教授。

他以第一作者或通讯作者身份已发表 SCI 论文 136 篇，这些论文被他引近 3000 次。获国家科学技术进步奖一等奖（2009）、中华医学科技一等奖和陕西省科学技术一等奖各 1 项，均为第一完成人；1996 年获"全国中青年医学科技之星"称号并获"国家杰出青年科学基金"资助；1997 年获政府特殊津贴；1998 年入选国家"百千万人才工程"；1999 年获中国科协"求是奖"；2002 年被聘为"长江学者奖励计划"特聘教授；2009 年获国家科学技术进步奖一等奖；2010 年获军队后勤科技突出贡献奖，被评为"全国优秀科技工作者"，荣立一等功；2014 年成为首批"军队科技领军人才"；2015 年获"军队杰出专业技术人才奖"。获国家发明专利 6 项、实用新型专利 12 项。

目前，已经培养博士后 6 名、博士研究生和硕士研究生 86 名，其中全国优秀博士论文获得者 1 名、军队优秀硕士和博士论文获得者各 1 名、陕西省优秀博士论文获得者 8 名。

三、育人管理严格，研究中心桃李芬芳

李云庆始终把教书育人作为首要工作，长期坚持工作在教学第一线。主编（译）著作和教材 12 部，曾获第三届国家音像制品奖、全国教育教学信息化一等奖、省部级教学成果特等奖和一等奖各 1 项；所领导的教学团队被评为"国家级教学团队"，负责的课程被评为"国家精品课程""国家级精品资源共享课"和"国家级精品视频公开课"。他本

人还获得了全军教书育人优秀教员、军队院校育才金奖、全国优秀博士学位论文指导教师奖、陕西省教学名师等荣誉和奖励。

1995 年，在第四军医大学梁铥琚脑研究中心成立之初，李云庆即担任副主任并于 2005 年开始担任主任至今。在他的拼搏和带领下，在老一辈专家教授的指导和帮助下，在研究中心团队的努力和协作下，梁铥琚脑研究中心于 1997 年成为国家"211 工程"重点建设学科，2001 年和 2007 年两次被确认为国家级重点学科，是西北地区唯一的医学"国家级继续教育基地"；研究团队成员中 95% 具有博士学位，全部有出国留学经历。该中心已经发表 SCI 论文 368 篇，分别获国家科技进步奖一等奖、国家科技进步奖三等奖和国家自然科学四等奖各 1 项，先后培养出"国家杰出青年科学基金"获得者 4 名、"长江学者奖励计划"特聘教授 4 名、国家"973"计划首席科学家 1 名、"全国优秀博士论文"获得者 2 名、"军队院校育才奖"获得者 5 名等优秀人才。

作为中国解剖学会历史上最年轻的理事长，李云庆在任职期间高度重视培养青年人才、提高学会整体学术水平和开展有效的国际交流，连续两次为我国争取到在国内举办国际解剖学界著名学术会议的主办权并担任会议主席主持召开会议。他当选为国际解剖学工作者协会联盟（IFAA）和国际形态科学大会（ISMS）的副主席，还于 2017 年被 ISMS 授予"优秀解剖学家奖"，成为 ISMS 大会成立 47 年以来获此殊荣的第 8 位学者，这些都实现了中国解剖学会"零"的突破，标志着我国已经跻身国际解剖学领域主导地位。

Awardee of Medical Sciences and Materia Medica Prize, Li Yunqing

Li Yunqing was born in Urumqi City of Xinjiang Uygur Autonomous Region in August 1961. He was conferred Bachelor's degree at the Fourth Military Medical University（FMMU）in 1984 and Doctor's degree at FMMU and Kyoto University in 1990 and 1993，respectively. Upon returning to FMMU from Japan in 1993，he was appointed as deputy director and associate professor of Human Anatomy Department. In 1996，he was selected as director of Human Anatomy Department，professor，supervisor for doctorial candidates and deputy director of the K. K. He became director of the Leung Brain Research Centre in 2005. He served as part-time professor of Kyoto University in Japan，National Institute of Physiology in Japan，Huazhong University of Science and Technology，Sun Yat-sen University，Jinan University，and Zhengzhou University. In addition，he was invited as guest graduate supervisor by West China Medical Center of Sichuan University，Fujian Medical University，and Guangxi Medical University. He has been devoting himself to the teaching of human anatomy and the research on the neural mechanisms underlying algesia and analgesia wholeheartedly. He has investigated the structure and function of central analgesia system, the opioid analgesia and its side-effects, and central regulation mechanism for visceral pain transmission for 35 years. He has published 136 research articles in SCI journals with the citation up to 3000 times. Furthermore, his findings which have provided useful guidance for pain treatment in clinical practice have been cited by such pain monographs as *Textbook of Pain* and *Science of Pain* and awarded the first prize of "National Science and Technology Awards in China". He was financed by "National Natural Science Foundation of China for Distinguished Young Scholars" in 1996 and selected as "Distinguished Professor of Cheung Kong Scholars Program" in 2002. He worked as president of the 31st and 32nd Chinese Society for Anatomical Sciences (CSAS). Currently he serves as vice chairman of the 25th International Committee for Symposium on Morphological Sciences (ISMS), and vice chairman of the 18th Executive Committee of the International Federation of Associations of Anatomists (IFAA). Meanwhile, he is chief editor of *Chinese Journal of Neuroanatomy* and associate editor of *Frontiers in Neuroanatomy*. He won "Excellent Anatomist Award" from the ISMS in 2017.

医学药学奖获得者

李 校 堃

李校堃，1964 年 2 月出生于陕西省富平市。1996 年毕业于中山医科大学微生物与生化药学专业，获博士学位。1999 年破格晋升教授、博士生导师。2004 年牵头申报并获批基因工程药物国家工程研究中心，担任首席科学家。2005 年 1 月—2015 年 7 月先后担任温州医学院（后更名为温州医科大学）药学院院长、温州医科大学副校长。2015 年 8 月至今担任温州大学校长。李校堃长期担任中华医学会创伤学分会创伤药物与转化应用委员会主任委员，中国生物工程学会转化医学专业委员会主任委员，中国医药生物技术协会副理事长，中国生物工程学会常务理事，中国医药质量管理协会副会长等学术职务。

李校堃从事蛋白质药物科学研究 20 多年，在成纤维细胞生长因子（FGFs）基因工程创新药物开发、产业转化以及基础研究方面做出了突出贡献。

一、FGFs 工程技术研究

李校堃围绕提高生长因子类功能蛋白表达水平和稳定性的关键工程技术开展了创新而深入的研究，在国际上率先开发了肝素亲和层析和疏水层析固相定点修饰技术，开发了一系列提高功能蛋白药用价值的新型制剂工艺，相关技术成功应用到多个生长因子功能蛋白中并已获得两项新药临床批文，相关技术孵化的皮肤护理项目已创造了显著的经济社会效益，技术水平达到国内领先平。

（1）采用 SUMO 融合技术建立了新型 FGF 可溶性分泌表达体系，成功实现了多个 FGFs 家族新成员（如 FGF7、FGF18、FGF20、FGF21 等）的可溶性高效表达，蛋白表达率均超过 120mg/L，完全达到了相关药物的工业化需求。

（2）针对 FGFs 家族具有重要临床价值的功能蛋白（如 FGF1、FGF2、FGF7、FGF10、FGF20、FGF21、FGF23C-Tail 等）普遍存在稳定性差、半衰期短的缺陷，率先开展了针对性的 FGF 蛋白结构改造和修饰研究，发明建立了多个固相特异性修饰体系（肝素亲和固相修饰、疏水色谱固相修饰、SUMO 吸附固相修饰），获得了稳定性和体内半衰期显著改善的系列 FGFs 长效功能蛋白。

（3）根据 FGFs 的结构和生物学特征，开展了 FGFs 新型给药途径及相关制剂工艺的研究。目前已获两项一类新药临床批文并进入临床 Ⅱ 期或 Ⅲ 期，1 项新药获临床受理，2 个创新制剂已完成临床前动物实验；与此同时广泛开展 FGFs 基础理论研究，为 FGFs 新药的临床研究和推广奠定了坚实的理论和实践基础。

在前期所获得的 FGFs 家族三个国家一类新药证书基础上，结合 FGFs 家族成员的结构和新作用特征，成功研制了 FGF10 冻干粉外用制剂、FGF7 冻干粉注射制剂、FGF10 滴眼液、FGF21 注射液和 FGF1 凝胶剂等。

围绕上述新药及形成的工程创新技术，李校堃曾获国家科技进步奖一等奖、国家技术发明奖二等奖、国家科技进步奖二等奖及 5 项教育部、中华医学会和中国药学会科技进步一等奖（均排名第一）。相关技术行业推广迅速，已被应用于重组生长激素、神经生长因子等基因工程药物的技术改造和大规模生产，带动了我国相关领域工程化技术的提升。

二、FGFs 新药的临床应用研究及新适应证拓展

FGFs 系列新药在国际上首次开展临床实验，先后在北京解放军 301 医院等 60 多家三甲医院进行了临床应用。*Lancet* 杂志首次报道了李校堃研制的 bFGF 临床试验结果，结果表明 FGFs 能够显著加快烧创伤、糖尿病溃疡等创面的愈合速度。对 FGFs 新药临床应用近 20 年的跟踪观察，未见过度增生和异常增生等不良反应。

在进行 FGFs 新药研发的同时，李校堃围绕新型内分泌 FGFs 亚家族创新药物开发及作用机制开展了大量开拓性的工作。

（1）蛋白结构生物学的突破：在国际上率先解析了生长因子受体与下游重要信号蛋白 PLCγ 复合物精确的晶体结构，对指导受体下游靶点创新药物的开发提供了重要的理论依据。该成果发表在 *Molecular Cell*（IF=13.958）上。

（2）发现 FGF21 治疗新靶点：李校堃研究发现 FGF21 能够对机体胰岛素产生增敏效应且通过胰岛素增敏激素——脂联素（Adiponectin）发挥作用。该研究首次揭示了 FGF21 对胰岛素增敏作用的机制。FGF21 具有降低机体血糖血脂、改善胰岛素抵抗、保护胰岛 β 细胞等多种糖脂代谢调控的功能，在 Ⅱ 型糖尿病、动脉粥样硬化等多种代谢综合征的临床应用方面极具潜力。该项研究不仅明确了 FGF21 对糖脂代谢的调控机制，而且对于开发肥胖、糖尿病的药物有重要意义。该研究发表于国际顶尖学术期刊 *Cell Metabolism*（IF=17.7）上。

（3）发现 FGF21 治疗动脉粥样硬化新机制：李校堃的研究首次发现 FGF21 可以明显减少粥样硬化板块的形成，通过进一步研究发现，FGF 可通过上调脂联素的表达和分泌来抑制动脉粥样硬化的形成作用，研究成果发表在 2015 年心血管顶级期刊 *Circulation*

（IF=17.202）上。

李校堃在国际上率先解决了 FGF 蛋白成药过程中的一系列基因工程技术难题，研制出具有自主知识产权的 3 个国家生物制品一类新药和一个Ⅲ类医疗器械（最高等级），为治疗严重创伤和难愈性溃疡提供了具有主动修复功能的创新药物。在 FGFs 组织修复和代谢调控研究方面，先后在 *Cell Metab*、*Circulation*、*Mol Cell* 等国际权威杂志发表 SCI 论文 257 篇；出版 FGFs 及生物药物专著 7 部；获得授权发明专利 55 项，转化 6 项；荣获国家科技进步奖一等奖（排名第四）、国家技术发明奖二等奖（排名第一）、国家科技进步奖二等奖（排名第三）、教育部高等学校科学研究优秀成果奖（自然科学）一等奖（排名第一）、中国知识产权局专利优秀奖和中国产学研合作创新奖等多项国家级、省部级奖项。

截至目前，李校堃共培养博士生 25 名、硕士生 150 名；主编教材、专著 7 部，其主讲的《生物技术制药》被评为国家级精品课程和国家精品资源共享课，其作为学科带头人的药学专业被评为国家特色专业。作为浙江省"药学重中之重一级学科"带头人，累计引进和培养国家千人计划专家 3 人（外籍 1 人）、浙江省千人计划专家 15 人、国家优青 2 人、中组部青年拔尖人才 2 人；带领团队先后入选教育部长江学者创新团队、浙江省蛋白质药物创新团队，团队累计主持获得国家重点研究计划项目 1 项、国家新药创制项目 4 项、国家自然基金立项 122 项，其中国家重大项目（培育）2 项。先后组建了浙江省生物技术制药工程重点实验室和温州市生物医药协同创新中心，为提升我国生物药物的研发和产业发展做出了突出贡献。

Awardee of Medical Sciences and
Materia Medica Prize, Li Xiaokun

Li Xiaokun was born in Fuping City of Shaanxi Province in February 1964. He obtained Ph.D in Microbiology and Biochemistry at Sun Yat−Sen University of Medical Sciences in 1996. He was promoted to full professor and Ph.D supervisor in 1999. In 2004，he spearheaded the effort in establishing the National Engineering Research Center for Genetically Engineered Drugs, and served as chief scientist. From Jan. 2005 to 2015，he served as the dean of the School of Pharmacy，Wenzhou Medical University，and later also the vice president of the University until Aug. 2015，when he was appointed as the president of Wenzhou University.

For over two decades，Dr. Li has led a team dedicated to the research and development of FGF−based protein drugs and made seminal contributions to the field spanning from basic research and protein engineering to pharmaceutical industry and clinical application. His team overcame several major bottlenecks for FGF protein engineering and recombinant production and licensed the first FGF recombinant protein drug in the world. Extensive basic and clinical research on FGFs has led to novel clinical indications and more effective route of drug administration/formulation. Several new FGF-based biologics with full intellectual property rights are currently under Phase II or III clinical trials.

In his continuing effort to better understand the biology of FGFs and to explore novel therapeutic indications, his team is among the first in the world to discover the link of FGF21 to type 2 diabetes, and its underlying mechanism via the PPARg/adiponectin signaling axis (*Cell Metab*, 2013). His team first shows that FGF21 signaling also prevents atherosclerosis (*Circulation*, 2015), a finding highlighted by Nature Reviews and is considered as one of the Top-10 groundbreaking discoveries of the FGF field (*Cell Metab*, 2015). Two recent papers from his team have unveiled a therapeutic potential of FGF1 toward diabetic nephropathy and a unique mechanism of uncoupling mitogenic and metabolic activity by tuning FGF1-FGF receptor dimer stability (*Kidney Int*, 2017; *Cell Report*, 2017), which will impact the future of drug discoveries targeting FGFs for the treatment of a variety of human diseases.

Dr. Li has trained more than 150 graduate students including 25 Ph.Ds. and authored in more than 250 research papers including some in the most prestigious journals. He has been granted 55 FGFs-related invention patents with 6 successful Technology/License Transfers. The FGFs series of drugs have been widely used in the clinical hospitals with revenue of more than 4 billion Yuan. He was named a Changjiang Scholar Professor by the Ministry of Education in 2006, and has been the recipient of several highly prestigious national awards on science/technology advancement and innovation. He has been a founding member and served as a leader in several national academic societies/organizations.

医学药学奖获得者

姜 保 国

姜保国，1961 年 4 月出生于辽宁省沈阳市。1992 年 10 月毕业于北京医科大学获医学博士学位。1990 年 9 月—1992 年 7 月为日本新泻大学医学部整形外科中日联合培养博士研究生。1987 年起在北京大学人民医院工作至今。1999 年创立北京大学人民医院创伤骨科，任科室主任。2005 年 1 月—2016 年 9 月任北京大学医学部副主任；2016 年 1 月起任北京大学人民医院院长。担任中国创伤救治联盟主席、北京大学创伤医学中心主任、北京大学骨科学学系主任、中华医学会常务理事、中华医学会创伤学分会主任委员等职。主持承担国家自然科学基金、北京市科委重大研究专项、国家"863"项目、国家"十一五"科技支撑计划、卫生公益行业专项、国家"973"项目等多项课题；2006 年度获国家杰出青年基金资助，2012 年作为团队学术带头人获得教育部创新团队，2013 年作为首席科学家获国家"973"项目。

姜保国在严重创伤规范化救治、周围神经损伤与修复、关节周围骨折等研究领域做出了一系列开创性研究工作。

一、率先研究并制定了中国严重创伤救治规范

姜保国于 2006 年创建了北京大学交通医学中心，在国内率先开展了全国范围的创伤数据采集和流程监测，针对创伤救治中的问题，在国家卫计委项目支持下组织国内百余家医院进行多中心研究，创新性提出在我国建立"以综合医院为核心的闭环式区域性创伤救治体系"核心理念，并率先提出在综合医院建立创伤救治团队替代独立的创伤救治中心的新模式。领导项目组专家完成制定了《严重创伤救治规范》等 11 项专家共识。自主研发了现场急救与救治医院间的信息联动系统，从根本上改变了中国严重创伤救治现状和流程，使创伤平均救治时间缩短了 50%、严重创伤救治院内平均死亡率下降了 40%（从 33.8% 下降至 20.9%。），核心理念以通讯作者在国际权威医学杂志《柳叶刀》等发表，被国内外同行认可为创伤救治的"中国模式"，2016 年该研究成果获国家科技进步奖二等奖。

现阶段，该成果得到国家政府部门的重视和认可，教育部将该成果推广列入国家十三五规划项目，并授权成立中国创伤救治联盟，姜保国为联盟主席；在教育部、卫计委、住建部等多个部门的大力支持下，由中国创伤救治联盟牵头，北京大学创伤医学中心、北京大学人民医院联合全国百余家大型医院以及地方卫生行政主管部门共同发起并启动了"安全中国，百县工程"，将在以全国县域为主的城市进行严重创伤救治规范的试点推广，建立区域性创伤救治体系的示范区，带动县域医疗卫生服务水平和公共卫生应急职能提升，让更多基层百姓受益。同时，创伤救治的"中国模式"也得到国际同行和政府的高度认可，2017 年 6 月，以姜保国为核心的专家团队应柬埔寨青年联合会医生联盟邀请，在国家卫计委带领下与柬埔寨联合开展了密切合作和学术交流，实现了创伤救治的中国模式在柬埔寨落地。以柬埔寨推广为开始，创伤救治"中国模式"将在"一带一路"框架下开展国际医疗合作，实现成果的国际性推广。

二、率先提出多项周围神经再生修复新理念，并开创性提出了周围神经修复新方法

姜保国潜心研究周围神经损伤与修复 30 余年，在国际上率先提出了替代传统神经外膜缝合的小间隙套接缝合技术，形成了再生效果好、避免形成神经瘤、外科操作简易的创新性修复技术，并研发了具有自主知识产权的生物管桥。研究成果以第一完成人获教育部技术发明一等奖。以此为基础上，在国际上率先提出了周围神经多芽再生、周围神经替代修复、周围神经修复过程中的中枢重塑等多项创新性假说。目前，在国家"973"项目支持下，正组织项目组专家进行脊髓及脑功能重塑的系统论证。2016 年 11 月，姜保国因周围神经损伤修复和创伤规范化救治方面的学术成就获国际顾氏和平奖。

三、首次提出内固定材料应基于国人的解剖数据进行设计，并率先提出了关节周围骨折的理念

通过系统的体内外研究，证实了关节周围骨折独特的愈合模式；设计完成具有自主专利权的符合国人解剖特点的内固定系统，获得自主知识产权 15 项，完成专利转让，形成临床产品。研究成果以第一完成人获教育部科技进步一等奖。

姜保国已培养硕士生、博士研究生 102 名，多名已成长为国内本专业的中青年技术骨干，其中 7 位已担任学科带头人；以第一作者或通讯作者在国内外学术期刊上发表学术论文共计 370 余篇，其中在国际 SCI 杂志 *The Lancet*、*Spine*、*Plos One* 等发表论文 71 篇；获国家发明专利 9 项、实用新型专利 15 项；主编主译《严重创伤救治规范》《关节周围骨折》等著作 21 部；以第一完成人获国家科技进步二等奖 1 项、省部级一等奖 2 项；2016 年获吴杨奖和国际顾氏和平奖；2017 年 8 月荣获"全国卫生计生系统先进工作者"。

Awardee of Medical Sciences and Materia Medica Prize, Jiang Baoguo

Jiang Baoguo was born in Shenyang City of Liaoning Province in April 1961. He earned his M.D. from Beijing Medical University in October 1992. From September 1990 to July 1992, he joined the China-Japan Joint Doctoral program and trained at the Department of Orthopedics, Niigata University. Prof. Jiang initiated his professional career at Peking University People's Hospital (PKUPH) in 1987. He became the founding director of the Department of Traumatology & Orthopedics at PKUPH in 1999.

He served as Vice President of Peking University Health Science Center from January 2005 to September 2016. Since January 2016, Prof. Jiang has been the President of PKUPH. He also holds concurrent positions as the President of China Alliance of Trauma Care, Director of Peking University Trauma Medicine Center, Dean of the Faculty of Orthopedics at Peking University, Executive Member of the Chinese Medical Association and President of Chinese Medicine Traumatic Academy. He is also responsible for the projects supported by the National Natural Science Foundation of China, the Key Projects in the National Science & Technology Pillar Program during the 11th Five-year Plan Period, the Special Fund for Health Scientific Research in the Public Interest, the National Key Basic Research Program of China (973 Program), etc. In 2006, he won the National Science Fund for Distinguished Young Scholars. In 2012, he was named as the academic leader of the Innovative Research Team Program of the Chinese Ministry of Education. In 2013, he was supported by the National Basic Research Program of China (973 Program) as a chief scientist.

Prof. Jiang has accomplished a series of pioneering work in standardizing procedures for severe trauma rescue and treatment, peripheral nerve injury and repair, periarticular fractures and etc.

1. Research & Development of the Standard Procedures for Severe Trauma Rescue & Treatment in China

Prof. Jiang led a team of experts to formulate 11 expert consensus documents, including "Standard Procedures for Severe Trauma Rescue and Treatment", independently invented the information exchange and linkage system between onsite rescue teams and in-hospital rescue teams, which has fundamentally improved the situation and procedures of severe trauma rescue and treatment in China.

Prof. Jiang has published his core concept as the corresponding author in such international authoritative medical journals as *The Lancet*. His core concept has been recognized as the "China's model of trauma rescue and treatment" by domestic and international peers. The research accomplishments were awarded the Second Prize of the Chinese National Science & Technology

Progress Award.

2. Research on Peripheral Nerve Injury and Repair

As a chief scientist of the National Basic Research Program of China (973 Program), Prof. Jiang is the first to propose the innovative hypotheses of peripheral nerve replacement repair and remodeling in the process of the peripheral nerve repair in the world. These hypotheses have been systematically validated. Prof. Jiang was awarded the First Prize of the Technology Invention Award of the Chinese Ministry of Education as the chief scientist of this research accomplishment.

With the support of the National Basic Research Program of China (973 Program), experts are organized to conduct systematic research on spinal cord and brain function remodeling. Due to his great academic accomplishments in peripheral nerve injury and repair, as well as trauma rescue and treatment standards development, Prof. Jiang was awarded the Gusi Peace Prize International in 2016.

3. Research on Periarticular fracture

Prof. Jiang is the first to propose that the internal fixation material of fractures should be designed based on the anatomical data of Chinese people. He is also the first to propose the theory of periarticular fracture, which validates a unique healing mode after periarticular fractures. Prof. Jiang has developed a patented internal fixation system, which is customized to fit the anatomical needs of Chinese patients. He also obtained 15 independent intellectual property rights, which has been translated into clinical devices after patent transfer. As the chief inventor, Prof. Jiang was awarded the first prize of Science and Technology Progress Award of the Ministry of Education.

医学药学奖获得者

王宁利

王宁利，1957年5月出生于青海省西宁市。1992年毕业于广州中山医科大学眼科学专业，获博士学位。1996年作为高级访问学者在新加坡国家眼科中心进行研究交流。1998年作为高级访问学者在美国加州大学圣地亚哥分校进行研究交流，并取得博士后学位。2002年至今在首都医科大学附属北京同仁医院工作，现任医院院长兼北京市眼科研究所所长、眼科中心主任，国家眼科诊断与治疗工程技术研究中心主任，首都医科大学北京眼科学院院长；国际眼科科学院院士，国际眼科理事会成员，世界青光眼协会执行和指导委员会委员，首位来自中国大陆的亚太眼科学会候任主席，中华医学会眼科分会主任委员（2013—2016）。

主持"863"等国家重大项目11项，主持国家重大防盲工程2项。培养博士后10名、博士生52名。主编眼科学教材及专著26部，制定标准规范12项，获发明专利20项。以第一作者或通讯作者发表论文429篇，其中SCI文章167篇，总引5388次，排名前2的国际眼科期刊25篇（第一/通讯）；在 *Nature Genetics* 发表4篇、*Nature Communication* 1篇；是青光眼领域发表论文国内第一、国际前十的专家。连续三年入选 Elsevier 高引学者榜，连续两次被英国眼科医师杂志评为全球最具影响力百名眼科医生（国内一人）。以第一完成人获得国家科技进步奖二等奖2项、全国创新争先奖1项、省部级一等奖4项。

王宁利从事眼科临床与科研工作34年，完成手术约2万例。在青光眼防治的理论研究、技术创新、设备研发等方面做出了一系列开创性研究工作。

一、阐明国人原发性闭角型青光眼（闭青）病因机制，研发了闭青防治所需的关键设备，创建适合国人的防治体系，使推广区致盲率下降35.4%，使我国闭青防治技术达到国际领先水平

闭青是国人最常见的不可逆性致盲眼病。针对因人种差异，西方传统理论与技术在国人闭青防治中效果不佳、致盲率高的问题，王宁利进行了系列研究。

自主研发闭青诊断的关键设备——全景高频超声生物显微镜（国际领先），实现对整个前房形态的实时动态观察和测量，为该病研究及诊断提供了关键设备，国内市场占有率70%。借助上述设备，首次发现国人闭青的发病机制不同于西方人，提出"房角关闭混合机制学说"。针对国人闭青机制多样性的特点，创建早期干预策略、闭青急性发作干预技术、慢性期循序渐进处理技术、复合式小梁切除术、新的激发试验等多项适合国人闭青防治的关键技术，形成适合国人闭青防治的技术体系，使推广区致盲率下降35.4%。组织亚洲闭青分子遗传学研究，在国内外首次发现8个易感基因位点和10个易感基因，为闭青早期筛查生物标志物的发现奠定了基础。哈佛大学Howe研究室主任Wiggs教授评价其研究为"里程碑式的研究、理解该致盲疾病分子机制的关键一步"。

成果纳入国际眼科理事会指南、世界青光眼学会专家共识，写入5部国外专著、国内5部眼科学教材和8部专著。新防治体系纳入卫生部十年百项、国家科技攻关项目和北京市科技计划项目推广。

二、在国际上首次发现低颅压是导致原发性开角型青光眼（开青）视神经损害的危险因素，创建了颅眼压力梯度学说，回答了传统眼压学说长期未能回答的科学问题，改变了临床实践

开青是另一类全球最常见的不可逆致盲眼病。传统眼压学说认为眼压升高是开青视神经损害的主要原因，但该学说无法回答：① 83%的开青患者眼压在正常范围，为何发生视神经损害？②高眼压症人群中为何近90%不发生视神经损害？

针对以上问题，王宁利创建"颅眼压力梯度学说"，首次发现眼压和颅压构成的跨筛板压力差增加导致了视神经损害，而非高眼压或低颅压单一因素所致，阐明开青视神经损害的重要科学问题。据此建立开青基于跨筛板压力差的新分类和治疗策略，提出治疗应以控制跨筛板压力差水平为标准，解决了正常眼压青光眼治疗不足和高眼压症过度治疗的问题，改变了临床实践。研究成果被国际眼科学者评价为Groundbreaking和Vital的研究。著名专著*Glaucoma*评价此研究"开辟了青光眼研究新方向"。同时，建立了跨筛板压力差无创测量技术。建立基于核磁的无创跨筛板压力差测量方法，为临床分类和监测提供关键技术；为人群筛查设计不依赖核磁的测量方法，被多项国内外流调工作采纳。剑桥大学脑研究中心Geeraerts教授专题撰文评价为"elegant study"。首次研发出适合国人的基于相干光学断层扫描技术的视神经结构定量检测设备，为开青早期诊断和病情监测提供了关键设备。上述技术和设备的应用使人群开青检出率由10%提高到95%。

成果纳入世界青光眼学会继续教育项目、美国眼科学会临床指南，写入4部国外专著、8项国内标准与规范共识。英国眼科医师杂志及世界青光眼学会前任主席Weinreb评价该研究是改变青光眼临床实践的里程碑式的发现。

三、通过技术集成、理论创新研发了房水流出通路重建手术，解决了传统青光眼滤过手术高并发症的技术难题，引领微创手术发展

针对青光眼滤过性手术并发症多、医源性致盲率高的难题，在长期临床实践总结基础上，王宁利创新性提出房水流出通道"储备区"理论，首次研发房水流出通道造影术及微创手术重要装置，建立房水流出通路重建术，将传统外滤过引流模式变为内引流模式，在保证手术成功率的同时杜绝了传统滤过手术相关并发症。针对传统手术多次失败的患者，以自主设计的发光套管针技术建立跨越既往手术破坏区小梁网的房水内引流手术，使手术失败的患者从"不可治"变成"可治"，新式式使多次手术失败的开青患者手术治疗成功率从40%提高到80%。自主设计发光微导管引导技术，用发光微导管引导及机械切割作用解决了精确定位和切开下方残存小梁网两个技术难点，实现360度全周及次全周小梁切开，扩大了生理引流范围；和传统手术相比，成功率从51.6%提高到81%，为先天性青光眼患儿提供了新的治疗机会。

上述3类手术在保证手术成功率的同时，彻底避免了滤过相关并发症，在国内外交流和现场演示25次。被亚太眼科学会 Ocular Surgery News 专题报道，获得国家专利6项，纳入5项标准规范和共识，写入国家继续教育教材及2部国内专著，推广至全国13个省市。

王宁利在担任中华眼科学分会主任委员期间，通过搭建国际交流平台、促进交流与合作，提高了我国眼科的国际地位，获中华眼科杰出成就奖及国际奖5项。主持并参与"光明行"等多项防盲公益项目，获全国防盲突出贡献奖。曾获周光召临床医师奖、中国医师奖、中国医学科学家奖，是卫生部有突出贡献专家、北京市有突出贡献专家、全国劳模。

Awardee of Medical Sciences and Materia Medica Prize, Wang Ningli

Wang Ningli was born in Xining City of Qinghai Province in May 1957. He is the President of Beijing TongRen Hospital，Director of Beijing Tongren Eye Center，Director of Beijing Institute of Ophthalmological and President-elect of Asia-Pacific Academy of Ophthalmology（APAO），President-elect of Chinese Ophthalmologist Association，President of Chinese Glaucoma Society and Governor of World Glaucoma Association（WGA）.

Prof. Wang was awarded Zhou Guangzhao Foundation Award for Science and Technology（2014）and Medical Doctor Award of Chinese Medical Doctor Association（2010），and was honored Young and Middle-aged Experts with Outstanding Contributions and The National Model Worker（2015）. As PI, he was awarded 2 National Science and Technology Progress

Second Class Awards and 4 Provincial Science and Technology Progress First Class Awards. He was listed as Elsevier's: "Most Cited Chinese Researchers" in 2014, 2015 and 2016, and The Ophthalmologist's "Top 100 most influential people in the world of ophthalmology" in 2014 and 2016). During his term as the President of Chinese Ophthalmological Society, he greatly promoted the international cooperation and exchange activities and increased the international influence of Chinese ophthalmic community, and thus was awarded Outstanding Achievement Award by Chinese Ophthalmological Society and 5 international awards. He led and participated in several major blindness prevention projects, including the "Brightness Action", and was awarded the National Award for Outstanding Contribution to Blindness Prevention.

(1) He explained the mechanism of primary angle closure glaucoma (PACG) in Chinese, and developed the key instrument and established the new PACG prevention and treatment system, which decreased the blindness rate of PACG in China.

(2) He found that low cerebrospinal fluid pressure (CSFp) is an important factor in glaucomatous optic neuropathy, which answered the long unresolved questions in Primary Open Angle Glaucoma (POAG) and changed clinical application.

(3) He developed the Aqueous humor outflow pathway reconstruction surgery, which resolved the problems of traditional surgery, like high complication rate and high iatrogenic blindness rate.

医学药学奖获得者

张 学

张学，1964 年 7 月出生于黑龙江省肇州县。1986 年中国医科大学临床医学专业本科毕业，获医学学士学位；1989 年中国医科大学医学遗传学专业研究生毕业，获医学硕士学位；1994 年中国医科大学细胞生物学专业研究生毕业，获医学博士学位。1992 年 10 月—1993 年 9 月在日本国立癌中心研究所研修，1996—1998 年先后在美国宾夕法尼亚大学医学院和哈佛医学院做博士后。1994 年被中国医科大学破格晋升为医学遗传学教授；1998—2002 年任中国医科大学基础医学院细胞生物学教研室主任；1999—2002 年任中国医科大学卫生部细胞生物学重点实验室主任；2001 年 6 月起任中国医学科学院基础医学研究所—北京协和医学院（原中国协和医科大学）基础学院医学遗传学系主任；2002 年至今先后担任中国医学科学院—北京协和医学院校长助理、研究生院副院长、科技管理处处长和副院校长；2004 年起任中国医学科学院—北京协和医学院遗传医学中心主任；2012 年起任中国医学科学院北京协和医院临床遗传学实验室主任。2001 年获国家杰出青年科学基金，2007 年入选教育部长江学者特聘教授。中华医学会医学遗传学分会第八届委员会主任委员，国家卫生计生委罕见病诊疗与保障专家委员会主任委员。

张学从事单基因病和基因组病的分子遗传学研究，在单基因病致病基因和基因组病致病 DNA 重排研究方面取得了系列原创性成果，以第一完成人获 2014 年度国家自然科学二等奖。

一、发现单基因病 9 个致病基因和基因组病 3 种致病 DNA 重排，揭示了多种罕见遗传病的分子基础

经典的单基因病和近年来发现的基因组病都可在家系内按孟德尔遗传方式传递，同属孟德尔病。该类疾病多为罕见病，病种多（超过 7000 种）、危害重，常具有先天性、终生性和家族性，人群中总患病率为 2%。目前尚有近 40% 孟德尔病的分子基础未知，无法进行基因诊断。

张学与国内外专家合作，依靠临床、面向临床，发现了家族性反常性痤疮的 3 个致病基因（*NCSTN*、*PSEN1* 和 *PSENEN*）、Marie Unna 型遗传性稀毛症的致病基因（*U2HR*）、家族性特发性基底节钙化的致病基因（*SLC20A2*）、V 型并指和一种新型短 – 并指综合征的致病基因（*HOXD13*）、单纯毛发 – 指甲型外胚层发育不良的致病基因（*HOXC13*）、家族性发作性疼痛致病基因（*SCN11A*）、先天性后极性和全白内障致病基因（*EPHA2*）、先天性全身终毛增多症中 17q24 拷贝数突变、X– 连锁神经管畸形 – 脊柱侧弯 – 先天性全身多毛综合征中 Xq27.1 常染色体插入和 IV 型并指中 7q36 微重复，在 *Science*、*Nat Genet* 和 *Am J Hum Genet* 等国际著名杂志上发表系列论文，其中有 5 篇论文被 F1000 推介。

上述发现揭示了多种罕见病的遗传基础，改写了国际上最权威的人类遗传病数据库 OMIM（Online Mendelian Inheritance in Man）的 13 个条目，为遗传病的基因诊断提供了系列新靶点，对预防严重遗传病患儿出生和降低出生缺陷发生率有重要应用价值。

二、发现"uORF 突变"和"回文结构介导的染色体间插入"两种新的致病突变机制

目前已知单基因病致病突变的 85% 都位于基因编码序列内。Marie Unna 型遗传性稀毛症是一种呈常染色体显性遗传的毛发疾病。国内外五个小组都将其致病基因定位于无毛基因 *HR* 所在的染色体 8p21 区域，但他们都没能在 *HR* 编码区找到致病突变。张学在 *HR* 的 5' 非翻译区内发现 4 个上游开放读码框（uORF），命名为 *U1HR–U4HR*；证明 *U2HR* 能抑制 *HR* 生理性开放读码框的翻译；在来自 10 个国家的 19 个 MUHH 家系中发现 *U2HR* 突变，进一步的功能研究显示突变导致 *HR* 翻译水平升高。本项发现不仅揭示了一种全新的遗传性脱发机制，更重要的是表明"uORF 突变"可以是某种单基因病的主要致病突变机制。论文在 *Nat Genet* 上发表，哈佛医学院两位专家在同期为论文撰写了评论。论文审稿专家评价该文是"a masterpiece""开辟了生物学新领域"。

微缺失和微重复是基因组病中最常见的致病 DNA 重排。张学发现染色体 17q24 微缺失和微重复可导致先天性全身多毛症（俗称"毛孩"），在国际上首先证明先天性全身多毛症属于基因组病。他领导的团队随后又在一个 X– 连锁神经管畸形 – 脊柱侧弯 – 先天性全身多毛综合征中国人家系中发现人类特异性回文序列介导的 Xq27.1 区域常染色体大片段 DNA 插入，同时在国外相关家系中验证了这种致病 DNA 重排新机制。以上两项工作都在 *Am J Hum Genet* 上发表。

上述两种遗传病致病突变新机制的发现，无论对基础研究中发现新致病突变，还是对基因诊断应用中提高致病突变检出率都具有普遍应用价值。美国实验皮肤病学会主席 Angela Christiano 教授将张学团队在毛发疾病遗传学上的新发现列入突显近百年皮肤生物学突破性进展的 "Milestone in Cutaneous Biology"。

三、揭示了家族性反常性痤疮的遗传和分子发病机制，证明该病与早发家族性 Alzheimer 病为等位基因病

一些常见复杂疾病会有少部分病例是家族性的，表现为典型的孟德尔遗传。利用这些家系发现致病基因，再根据致病基因的已知功能和致病突变的性质，可揭示常见复杂疾病的发病机制和治疗新策略。

反常性痤疮（acne inversa，AI）又称化脓性汗腺炎或毛囊闭锁三联征，是一种慢性、反复发作的毛囊自身炎症性疾病，常形成脓肿、窦道和瘢痕，为最严重的皮肤病之一，对患者身心健康伤害极大。自 1839 年被首次报道以来，对其命名国际上长期争论，发病机制不清。家族性 AI 表现为常染色体显性遗传，致病基因未知。张学与王宝玺及沈岩合作，在 6 个家族性 AI 中国人家系中发现 g- 分泌酶亚单位基因 *NCSTN*、*PSEN1* 和 *PSENEN* 的丧失功能突变，确定家族性 AI 发生的遗传机制为 g- 分泌酶亚单位基因的单倍性不足，提出其分子发病机制为 g- 分泌酶 -Notch 通路的功能缺陷，证明早发家族性 Alzheimer 病和家族性 AI 可以是早老素基因 PSEN1 不同性质突变引起的等位基因病。本项发现为确定 AI 源于毛囊而非大汗腺提供了关键证据，为 AI 的治疗药物研发提供了新思路，也为重新评价基于 g- 分泌酶的 Alzheimer 病分子发病机制和治疗策略提供了理论依据。

上述发现以亮点文章在 *Science* 上发表，同期特别配发了哈佛医学院两位教授撰写的展望评述。三位 F1000 专家给予了高度评价和推介，其中 *Br J Dermatol* 主编 Alex Anstey 指出"本文在皮肤病学、神经病学、老年护理和神经精神医学领域引起了轰动"。Orly Reiner 教授在 F1000 推介中认为"继本项发现后，g- 分泌酶在 Alzheimer 病之病理生理学中的确切作用需要重新考虑"。

张学的研究成果被编入 *Emery and Rimoin's Principles and Practice of Medical Genetics*、*Human Genetics：Concepts and Applications* 和 *Gene Control* 等多本世界著名教科书、参考书和专著。他十余次应邀在国际学术会议上作报告，先后担任 *Am J Hum Genet* 等 8 家国际专业学术杂志的编委，为提升我国医学遗传学的国际影响力做出了贡献。

Awardee of Medical Sciences and
Materia Medica Prize, Zhang Xue

Zhang Xue was born in Zhaozhou County of Heilongjiang Province in July 1964. He is the professor and chair of medical genetics at the Chinese Academy of Medical Sciences & Peking Union Medical College（CAMS & PUMC）. He got a medical degree in 1986, received a master degree in medical genetics in 1989, and obtained a PhD in cell biology in 1994, all from China

Medical University located in the Shenyang city of China. He subsequently did his postdoctoral training in cancer genetics at the University of Pennsylvania and at Massachusetts General Hospital / Harvard Medical School. In 1998, he was appointed as the department head of cell biology at China Medical University. In 2001, he was recruited to CAMS & PUMC, serving as the chairman of the Department of Medical Genetics, Institute of Basic Medical Sciences. He became the scientific director of the McKusick–Zhang Center for Genetic Medicine at CAMS & PUMC in 2004 and the director of the Laboratory of Clinical Genetics at PUMC Hospital in 2012. In CAMS & PUMC, he served as an assistant president for international affairs from 2002 to 2009, and director of the Department of Research Affairs from 2013 to 2014, and was promoted to vice president for research and graduate studies in 2017.

After moving to CAMS & PUMC, Dr. Zhang switched his research interest to the molecular basis of Mendelian disorders. He has discovered the disease genes for several monogenic disorders, including familial acne inversa (AI), Marie Unna hereditary hypotrichosis (MUHH), familial idiopathic basal ganglia calcification and syndactyly type V, and identified the pathogenic genomic rearrangements for congenital generalized hypertrichosis terminalis, X–linked congenital hypertrichosis syndrome and syndactyly type IV.

In congenital hair growth disorders, Dr. Zhang has found two distinct mutations mechanisms. He led an international collaboration and showed that loss–of–function mutations in an inhibitory uORF of the *hairless* gene (*HR*) could cause MUHH. He discovered that X–linked congenital hypertrichosis syndrome resulted from interchromosomal insertions mediated by a human–specific palindromic sequence near *SOX3*.

Dr. Zhang has provided the first insight into the molecular pathogenesis of AI. In familial AI, he identified loss–of–function mutations in the γ–secretase component genes *NCSTN*, *PSEN1* and *PSENEN*, establishing the haploinsufficiency of a γ–secretase component gene as the genetic mechanism and the impaired γ–secretase–Notch pathway as the molecular mechanism of pathogenesis, and demonstrating that familial AI can be an allelic disorder of early–onset familial Alzheimer's disease.

Dr. Zhang serves as the president of the Chinese Society of Medical Genetics from 2013 to 2016. He has been on the editorial board of eight international journals, including the *American Journal of Human Genetics*, *Annual Review of Genomics and Human Genetics*, *Journal of Medical Genetics*, *Clinical Genetics*, and *Journal of Investigative Dermatology*.

医学药学奖获得者

赵铱民

赵铱民，1956年10月出生于陕西省汉中市。1983年毕业于第四军医大学口腔医学系，1991年于同校获医学博士学位并留校任教。1996年任教授、主任医师、博士生导师。1996—1997年在日本爱知学院大学齿学部任特别研究员。2002—2003年在美国UCLA牙科学院任客座教授。2004年起任第四军医大学口腔医院院长。2012—2015年任第四军医大学副校长、代校长。2014年起任军事口腔医学国家重点实验室主任。先后担任日本大阪齿科大学名誉教授、日本爱知学院大学齿学部客座教授、美国UCLA牙科学院客座教授、中央保健委专家、国务院学科评议组成员、世界军事齿科学会主席、国际颌面修复学会主席、中华口腔医学会名誉会长。《中华口腔医学杂志》总编辑，第十一、第十二届全国政协委员。

赵铱民长期从事口腔颌面缺损修复的临床和研究工作，在口腔颌面缺损的数字化修复研究、颌面缺损仿真修复和咀嚼功能重建以及修复体固位技术方面做出了重要贡献。

一、建立了颜面缺损仿真修复技术体系，实现了赝复技术根本性的革新与进步

传统颜面缺损赝复完全依赖医生的临床经验和手工操作，工艺复杂，过程烦琐，医生培养周期长，技术难以普及。赵铱民率先开展颜面缺损数字化修复研究，从根本上解决了上述问题。

（1）创建了颜面赝复体智能化仿真设计和快速制作方法。赵铱民1996年提出数字修复、功能修复、远程修复的颌面修复新理念，研制数字化颜面印模技术，建立了中国人颜面器官三维形态数据库，形成了基于数据库与逆向复原技术的赝复体智能化仿真设计和以阴模成形为主体的快速成形技术，于2003年自主研发出国际上首个颜面赝复数字化医疗系统，可对任一颜面缺损进行智能化仿真修复，恢复患者原有容貌，并在全世界率先用于临床。现已成为常规技术，使治疗步骤缩减一半、治疗周期缩短4/5、技术培训由

5～8年缩短至7天，还实现了远程修复。国际颌面修复学会前主席John Beumer评述"中国团队首先创造了颜面赝复体的计算机仿真设计和快速制作方法……中国同行正在引领世界颌面修复领域的发展……"。这一成果被编入美国颌面赝复学教科书相关内容。

（2）提出"共混－复合"设计理念，研制出新型赝复材料。针对原赝复材料存在抗撕裂强度弱、仿真性差等缺陷，赵铱民提出了"共混－复合"的新材料设计理论，即将含有不同官能团的材料按比例共混后，再对不同组合材料进行复合处理，形成与颌面组织质感相似的系列仿真材料。据此研制出ZY系列加成型硅橡胶赝复材料，实现了颜面缺损修复的"质感仿真"。成果获美国颌面修复学会学术一等奖（2007）。

二、建立了系统的颌骨缺损咀嚼功能重建技术，显著提升了修复后患者的咀嚼效能

咀嚼是颌骨最重要的功能，但传统颌骨缺损赝复体只能恢复外形，不能重建咀嚼功能。赵铱民建立了系统的颌骨缺损种植修复技术，实现了咀嚼功能重建。

（1）建立了系统的颌骨缺损种植修复理论和技术方法。提出了颌骨缺损后生物力学体系重构再平衡的理论，建立了首个国人颅颌骨种植数据库与全颅颌骨三维有限元模型；精确测量了国人颅颌骨骨质、骨量，制定了颅颌骨种植体定位图谱，为颅颌面缺损种植修复奠定了理论基础；优选出不同类型颌骨缺损种植修复设计方案；提出了"基于功能重建目标逆向设计修复颌骨缺损"的新治疗理念；创造了"种植体－研磨杆修复上颌缺损"等7项修复新技术，在多个国家推广应用。

（2）制定了颌骨缺损赝复诊疗规范，实现了颌骨缺损后咀嚼效能重建。制定了我国首个颌骨缺损赝复临床诊疗规范和临床路径，成功治疗了包括世界首例"先天性颧骨－全上颌骨缺失"病例在内的大型颌骨缺损患者群，患者咀嚼功能从传统修复体的10%提高到80%以上。

三、发展了种植体固位技术，提高了牙、颌面种植修复成功率

种植体是缺牙和颌面缺损修复的重要固位方式，但放疗后骨组织的失败率仍较高。赵铱民通过系列研究，提高了牙、颌面种植修复成功率。

（1）发展了种植体表面处理技术。研究应用微弧氧化、纳米管、组织工程等技术修饰钛种植体，显著扩大了种植体表面面积，筛选出最适于骨细胞附着的表面孔隙率，显著提升了种植体与骨组织的结合率，缩短了骨结合时间；研究放疗患者种植体植入的时效影响，制定此类患者种植体植入的临床规范，使放疗后骨组织的种植体植入成功率由65.1%增加到89.4%。

（2）创造了种植磁附着固位技术。赵铱民将种植体与磁附着技术结合形成新型种植体上部结构，创造了种植磁附着固位技术。此技术固位可靠、取戴便捷、安全易行，可解决多种赝复体及义齿的固位难题，被国际修复学界称为"Chinese way"，目前已为国际同行广泛应用。

（3）研制出国际首台主动式种植牙机器人并用于临床，实现了种植牙修复的精确设计、在非直视条件下的自动精细手术和多牙缺失的精准即时种植修复，是口腔种植修复领域的重大创新。

四、创建并促进中国颌面赝复学发展，推动我国该学科跻身于国际先进水平

（1）创建了我国的颌面赝复学。赵铱民是我国颌面赝复学的创始人，首先开设《颌面赝复学》课程，培养了我国颌面赝复方向首批研究生，著有该领域首部教科书和系列专著，培养了我国 90% 以上的颌面赝复人才。建立了中华口腔医学会口腔颌面修复专业委员会，还建成了国际知名的口腔医学博物馆。

（2）促进了颌面赝复学国际学术交流与发展。赵铱民及其团队是国际颌面修复领域的领跑者，4 次获得国际颌面修复学会学术奖；建立了国际颌面赝复培训基地，为多个国家培训修复医师。

赵铱民一直工作在科研、教育、教学第一线，共主持国家科技支撑计划、国家自然科学基金重点项目等国家、军队重点课题 15 项；领衔获得国家科技进步奖一等奖（排名第一，2011）1 项、国家科技进步奖二等奖 2 项（排名第三，2000、2004）、军队科技进步一等奖 2 项（排名第一、第二）；以第一作者或通讯作者发表论文 280 篇，其中 SCI 收录 46 篇；出版专著 3 部；以第一完成人获得国家发明专利 7 项。先后被授予全国优秀科技工作者、中国医师奖、中国杰出口腔医师奖、军队专业技术杰出贡献奖。2013 年荣立个人一等功。

Awardee of Medical Sciences and
Materia Medica Prize, Zhao Yimin

Zhao Yimin was born in Hanzhong City of Shaanxi Province in October 1956. He graduated from School of Stomatology, the Fourth Military Medical University in 1993 and received his PhD from the same school in 1991. He was promoted to full professor, chief-physician and doctorate supervisor in 1996. He worked in School of Dentistry, Aichi Gakuin University during 1996–1997. He was visiting professor at School of Dentistry, UCLA in 2002 and 2003. He became dean of School of Stomatology, Fourth Military Medical University in 2004. He was vice president and acting president of the Fourth Military Medical University from 2012—2015. He has been director of State Key Laboratory of Military Stomatology since 2014. He was invited as honorary professor of Osaka Dental University, visiting professor of Aichi Gakuin University and UCLA School of Dentistry. He was Chairman of World Military Dental Association & FDI Section of Denfense Forces Dental Services. He is member of State Academic Degree Committee Discipline Evaluation

Group, honorary chairman of International Society of Maxillofacial Rehabilitation, honorary chairman of Chinese Stomatological Association, editor-in-chief of Chinese Journal of Stomatology and member of the National Committee of the Chinese People's Political Consultative Conference.

Zhao Yimin has long endeavored to the clinical work and research of oral and maxillofacial defects rehabilitation. He has contributed greatly to the research of digital and mimic rehabilitation of oral and maxillofatial defects, reconstruction of masticatory functions and the retention techniques of prosthesis.

(1) He established a mimic rehabilitation system for oral and maxillofacial defects, the system completely renovated rehabilitation techniques. He established the intelligent-artificial method to design and a new method to rapidly fabricate the prosthesis, and invented the "Mingle-complex" design concept and found new prosthetic materials.

(2) He established the functional rehabilitation technique to systematically reconstruct the masticatory functions. This technique greatly improved masticatory function of maxillo-mandibular defects patients. He established systematic implant rehabilitation theory and technique for oral and maxillo-mandibular defects. He made guidelines for diagnosis and rehabilitation treatment for oral and maxillo-mandibular defects and realized functional recovery of mastication.

(3) He developed the retention technique for implants and improved the success rate of tooth and maxilla implants. He developed the micro arc oxidation surface treatment technique for implants and magnetic-retention technique for implants. He designed and made the first robot to be used for dental implants.

(4) He established and promoted the development of oral and maxillofacial prosthetics in China, and promoted international exchange and development in the field. He facilitated the discipline's development.

Prof. Zhao Yimin has got 15 research projects, including State Science & Technology Supportive Plan project, Key project of NSFC, Key projects from the PLA. He won First Class State Science and Technology Progress Award (2011), Second Class State Science and Technology Progress Award (2004, 2000), PLA First Class Science and Technology Progress Award. He has published 280 peer-reviewed papers, including 48 in SCI journals. He has published 3 books. He got 7 inventory patents. He is honored as National Outstanding Scientific Researcher, Chinese Outstanding Dentists and received PLA Outstanding Professional Contribution Award. In 2013, he won the First Class Service Medal from the PLA.

机械电力技术奖获得者

刘　宏

刘宏，1966 年 12 月出生于安徽省合肥市。1993 年毕业于哈尔滨工业大学机械电子工程专业获工学博士学位，其间在德国宇航中心博士联合培养一年半。1993—1999 年任德国宇航中心研究员；1999—2004 年获教育部首批长江学者计划支持；2004—2010 年任德国宇航中心终身研究员；2010 年入选中组部"千人计划"，全职回到哈尔滨工业大学工作；2013 年起任机器人技术与系统国家重点实验室主任；2015 年至今任哈尔滨工业大学校长助理。军委科技委智能无人平台主题专家组首席科学家，原总装备部载人航天技术预先研究主题专家组副组长，国家自然科学基金委重大研究计划"共融机器人"指导专家组成员。

刘宏长期从事空间机器人基础理论和关键技术研究，在灵巧操作与在轨维修等方面取得创新成果，主持研制的我国首台空间机械臂系统和空间灵巧手系统成功应用于"试验七号"卫星和天宫二号空间实验室，为空间服务做出了重要贡献。获国家技术发明二等奖 3 项，出版专著 3 部，发表 SCI 论文 57 篇、EI 论文 81 篇；授权发明专利 44 项（美国专利 1 项、德国专利 5 项）。

一、主持研制了我国首台空间机械臂系统

空间机械臂安装在航天器外侧，暴露在太空，工作环境恶劣。它具有六维空间精确定位和手爪精细操作能力，是航天器在轨维护的核心装备，世界上仅美国具备这个能力。自 1999 年以来，刘宏发明了具有冗余容错，集机、电、热、控于一体的模块化关节，并在此基础上提出了可折叠机械臂构型，实现了最小空间的发射锁紧配置；建立了柔性关节的空间机械臂动力学模型，有效抑制了机械臂的末端残余抖动，实现了机械臂的精确定位；提出了动基座下动目标的相对运动预测方法，实现了浮动基座情形下大时延的运动目标自主视觉伺服跟踪；提出了重力环境下物理半物理相融合的方法，建立了机械臂

模拟空间微重力环境的三维空间运动综合平台，攻克了机械臂地面测试的技术难题。

空间机械臂于 2013 年作为"试验七号"卫星核心载荷成功发射，首次成功完成了空间机械臂在轨操作等空间维护技术科学试验，使我国成为继 2007 年美国轨道快车后第二个拥有该项技术的国家，为我国空间机器人系统跻身世界前列做出了重要贡献。

美国官员披露："安装有机械臂的卫星最令人担忧，严重威胁美国卫星，该卫星可执行近距离观察与攻击任务，拔下美卫星系统元件送回中国大陆，或是贴近美国卫星植入中国大陆系统，而抓取方式不产生太空碎片，无害中国大陆卫星。"

相关成果获 2015 年国家技术发明二等奖并入选 2013 年中国高校十大科技进展，出版专著《空间机器人及其遥操作》获国家"三个一百"原创图书出版工程。

二、主持研制了我国首台具有多种感知功能的五手指空间灵巧手，成功应用于我国天宫二号空间实验室人机协同维修任务

空间站的装配、检测与维修以及大量科学试验载荷照料等维护任务对空间机器人的精细操作能力提出了严峻挑战，迫切需要机器人具有仿人手的灵巧操作功能，其典型特征是机械手的自由度多、感知能力强。多指仿人灵巧手是国际机器人领域的前沿方向，目前仅有美国 NASA 的 5 手指 12 自由度灵巧手在国际空间站上服役，但驱动器置于灵巧手外部，通过绳索驱动手指，重量 4.5 千克。自 1986 年以来，刘宏基于人手多模式运动谱解析揭示了人手灵巧作业过程中多个手指的协同作业机理；针对传统驱动外置式灵巧手重量大、动态响应慢的问题，提出了驱动内置型灵巧手的设计方法，发明了将所有驱动器置于手指指部或根部的模块化手指，根部两驱动器差分传动、转轴垂直相交，实现了指尖输出力倍增，灵巧手重量仅 1.8 千克；发明了集成于手指非规则曲面的柔性触觉传感器和适于 MEMS 加工的手指尖全平面式微型六维力传感器弹性体，实现了精细操作的物理接触感知；基于关节力矩、指尖力和触觉等多传感器信息，提出了指尖任意笛卡尔方向上可编程阻抗控制方法，实现了手指柔顺控制；提出了基于几何分析的多指力封闭抓取方法，实现了多指实时协调控制。

主持研制了具有 15 个驱动器、5 个手指、140 个传感器的空间灵巧手，于 2016 年随天宫二号空间实验室发射入轨，国际上首次成功完成了灵巧手在轨精细维修操作等任务。与美国 NASA 手相比，空间灵巧手的传感功能更丰富，重量减轻 50% 以上。

IEEE Control System 杂志封面刊登了灵巧手照片；ICRA2001 论文被引 813 次，是该领域十年来被引次数最多的论文之一。瑞典皇家工学院 Wikander 教授称"该灵巧手无论是在机构构型还是在控制效果上都是当今世界上最精巧的机器人手之一，所实现的阻抗控制对完成更加自主的任务是决定性的。"IEEE 机器人和自动化学会原主席 Siciliano 教授在编著里称"灵巧手具有很好的灵巧功能，逼近了人类手的特征"。

相关成果获 2008 年国家技术发明二等奖、2007 年欧盟机器人技术和转化一等奖（中国学者首次）、2009 年国际 IF 设计奖，出版专著《仿人多指灵巧手及其操作控制》。

三、突破生机电一体化仿生手关键技术，主持研制出残疾人智能假手并应用于多例肢残患者实验

残疾人假肢是重要的民生工程。传统假手外观与正常人手相近，但仅能完成单自由度握拳动作，严重影响残疾人正常生活。智能假手是国际前沿研究领域。刘宏发明了基于物体外形自适应抓取的欠驱动/耦合假手机构，发明了具有空间运动轨迹的单驱动拇指机构，假手重量484克；发明了基于肌电信号的智能假手嵌入式控制系统，实现了正确率高于98%的运动模式识别。

研制出具有5个驱动器、5个手指、15个耦合关节的智能假手，完成了12例肢残患者实验。*IEEE RAM*主编Stamigioli教授在其综述性论文中，将本成果列为国际上智能假手领域最具代表性的7项研究成果之一。相关成果获2016年国家技术发明二等奖，并出版专著《仿人型假手及其生机交互控制》。

Awardee of Machinery and Electric Technology Prize, Liu Hong

Liu Hong was born in Hefei City of Anhui Province in December 1966. He received his bachelor degree and doctor's degree from the Harbin Institute of Technology in 1986 and 1993, respectively. Prof. Liu's research interests include dexterous robot hand, space robot and biomechatronics. His research excellence has been well recognized and clearly indicated by the awards he has received, including three National Technology Invention Awards (second prize), an EURON/EUnited Robotics Technology-Transfer Award (First prize), and several Provincial & Ministerial Awards. He has published more than 100 SCI/EI papers in robotics. A large number of patents are also authorized in Germany (5), USA (1) and China (38).

(1) The space robot: Prof. Liu was the prime investigator of the first Chinese space robot arm and also among the earliest researchers studying on space robot, especially the light weight manipulator and multifunction end-effector for various space applications. The precision control of manipulator is achieved by vibration suppression based on the dynamics of space flexible manipulator. The on-orbit experimental results indicate the proposed methods are applicable to space service operations. The work had a significant impact on the research of space robot applications, awarded National Award for Technological Invention 2nd Prize from the State Council of the People's Republic of China in 2015.

(2) The dexterous robotic hand: Prof. Liu and his research team developed the 4 and 5 fingers dexterous robot hands which integrated mechanical, electrical, sensing and control system into one finger to realize humanlike manipulation with 12 or 15 DOFs, based on the modularization

idea. In his early work, he also presented a multi-control strategy to solve the smooth switch of the planning strategy from the free space to constraint space, as well as the form closure grasping strategy with multi-fingers based on the geometric analysis. Moreover, to restore the hand function for amputees, he and his team developed a prosthetic hand with multiple DOFs integrated with force/position and tactile sensor. They proposed a pattern recognition based intuitive EMG control scheme that can realize an on-line control over 18 active hand gestures. The works laid the foundation of the theory and methodology for dexterous robot hand analysis and design and manipulation, which have been widely cited by researchers all around the world.

电子信息技术奖获得者

何　友

何友，1956 年 10 月出生于吉林省磐石市。1982 年毕业于海军工程大学指挥控制专业，获学士学位。1988 年毕业于海军工程大学指挥系统专业，获硕士学位。1991 年 10 月赴德国布伦瑞克工业大学信息技术研究所做高级访问学者。1997 年毕业于清华大学通信与信息系统专业，获博士学位。历任原海军航空工程学院教研室主任、系主任、副院长、院长等职务，2007 年晋升为海军少将军衔。现任海军航空大学信息融合研究所所长，海战场信息感知与融合技术军队重点实验室主任，清华大学双聘教授、博导。兼任 IET Fellow，国家 "863" 先进防御技术领域专家委员会委员，国务院学科评议组成员，国家杰出青年科学基金评审委员会委员，国家自然科学基金委信息学部咨询专家委员会委员，军委科技委兼职委员，军委装备发展部雷达探测技术专家组成员，中国电子学会、中国航空学会、中国指挥与控制学会常务理事，中国航空学会信息融合分会主任委员。2013 年当选中国工程院院士。

何友 30 年来一直致力于信息融合的技术研究、工程建设与人才培养，为我国信息融合理论和关键技术的发展与应用做出了突出贡献，是我国信息融合领域的学科带头人。主持完成国家自然科学基金重点项目、"973" "863"、军内科研等国家、军队级项目 40 余项；在雷达目标融合检测、多传感器融合、信息融合综合工程应用等方面取得恒虚警检测统一模型、多传感器航迹关联等 5 项主要技术突破；主持研制 331G 雷达、轰六 G 任务系统训练机等 6 型工程系统；以第一完成人获国家科技进步奖二等奖 4 项，国家级教学成果一、二等奖各 1 项，省部级科技进步一等奖 7 项，省部级科技发明一等奖 1 项；授权国家发明专利和软件著作权 46 项；在 IEEE 会刊等发表论文 260 余篇，出版专著 6 部，论著他引 10000 余次；获全国百篇优秀博士学位论文奖。相关成果被应用于国内主要雷达厂所的 19 个型号 847 部雷达装备生产和航母指控等我国重大工程项目中，军事、经济和社会效益显著。

一、在雷达目标融合检测方面取得系列创新成果，主持研制的 331G 雷达批量装备部队

提出了广义有序统计类恒虚警融合检测算法，经过长期研究建立了该背景下恒虚警融合检测统一模型，使原来所有模型都成为它的特例且衍生出众多新模型。德国雷达学会主席 H. Rohling 等专家认为该模型计算量小、性能好，是该领域的重大研究进展。

强海杂波背景下群目标的检测与跟踪取得重要突破，提出距离扩展目标检测新方法，IEEE 会士 B. Himed 等认为该方法为解决群目标检测这一富有挑战性的难题开辟了新途径，提升了检测鲁棒性。

主持研制 331G 地面跟踪雷达，自主设计 P/B 和 A/B 组合光栅显示系统，明显改善了雷达终端性能，达到当时国内同类产品的领先水平，并装备到所有岸导部队，配套研制的实时雷达标校设备已生产 30 余套。

相关成果获国家科技进步奖二等奖 1 项、山东省技术发明一等奖 1 项、军队科技进步一等奖 2 项，均排名 1；出版专著 2 部，授权发明专利 20 项、软件著作权 1 项。

二、多传感器融合理论与技术研究取得多项开创性成果，推动了我国军事信息融合领域的发展

系统发展和建立了多传感器航迹关联理论与方法，提出的序贯、不等维、模糊、灰色、MDCA 等航迹关联算法解决了分布式信息融合中长期存在的航迹重复、丢失、间断等难题，突破了目标密集、交叉、机动等复杂环境下的航迹关联技术；序贯法的正确关联率比首届国际信息融合学会主席 Bar Shalom 的方法提高 34%，第 4 届国际信息融合学会主席 P. K. Varshney 认为序贯法是非常原创性的方法；专家鉴定认为序贯法等成果达到国际领先水平。

提出了双 / 多基地雷达测量数据最优估计定理。双 / 多基地雷达如何实现测量数据最优估计一直无理论依据。何友基于双 / 多基地雷达定位误差的相关性，建立了测量子集划分和选取准则，提出了测量数据的最优估计定理，消除了定位无解的现象，定位误差降低 2 ~ 4 倍。

突破了电磁辐射源快速融合识别的关键技术，提出了基于模糊贴近的辐射源识别新模型，建立了基于不确定推理的快速融合识别新方法，与工程上常用的模板匹配法相比，正确识别率提高 10% ~ 28%。

上述成果已成功应用于×××工程、×××海空情、舰艇编队指控、×××雷达网等融合系统中，显著提升了系统的性能，复杂环境下航迹关联的正确率最高可提高 20%，辐射源正确识别率可达 85% 以上。

相关成果获国家科技进步奖二等奖 1 项、军队科技进步一等奖 2 项，均排名第一；出版专著 2 部（1 部获国家"三个一百"原创图书工程奖），授权发明专利 10 项、软件著作权 3 项。

三、信息融合综合工程应用

针对我军新型飞机信息化程度高、技术复杂、作战训练难度大等突出问题，综合运用信息融合的研究成果研制了 ××× 任务系统训练机、歼 ××× 全任务训练机等多种大型综合训练机。提出了与三维数字地形匹配的机载雷达图像生成新方法，建立了大范围地景数据库融合处理和调度策略，解决了大视场地形条件下动态雷达图像实时产生和多种目标信息融合显示的难题；提出了雷达、通信、电子侦察和干扰设备全系统的信号处理、分选及特征识别等仿真建模方法，指导实现了东南沿海和周边地区复杂电磁信号态势的动态实时模拟；提出了与硬件结构无关的战场信息处理流程，实现了飞机平台战场态势感知与融合过程的仿真。这些成果实现了大型航空信息装备从程序训练到以任务为中心的战术训练方式的跨越，解决了在敏感地区无法用实装进行作战训练的难题，3 型装备共节省飞机燃油和折旧费约 3.3 亿元。

针对我国舰载直升机装备建设和发展的迫切需求，创建了舰载直升机测试信号系列模型和通用技术支援平台，突破了舰载直升机机载设备通用检测、分布式远程测控、跨地域协同诊断等多项关键技术，形成了我国舰载直升机多机型、多专业分布式跨地域联合技术体系，总体技术居同领域国内领先，达到国际先进水平，改善了我国舰载直升机装备保障的落后局面。

相关成果获国家科技进步奖二等奖 2 项、省部级科技进步一等奖 3 项，均排名第一。出版专著 2 部，授权发明专利 4 项、软件著作权 8 项。培养博士、硕士 110 余人，其中 3 人获全国百篇优秀博士学位论文和提名奖、22 人次获省部级优秀博士 / 硕士论文奖；带领的团队获山东省优秀创新团队和军队科技创新群体奖。何友本人入选国家百千万人才工程，荣获"求是"工程奖、全国留学回国人员成就奖、军队专业技术重大贡献奖等，被评为全国优秀讲师，享受政府特殊津贴，荣立二等功 5 次，任十七大党代表和十二届全国政协委员。

Awardee of Electronics and Information Technology Prize, He You

He You was born in Panshi City of Jilin Province in October 1956. He graduated from the Command and Control department of Naval University of Engineering in 1982 with a bachelor's degree and the Command System department of Naval University of Engineering in 1988 with a master's degree. In October 1991, he was a senior visiting scholar at the Information Technology Research Institute of Technische Universität Carolo–Wilhelmina zu Braunschweig in Germany. In 1997, he got his Phd from Qinghua University with a degree in Communication and Information

Systems. He was the Department Director, Department dean, Vice Dean, Dean, etc for the Naval Aeronautical and Astronautical University, and in 2007, he was promoted to the rank of Rear Admiral. He is now Director of the Information Fusion Research Institute of Naval Aeronautical University, Director of key laboratory for Information Perception and Fusion Technology Army, and a dual professor and director of Qinghua university. At the same time a IET Fellow, a National Outstanding Youth Science Fund review committee member, committee elected academician of Chinese Academy of Engineering in 2013.

In the past 30 years, He You has been committed to the technology research, engineering construction and personnel training in Information Fusion domain. He made great contributions for the development and application of Information Fusion Theory and key technology in our country, and is the leader in the field of Information Fusion in China. He presided over more than 40 national and military level projects, including the key projects of the National Natural Science Fund, 973, 863, military research, etc. He is the first to win four Second Prize for National Scientific and Technological Progress, First and Second Prize for National Teaching Achievement, seven First Prize for Provincial Scientific and Technological Progress, First Prize for Provincial Scientific and Technological Inventions; 46 authorized national invention patent and software copyright; more than 260 published articles in IEEE conference and other publications, and 6 published treatises, being cited over 10000 times; won the National 100 Excellent Doctoral Dissertation Award. His research results have been applied to aircraft carrier charges and other major engineering projects in China, and gained significant military, economic and social benefits.

He You has trained more than 110 doctor and master students, 3 of them have won the National 100 Excellent Doctoral Dissertation Award or nominees. Selected into the national pacesetter program, he won the "Realistic" Engineering Award, Major Military Professional Technology Contribution Award, etc., and was named the National Excellent Lecturer, was awarded with special government allowances, won the second-grade merit 5 times, and was party congress delegate for the 17th NCCPC and member of 12th CPPCC national committee.

电子信息技术奖获得者

刘　　明

刘明，女，1964 年 4 月出生于江西省丰城市。1981—1988 就读于合肥工业大学应用物理系半导体物理与器件专业，先后获得学士和硕士学位；1995—1998 就读于北京航空航天大学材料学院，获得博士学位。1998—1999 年为中国科学院半导体研究所和微电子中心联合博士后研究人员；1999—2000 年任中国科学院微电子研究所副研究员；2000 年至今任中国科学院微电子研究所研究员。中国科学院大学教授，英国卢瑟福实验室和日本东京理科大学访问教授，中国科学院院士。

刘明长期从事新型存储器和集成电路加工技术的研究。在非易失存储器材料、器件结构、算法、电路设计、三维集成等方面取得了一系列原创性成果，获国家自然科学奖二等奖 1 项（排名第一）、国家技术发明二等奖 3 项（分别排名第一、二、四）、国家科技进步奖二等奖 1 项（排名第四）、真空科技成就奖和科学院杰出成绩奖等奖项。获得授权发明专利 216 件（含美国 14），主要专利转让（许可）给国内重要集成电路制造企业中芯国际和武汉新芯。

一、建立阻变存储器（最重要的新型存储器技术之一）物理模型，提出并实现高性能 RRAM 和集成的基础理论和关键技术方法，产生重要国际影响

存储器是集成电路的核心和重要基础，阻变存储器（RRAM）是新型存储技术的国际竞争重地，但研究初期其存储机理不明、性能难以调控和集成中存在严重串扰等基础性难题，亟待解决。在机理模型方面，刘明阐明导电通路形成 / 破灭是阻变的物理本质，发展了导电通路微观动态表征技术，揭示了阻变动力学过程，建立了阻变存储器模型。在性能调控方面，阐明阻变起源，发现阻变功能层缺陷产生 / 分布均匀性对存储性能的影响规律，提出功能层掺杂的器件设计新技术；提出局域电场增强控制导电通路有序生长、有效提高参数均匀性，使存储器性能调控从实验探索上升到理性设计和可控实现。在集成方面，阐明阵列集成中串扰产生的物理机理，发现 RRAM 自整流效应和肖特基接触对其影响的内在规律，揭示了自整流效应的物理本质，进而提出抑制阵列集成串扰的新技术，实现了 8×32 八层的三维集成。目前，刘明和她的小组基于中国最先进半导体代工厂的 28nm PolySiON/HKMG 制造工艺，致力于 RRAM 的产业化开发，这一新技术的开发将使中国在 RRAM 应用领域处于国际领跑地位。

二、拓展新型闪存材料和结构体系，提出可靠性表征新技术、物理机理和失效模型，为存储器产业发展提供了关键理论和技术基础

闪存是目前占主导地位的非易失存储器，但随着尺寸缩小，其存储性能和可靠性的矛盾日趋严峻，成为制约闪存进一步发展的瓶颈。在新材料结构方面，刘明针对多晶硅存储层的限制，引入纳米晶 / 高 k 等新材料体系优化闪存综合性能，提出成核和生长分离的二步低压化学气相沉积纳米晶材料制备新工艺和在线检测技术，在 8 寸生产线获得尺寸 / 密度均匀可控的材料；发展了新型复合存储层结构，综合优化阻挡层 / 存储层 / 隧穿层，解决了存储性能和可靠性的矛盾。在机理可靠性方面，建立了存储性能和可靠性表征平台，理论分析并实验验证了纳米晶等新材料引入后的存储机理和物理模型（多层介质载流子输运、俘获 / 释放模型）及可靠性模型（保持、耐久性和串扰）；发展了结辅助的低压编程技术，改善了存储性能和可靠性。在闪存新技术方面，基于新材料和机理，在 8 寸生产线自主开发了纳米晶存储材料 / 集成工艺 / 器件 / 可靠性 / 电路等成套技术，研制 8M 纳米晶芯片，列入企业发展计划；牵头国内研产学开发了 32nm 闪存技术；研制了 128M 和 1G 芯片并实现了技术的产品转化。

三、发展了集成电路的微纳加工技术并拓展到禁运的短波衍射元件研制中，重要指标达到国际先进水平，促进了集成电路工艺技术的自主发展

微纳加工是集成电路的基础和驱动力，广泛应用于信息、制造和科学研究等领域。提高分辨率特别是不严重依赖设备更新的分辨率增强技术，并拓展其应用是该领域追求的核心目标。在分辨率 / 效率增强方面，刘明提出不依赖线宽测量精度的散射参数提取技术，同时提高了参数提取精度和图形修正效率；发展了大小 / 疏密图形保真制造的混合和匹配曝光技术，提高了加工精度和效率。在移相掩模方面，提出双移相器结构，解决了传统移相掩模光强分布不均衡的难题，提高了信噪比，将分辨率进一步提高 30%。为我国首台 193nm 投影光刻机提供成套镜头检测掩模，制定了 7 项掩模制造国家标准。在短波衍射元件方面，短波衍射元件是特指工作波段在 0.01 ~ 10nm 的器件，是激光聚变等国防武器重要领域急需核心元件，对中国禁运。其制造难题为自支撑薄膜应力控制和大高宽比纳米结构制造，对此刘明等提出二步亚胺化工艺和杂环形成技术控制自支撑薄膜应力；提出并实现电子束加工纳米结构和 X 射线复制增大高宽比的自主技术，解决了系列制造难题并获得广泛应用，如衍射光栅、微聚焦波带片、螺旋波带片等短波元件批量应用到激光聚变实验等国家重大工程中。

Awardee of Electronics and Information Technology Prize, Liu Ming

Liu Ming, female, was born in Fengcheng City of Jiangxi Province in April 1964. She received the B.S. & M.S. degrees in semiconductor physics and device from Hefei University of Technology in 1985 and 1988 respectively, and the Ph.D degree in Material Science from Beijing University of Aeronautics and Astronautics in 1998. Currently, she is a professor and the director of CAS Key Lab. of Microelectronic Device and Integration Technology at the Institute of Microelectronics of CAS. She was elected Member of the Chinese Academy of Science in 2015.

Her current research interests are Micro/nanofabrication, memory device and integration, nano-electronics and molecular electronics. She holds more than 216 Chinese patents and 14USA patents (more filed and pending), and has published 8 books (collaborate with others). She has authored and coauthored more than 200 journal papers, and more than 60 papers (including 38 keynote or invited papers) in international and national conference. Prof. Liu is an IEEE Senior Member. She has served as an IEEE Electron Devices Society (EDS) distinguished lecturer since 2012 and is currently the Chair of ED Beijing Chapter. She received State Science Award (second level in 2016), State Invention Award (second level, in 2005, 2007 and 2013) and State S&T Progress Award (second level in 2009) as well as other Awards from Beijing Government and Ministry of Education.

1. The systematic works on Resistive Switch Random Access Memory (RRAM)

They first observed the morphology, microstructure, composition, and growth/rupture of the conductive filament (CF) of RRAM at nanoscale by in-situ TEM. Liu's group proposed a method for adjusting the memory performances by doping in the functional layer, which solves a difficult issue of low yield and poor performances of previous RRAMs. They designed and fabricated the corresponding devices, whose parameter uniformity has been greatly improved. To achieve high density integration, they have proposed a high performance self-selective device (SSC) with built-in nonlinearity for VRRAM integration. Furthermore they experimentally demonstrated a bit cost scalable (BiCS) 8-layer 3D vertical RRAM with ultimate scalability.

2. A series of new materials and structures of Flash was developed and new characterization method/ memory physical mechanism and reliability model were proposed

Liu's group developed a series of new materials and structures to enhance the performance of charge trapping memory (CTM), which is the basic device for 3D NAND. They also made significant contributions to the study of nitride storage type flash from the fabrication of high quality charge storage layer, to the cell optimization and Chip Design. Not only on the fundamental study, also in a strong collaboration with the industry, she successfully made numerous efforts to commercialize the memory products. Her group also jointly developed 32nm SONOS process modules with SMIC, and also developed several flash memory chips based on 65nm EOTOX technology with design house. All of these chips were in a great success that is widely used in smart card, mobile communication, etc. Her group's patents and related memory technology were transformed to XMC and become the foundation for Chinese Industry to kick off 3D NAND mass production development.

电子信息技术奖获得者

王 立 军

王立军，1946 年 7 月出生于吉林省舒兰市。中国科学院院士，激光与光电子技术专家。他从事激光理论、技术及工程化应用研究四十多年，主持及主要参与承担国家及省部级重大、重点项目 18 项（其中国防重大型号 1 项、重点型号 2 项，重大重点预研 4 项）；在大功率垂直腔面发射激光器、大功率无铝量子阱边发射激光器及其合束技术等方面取得了系统性、创造性学术成就，既有较深的理论造诣，又为我国国防应用等做出了重大贡献。获国家技术发明二等奖 1 项、国家科技进步奖二等奖 1 项、吉林省技术发明一等奖 1 项、吉林省科技进步一等奖 2 项、世界华商创新奖 1 项，均为第一完成人；发表 SCI、EI 论文 305 篇；合著专著 5 部；获授权发明专利 57 项，其中一项获得"中国专利优秀奖"；获全国优秀科技工作者等荣誉称号。

一、创新实现垂直腔面发射大功率激光器及高光束质量集成面阵

（1）他带领研究团队突破了前人认为垂直腔面发射激光器（VCSEL）只适于在毫瓦至几十毫瓦级低功率下运作的旧框架，从理论上详细阐明了瓦级大功率运作的可行性。首次提出多增益区、组分渐变、调制掺杂 DBR 等多项设计理念，攻克了芯片制作、器件封装等系列关键技术，并于 2004 年国际首创实现了光功率密度 33.4kW/cm^2 单管 VCSEL 脉冲峰值输出（10ns，100Hz 条件）；国际首创实现了 1.95W 单管 VCSEL 连续波输出，与以前传统结构相比，光功率提高近百倍，显著拓宽了其应用领域。

（2）突破了 VCSEL 正面发射的传统结构，在国际上首次提出张应变宽带隙势垒背面衬底发射的 VCSEL 新结构和设计思想，找到了一种增强器件散热能力和提高输出功率的有效途径。于 2011 年研制出 92 瓦脉冲输出单管背面衬底发射激光器，结果被 *Semiconductor Today* 以"垂直腔面发射激光器取得 92 瓦输出记录"为标题给予评价，此外 *Laser Focus World* 杂志评价为"在 60ns、110A 脉冲电流驱动下，脉冲峰值功率达

92W""一个单管面发射激光器记录"。

（3）提出了 GaAsP 高势垒增强载流子限制的设计思想，研制出 4×4 二维 VCSEL 面阵，在 110A 电流下脉冲功率达到 123 瓦，被美国 *Semiconductor Today* 评价为"主要区别是 GaAsP 替代 GaAs 势垒……是数据通信和泵浦源应用的更好选择"。提出并实现了大功率 VCSEL 集成面阵与其 GaAs 衬底材料制成的微透镜面阵单片集成，使面阵单元器件发散角由 14.8 度降到 6.6 度，光束质量获成倍改善。他所研制的各种 VCSEL 已陆续用于激光泵浦、激光引信、激光测距等领域，上述开创性工作为 VCSEL 领域研究奠定了基础，推动了本领域发展。

二、边发射无铝量子阱激光器及其合束技术工程化对国防建设的重要贡献

（1）他非常关注研究成果的工程化应用，创新思路的提出也都立足重点应用需求，更注重国防急需。针对当时国外禁运、国内传统大功率半导体激光器使用寿命短等情况，1995 年回国后，他优化设计出无铝量子阱激光器新结构，攻克了激光器腔面氧化导致器件失效、使用寿命短等难题，在国内率先研制出 3.2 瓦无铝量子阱单管激光器；2004 年开发出两种激光光纤耦合模块，分别被评价为当时国内报道最高亮度和最大功率；当时 50 瓦光纤耦合模块工作寿命突破 2 万小时，被评价为寿命指标国际先进水平。他提出了半导体激光叠阵双面封装方法，攻克了几十层叠阵封装的技术难题；在国内率先开发出单管、线阵、叠阵、光纤耦合模块四大系列长寿命无铝量子阱激光器产品，作为泵浦光源批量用于国防、核能源建设及激光制造业等领域；获相关授权发明专利 15 项，所在单位将其中 9 项专利技术和 2 项专有技术作价 3280 万元投入到三家公司。无铝量子阱激光器已经成为目前国内主流产品之一和重要发展方向。

（2）边发射激光器输出功率密度低、光束质量差的缺点使它很难作为千瓦、万瓦乃至更大功率高光束质量的直接光源在国防和加工等领域应用，已成为国际上重大瓶颈问题。王立军提出了 1/4 波片和偏振棱镜一体化激光偏振合束、自偏振合束以及基于二向分色的偏振合束三种方法，攻克了激光线阵、激光叠阵的合束难题，首次研制出千瓦至万瓦级高光束质量半导体激光光源，在激光加工及国防等领域得到重要应用。发明并实现了基于透射光栅技术的外腔半导体激光光谱合束方法，研制出大功率高光束质量激光光源，应用于激光对光学成像×××系统的国防某重点型号任务中，使用单位评价"激光合束技术的突破，满足了国防应用特殊需求，为其在小型化、轻量化、高效率、高可靠性的车载激光对抗中应用奠定了基础。"激光合束成果是王立军获 2011 年国家发明二等奖的主要内容之一。目前在国际上，激光合束技术已成为获取万瓦乃至更大功率半导体激光光源的重要途径之一。

（3）武器中激光点火的优点是有效增强武器抗电磁等外界干扰能力，解决了传统电点火在武器总装、测试、运输、作战等过程中的安全性问题。继美国、俄罗斯将激光点火应用于导弹、火箭之后，王立军作为激光点火系统项目负责人，带领研究团队突破了

多路、小型化、集成化、全金属化封装等系列关键技术，解决了 –45℃ ~ 75℃宽温度范围高可靠性工作等技术难题，提出并实现了一种点火装置高精度快速检测方法，首次研制出工程化半导体激光点火装置，应用于我国某重大任务中。被评价为"该项目研制难度大、技术复杂、有多项创新，成果达到国际先进水平，对提升我国航天……系统火工品点火的先进性和安全性具有重要意义"。在此基础上，他又研制出双路远程控制激光点火装置并应用在其他重大项目中，被评价为"是我国首次……点火方式由电点火升级为激光点火奠定坚实的基础，具有里程碑式的重要意义"。

Awardee of Electronics and Information Technology Prize, Wang Lijun

Wang Lijun was born in Shulan City of Jilin Province in July 1946. He is academician of Chinese Academy of Sciences, an expert in laser and optoelectronics technology, has been engaged in research and application of theory, technology and engineering of laser in recent 40 years. He hosted and mainly participated in 15 major and key projects of national and provincial class and has made systematic and creative academic achievements in high–power vertical cavity surface emitting lasers, high–power aluminum–free quantum well edge emitting lasers and laser beam combining technology. He has not only made deeper theoretical attainment, but also made great contributions to the application of national defense.

For vertical cavity surface emitting laser, he proved that it could realize watt–level high power laser output with micrometer–class short optical cavity surface emitting structure. For the first time in the world, he developed three kinds of watt–level high power vertical cavity surface emitting laser devices, which have had important influence in the world. For the first time in China, he solved series of problems such as working lifetime for the aluminium–free quantum–well high power lasers, proposed four methods of laser beam combining and developed series of high power semiconductor laser light source with output power from kilowatts to tens of kilowatts class. The high power lasers have had important applications in national defense, aerospace and industrial fields, resulting in significant economic and social benefits.

He had won second prize of National Technology Invention Award, second prize of National Science and Technology Progress Award, first prize of Technology Invention Award of Jilin province, two first prize of Science and Technology Progress Awards of Jilin province, and World Chinese Merchant Innovation Award. He was the first prize winners of all the awards. He co–authored 5 books and published 305 papers on SCI and EI included journals. He was authorized 57 invention patents, in which a patent was awarded "Chinese patent Excellence Award". He won the award of "national outstanding scientific and technological worker".

电子信息技术奖获得者

张 文 军

张文军，1963 年 10 月出生于山东省青岛市。1989 年毕业于上海交通大学电子工程系获工学博士学位。1990—1993 年在德国 PHILIPS 通信工业公司任工程师。1993 年 7 月回到上海交通大学工作至今。曾先后担任上海交通大学电信学院副院长、院长，上海交通大学副校长。同时担任 IEEE Fellow、中国电子学会会士、数字媒体处理与传输上海市重点实验室主任、数字电视国家工程研究中心首席科学家、国家基金委数字媒体通信创新群体带头人。张文军一直专注于数字电视广播系统和标准技术研究，为我国电视广播数字化进程的成功开启、首个地面数字电视强制性国标的确立及广泛应用、网络化时代广播与互联网协同传输机制的建立，做出了开拓性和持续性的贡献。获得国家科技进步奖二等奖 3 项（均排名第一）、省部级一等奖 5 项，授权发明专利 85 项，发表 SCI 论文 92 篇。指导的博士生曾分别获得全国百篇、中国电子学会和上海市的优秀博士论文。

一、主持研制成功我国首套高清电视数字编码传输系统，用于国庆 50 周年庆典高清现场转播，实现了我国数字电视地面广播从无到有的历史性跨越

率领团队完成了总体方案设计，研制了高清视音频编解码、系统复用、无线信道调制解调、发射机及调谐器等 7 个关键子系统。①提出了面向视频子图并行处理的视觉优化码率分配和控制机制，建立了高清视频编码十字划分并行处理架构，发明了视频子图重叠区数据处理与合成方法，解决了高清视频编码效率和处理带宽的相互制约难题，保证了视觉重建质量；②提出了利用传送协议扩展字段的在线实时检测方案，设计了专用测试器，在不影响数据载荷正常传送的同时在线传送测试图案集，解决了系统全运行周期内的错误精准实时定位问题，实现了各分机的高效联试和系统可靠性测试。该系统用于国庆 50 周年庆典，首次实现了我国高清电视的现场转播，被评为"九五"国家科技攻关重大科技成果。工信部验收意见认为"该项目使我国成为继美、欧、日之后拥有较完整数字电视系统技术的国家，为我国后续相关标准制定和产业化工作的开展做出了开创性贡献。"

二、突破高速移动接收和时频域同构处理关键技术，成为我国首个强制性地面电视国标的重要组成部分，丰富并发展了数字电视无线传输技术体制

1. 发明了一阶循环数据帧结构和基于虚拟中心的系列信道均衡算法，攻克了单载波高速移动接收难题，用于我国载人航天神舟系列返回舱着陆任务保障

从系统设计和核心算法两个层面提出了一种单载波传输技术体制。该体制不同于国外标准的帧场段结构设计，是由预置信息、系统信息和负载数据直接构建的一阶循环数据帧结构，既保持了高传输效率，又提供了恰当数量的训练数据来跟踪信道快速变化；发明了基于虚拟中心的重叠均衡器结构和误差反旋、内码辅助等快速收敛算法，将中心抽头设置于信道能量集中区域并通过重采样平滑调整其位置，避免了传统均衡器将中心对应于主径而频繁发生的主、副径切换问题，实现了对抗动态强多径的能力。经磁浮列车430千米/小时实测验证，该单载波技术实现了高速移动电视接收，具有国际领先水平。研制的专用装备用于神舟系列返回舱着陆过程的直升机追踪视频高速无线传输任务。该体制的发端方案已成为首个地面电视广播国标的单载波工作模式，经工信部评估，贡献的系统发明专利数目占国标核心必要专利池的一半。2008年起，我国使用国标单载波模式在京沪等主要城市开路播出高清电视节目。

2. 发现了单多载波实现高效信道均衡的共同依赖路径，提出了统一的时频混合迭代处理方法，实现了双模国标的高性能低成本广泛应用

通过对国标单多载波接收的理论分析，发现要实现对两者的高效信道均衡，都应依赖"信道参数的时域表达和负载数据的频域滤波"这一共同路径。据此提出了一种数据判决反馈辅助的时频混合迭代处理方法——利用前述发明的一阶循环结构所形成的数据循环前缀特征，单多载波均使用预置信息统一在时域进行初始信道估计，然后对负载数据统一在频域进行初次均衡，再利用数据判决信息统一在时域加窗和滤波完成精确信道估计，最后再统一转换到频域进行迭代信道均衡。该方法使国标单多载波模式在接收端能共用约90%的信号处理资源，并确保了各自的接收性能。通过将时域判决数据转换至频域辅助均衡，还进一步提升了单载波模式对抗恶劣多径信道的性能达3dB。基于上述方法，张文军主持研制出系列国标双模接收芯片，成本已下降到与国外单模标准产品相当，获2011年国家重点新产品奖，直接销售超过1500万片并实现了向多家境内外芯片公司的IP核授权，被广泛应用于全国主要大中城市的地面电视固定覆盖和"户户通"工程。

三、提出地面广播与互联网协同传输的系统架构和协议模型，解决了视频内容通过多网传输的同步呈现难题，多项专利技术被新一代国际标准采纳

率先提出地面广播与互联网协同传输的系统架构和协议模型，据此建立了高清视频

网络化即时传送和服务验证平台，形成了相关协议和标准方案。①针对高清视频多网络传输带来的延时和同步问题，提出了基于 IP 的多网协同媒体传送协议，发明了多源内容异构网络时延预测及同步方法、视频分片多通道并行传输方法、异构网络下跨层容错与增强编码、视频分级传输呈现技术，解决了低延时、高可靠的多源视频内容服务难题，被应用于多项重大活动新闻视频的网络化回传及上海电信 4K 电视网络播出服务，其中两项技术被 MPEG-H 标准采纳；②针对协同传输的入口信号设计与双向机制建立问题，发明了面向广播与宽带网协同传输的系统信息前导字、逼近香农极限的 BICM 映射交织、反向信道传输方案。通过与高通、三星和索尼等国际公司的激烈竞争，该三项专利技术方案被美国新一代数字电视标准（ATSC3.0）采纳，首次打破北美数字电视市场的标准专利壁垒。

Awardee of Electronics and Information Technology Prize, Zhang Wenjun

Zhang Wenjun was born in Qingdao City of Shandong Province in October 1963. He graduated from Shanghai Jiao Tong University in 1989 and received his Ph.D. in Electrical Engineering. From 1990 to 1993, he was an engineer at PHILIPS Communication Industries in Germany. Since he came back China in July 1993, he has been working in the School of Electronic Information and Electrical Engineering (SEIEE) of Shanghai Jiao Tong University, and later served as dean of the school and vice president of the university respectively. He is an IEEE Fellow, a Chinese Institute of Electronics Fellow, director of Shanghai Key Laboratory of Digital Media Processing and Transmission, chief scientist of National Engineering Research Center of Digital Television and the leading PI of NSFC research cluster in digital media communications.

His research has been focusing on digital television broadcasting systems and standards. In the past 24 years, he has made a pioneering and sustained contributions to the establishment and extensive applications of the first terrestrial digital television broadcasting mandatory national standard, as well as the establishment of a collaborative transmission mechanism between broadcast channel and broadband networks. He won three times national science and technology achievement prizes, and five times provincial and ministerial level achievement prizes. He holds 85 patents and publishes 92 journal papers. Several students supervised by him were awarded the excellent doctoral thesis title from the Ministry of Education, Chinese Electronics Society, and Shanghai municipal government, respectively.

交通运输技术奖获得者

汪双杰

汪双杰，1962年4月出生于安徽省安庆市。1983年毕业于原西安公路学院，2005年获东南大学工学博士学位。1983年至今一直在中交第一公路勘察设计研究院工作，历任测设队长、总工办副主任、技术处处长、副总工程师、科技中心主任、副院长等职务。现任中国交建集团副总工程师、中交一公院副总经理、高寒高海拔地区道路工程安全与健康国家重点实验室主任、多年冻土区公路建设与养护技术交通行业重点实验室主任、中国科学院寒区旱区环境与工程研究所兼职教授、博士生导师。

汪双杰是交通运输部专家委员会委员、中国公路学会副秘书长、地质和岩土工程分会理事长、中国岩石力学与工程学会理事、国际岩石力学学会会员、中国公路勘察设计协会常务理事、岩土工程设计分会理事长、陕西省岩石力学与工程学会副理事长、国家重点实验室学术委员、特殊地区公路工程教育部重点实验室学术委员、青藏高原重大冻土工程的基础研究专家组成员、国家科技支撑计划"高寒高海拔多年冻土高速公路建设技术"研究项目首席专家。

汪双杰长期从事交通领域冻土工程的科研和工程设计，面对全球最不稳定的青藏高原高温多年冻土的世界性难题，克服高寒缺氧、气候恶劣的严酷考验，30多年来坚守青藏高原，专注于公路修筑技术领域，破解大尺度沥青路面公路在高原超强太阳辐射下吸热储热、路基传热加剧冻土地基融化下沉的尺度效应，创建公路冻土尺度效应理论；创新大尺度公路冻土路基在时、空维度下能量导入与耗散过程的平衡设计理念、方法和技术，为高寒高海拔青藏区域交通发展做出了重大贡献。获国家科技进步奖一等奖1项，省部级特等奖4项、一等奖8项，获国家优秀设计金、银奖3项；主编交通行业标准规范6项，出版专著8部（译著1部），发表论文100余篇；获专利21项（国际1项）。

一、在国际上率先提出冻土工程尺度效应研究方向，创建公路冻土工程尺度效应理论，填补冻土工程理论空白

占我国 1/6 国土的青藏高原高海拔低纬度多年冻土，温度处 –1.5℃ ~ 0℃极不稳定区，与西伯利亚、北美 –2.5℃以下低海拔高纬度多年冻土相比，具有极高的工程风险。国际上仅我国在多年冻土区修筑沥青公路，揭示公路 35% 左右的高病害率发生机理、提出工程对策依据成为亟待解决的重大问题。

开展青藏公路三维冻土地温场模拟与长期观察数据的研究验证，发现公路冻土病害 80% 以上由路面强吸热导致公路中心下融化盘融沉引起，解决了冻土病害成因与类型辨识问题。

建立了基于地 – 气耦合的热学边界条件，突破了传统的"附面层原理"边界近似计算的局限，首次解决了冻土路基设计中能量交换的数值计算方法；发现沥青路面公路吸热量 5 ~ 8 倍于铁路，揭示了大尺度公路冻土路基能量聚集耗散平衡过程及强度，解决了公路冻土工程特殊路基结构设计依据问题。

发明大尺度冻土路基路面能量调控特殊结构，发现建设过程需要 3 ~ 5 年的能量导入、耗散平衡过程的时间效应，首次提出冻土区公路工程二次建设的原则，解决了公路冻土工程建设路基稳定问题。

出版专著 3 部，《多年冻土地区公路修筑技术》获"三个一百"创新奖。"多年冻土青藏公路建设和养护技术"获国家科技进步奖一等奖。

二、首创公路冻土路基能量平衡设计理念与方法，攻克大尺度冻土路基稳定技术，冻土工程技术水平居国际前沿

2010 年玉树大地震后，国家决策建设共玉高速公路。青藏铁路、青藏公路窄幅冻土路基成功的导冷阻热特殊结构，在高速公路约 25 米宽度大尺度路基上存在因尺度效应导致的结构失效问题。大尺度冻土路基设计方法、技术、参数国际无先例，成为工程建设的重大技术难题。

汪双杰突破以控制冻土上限为目标的传统设计方法，描述以路基基底面传入能量与导出能量平衡为出发点的时间尺度、空间尺度两个维度，建立了包括时、空因子的冻土路基合理高度算法。

提出不同冻土路基结构间的能量平衡点及相应等效结构尺度，创新新建高速公路特殊路基结构设计参数体系。攻克冻土工程效能控制难题，高温高含冰量路基平均填高由 6 米以上降至 3 米左右。

在时间尺度上提出能量平衡近（施工期）、中（设计年限）、远（全寿命）3 阶段工程策略；在空间尺度上，能量平衡从路堤高低、特殊结构效能、以桥代路 3 方面提出工程设计准则。

出版专著 2 部，作国际冻土工程会议等主旨报告 3 次。"青海省共玉公路建设技术"等获省部级特等奖 3 项（均排名第一）。

三、30 年坚守青藏高原开展研究，解决国家重大工程建设、养护系列关键技术难题

汪双杰主持青藏公路等 4 条主要进藏国道干线约 4000 千米的冻土工程病害整治以及中印边界天空防区 650 千米边防公路冻土工程保障，建立冻土路基路面综合整治技术，工程病害率比国际上降低 50%，攻克多年冻土区公路长期形成的高病害率难题，保证了青藏等公路的全天候通车，达到了全球多年冻土公路建养水平新高度。

建立冻土分段危害性评价标准，研发冻土特殊路基结构及设计技术，建立工程材料要求、施工时间、工艺及流程，主持设计并建成全球首条多年冻土区高速公路——青海共玉 250 千米高速公路，为玉树灾后重建打通了生命通道，一期工程四年病害率仅 7%，实现了国际冻土工程新突破。

主持青藏高速公路的前期工作，为国家重大决策和工程设计提供了重要技术支撑；主持黑龙江漠河机场的技术咨询和方案制定，首次将隔热层技术应用于机场建设，成功解决了冻土机场道面的基础稳定难题。研究成果还成功应用于黑北公路、青藏铁路、哈大铁路以及巴基斯坦喀喇昆仑公路等"一带一路"工程项目，共约 6600 千米。

先后获交通部十百千人才工程人选、交通青年科技英才，国务院政府特殊津贴，第一届中国公路学会青年科技奖，新世纪百千万人才工程国家级人选，陕西省有突出贡献专家，首届全国创新争先奖等荣誉。创立"高寒高海拔地区道路工程安全与健康"国家重点实验室、"多年冻土区公路建设与养护技术"交通行业重点实验室，团队获交通运输部"2013 年感动交通十大年度人物"。

我国多年冻土面积占国土面积 22%，"一带一路"沿线冻土区公路两万多千米，未来公路建设任务依然艰巨。汪双杰的创新成果技术将支撑国家高速公路网的收官之作——跨越 550 千米多年冻土的青藏高速建设，同时也将为青藏两省区规划的多年冻土区约 3000 千米高速公路、7000 千米国省道以及"一带一路"沿线 2 万多千米的公路建设提供技术保障。

Awardee of Communication and Transportation Technology Prize, Wang Shuangjie

Wang Shuangjie was born in Anqing City of Anhui Province in April 1962. He is a chief expert in the field of transport in China. The engineering construction is very challenging in permafrost regions since it is cold and oxygen–poor and the climate is harsh. Wang Shuangjie established the scale effect theory of road permafrost and proposed the energy-balance design principle, method and technology for large-scale permafrost road embankments. He has presided over the distress mitigation projects of 4 highways leading to Tibet with a total length of over 4000km, as well as the design of 250km long freeway in permafrost regions. He has won 1 first-class prize of the National Science and Technology Progress Award, 4 special-class prizes and 8 first-class prizes of provincial- and ministerial-level science and technology progress awards. As the chief editor, he has participated in writing 6 dominant industrial standards, published 8 monographs (including 1 translation) and over 100 papers, and was granted 21 patents (including 1 PCT). Wang Shuangjie has been granted the state level person for New Century Talents Project, Expert with Outstanding Contributions in Shaanxi Province, and expert enjoys the Special Allowance of the State Council.

1. Wang for the first time presented the research direction of scale effect of permafrost engineering in the world

Wang found that over 80% permafrost road distresses are induced by thawed bulb at the center of road caused by the strong heat absorption of asphalt pavement, which solved the issues of permafrost embankment distress cause and its recognition. He discovered the scale effect issue of road permafrost and established ground-atmosphere coupling thermal boundary conditions. He for the first time revealed the spatial effect, temporal effect, and structure effect.

2. Wang presented the concept and method of energy-balance design for permafrost road embankment

He proposed a computational method for rational permafrost embankment height taking temporal and spatial factors into consideration. He proposed the design parameter systems for special new-built freeway embankment structures. It is widely agreed by international peers that the energy-balance design method will have profound significance in the area of permafrost engineering research.

3. Wang has been sticking to the Qinghai-Tibet Plateau for 3 decades, and solved a series of key difficulties of major engineering construction and maintenance

He has overcome the high distress rate difficulty of the Qinghai-Tibet Highway. He suggested an integrated embankment-pavement maintenance technology, which decreased the distress rate by 50% referring to international average, and ensured 24-hour traffic of the Qinghai-Tibet Highway 60 years after its construction.

冶金材料技术奖获得者

范 景 莲

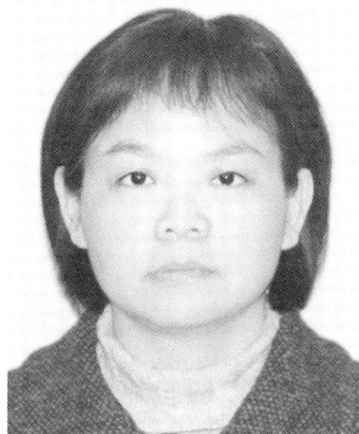

范景莲，女，1967年7月出生于湖南省澧县。1986—1993年在中南大学粉末冶金专业攻读本科、硕士；1993—1996年在广州冶金所及广东省南山工业集团担任厂长、总经理助理；1996—1999年在中南大学攻读博士学位；2000—2001年在中南大学冶金工程进行博士后研修，2001年破格评为中南大学教授；1999年、2002年分别前往美国INJECTAMAX CORP和美国RUTGERS大学担任高级访问学者。现任中南大学难熔金属所所长、湖南省纳米材料工程中心常务副主任；兼任总装专项、国防科工局专家，国家奖励计划专家，国家核聚变专项专家组组长，硬质合金国家重点实验室学术委员，美国粉末冶金协会会员，中国钨协理事，《中国钨业》和《硬质合金》编委。荣获国家杰青、中组部"万人计划"、教育部"长江学者"、全国创新争先奖、全国优秀科技工作者，享受国务院特殊津贴。

20多年来一直从事高性能难熔金属材料研究，针对新型飞行器、发动机、原子能等领域对难熔金属的需求和现有难熔金属强韧性不足、高温抗烧蚀差的问题，范景莲提出"纳米原位复合/微纳复合"设计思想，开辟"纳米/微纳复合高性能难熔金属基复合材料"新领域，取得了系列重大突破。

一、原创发明超高温轻质难熔金属基复合材料，为新型飞行器和发动机提供高性能关键高温材料保障

新型超高速飞行器研制是目前世界各空天强国重点探索的领域，代表了国际空天技术发展的重大方向。新型飞行器在近地空间以5～20倍声速长时间飞行，与空气产生剧烈的摩擦和冲击，其前端关键结构部件表面将产生2000～3000℃高温、承受强表面氧化和高动压高过载冲击。这对热端构件提出了极为苛刻的使用要求，要求具有优异的高温强韧、长时间抗氧化与轻量化等综合性能，是国际公认的最突出技术难题。现有高温材料因高温强度低、抗氧化烧蚀差或密度高等不足而无法应用，成为飞行器研制的关键技术瓶颈。

针对这一重大需求和瓶颈，范景莲创新提出"微纳复合"设计思想，采用超高温陶瓷相微纳复合增强难熔金属，综合难熔金属的高温强韧和超高温陶瓷的耐高温和轻量化的优势，并采用微纳复合技术解决两者界面不相容问题，实现了难熔金属和超高温陶瓷的完美融合。在此基础上，开发出多相超高温陶瓷在难熔金属表面原位自生长的热防护涂层，最终制备出超高温轻质难熔金属基复合材料。该材料经过风洞和发动机反复试验验证，材料基体无破坏、表面基本无烧蚀，从而实现难熔金属的高温强韧、长时间抗烧蚀和轻量一体化。其高温强度比现有超高温材料提高 5 倍以上，密度降低 1/2。该技术成果为国内外原创，填补了世界空白，为我国超高速飞行器前缘热端部件研制提供了关键高温材料保障，同时拓展应用于航空航天和兵器高性能新型发动机动力系统，满足了发动机在大推力、高动压、耐 3000℃以上的强的抗冲刷、抗冲击和抗烧蚀性能要求，成为多项国家重大高新工程的定型产品。

二、发明新型细晶高性能钨基复合材料，成功应用于国防科技、新能源、微电子信息、原子能等高端制造，推动行业领域的发展

高性能钨基复合材料具有高密度、高强韧等特性，是国防军工和国民经济诸多领域难以替代的关键材料。现有制备技术存在晶粒粗大、性能低、规格尺寸小等缺陷，难以满足尖端技术发展要求。为解决这一重大难题，范景莲提出"纳米原位复合"思想，发明金属盐溶液混合 – 快速喷雾干燥实现粉末超饱和固溶和合金化，突破传统 W、Cu 不相溶和 W 渗 Cu 理论禁锢与技术缺陷，解决了现有 W-Ni-Fe（Cu）材料强韧性低、晶粒粗大、组织不均匀的问题，晶粒细化 4～10 倍，强度提高 30%，延伸率提高 2～5 倍。建立了"纳米原位复合"细晶钨基复合材料相关理论模型，获国际钨领域权威 German、Hausselt 多次引用和积极评价。通过技术和装备集成创新，研制出系列新型高性能钨基复合材料和超大尺寸钨材，形成了多种规格和品种的产品，成功用于我国 10 多项重点、重大工程，为保障国家安全做出了重要贡献；超大规格钨材在国内 11 家企业推广应用，同时产品出口国外，应用于新能源、微电子信息等高端技术领域，经济效益十分显著，性能达到国际先进水平，引领我国钨材向高、精、尖方向发展，支撑了新能源、微电子信息、原子能等高端制造产业的发展，提升了我国国际竞争力。

三、发明未来核聚变堆面向等离子体最关键全钨偏滤器材料和部件制备技术，将我国钨材料研究推向国际最前沿领域

核聚变能与核裂变能相比，具有无核辐射危险、释能大等显著优点。为解决核聚变能的可控利用，中、美、欧盟、韩、日、印七方成立了目前最大的国际合作项目——国际热核聚变实验堆（ITER），我国也已启动了中国聚变工程实验堆（CFETR）建造计划，

这将开启人类未来能源的理想途径。聚变堆面向等离子体材料在运行时，承受高能等离子体持续长时间轰击，并在表面产生 2000℃ 以上的高温，对材料高温性能和化学稳定性提出了极高要求。钨由于极高的熔点、良好的化学稳定性等优点，被认为是未来聚变堆最理想的面向等离子体最关键高温结构材料部件。但现有钨材料晶粒粗大、性能差，难以满足未来聚变堆的苛刻服役环境要求。针对这一难题，创新发明提出"纳米/微纳复合增强"和"纳米梯度复合扩散连接"技术制备细晶全钨偏滤器材料及部件。采用微量稀土氧化物和碳化物纳米/微纳复合增强钨，实现其高强韧和高抗热冲击，与当前国际最先进商业钨相比，抗热冲击性提高 50% 以上。采用纳米梯度复合扩散连接技术，实现钨与热沉结构材料高强度冶金结合，连接强度比传统连接强度提高 2 倍。研究成果获国际钨领域最权威刊物 *RM&HM* 主编 H. Ortnal 评价"钨领域重大技术进展"，国际核聚变权威机构 CEA 法国原子能委员会评价"为全钨偏滤器提供全新技术途径"，将我国钨研究引入国际最前沿系列。

研究成果发表论文近 400 篇，出版专著 2 部，申请发明专利 54 项，获国家科技进步二等奖 2 项、省部级一等奖 3 项、省部级二等奖 5 项。高性能钨基粉末和大尺寸钨材技术分别在江钨华茂、中国五矿株洲硬质合金集团公司实现产业转化，累计新增销售收入 8.18 亿元；高性能钨、钼基复合材料技术成果受到宁乡高新区高度关注和重视，目前已在宁乡高新区支持下组建"长沙微纳坤宸新材料有限公司"，将超高温轻质难熔金属基复合材料和高性能钨基复合材料从实验室推向工程产业化，为我国新型飞行器、发动机、新能源、微电子信息、原子能等高端制造领域提供了关键工程新材料支撑。

Awardee of Metallurgy and Materials Technology Prize, Fan Jinglian

Fan Jinglian, female, was born in Li County of Hunan Province in July 1967. She was a bachelor and master of Powder Metallurgy Research Institute, Central South University（CSU）in 1986—1993; a factory manager and assistant to the general manager of Guangzhou metallurgical institution and Guangdong Nanshan industrial group 1993—1996, respectively; a doctor of CSU 1996—1999; a postdoctor of Central South University 2000—2001 and was promoted to professor at 2001. She was senior visiting scholar to Injectamax Corp（America）and Rutgers University at 1999 and 2002, respectively. Now, she is the director of Refractory Metals Institute at CSU, and deputy director of Hunan Nanomaterial Engineering center, a specialist in Special Assembly and State Administration of Science, Technology and Industry for National Defense, a group leader of national nuclear fusion project, a academic member of State Key Laboratory of Hard Alloy, a member of American Powder Metallurgy Association, a director of China Tungsten Association. At the same time, she is the winner of national natural science fund for distinguished young scholars, Central Organization "million people plan" "Changjiang Scholar" by Ministry of Education, National Innovation Awards, National Excellent Scientist. She also enjoys the special allowance of the State Council. For more than 20 years, Fan Jinglian has been engaged in the research of high performance refractory metal materials. Refractory metals are used in new types of aircraft, engines, atomic energy and other fields. But the existing refractory metals are weak in strength and toughness, and have poor ablation resistance at high temperature. Fan Jinglian proposed "nano in situ composite & micro/nano composite" design ideas, opened up a new field of "nano/micro-nano composite high performance refractory metal matrix composite" and achieved a series of major breakthroughs.

Fan jinglian has published about 400 research papers and 2 monographs. 58 national invention patents are gained. The winner won 2 second prize of National Scientific and Technological Progress Award and 3 first class provincial-level prizes. The technology of preparing high performance tungsten powder and large size tungsten matrix realize industrial transformation in Jiangwu Huamao Corporation and Zhuzhou Cemented carbide group. Cumulative new sales revenue are ¥818 million.

冶金材料技术奖获得者

王 玉 忠

王玉忠，1961 年 6 月出生于山东省文登市。1994 年在四川大学获得博士学位后，一直在四川大学化学学院任教至今，1995 晋升教授，1997 获得博士生导师资格。1999 年受 DAAD 资助，在德国 Max Planck Institute for Polymer Research 作访问教授；2002 年受英国皇家学会资助，在英国 The University of Nottingham 作访问教授。创建了环保型高分子材料国家地方联合工程实验室、教育部环境友好高分子材料工程研究中心、降解与阻燃高分子材料四川省高校重点实验室及相应领域的四川省国际合作研究基地（国际联合研究中心）和协同创新中心并任主任。中国工程院院士，教育部科技委学部委员，中国科学院学术委员会专委会委员。荣获"全国优秀科技工作者"称号，入选"新世纪百千万人才工程"国家级人选、国家杰出青年科学基金获得者、教育部"长江学者奖励计划"特聘教授、教育部创新团队带头人，获得中国工程院光华工程科技奖青年奖（2004）、四川省杰出青年科技创新奖、四川省优秀研究生指导教师称号、宝钢教育奖优秀教师奖、四川大学首届"最受学生欢迎教师奖"、四川大学首届产学研合作年度杰出贡献奖一等奖。

王玉忠主要从事有机高分子材料研究，在阻燃材料、生物基与生物降解高分子材料及高分子材料循环利用等领域做出了一系列开创性研究工作。

一、高分子材料无卤阻燃高性能化的新原理和新技术

针对量大面广的通用高分子材料易被引燃导致火灾、对人民生命财产造成严重威胁的问题，王玉忠通过多年潜心研究，从燃烧和阻燃机理研究入手，对高分子材料无卤阻燃化遇到的技术难题和瓶颈进行研究和攻关，提出和发展了多项阻燃新原理和阻燃新技术。①出版了国际上首部《聚酯纤维阻燃化设计》专著，发明了最大合成纤维品种聚酯纤维的高效无卤阻燃技术，建成了我国第一条无卤阻燃聚酯工业化生产线，并且采用该项技术生产的阻燃聚酯在全球市场占有率超过 80%，使我国在该领域处于国际领先

地位；②提出了智能化高温自交联成炭阻燃学术思想，发明了"无传统阻燃剂"的全新阻燃技术，解决了聚酯阻燃与抗熔滴相矛盾这一长期未解决的技术难题，被国际权威同行专家评价为是"开创性"的工作，"开辟了全新的绿色阻燃技术"；③突破了现有膨胀阻燃理念，发明了由超支化成炭剂/金属络合物等构成的多相协效膨胀阻燃技术，解决了最大通用塑料品种聚烯烃无卤阻燃的高效化难题，生产出目前最高效的聚烯烃无卤阻燃剂，开始替代长期使用的有害含卤产品，同行专家评价该技术处于"国际领先"水平；④提出了液晶高分子原位增强阻燃的学术思想，发明了同时实现阻燃与增强的全新阻燃技术，解决了添加阻燃剂不可避免导致材料力学性能下降这一技术难题，被国外同行评价为阻燃领域的"重要成就"。他在阻燃领域取得的发明专利中，已有30余项得到实施，在国内外企业中得到广泛应用，涉及纤维与纺织品、通用塑料、工程塑料、橡胶/弹性体与电线电缆、热固性塑料、涂料、建筑保温材料等各种高分子材料的阻燃技术，多个产品获得国际认证，在国际市场上具有很高的占有率，获得了显著的经济与社会效益。相关成果先后获国家技术发明奖、国家科技进步奖、教育部和四川省科技成果奖8项。王玉忠是我国发展无卤阻燃技术的倡导者、开拓者和践行者，为推动我国阻燃科技发展、提升行业技术进步和国际竞争力做出了杰出贡献。

二、新型可生物降解和可循环利用塑料

绝大多数高分子材料存在生物降解难、回收率低、易造成环境污染等问题。对于一次性使用塑料制品，发展生物降解材料是缓解塑料对环境造成压力的有效途径。王玉忠瞄准该领域中的重大需求，多年来坚持攻克降解塑料存在的技术瓶颈和难题。①提出发展可高回收率回收聚合单体的完全生物降解高分子材料是解决一次性使用塑料制品废弃物造成环境污染和资源浪费的有效途径，发明了可反复循环利用并且可完全生物降解的高分子材料新技术。以二甘醇为原料一步高产率获得对二氧环己酮单体的新合成路线和催化体系，并实现了可控聚合合成聚对二氧环己酮及其通用成型加工。该材料性能好，废弃后可热解回收单体，单体回收率最高可达到99%，回收单体可再聚合实现循环利用；对不宜回收的应用领域，该聚合物可完全生物降解；这是高分子家族中少有的既可完全生物降解、又可高收率回收单体，并且具有优异的加工性能、热性能和力学性能的高分子品种。该技术已形成18件发明专利，涉及催化剂、单体合成、聚合、成形加工、回收单体等各个过程的完整知识产权保护体系。北美和韩国的生物塑料协会主席对该成果给予了高度评价，认为其"开辟了一新兴领域"。②发明了新型生物基降解塑料，研发出一步完成淀粉细化、糊化、破结构和改性的原位改性技术，使非粮蕉藕淀粉制备的生物基塑料的成本低、性能好，既节约了化石资源又可以生物降解，适用于不易回收的应用领域，被列为国家级重点推广成果；采用生物基单体、天然大分子设计制备了一系列生物基脂肪族共聚酯、淀粉/纤维素/木质素复合物等生物降解材料，从控制生物降解高分子材料的不同层次高分子结构出发，实现对材料性能的调控，特别是通过分子设计精确控

制高分子的拓扑结构，在不破坏生物降解性的前提下解决了加工性、耐水性和力学性能差的难题，相关成果具有国际领先水平。该系列研究成果分别获得了 1999 年教育部科技进步一等奖、2006 年教育部技术发明一等奖和 2012 年四川省科技进步一等奖。

王玉忠先后承担了 40 余项各类国家计划项目、省部级项目、人才基金和大量国内外企业合作项目，获授权发明专利 110 余项，已实施 42 项，取得了显著的经济效益；出版专著、教材和手册 6 部，在国内外期刊发表论文 537 篇，其中 SCI 论文 465 篇，SCI 引用上万次，两项基础研究成果入编《国家自然科学基金资助项目优秀成果选编》；以第一完成人获 11 项国家和省部级科技成果奖，其中国家级二等奖 2 项、四川省和教育部自然科学、技术发明和科技进步一等奖 5 项；应邀在境外国际学术会议作 Plenary 和 Keynote 邀请报告 20 余次，多次担任国际性学术会议大会主席；担任 12 个中英文期刊编委。

Awardee of Metallurgy and Materials Technology Prize, Wang Yuzhong

Wang Yuzhong was born in Wendeng City of Shandong Province in June 1961. He earned his Ph.D. degree at Sichuan University in 1994, where he was promoted to a full professor in 1995. He was a visiting professor at the Max-Planck Institute for Polymer Research (Germany) supported by the DAAD in 1999 and at the University of Nottingham (UK) in 2002 supported by the Royal Society. He is now the Director of the National Engineering Laboratory for Eco-Friendly Polymeric Materials (Sichuan) and the Center for Degradable and Flame-Retardant Polymeric Materials, which were founded by himself. He is the Honorary President of China Flame Retardant Society, the Vice President of Degradable Plastic Committee of China Plastics Processing Industry Association (CPPIA), and the Associate Director of the National Technical Committee for Standardization of Bio-Based and Biodegradable Products. He was awarded the National Science Fund for Distinguished Young Scholars (2005), Cheung Kong Scholar of Ministry of Education of China (2006), State Talent of China in 21st Century (2006), Younger Prize of Guanghua Engineering Science and Technology of Chinese Engineering Academy (2004), Excellent Postgraduate Supervisor of Sichuan Province (2000), Outstanding Younger Innovation Prize of Sichuan Province (1998) and ten National and Provincial governmental Science & Technology Awards during 1992—2012. He was elected as a Member of Chinese Academy of Engineering in 2015.

Wang's researches focus on fire-retardant polymeric materials, bio-based and biodegradable polymers, and polymer recycling and reuse, where a series of pioneering research work has been done. He has earned eleven National and Provincial governmental Science &Technology Awards during 1992—2017. He has put forward and developed many new flame-retardant technologies and principles to overcome the difficult problems in flame-retardant science, which are commented as "great achievement" by famous foreign counterparts. Many of his works have been industrialized and well accepted by customers. For example, halogen-free flame-retardant polyester products have been sold all over the world with the market share of >80%, breaking the 20-year monopoly of the Germany's rival products and forcing the company to halt production. Meanwhile, he has proposed some innovative technologies of recycling polymer materials and invented a new series of biodegradable plastics. He has created a novel synthetic route and a catalytic system for the synthesis of fully biodegradable poly (p-dioxanone) (PPDO), making the controlled polymerization and general processing of PPDO possible. These technologies are appraised as "opening a new field" by the Chairman of North American bioplastics Association.

Until now Wang has published over 500 refereed journal papers, 6 books and chapters, 110 authorized patents, in which 42 patents have been assigned. Additionally, Wang has presented over 20 Plenary and Keynote lectures in international conferences. As a chairman, he has organized two international and national academic conferences, such as the International Symposium on Flame-Retardant Materials & Technologies. Wang serves now as a vice-chief editor for Chinese Chemical Letters and an editorial board member for 12 English and Chinese journals.

资源环保技术奖获得者

侯 立 安

侯立安，1957 年 8 月出生于江苏省徐州市，环境工程专家。2006 年 7 月毕业于防化研究院获工学博士学位。2009 年 12 月当选中国工程院院士。现任火箭军工程大学三系教授，教育部高等学校环境科学与工程类专业教学指导委员会副主任委员，中国膜工业协会名誉理事长，中国环境科学学会顾问。

侯立安是我国特种污染防控工程技术的开拓者之一，长期致力于我国水安全、特种水污染防控和特殊区域生命保障的理论及环境工程技术研究，率先提出并开展了核生化条件下特殊区域环境污染控制工程技术体系和人员生存保障系列装备研究，取得多项突破性成果和富有创造性的成就。获国家科技进步奖 6 项、军队省部级科技成果奖 26 项、国家专利 32 项，出版专著 5 部，发表论文 300 余篇；荣立一等功 1 次、三等功 4 次。曾获全军首届杰出专业技术人才奖、全国科普工作先进工作者和全国优秀科技工作者。

一、在特殊环境的污染治理、战斗人员生存防护方面，率先提出并开展了密闭空间有毒有害气体净化技术研究，推动了我国特殊环境空气净化技术的发展

针对特殊区域防护条件差、人员无法长期生存的问题，在无国外技术可供借鉴、国内相关领域研究尚少的情况下，侯立安自主创新，牵头开展密闭空间有害气体净化系统研究，提出并开展了密闭空间人员生存条件限值、环境监测、有毒有害气体净化和生命保障装备等系统研究，确立了地下工程人员生存环境条件限值，建立了水处理和空气净化装备保障模式，攻克了静态吸附与动态吸附相结合、低温等离子体特效纤维负载吸附空气净化、化学毒剂和伪装防护于一体、臭气封堵、有毒有害气体污染治理和改进金属表面防腐处理方法等密闭空间环境污染防控的关键技术。解决了密闭环境大空间、多人员、长时间与外界空气隔绝时有毒有害气体净化的技术难题，为已建工程改造升级和新建工程建设提供了科学依据，具有重大军事价值和社会效益。

在开展科技创新的同时，侯立安注重成果的推广应用和科技领域军民融合，积极将密闭空间有毒有害气体净化理念应用到室内空气 PM2.5 污染防控和生态环境保护等人居环境中，围绕室内与典型工业厂区空气污染和防控技术现状，分析空气污染特征，提出源解析重点任务、健康风险评估、污染控制先进技术与设备研发、综合防控等任务的发展战略，为室内与典型工业厂区的空气污染控制提供了科技支撑。

二、在饮用水安全保障、核生化沾染水处理方面取得多项重大技术突破，构建了我国特种水污染防治体系

针对我国特种水污染的特点，作为总负责人和第一完成人承担了"放射性废水等特种污染控制"研究课题，先后开展了多种类型工艺、不同时期居国际领先或国际先进水平的核生化沾染水处理技术研究和系列装备研制。发明了纳滤饮用水净化和以"预处理－纳滤膜－后处理"组合工艺净化水体中的"三致"物质及处理核生化沾染水的方法和系列水处理装置，研究并建立了以"浓缩－膜分离－连续电除盐"的组合工艺路线，研究了组合工艺各单元对不同类型核素的去除机理及长期稳定运行机制，可有效去除水体中"致癌、致畸、致突变"物质和对人体有害的核生化特种污染物，实现了废水的达标排放。研制了纳滤饮用水净化装置、放射性废水处理装置、漂浮填料、微孔曝气器、一体化污水处理装置，在有限空间内实现了催化消毒、核生化沾染水处理、局部洗消、淋浴、防化、伪装、自供电、自装卸等功能为一体的可伸缩核化沾染洗消方舱。这些装置的研发对推动我国核生化沾染水处理工艺研究具有积极作用，并为未来战争、反恐维稳和饮用水安全保障提供了实用技术和系列装备，是重要的战略技术储备。开发了低放射性污染饮用水源的强化净化技术、突发性核污染应急处理关键技术与装备，放射性浓缩废液、废渣等处理处置技术；强化了集中式水厂工艺去除放射性物质的能力和突发放射性污染应急处理能力，为应对可能遭遇的突发性水源放射性污染、保障广大民众饮用水安全提供了技术支撑。

三、开创特殊环境的污染防控理论研究新领域，丰富了我国密闭空间环境保护理论，为确立特殊环境污染防治体系奠定了理论基础

为了切实保障军事环境安全，确保官兵身心健康，提升军队战斗力，深入研究了特殊环境生命保障系统的理论，研究了密闭空间特殊污染物的来源、成因和防控对策，系统分析了特殊环境中放射性物质和生化战剂对水及大气的污染种类、成因和危害，提出了机动、快速、全面与应急、便携相结合的环境污染监测模式，确定了密闭空间特殊污染物的源解析和排放源清单，探索并确立了人员在密闭空间内的生存规律、环境条件限值和污染治理装备保障模式；建立了"接触曝气法处理间歇流小规模生活污水的动力学模型"；发现了纳滤膜截留放射性核素、化学毒剂和生物战剂的机理，创立了"临界膜污染点"动态模型；探明了密闭空间低温等离子净化挥发性有机、无机污染物的机理；确定了密闭空间中二硫化碳的来源和表征。研编了国家军用标准 5 项，为特殊环境的污染治理提供了重要依据，发挥了基础性、先导性、全局性作用。

针对饮用水安全、室内空气 PM2.5 污染防控和生态环境保护等民生问题，牵头或参与起草了《受放射性沾染饮用水安全保障与应急系统建设》等十余份咨询建议，受到党和国家部委分管领导的高度重视，被国家相关部门采纳。先后发表学术论文 300 余篇，在国内外高端学术会议作特邀或主题报告 200 余次。结合工作实践和专业特长，热心为大众解读环保焦点和民生热点，围绕"生命之水""军民融合""生态文明"和"绿色发展"等主题开展科普专题讲座，收到良好效果。

侯立安从部队建设的全局出发，抛家舍业，告别工作生活 30 余年的首都，由北京研究院副总工程师岗位远调西安大学任普通教授。同时积极组织国家、军队和省部级重大、重点项目申报，获得科研经费资助 3000 余万元。牵头创建了具有我国特色的核生化沾染水处理和密闭空间有毒有害气体净化为优势学科的博士后科研工作站，培养博士后和研究生 60 余名，带教军队专业技术领军、拔尖人才培养对象 9 名，使其成为相关领域的专业技术骨干和在军内外具有一定知名度的专业学科带头人；建立和培养了特种污染防控研究队伍，为国家、军队特种环境污染防控后继有人奠定了基础。

Awardee of Resources and Environmental Technology Prize, Hou Lian

Hou Lian was born in Xuzhou City of Jiangsu Province in August 1957 and is famous as an expert in environmental engineering. In July 2006, he was graduated from PLA Institute of Chemical Defense and received a doctorate in Engineering. In December 2009, he was elected as academician of Chinese Academy of Engineering. At present, he works as a professor and doctoral supervisor in Engineering University for Rocket Force. Moreover, he serves as an advanced expert directly connected with central authorities, the consultant of Chinese Society of Environmental Sciences, the vice-chairman of Expert Committee of the Membrane Industry Association of China and the vice-chairman of Beijing Association of Inventions, etc.

Dr. Hou Lian is one of the famous pioneers for the prevention and control technology against the special pollution in China. During the basic research, project design and technical management in the environmental science and engineering for several decades, he firstly proposed and successfully developed a set of advanced techniques and serial equipment in the safeguard for the water security, the domestic sewage treatment for the scattered point source and the air purification for the human settlement, and made several great breakthroughs and significantly creative achievements. In addition, he was entitled with the National Award for Progress in Sci-Tech for six times, the Military and Provincial Award for Progress in Sci-Tech for twenty-six times. Moreover, he was authorized twenty-five national patents and endorsed four books. He has compiled five national military standards and published more than 300 papers. At present, he has won the State Council Special Allowance, the "Truth from facts" Outstanding Youth Award of China, the Invention and Entrepreneurship Prize and the Outstanding Personnel Award in Professional Skills, and elected as the Advanced Workers in National Popularization of Science and the Advanced Sci-Tech Workers of China.

(1) For the pollution control in the special environment and survival protection of combatants, the technologies for treating poisonous and harmful gas in the confined space was systematically studied, which promotes the development of purification technologies for the special environment in China.

(2) For the safeguard of drinking water safety and the treatment of NBC contaminated water, several breakthroughs in technology has been achieved, which builds up the prevention and control system for the special water pollution.

(3) For the theoretical research on pollution prevention and control in the special environment, the theories on environment protection in the confined space had been greatly enriched, which establishes a sound theoretical foundation for the construction of pollution prevention and control system for in the special environment.

资源环保技术奖获得者

庞 国 芳

庞国芳，1943 年 10 月出生于河北省滦南县。1968 年毕业于河北大学化学系。1968—1982 年在河北大学任教。1982—2009 年在秦皇岛出入境检验检疫局从事农产品进出口贸易中农药、兽药残留分析技术研究与应用。2007 年当选中国工程院院士。2009 年至今任中国检验检疫科学研究院首席科学家，从事高分辨质谱－互联网－数据科学／地理信息（GIS）三元融合技术研究。担任中国食品安全国家标准审评委员会副主任，中国国家食品安全风险评估专家委员会副主任，AOAC Fellow，中国农业大学、燕山大学、北京工商大学兼职教授。研制国际国家标准 142 项，出版农药兽药残留分析技术专著 12 部，荣获国家科学技术进步奖二等奖 3 项、国际 AOAC 科学技术奖 8 项，包括国际 AOAC 最高科学技术奖哈维威利奖（Harvey W. Wiley Award）。

庞国芳从事农药化学污染物微量分析基础理论、应用技术和方法标准化研究，在农药化学污染物残留微量分析技术领域进行了一系列开拓性的研究工作。

一、构建六类色谱－质谱数据库基础理论研究

用六类色谱－质谱技术（气相色谱－质谱、气／液相色谱－串联质谱、气／液相色谱－四极杆－飞行时间质谱、线性离子阱－电场回旋共振轨道阱组合质谱）评价了世界常用的 1200 多种农药不同条件下的质谱特征，建立六类质谱数据库和图谱库，为农药残留高通量高分辨检测技术开发奠定了理论和方法基础。这项研究已出版系列专著 5 卷，现已成为世界常用 1200 多种农药六类色谱－质谱基本参数的工具书、未知化合物鉴定的权威参考书、研究新分析方法的技术指导书。

二、检测技术标准化研究提升食用农产品质量，促进国际贸易发展

（1）用气／液相色谱－质谱研究建立了适用于水果、蔬菜、粮谷、茶叶、中草药、食用菌、动物组织、水产品、原奶及奶粉、蜂蜜、果汁、果酒、蜂王浆等基质中 1000 多种农药残留和 200 多种兽药残留检测技术，建立了 139 项检测技术国家标准。其中 20 项农药残留检测技术国家标准经 10 年应用，促进了农药残留检测能力的提升。2016 年国家卫计委、农业部和食药总局发布其中 9 项由原推荐性国家标准转化为强制性食品安全国家标准，成为食品农产品中农药残留限量法定检测方法，在食品安全监管中发挥了重要作用。

（2）3 次领导组织共计 17 个国家和地区 62 个实验室参加国际协同研究，用气/液相色谱 – 串联质谱 3 种技术研究建立了 3 项国际 AOAC 标准，开创了我国学者研究建立国际 AOAC 标准的先河。其中，茶叶中 653 种农药多残留 AOAC 标准的研究第一次将具有自主知识产权的茶叶净化材料写入了国际 AOAC 标准，展示了我国学者在农药残留高通量检测技术领域的水平和能力，提高了国际标准制定中的话语权，扩大了我国在该领域的国际影响。基于对各类食品农产品中 1000 多种农药残留研发色谱 – 质谱所做出的杰出贡献，庞国芳于 2014 年荣获国际 AOAC 最高科学技术荣誉奖哈维威利奖。

三、研究每种农药的电子身份证，实现了农药残留检测电子化

用液相色谱 – 四极杆 – 飞行时间质谱和气相色谱 – 四极杆 – 飞行时间质谱研究建立了世界常用 1200 多种农药的精确质量数据库和碎片离子谱图库。在此基础上，为 1200 多种农药的每种都建立了一个自身独有的电子身份证，实现了以电子标准取代农药实物标准作参比的传统鉴定方法，同时也实现了农药残留由靶向检测向非靶向筛查的跨越式发展。这是供给侧改革在农药残留分析领域的一项创新成果。

经全国各地 10 个示范实验室对侦测新技术方法效能验证，对全国 31 省会/直辖市（含 284 个区县）638 个采样点 22328 例水果和蔬菜样品检测，其发现能力达到 1200 多种农药，方法适用于 18 类 140 多种水果蔬菜中农药残留的监测，占国家标准规定的 85% 以上，满足欧盟 MRL 要求超过 95%，验证了方法的高速度、高精度和高可靠性。现已完成 31 个省会/直辖市市售水果蔬菜农药残留侦测报告 31 套，反映出我国"菜篮子"中残留农药的品种、类别、毒性、残留水平、分布区域等规律，为我国农药科学施用与治理提供了重要科学数据支持。

四、研究开发了高分辨质谱＋互联网＋数据科学三元融合技术，实现了农药残留检测报告生成自动化

针对食品农药残留检测数据分析中目前难以解决的数据维度多、数据关系复杂、分析要求高等难题，解决了"多国 MRL 标准 – 农产品分类 – 千余种农药特性"的关联存储与查询关键技术。①建立了多国 MRL 标准等四大基础数据库，实现了农药残留基础数据的关联存取与调用，为农药残留侦测结果的判定提供标准依据。②自主研发了农药残留数据采集系统，构建了国家农药残留侦测结果数据库，提出的"数据获取 – 信息补充 –

衍生物合并－禁药处理－污染等级判定"的数据融合与处理模型实现了对农药多残留检测结果数据进行快速在线采集、融合；同时参照多国 MRL 精准判定，实现了农药残留侦测结果数据库的动态添加与实时更新，为国家食品安全决策提供了科学数据支持。③自主研发了农药残留海量数据智能分析软件，提出了面向海量农残检测数据的多维度交叉分析方法、农药残留污染综合评价与预警模型，实现了 20 项农药残留指标自动统计，最终实现"一键导出"一本图文并茂的农药残留侦测报告 20 ～ 30 分钟自动生成，极大提高了侦测报告精准度，为国家农药残留大数据分析提供了有效工具。

五、研发高分辨质谱＋互联网＋地理信息系统（GIS）三元融合技术，实现了农药残留风险溯源视频化

将农药残留数据与地理数据相关联，完成了农药残留数据驱动方式下中国地图的新应用，采用高分辨质谱＋互联网＋地理信息系统多元技术融合，设计编制了目标农药－食品名称－食品产地等多维空间特征的可视化系统，现已形成两个产品：① 31 省会／直辖市市售水果蔬菜农药残留水平地图集；② 31 省会／直辖市市售水果蔬菜农药残留在线制图系统。实现了一册图集在手，我国市售水果蔬菜农药残留概况总览无余；实现了农药残留监控像天气预报一样实时可视化，使我国农药残留数据规律展示一目了然。从而实现农药残留检测、溯源和预警三个关键点的"智慧一张图"管理，为产业自律、政府监管和第三方监督提供了基于空间可视化的科学数据支撑，构建了面向"全国－省－市（区）"多尺度的开放式专题地图表达框架，可实现现有数据汇聚和未来数据动态添加及实时更新。

庞国芳在基层单位工作 30 多年，培养带出了一支包括 5 名二级研究员、6 名享受政府特殊津贴专家、2 名百千万人才工程国家级人选、1 名第二批国家"万人计划"领军人才的研究队伍。

Awardee of Resources and Environmental Technology Prize, Pang Guofang

Pang Guofang was born in Luannan County of Hebei Province in October 1943 and graduated from Department of Chemistry of Hebei University. From 1968 to 1982, he worked as a lecturer in Hebei University. From 1982 to 2009, he was engaged in the research and application of pesticide and veterinary drug residue analytical techniques for import and export agricultural products. He was selected to be Academician of Chinese Academy of Engineering in 2007 and the chief scientist of CAIQ, deputy director of Risk Evaluation Expert Committee of China National Food Safety, deputy director of Review Committee of China National Food Safety Standards, Fellow of AOAC, recipient of the 2014 Harvey W Wiley Award.

Over the past 30 years, he has been engaged in the research of fundamental theories of trace elements analysis, application techniques and method standardization of pesticides and chemical contaminants, and has undertaken a series of pioneering research work in the trace element analysis of pesticide and chemical contaminants.

(1) Six categories of MS databases and spectra library were developed, which lay a theoretical and methodological foundation for the development of high throughput and high-resolution analytical techniques for 1200 pesticide residues. On such a basis, a unique electronic identity was established for each of the 1200 pesticides, with the realization of pesticide residue detection of electronic standard taking place of the conventional method of using substantial pesticide standards as reference. In the meanwhile, a frog-leap development was also achieved for pesticides residues analysis from target detection to non-target detection. This can be called an innovative result of supply-side reform in the area of pesticide residue analytical techniques.

(2) GC/LC-MS study was adopted to develop analytical techniques for over 1000 pesticide residues and over 200 veterinary drug residues in edible agricultural products, and 139 national standards have been formulated for these analytical techniques. In the meanwhile, he led and organized the international collaborative studies attended by 62 laboratories from 17 countries and regions, and 3 technologies of GC/LC-MS/MS were used to develop 3 AOAC official methods, being the pioneers in the Chinese scholars developing AOAC standards.

(3) Development of the tri-element merging technology of high-resolution MS-internet-digital science and realization of the automation of the generation of detection report of pesticide residues. Development of high-resolution MS-internet-geographical information system tri-element technology and realization of visualization of source tracing of pesticide residues.

Based on the remarkable achievements he had made to the development of LC-MS technology for the analysis of over 1000 pesticide residues in edible agricultural products, he won many awards including 3 Prizes of National Scientific and Technological Progress, and 8 AOAC International Scientific and Technical Awards inclusive of the top AOAC prize of Harvey W. Wiley Award for science and technology, as well as 12 scientific and technical works and over 100 papers published.

工程建设技术奖获得者

范 瑞 祥

范瑞祥，1965年6月出生于甘肃省武威市。1991年毕业于哈尔滨工业大学材料科学与工程系获工学博士学位。毕业后一直在中国运载火箭技术研究院工作，现任长征七号运载火箭总设计师。2001年10月—2004年6月任长征二号丙运载火箭和某新型洲际导弹副总设计师，2004年6月—2009年5月任长征二号丙运载火箭和某新型洲际导弹总设计师。中国人民解放军原总装备部第一届航天运载技术专业组组长，中央军委科技委航天领域专家委员会成员，国际宇航科学院院士。

范瑞祥长期从事多个国家重点航天型号的研制，在运载火箭和战略导弹总体设计领域进行了创新性研究和工程实践。

（1）他带领研制团队攻克了分导式洲际导弹多目标打击策略优化、多载荷分离释放、分导机动飞行姿态控制等关键技术，解决了分导飞行试验考核的难题，填补了我国战略导弹分导技术的空白，大大提高了导弹的突防能力，使我国战略导弹技术水平实现了新跨越。成果获国家科技进步奖一等奖（排名第一）。

一方面，提出了多种有效载荷多批次按顺序分离释放的设计方法，建立了有效载荷分离过程中导弹末级多模式的姿态控制模型，优化设计出百余个飞行时序动作，解决了多种有效载荷分离释放、分离冲击及姿控喷管羽流对有效载荷工作可靠性影响等难题。

另一方面，提出基于有限数量的落区、多个落点的"往复机动飞行"的设计方案，解决了我国开展洲际导弹分导飞行试验所遇到的弹头落区必须在境内、落区选择受限制等难题，实现了对导弹完整飞行程序的考核。

（2）长征七号运载火箭是我国空间站工程中为发射货运飞船及未来新型载人飞船、同时兼顾未来大中型卫星的发射任务，按载人航天标准全新研制的新一代高可靠、采用无毒推进剂的中型运载火箭。他带领研制团队攻克了长征七号运载火箭系列构型优化、发动机多机并联布局及级间分离、大长径比助推器捆绑和分离、底部热环境及防热结构设计、控制系统和液氧煤油低温动力系统高可靠性设计、新型箭体结构三维数字化设计与制造等一系列关键技术，针对新建成的海南文昌发射场高温、高湿和浅层风大等自然环境，攻克了火箭防水防潮、防风减载及新型活动发射平台设计与防护等难题。经过 8 年艰苦攻关，2016 年 6 月长征七号火箭首次飞行试验获得圆满成功，使我国运载火箭近地轨道运载能力由 8.6 吨提升至 14 吨，达到国际先进水平。2017 年 4 月该火箭第二次飞行成功将我国第一艘货运飞船"天舟一号"准确送入预定轨道，实现了载人航天工程空间实验室阶段发射任务的圆满收官。

第一，提出了我国新一代中型运载火箭系列化、模块化发展的路线。基于两种新型液氧煤油发动机和一种 9 吨级推力的液氢液氧发动机，以 3.35 米直径的芯级模块和 2.25 米直径的助推器模块构建出了运载能力全面覆盖和超越现役运载火箭、绿色环保且能够在内陆及濒海发射场发射的新一代中型运载火箭系列。

第二，为了实现新一代中型运载火箭系列构型和运载能力优化的目标，长征七号火箭采用大长径比液体助推器。但大长径比助推器低频模态密集且与芯级强耦合，给火箭姿态控制系统设计带来了难题。为此，他提出采用三支点超静定捆绑和分离的设计新方法。与传统的两支点静定捆绑设计方法相比，将助推器固有频率提高 100%、弯矩载荷减小 38%，既优化了火箭总体设计、减轻了结构重量，又提高了姿态控制系统的设计可靠性。

第三，国内外运载火箭飞行失利和重大故障统计表明，动力系统占比超过 30%，且该系统普遍存在单点失效故障模式。长征七号火箭采用全液氧煤油低温动力系统，该系统组成复杂、设计难度大。为此，范瑞祥提出了推进剂贮箱系统级冗余的柔性增压控制方案，实现了火箭飞行全过程满足发动机工作要求、增压能量最省、贮箱薄壳结构轴向载荷优化等多目标优化，提高了动力系统的可靠性和强壮性，达到了载人航天运载火箭高可靠性的要求。同时，提出通过调节蓄压器的容量、对火箭动力系统固有频率进行上限控制的方法，成功抑制了大推力液氧煤油发动机液氧入口 5 ~ 10Hz 低频压力脉动，消除了火箭飞行过程中因固液耦合振动导致结构低频响应破坏和发动机异常工作的隐患。

第四，提出火箭推进剂贮箱结构三维设计 / 制造新方法、箭上小导管密封冗余设计方法，使贮箱承载能力提高 15%，提高火箭运载能力 340 千克以上，同时大大提高了火箭管路密封的可靠性。提出设计思想和技术方案，并带领团队研制成功可折叠、大跨距和可重复使用的火箭防风减载机构，使火箭转场过程中地面风载造成的根部弯矩减小 48%，解决了海南发射场地面浅层风大的气象环境条件带来的火箭设计难题。

（3）在担任长征二号丙运载火箭副总设计师、总设计师期间，带领团队研制成功两种新型固体上面级，攻克了固体上面级自旋稳定、上面级双星异轨部署、整流罩低空分离、二级钝化和离轨等多项新技术，形成了长征二号丙系列运载火箭，使其成为我国唯一能够同时承担近地轨道、太阳同步轨道和大椭圆轨道卫星发射任务的运载火箭，且能够在国内三个内陆发射场执行发射任务，显著提高了火箭对不同任务的适应能力。圆满完成了以地球空间探测双星、育种卫星、环境监测卫星（A、B双星）为代表的多颗卫星发射任务。成果获国防科技进步二等奖（排名第二）。

（4）我国在载人运载火箭长征二号F中首次研制逃逸系统，该系统内结构和各项机构组成及受力形式复杂，逃逸飞行器薄壳结构除承受轴向载荷外，还承受栅格翼和支撑机构传来的28个径向集中载荷作用。作为主任设计师，提出火箭箭体结构轻质化设计和薄壳结构集中力扩散设计方法，攻克了逃逸飞行器结构和各项机构研制的关键技术，提高火箭运载能力380千克。成果获国家科技进步特等奖（排名第十七）。

范瑞祥获国家科技进步特等奖1项、一等奖1项，国防科技进步特等奖1项、一等奖2项，二等奖4项。申请并获授权国防发明专利18项。在国内学术期刊上发表论文14篇（其中10篇为第一作者），在原总装备部科技委年会上发表论文5篇；参与编写著作2部。培养博士生1名、硕士生2名、型号副总设计师19名、主任设计师29名。

Awardee of Engineering and Construction Technology prize, Fan Ruixiang

Fan Ruixiang was born in Wuwei City of Gansu Province in June 1965 and received his Ph.D degree in the Department of Material Science and Engineering from Harbin Institute of Technology. He has been working at China Academy of Launch vehicle Technology since 1991. Now, he is the chief designer of the Long March 7 launch vehicle. From 2004 to 2009, he has served as the chief designer of the Long March 2C launch vehicle series and one type of intercontinental ballistic missile. Besides, he has been a member of the Expert Committee of the Space Commission of the CMC and a member of the International Academy of Astronautics.

Dr. Fan Ruixiang has long been engaged in the development of core aerospace projects and made innovative contributions in the field of systems engineering of launch vehicle and intercontinental ballistic missile.

He and his team have conquered the optimization of multi target attacking strategy for Multi Independent Reentry Vehicle（MIRV）of intercontinental missile, multi payloads deployment, independent maneuvering flight attitude control etc. key technologies, which filled the gaps in Chinese MIRV intercontinental missile technology.

The Long March 7（LM-7）, as a new generation of medium and basic launch vehicle based on the design concepts of non-toxic and non-polluting, was developed for the purpose of launching cargo spacecraft and new type of manned spacecraft to the Chinese space station. Dr. Fan and his team have made breakthrough in a series of critical technical challenges such as high slenderness booster separation with hyper-static strap-on structures, final stage injection with high accuracy, robust control of pressurization system. On 25th June 2016, the success of LM-7 maiden flight signified that the low earth orbit launch capacity of China has risen from 8.6 tons to 14 tons. On 20th April 2017, the successful launching of Tianzhou-1 cargo spacecraft by LM-7 marked a prelude for the space lab mission of Chinese manned spaceflight program.

Dr. Fan and his team have successfully developed two types of upper stages with solid rocket motor for the Long March 2C series. It enables to carry out launch mission of low earth orbit, high elliptic orbit and sun synchronous orbit at Chinese three inland launch sites. Typical missions include Double Star exploration mission (TC-1/TC-2 satellites), and environmental monitoring satellite mission (HJ-1A/B satellites).

Dr. Fan Ruixiang is moral, cultured, patriotic and innovative. He have awarded one special and one first-class National Science and Technology Progress Award, one special, two first-class National Defense Science and technology Progress Awards.

工程建设技术奖获得者

李 清 泉

李清泉，1965 年 1 月出生于安徽省天长市。1988 年毕业于武汉测绘科技大学，获工学硕士学位，留校从事工程测量教学科研工作。1998 年获得武汉测绘科技大学摄影测量与遥感专业工学博士学位，同年被聘为教授。2000 年 8 月—2012 年 6 月任武汉大学副校长、常务副校长，2012 年 7 月起任深圳大学校长。现任国家测绘地理信息局海岸带地理环境监测重点实验室主任、教育部科技委委员、中国测绘学会副理事长、中国地理信息产业协会副理事长、百千万人才国家级人选、欧亚科学院院士等职。先后到香港理工大学、美国加州大学圣巴巴拉分校作访问研究。历任"973"首席科学家、"863"领域专家、国际摄影测量与遥感协会智能空间辅助决策工作组主席、教育部科技委地学与资源环境学部常务副主任等职。主持科研项目 50 余项，获授权发明专利 26 项，出版专著 5 部，发表期刊论文 300 余篇，引用超过 6600 次、H-index 39（Google Scholar）。获国家级科技奖励三项、省部级科技进步一等奖五项以及中国青年科技奖。培养博士研究生 30 人、硕士研究生 50 人。

李清泉长期从事动态精密工程测量的理论与应用研究工作，经过近 30 年的探索和实践，形成自己独特的研究思路和模式：一是将测绘理论、信息技术与工程应用结合开展交叉学科研究；二是构建动态精密工程测量理论与方法，实现从基础研究（论文）到技术方法（专利）再到装备研制（产品）的系统性创新；三是产学研紧密结合推动相关行业技术进步和测绘高新技术产业发展。

一、道路动态弯沉测量

道路弯沉是评估道路承载能力的关键指标，其含义是对路面施加标准力（100KN）时测量路面充分变形后的位移量，弯沉值是表征道路结构强度的重要指标。弯沉直接测量无法快速进行，只能采用人工抽检方法，效率低下且事故频发。高动态条件下的道路弯沉高精度测量是亟待突破的世界性难题。

李清泉带领团队发展了测量滚动载荷作用下的测量载体上多点相对位移以及载体与路面相对姿态的技术，解决了运动载体的微弱变形形成的动态测量误差问题；提出了基于波动周期的微弱变形信号提取算法，结合测量载体对地相对姿态、绝对姿态与变形信息，实现强噪声信号中 0.01 毫米级微弱变形量的提取；发明了基于变形速度的弯沉反演方法，进行路面弯沉值准确计算，实现了道路弯沉实时、非接触、动态高速测量。研制了唯一适合我国道路环境的激光动态弯沉测量技术装备，测量速度由传统的 1 ～ 5km/h 提升至 15 ～ 90km/h，测量精度达到 0.01 毫米，填补了国内空白，彻底改变了我国道路弯沉测量的现状，在十多个省、市推广应用，累计测量里程达到数百万千米。

二、高精度三维测量

传统工程测量方法存在测量精度差、采样点稀疏、三维重建模型粗糙以及作业效率低下等缺点，不能满足现代大型基础设施对工程测量大范围、连续、动态、高精度的实际应用需要。

李清泉带领研究团队提出基于线扫描成像的高精度三维测量方法，发明了基于 FPGA 的断面数据实时预处理和压缩传输算法，实现了高精度线扫描高频率和大数据量三维数据连续采集；提出基于断面的自主轮廓计算、断面点分类和点云目标匹配方法，发明了基于深度学习的种子点云分类算法和基于感知编组的线性目标提取算法，实现了高效可靠的目标三维特征自动提取；发明传感器自动标定技术，标定粒度达 1/64 像素，解决了三维测量传感器精密标定的技术难题。研制了适用于多种行业应用的高精度三维测量传感器，线扫描频率优于 10KHz，在测量高程范围内精度达 0.1 ～ 0.35 毫米，打破了国外公司的技术垄断，满足了我国在道路路面病害检测、机场跑道病害检测、高铁轨道伤损检测等领域的应用需求。在此基础上开发的应用系统获中国专利优秀奖和国家重点新产品奖，在全国三十多个省（自治区）、市六十余家单位投入使用 100 余台（套），检测历程累计超过 1000 万千米，直接经济效益数亿元，间接经济效益数十亿元，确立了我国在大范围三维动态测量领域的国际领先地位。

三、文化遗产数字化复原

随着我国经济建设速度加快和自然环境变化加剧，大量的珍贵文化遗产正以不可逆的方式快速消亡，而文化遗产数字化保护是实现文化遗产"永生"的唯一途径。实现高精度、高效率、低成本的数字化复原是文化遗产数字化保护的重要基础。

李清泉带领研究团队在几何重建、色彩复原、知识发现、个性化展示等方面开展系统性研究。提出复杂对象的几何与纹理数据多尺度采集与建模方法，发明了无人机高精度三维激光测量系统，并首次成功应用于遗址发现（荆州大遗址）；在国际上率先提出面向对象的真三维空间数据模型及其数据结构，建立了复杂对象的层次化构建模式，解决了多尺度复杂对象几何、属性、语义精细计算的难题；提出基于机器学习的壁画语义（绘画风格、艺术演变规律等）分析方法，实现了壁画时代风格的智能判别，并成功应用于敦煌壁画时代分析研制不可移动文化遗产高精度测量与三维重建系统，应用于敦煌莫高窟、靖江王陵、云冈石窟、成都武侯祠、韩国崇礼门等数十处不可移动文化遗产保护工程，推动了文化遗产保护从传统模式向数字模式的跃升。研究成果列入"973"代表性成果。

四、城市时空数据分析

对城市动态变化规律的精确把握是实现城市精细化管理与运营的前提，而传统地理信息技术只能以静态方式表达和分析城市。城市时空数据是典型测量大数据，数据的挖掘和分析尚未形成完善的理论和方法。

李清泉带领团队提出面向复杂异构城市时空数据的一体化时空模型，实现多源城市时空大数据的精准耦合、统一管理和动态更新，攻克了多源城市时空数据实时在线处理与分析的技术瓶颈；发展多种城市时空数据（移动通信数据、智能交通数据、社交网络数据等）的融合方法，提出一系列顾及动态特征的城市时空数据分析方法，实现了面向复杂城市问题的时空大数据深度理解；发展基于时空邻近性的高效优化技术，突破了大规模物流车辆路径优化的计算密集性难题，服务于箭牌中国配送、华南农业物流、深港跨境物流等；发展众源数据支撑下的室内外一体化定位与导航方法，应用于大型机场、商业中心、高铁枢纽等十余个位置信息服务系统。研究成果突破了城市大规模移动对象的动态监测与在线分析技术，实现了对城市动态变化规律的感知，为智慧城市精细化管理与运营提供了有力的技术支撑。

Awardee of Engineering and Construction Technology Prize, Li Qingquan

Li Qingquan was born in Tianchang City of Anhui Province in January1965. Doctoral degree in Engineering from Wuhan Technical University of Surveying and Mapping. He was the Vice President and Standing Vice President of Wuhan University from August 2000 to June 2012, and then the President of Shenzhen University since July 2012. Currently Prof. Li is the director of Key Laboratory for Geo-Environment Monitoring of Coastal Zone of the National Administration of Surveying, Mapping and Geo-Information, Member of Science & Technology Commission of Ministry of Education, Vice President of China Society for Surveying, Mapping and Geoformation, Vice President of China Association for Geographic Information Society, and Academician of International Eurasian Academy of Science. He has served successively as Chief Scientist in

National Basic Research Program of China（973 Program）, Member of Modern Transportation Expert Boards for National High-tech R&D Program of China（863 Program）. Prof. Li has led over 50 research projects, obtained 26 authorized patent of invention, and published 5 monographs and more than 300 journal articles and papers, which have been quoted for 6600 times and more. He is with H-index 39 level on Google Scholar and has been awarded 3 National Science & Technology Awards, First Prize of Provincial and Ministerial Level Scientific and Technological Advancement Reward, and Chinese Young Technology Award. He has supervised 30 PhD students and 50 master students.

Prof. Li Qingquan has long engaged in the theoretical research and practical application concerning Precision Engineering Survey. After 30 years of exploration and practice, he has formed his unique research approach and pattern: ① to combine theories of Mapping and Surveying with Information Technology and Engineering Applications and thus conduct interdisciplinary research; ② to construct theories and methods on Precision Engineering Survey, thus realizing systematic innovation from basic research（Paper）to technical approach（Patent）to Equipment Development（Product）; ③ to rigorously combine Industry-University-Research, promote technological advancement of relevant industries, and develop the high-tech industry of Surveying and Mapping. His major research findings are Dynamic Road Deflection Measurement, High-Precision Three Dimensional Measurement, Digital Restoration of Cultural Relics and Urban Spatial-temporal Data Analysis.

工程建设技术奖获得者

宋保维

宋保维，1963 年 7 月出生于辽宁省锦州市。1999 年毕业于西北工业大学获工学博士学位。1989—2002 年在西北工业大学航海学院先后任助教、讲师、副教授、教授，2002 年 6 月—2013 年 4 月担任西北工业大学航海学院院长，2013 年 5 月—2015 年 3 月担任西北工业大学校长助理兼科学技术管理部部长，2015 年 4 月至今担任西北工业大学党委常委、副校长。兼任军委科技委领域专家、教育部科学技术委员会委员、国务院学位委员会兵器科学与技术学科评议组召集人、国家高技术计划（"863"计划）主题专家组责任专家、全国高等学校兵器类专业教学指导委员会委员、中国造船工程学会副理事长、中国兵工学会常务理事，入选国家教学名师、新世纪百千万人才工程国家级人选。

宋保维从事无人自主水下航行器研究，在新概念水下航行器设计、多学科优化与可靠性设计、水下仿生表面减阻等方面做出了开创性研究工作。

一、我国自航水雷体系创建者之一，解决了多型水雷总体关键技术

自主水下航行器是支撑探查和开发海洋资源、海洋科学研究、海洋工程作业的重要技术手段和装备。针对我国自主水下航行器技术水平还达不到国家战略要求等诸多问题，宋保维团队在国内率先提出多型新型自主水下航行器的概念与技术方案，相关技术已应用于自航水雷型号研制，实现了我国自航水雷技术的跨越式发展。

（1）团队在国内率先提出并开展"某新型水雷"关键技术研究，重点解决了水雷低阻远程与低噪隐身外形、载荷安全分离、高效双转螺旋桨等关键技术，完成了原理样机湖海实航试验，使我国水雷技术实现了跨越式发展。成果于 2005 年获国家科技进步奖二等奖。

（2）作为第一副总设计师，重点突破了低阻低噪流体动力外形与总体稳健衡重布局、低速航行鳍舵组合控制和推进转轴动态密封、载荷与运载体快速动态分离等关键技术，

研制了我国第一型具有自主知识产权的远程自主水下航行器，具有航程远、导航定位精度高、载荷与运载体可分离等特点，已批量生产。党和国家领导人先后亲临研制现场视察指导，对研制工作给予充分肯定和高度评价。研究成果获 2010 年国家科技进步奖二等奖。

（3）作为负责人，提出并主持开展了我国新型多载荷多次分离的远程自主水下航行器研究，突破了多载荷总体多目标优化及流体动力布局、双轴对转异型电机总体优化设计等关键技术，完成原理样机湖上实航验证，实现两个载荷分别定点布放，成果获 2015 年国家技术发明二等奖。相关技术研究成果已应用于某重大工程型号（任第一副总设计师），型号已定型批量生产。

二、创建了水下航行器多学科优化设计与可靠性理论体系

（1）在国内率先提出水下航行器总体多学科设计优化方法，建立了总体、外形及结构等多学科高保真自动设计优化模型；基于协同优化算法和中心数据库技术，构建了国内第一套水下航行器多学科集成优化平台，解决了型号研制中的总体系统优化设计问题。研究成果获省部级科技进步三等奖 2 项，并出版我国水下航行器领域第一部多学科优化设计学术专著《鱼雷多学科优化设计理论与应用研究》。

（2）针对水下航行器装备可靠性小子样问题，基于分系统折合的小子样产品可靠性抽样和序贯验后加权检验方法，创建了适用于水下航行器装备的可靠性评定模型。研究成果获部级科技进步二等奖 2 项、三等奖 1 项，入选全国优秀博士学位论文 1 篇，出版普通高等教育本科国家级规划教材《系统可靠性设计与分析》和国防特色学科专业专著《鱼雷系统可靠性理论与方法》，并获全国优秀教材一等奖 1 项。

三、揭示了水下随行波／条纹沟槽／疏水表面等仿生减阻规律

在国内率先开展了仿沙漠等自然界随行波表面、条纹沟槽表面及仿鲨鱼等海洋生物脊状表面的水下减阻方法研究，提出了随行波／条纹沟槽／脊状表面微观流场理论计算方法，突破了近壁区流场测试、加工工艺等关键技术，建立了一套水下减阻试验的评估与分析方法，揭示了不同工况下随行波／条纹沟槽／脊状表面的减阻规律和减阻机理。

为了实现水下长时防污及减阻技术的工程化应用，探索了仿荷叶等植物疏水／超疏水表面水下减阻特性及减阻机理，提出了利用亲疏水相间结构构筑无限边界气环，实现水下气膜层高效稳定封存的技术。在无外来气体持续补充的条件下，在旋转圆柱表面上成功封存住亚毫米厚度的连续气环层获得显著减阻效果，为解决目前仿生超疏水材料减阻失效问题提供了崭新的技术思路，为突破远航程、长航时水下航行器减阻技术瓶颈提供了一种有效的方法。成果已发表在 *Science Advances*，受到学者的高度评价。

四、创建了自主水下航行器国家级教学与科研团队

（1）创建了"鱼雷技术专业课程"国家级教学团队。提出了以教学团队进行课程建

设、教材建设、实验室建设和人才培养的模式，构建了创新人才培养体系，开辟了在科学研究和学科建设中培养创新型人才的途径。研究成果"结合学科建设和科学研究，构建创新人才培养体系"获国家教学优秀成果一等奖，"鱼雷技术专业课程"教学团队被评为首批国家级教学团队，建设的《鱼雷技术基础》课程被评为首批国家精品课程，所指导的本科生班被授予全国"先进班集体"称号。

（2）创建了"自主水下航行器"科技创新团队。依托水下信息与控制国防科技重点实验室，建立了一支以总体与动力、控制与导航、探测与通信等为主要研究方向的自主水下航行器科技创新团队，主要开展远程自主水下航行器基础技术研究、关键技术攻关与工程型号研制。所带领的团队先后被授予首批"国防科技创新团队"、首批"国家级教学团队""长江学者和创新团队发展计划"创新团队，并荣获"全国教育系统先进集体"称号和"国防科技创新团队奖"。

Awardee of Engineering and Construction Technology Prize, Song Baowei

Song Baowei was born in Jinzhou City of Liaoning Province in July 1963. He received his Ph.D. in 1999 from Northwestern Polytechnical University（NPU）. From 1989 to 2002, he worked as a teaching assistant, lecturer, associate professor, and then professor at School of Marine Science and Technology, NPU. He worked as the dean of School of Marine Science and Technology from June 2002 to April 2013, followed by taking over as the assistant president of NPU from May 2013 to March 2015. Since April 2015, he has held the position of the member of the Standing Committee and the vice president of NPU. Meanwhile, he also holds several concurrent positions, such as an expert of Commission of Science and Technology, the member of Science & Technology Commission of Ministry of Education, the convener of discipline appraisal group of Armament Science and Technology of Academic Degrees Committee, the specialist of the subject expert group of National High Technology Research and Development Program（863 Program）, the member of Armament Teaching Advisory Board under the Ministry of Education, the vice chairman of The Chinese Society of Naval Architects and Marine Engineers and the executive director of China Ordnance Society. In addition, he has be selected as the national prominent educator, and the state class talent of the New Century Talents Project.

His research focuses on the development and application of the autonomous underwater vehicle（AUV）. He has achieved a series of groundbreaking research results in many fields, such as the design of novel underwater vehicles, the multidisciplinary optimization and the reliability design, the underwater bionic surface drag reduction, etc. The related research results have placed second prize of the National Scientific and Technological Progress Award in 2005/2010, and placed second prized of State Technological Invention Award in 2015.

He has created the autonomous underwater vehicle technology innovation team. Relying on the key laboratories for national defense science and technology for underwater information and control, Song has established a scientific and technological innovation team of autonomous underwater vehicle, which is mainly oriented to power, control and navigation, detection and communication. This team mainly deals with the basic and key technology research and engineering model development of remote autonomous underwater vehicles. His team has been awarded the titles of First Batch of National Defense Science and Technology Innovation Teams, First Batch of National Teaching Teams, Innovation Team of Yangtze Scholars and Innovation Teams' Development Program, the awards of Advanced Collective National Education System and National Defense Science and Technology Innovation Team.

工程建设技术奖获得者

杨 伟

杨伟，1963 年 5 月出生于北京市。1985 年 5 月毕业于西北工业大学空气动力学与飞行力学专业，获工学硕士学位。1985—2008 年在中国航空工业集团公司成都飞机设计研究所（第 611 设计研究所）工作，历任专业组长、研究室主任、副所长、总设计师、所长，飞控系统总设计师、飞机总设计师，研究员、博士生导师；2008 年起历任中国航空工业集团公司副总工程师、中国航空研究院副院长、中国航空工业集团公司科技委副主任、国防科技工业航空技术创新中心主任。中央军委装备发展部武器装备探索研究专家指导委员会委员、中央军委科学技术委员会空战领域专家委员会委员、国务院中央军委军工产品定型委员会专家咨询委员会委员、中国系统工程学会常务理事、中国航空学会理事会理事、国防科技出版基金评审委员会委员等。

30 多年来，杨伟一直坚持在科研一线开展战斗机的设计与研发工作，是我国第四代战斗机歼 -20 飞机的总设计师，是我国第三代战斗机歼 -10 的系列改进型歼 -10 双座机、歼 -10A、歼 -10B、歼 -10X 飞机的总设计师，是我国与巴基斯坦联合研制的枭龙单、双座战斗机的总设计师，为我国航空工业和武器装备的发展做出了重大贡献。

一、主持研制成功我国最先进的歼 -20 战斗机，使我国成为世界上第二个装备第四代战斗机的国家

他主持研制成功我国最先进的歼 -20 飞机，实现了我国航空武器装备自主创新能力的历史性跨越，使我国成为世界上第二个装备第四代战斗机的国家，对捍卫国家的主权和发展权起到重要作用，同时引领了航空工业以及军工电子工业的科技创新发展。

为突破歼 -20 的隐身、高机动性、大航程等综合性跨代关键技术，他在多年预研和歼 -10、枭龙飞机研制的基础上，创新性地研发了"升力体边条鸭式气动布局"，综合发挥了鸭式布局和边条布局的优势。首次采用倾斜全动双垂尾，既降低了雷达反射截面，又提高了飞机的航向乃至纵向控制能力。探索了以压缩曲面产生的锥形激波在曲面边缘的附着原理，研发了两侧三边蚌式进气道，成功突破了蚌式进气道技术。主持研究了多种隐身方案与措施，使歼-20的隐身气动性能处于国际一流水平。

为实现歼-20飞机高度信息化、智能化的要求，他提出了全新的两级分布式飞机管理系统架构，打破专业界限，对全机十余个机电系统实施集中管理、按区域分布控制，既大幅度减轻了系统重量，又提高了系统可靠性和测试性。他主持建立了基于统一光纤互联的开放式、模块化新一代航电系统体系架构，可有效实现"综合探测、综合识别、综合干扰、综合打击"。构建了信息高度融合的统一管控的飞机大系统架构，极大地提高了系统效能。

二、突破容错数字式电传飞行控制，主持歼-10的持续深度改进，使其从第三代制空战斗机跃升为第三代半的制空/制海/制面多用途战斗机

主持开展容错数字式电传飞行控制系统研究，突破了余度管理、故障重构、四通道同步、静不稳定控制等关键技术，使我国电传飞行控制技术达到国际先进水平。

作为歼-10的系列改进型飞机的总设计师，他主持对歼-10进行不断的深度改进，拓展了歼-10的族谱，使其从第三代制空战斗机跃升为第三代半的制空/制海/制面多用途战斗机，飞机的综合作战效能得到大幅提升，并成为我国现役的主力战机。

为提升歼-10飞机的气动隐身性能以及全疆域部署能力，他对飞机的总体气动布局进行了一系列的优化改进，包括采用更大孔径的先进雷达；内埋通风进气口，降低飞机的阻力；采用无隔道腹部蚌式进气道，在提高总压恢复系数的同时兼容多型发动机；改进起落架和救生系统，使飞机能够在我国最高的高原机场起降等。

他主持加装、换装、升级改进包括雷达、电子战、红外搜索与跟踪系统、数据链等一系列探测、对抗、协同作战的关键设备，改进了飞行员的人机功效，加装了新型的超视距导弹与红外近距格斗导弹以及防区外对面/对海精确打击武器。

三、主持研制成功我国新一代外贸机枭龙飞机

主持研制了针对21世纪作战环境、面向国际市场、性价比优异的第三代先进战斗机枭龙飞机，实现了中国军机出口由二代机向三代机的重大跨越，使中国在军贸飞机国际市场占有了前所未有的重要位置。目前已出口100架，创汇20余亿美元。

采用先进的设计与制造技术，使研制过程全面实现数字化。攻克了先进的边条翼加无隔道蚌式进气道的气动布局，有效提升了飞机总体性能。突破了多种体制的飞控系统在同一架飞机上协同工作、综合化的机电管理系统以及先进的机电系统等先进关键技术。主持研究了基于"灵巧"显示机制的高度综合化航电武器系统、"玻璃化座舱"和多种新型攻击模式，增强了系统的综合化程度，极大地提高了人机工效。

四、引领技术发展，创新研发体系，建设卓越团队

除了主持型号飞机研制工作，杨伟还积极推动基础较弱的机电系统研发水平的提升，组织相关单位交流新技术新方法、传播好经验。大力推进军民融合技术的发展，积极推动国产碳纤维等民用技术的应用，同时积极将取得的相关技术成果向航空装备体系广泛辐射。

他积极健全完善以需求为牵引的飞机研发模式，领衔创建了基于全三维模型产品定义（MBD）的面向飞机设计与制造过程的全新研发体系，积极推动基于数字样机的虚拟产品研发技术、系统设计与仿真技术等应用；同时积极推进面向产品分解结构的项目管理、系统工程管理和关键设计评审（CDR）、飞行准备状态评审（FRR）等先进质量管理方法。

在他的带领下，一批具有先进设计理念、掌握先进技术的优秀技术和管理人才已经形成梯队，成为推动我国航空工业科技持续创新、向前发展的动力源泉。杨伟先后获得国家科技进步特等奖1项、二等奖1项，国家管理创新一等奖1项，国防科技进步一等奖2项、二等奖3项，集团科技进步奖8项。先后荣获全国先进工作者、全国先进科技工作者、全国五一劳动奖章、中国青年五四奖章、全国创新争先奖章和"国防科技工业杰出人才奖"等荣誉，并荣获巴基斯坦总统亲自颁发的"卓越之星"国家荣誉勋章。

Awardee of Engineering and Construction
Technology Prize, Yang Wei

Yang Wei was born in Beijing City in May 1963. He was admitted to Northwestern Polytechnical University（NPU）majoring in aerodynamics and flight dynamics at the age of 15. After graduated with Master's Degree of Science in Engineering in 1985, he joined Chengdu Aircraft Design & Research Institute（CADI）and engaged on the design of Digital Fly-by-Wire（FBW）Flight Control System of J-10. In 2000, he became the chief designer, and then the president of CADI. Since 2008, he has been appointed successively as deputy chief engineer of Aviation Industry Corporation of China（AVIC）, vice president of Chinese Aeronautical Establishment（CAE）, deputy director of AVIC's Science and Technology Committee, and director of Aeronautical Technology Innovation Center of National Defense Science & Technology Industry.

For more than thirty years, Yang Wei has devoted himself to design and development of fighter aircraft. He is the chief designer of Chinese 5th generation fighter J-20, the upgraded variants of Chinese 4th generation fighter J-10, including J-10S（dual-seat）/J-10A/J-10B/J-10X, and the single-seat/dual-seat JF-17 jointly developed by China and Pakistan. He has made meritorious contributions to the Chinese aviation industry.

In order to fulfill the remarkable requirements of J−20 with stealth, information superiority, high maneuverability, supersonic cruise, and long range etc., together with his team, he developed the unique canard−strakes lifting body aerodynamic layout, and established the advanced system architecture featuring in centralized management & distributed control of aircraft systems and open/ modularized/optical fiber interconnected avionics system, rendering China the second country in the world equipped with the 5th generation fighter.

Under his leadership, breakthrough was made in fault tolerant FBW flight control technology which played a critical role in successful development of J−10. As the chief designer, he developed the first 4th generation Combat/Training fighter J−10S in China. With a mass of the new technology adopted in J−10B and J−10X, the new J−10s became the 4th and half generation multirole fighter and the combat effectiveness was enhanced dramatically. With the optimum technology, he made JF−17 a most cost−effective, advanced, and light−weight fighter.

Furthermore, a brand new aircraft R&D system based on 3D digital model was established under his supervision, which promoted the transformation of aircraft R&D methodology.

Yang Wei has been conferred with several National Prizes for Progress in Science and Technology. He has received many honors such as National Advanced Worker, National Labor Medal, National Innovation Medal and Outstanding Talent in Defense Science & Technology Industry etc. In addition, he was granted with "Sitara−i−Imtiaz" (Star of Excellence) Award by the president of Pakistan.

何梁何利基金科学与技术创新奖获得者传略

PROFILES OF THE AWARDEES OF PRIZE FOR
SCIENTIFIC AND TECHNOLOGICAL INNOVATION OF
HO LEUNG HO LEE FOUNDATION

青年创新奖获得者

陈 小 武

陈小武，1972 年 5 月出生于湖南省安仁县。1994 年在北京航空航天大学应用数理系获理学学士学位，1997 年、2001 年在北京航空航天大学计算机科学与工程系分别获工学硕士学位和工学博士学位，2001—2002 年在加拿大多伦多大学从事博士后研究。2002 年至今在北京航空航天大学计算机学院、虚拟现实技术与系统国家重点实验室工作。2013年获国家杰出青年科学基金项目，2014 年入选国家万人计划科技创新领军人才，被聘为2015 年度长江学者特聘教授，2016 年获评国务院政府特殊津贴专家。现兼任国务院学位委员会学科评议组成员（计算机科学与技术）、中国计算机学会常务理事及虚拟现实与可视化技术专业委员会主任。

陈小武主要从事虚拟现实、可视计算、大数据与智能计算等研究。爆炸式增长的大数据约 80% 为图像视频、三维模型等可视大数据，然而图像视频编辑、三维模型构建与场景内容标注经常依赖人工编辑、人工建模与人工标注，耗费大量的人力、物力与财力，制约了许多行业领域的应用推广。针对上述问题，陈小武以可视大数据内容及其蕴含的特征规律为驱动，在图像视频场景自动编辑生成、三维模型场景自动构建生成、可视数据内容自动语义解析等方面取得了理论和技术创新。

陈小武主持了国家自然科学基金重点项目、国家"863"计划主题项目等 10 余项科研任务，主持研制了数据驱动的可视场景自动生成技术系统，研究成果已应用于信息产业、航空航天、公共安全、智能制造、教育体育、影视制作等领域。获 2014 年度国家技术发明二等奖（第一完成人）、2012 年度教育部技术发明一等奖（第一完成人）、2016 年第十一届光华工程科技奖青年奖、2012 年度中国计算机学会青年科学家奖。发表领域顶级国际期刊与顶级国际会议论文 28 篇，发表 SCI 论文 51 篇，获 ACM、IEEE、ASME、IAPR 等 Fellows 署名论文的引用和积极评价。获中国发明专利授权 46 项、美国发明专利授权 6 项。

一、图像视频场景自动编辑生成

针对生成内容失真、计算内存限制、窗口参数估计等问题，提出了特征结构保持的图像视频场景编辑自动传播模型及其稀疏表达字典学习模型，克服了过渡区域的颜色裂变和抖动难题，平均可节省90%的计算内存，突破了计算设备对高分辨率场景编辑的内存限制，大幅度拓展了适用范围，为对象颜色变换、场景基调变换、灰度场景着色、场景融合生成等技术方法提供了新的理论模型；提出了邻域与特征域平滑先验嵌入的图像视频对象精准提取方法，解决了难以估计卷积窗口参数的问题，在国际公开的性能评测系统上，其SAD、MSE、Gradient三项精准度性能持续约20个月均位居第一。

二、三维模型场景自动构建生成

针对数据驱动建模的难点问题，尤其是可视数据内容及9类属性的分布规律、特征聚合与约束变换，学习出场景布局结构、对象组成结构、属性特征分布等描述模型，建立了特征聚合的场景三维构建规则、对象及部件三维变形模板、场景属性映射规则，提出了规则联合的三维场景自动构建生成、模板联合的三维人体及服装自动构建生成、特征保持的场景光影迁移生成等方法。仅需输入单幅图像或单目视频，适用于单相机条件下（尤其是互联网的可视大数据）三维场景建模，探索出数据驱动的三维场景构建生成技术的新途径。

三、可视数据内容自动语义解析

针对可视大数据内容的场景级、对象级、部件级语义解析难题，提出了监督测地线传播的图像视频场景语义标记、检测器指导的弱标注视频对象语义分割、三维几何特征嵌入的图像对象部件语义分割、深度卷积神经网络的三维模型部件语义标记等方法，显著提高了解析准确率，部分指标国际领先。通过语义属性解析，尤其是富有挑战性的部件级语义解析，促进了跨类别可视数据的多尺度内容理解与关联，推动了可视数据内容的知识图谱构建。

在此基础上，陈小武主持研制了数据驱动的可视场景自动生成技术系统，其中包括31个具有自主知识产权的软件与装置、千万级样本的数据集。研究成果已应用于飞行器对地制导、无人机态势感知、航天器空间试验、公安局视频侦查、网络内容安全监测、智能化自动建模、奥运会项目备战、电大远程教育和影视后期制作等方面，大幅降低了人工操作与人力成本，社会经济效益显著。

Awardee of Youth Innovation Prize, Chen Xiaowu

Chen Xiaowu was born in Anren County of Hunan Province in May 1972. From Beihang University, he received B.S. degree in Applied Mathematics in 1994, M.S. degree and Ph.D. degree in Computer Science in 1997 and 2001 respectively. During 2001 and 2002, he was engaged in postdoctoral research in University of Toronto, Canada. Since 2002, he has been working in the State Key Laboratory of Virtual Reality Technology and Systems, School of Computer Science and Engineering, Beihang University.

In 2013, Chen Xiaowu was awarded the National Science Fund for Distinguished Young Scholars, from the National Natural Science Foundation of China. He was elected into the Ten Thousand Talent Program as a leading talent in science and technology innovation in 2014, and received the appointment of the distinguished professor of Chang Jiang Scholars Program in 2015. Since 2016, he started to receive the Special Government Allowances from the State Council. Currently, Chen Xiaowu is a consultative group member (Computer Science discipline) of the Academic Degrees Committee of the State Council. He is also an executive member of the Council for China Computer Federation as well as the director of the professional committee for Virtual Reality and Visualization.

Chen Xiaowu mainly focuses on the research in virtual reality, visual computing, computer graphics, computer vision, big visual data and intelligent computing. He has served as the Principal Investigator of more than ten research projects, such as the Key Program of National Natural Science Foundation of China and the National High Technology Research and Development Program of China. With the big visual data such as images, videos and 3D models, he has achieved multiple theoretical and technical innovations in automatic data-driven modeling, editing and parsing of visual scenes. He has led the successful development of a system that can automatically generate visual scenes in a data-driven manner. This system consists of 31 software tools and devices with intellectual property rights, a large-scale dataset with more than ten million samples. The technologies invented by him have been applied in many areas such as information industry, aeronautics and astronautics, public safety, intelligent manufacturing, education and culture industry.

In the past five years, Chen Xiaowu has ever won several awards. For example, he won the National Technology Invention Award (second grade) from the State Council of China in 2014 (first winner), the Technology Invention Award (first grade) from Ministry of Education of China in 2012 (first winner), the Eleventh Guanghua Engineering Science and Technology Prizes (Youth Award) in 2016, and the Young Scientist Award of China Computer Federation in 2012. Furthermore, he has published 69 papers, including 28 papers published in top journals and top conferences such as TOG, TPAMI, TIP, TVCG, IJCV, CVPR, ICCV and MM. Moreover, he has 52 patents issued, including 6 US patents.

青年创新奖获得者

姜　澜

姜澜，1972 年 7 月出生于四川省自贡市。国家"万人计划"首批科技创新领军人才、教育部长江学者特聘教授、国家杰出青年科学基金获得者、科技部"973"首席科学家、科技部"863""十二五"主题专家、教育部创新团队带头人、教育部科技委学部委员、科技部中青年科技创新领军人才，任"增材制造与激光制造"国家重点研发计划总体专家组组长、非硅微纳制造工信部重点实验室主任，兼任 *Microsystems & Nanoengineering*、*Scientific Reports* 等 5 个学术期刊编委。作为项目负责人，承担了科技部"973"项目、国家重大科技专项课题、国家自然科学基金委重大研究计划集成/重点项目、国家杰出青年科学基金等。迄今共发表 SCI 检索论文 205 篇，封面文章 3 篇。获得授权发明专利 18 项，申请发明专利 67 项。作主流国际大会 Keynote/Plenary/Invited 报告 72 次。曾获国家自然科学二等奖（第一完成人）和教育部自然科学奖一等奖（第一完成人）。所指导的博士生夏博获第六届上银优博银奖、王聪获第五届上银优博铜奖、李本业获第四届上银优博优秀奖。

姜澜主要从事激光微纳制造领域的科研工作，在飞秒激光与材料相互作用理论、超快激光微纳制造新方法、面向国家重大需求和国民经济中关键结构制造的应用方面取得了诸多研究成果。

一、飞秒激光与材料相互作用理论模型

1. 针对飞秒激光加工非金属，提出并建立了一个等离子体量子模型用以揭示超快激光与非金属相互作用的多项基本原理

（1）该模型大幅提高了理论预测精度，首次能够预测超快激光烧蚀形状。

（2）预测在一定条件下高斯型飞秒激光单脉冲在非金属上会形成平底结构，这一与传统观点相反的预测被十余个国家多个研究组的实验所确认。

（3）预测在飞秒激光与材料相互作用中存在小于衍射极限的纳米（数十到数百个纳米）稳定烧蚀深度区域。该预测被大量实验验证。该成果指导激光微加工大幅提高了飞秒激光脉冲序列纳米加工的精度和可重复性，揭示了飞秒脉冲序列脉冲绝缘体加工机理，推动了机械与材料、化工等其他相关学科的交叉融合。

2. 针对飞秒激光加工金属，以量子力学为工具改进了著名的"双温度方程"（该方程为微／纳热传导的基石之一）

改进算法将双温度方程的应用范围从电子温度小于费米温度的 1/10 区域拓展到了任意电子温度范围。该成果解决了 1993 年以来一直未能突破的一个难题——经典双温度方程不能正确描述高能量密度情况下超短脉冲与金属相互作用。应用该方程建立了飞秒激光脉冲序列金属加工的理论方法。

二、电子动态调控的超快激光微纳制造新方法

1. 制造新方法实验验证

应用前述模型，揭示了制造中超快激光对局部瞬时电子动态及其对应材料特性的调控规律，以大量实验证明了新方法的有效性。

（1）提出采用超快激光脉冲序列调控电子密度分布及材料局部瞬时特性，当激发产生的自由电子等离子体振荡频率（与自由电子密度相关）与入射激光频率相等／相近时，可实现等离子体与激光的共振吸收／近共振吸收，大幅提高加工效率。微通道体积加工效率可提高 5 ～ 56 倍。

（2）提出超快激光脉冲序列控制自由电子产生，使材料的瞬时局部特性发生变化，进而改变其物理性质（如反射率变化）和化学性质（如化学键变化），控制材料结构改性程度，后续化学刻蚀效率提高 37 倍。

（3）提出优化脉冲序列以调控自由电子密度，使其略高于临界密度，从而令库仑爆炸及静电烧蚀等非热相变效应为主要的相变机制，从而抑制熔化及其重铸，有效提高加工质量，使重铸层高度降低了约 60%。

（4）提出超快激光空间整形调控瞬时局部电子密度，从而调控激光与金属薄膜材料相互作用过程，实现了局部可控的纳米级材料去除，可完成高分辨率（约波长的 1/14）、高电导率（达体材料的 1/4）、任意形状突破衍射极限的金属纳米线结构制备。

（5）提出通过设计超快激光脉冲序列调控电子电离及复合过程，改变表面等离子体生成过程及其与激光的相互作用，有效控制了材料表面纹理结构的周期、方向、结构。

2. 制造新方法观测验证

提出并首次实现了超快激光与材料相互作用飞秒—皮秒—纳秒—毫秒—秒跨越 12 个时间数量级的电子动态演化全景过程观测，实现了超快激光加工过程从电子电离（飞秒—皮秒尺度）、材料相变（皮秒—纳秒尺度）到组织性能演化（纳秒—毫秒尺度）多时间尺度实验观测，为新方法提供了直接实验证据。

三、制造新方法在国家重大需求和国民经济中关键结构的制造

1. 新方法被选定为国家某重大工程中核心构件的加工工艺

针对国家某重大工程中核心结构微孔加工的技术挑战（如材料特殊、深径比大、孔型质量要求高、极小化重铸层/溅射物/腔内残留物等），对加工过程中自聚焦效应、光丝传播、等离子体膨胀等多种物理化学过程进行了有效调控。例如，提出采用时空整形以形成长焦深、小焦斑光束，调控聚焦点处局部瞬时电子密度分布及其随时间的演化，加工出了直径 1.6μm、深径比 330：1 的深小孔。相比于传统超快激光加工，深径比极限提高了 30 余倍，建立了球壳上用于充气的深小孔加工工艺，目前仅有中美两国可实现该结构的制备（不同技术路线），且新方法所加工的微孔总体质量显著优于美国所公布的微孔加工结果。目前，该新方法已被该国家重大工程选定为其核心结构微孔加工工艺。

2. 制造新方法应用于加工新型光纤微传感器

提出、设计并利用激光微纳制造新方法在光纤上加工了多种新型马赫曾德尔微传感器，能够实时在线检测温度、压力、应变、振动、浓度、折射率等参数。在提高光纤传感器的耐高温性、灵敏度等参数方面取得突破，与当前商品化的光纤光栅相比较，所研发的新型传感器灵敏度提高了 100 ~ 1000 倍，工作极限温度从 350℃提高到了 1200℃，克服了各物理量之间的交叉敏感问题，正在市场推广。

Awardee of Youth Innovation Prize, Jiang Lan

Jiang Lan was born in Zigong City of Sichuan Province in July 1972. He is Changjiang Professor of Mechanical Engineering at the Beijing Institute of Technology. He received the National Outstanding Young Scientists Award National Natural Science Foundation of China in 2010; First Prize Natural Science Award（the leading PI）Ministry of Education, China in 2014; and Second Prize, National Natural Science Award（the leading PI）in 2016. He was elected the Leader of the Innovation Group, Ministry of Education in 2013. Dr. Jiang served as a panelist in the National High-Tech R&D Program（863 Project）of the Ministry of Science and Technology of China. Dr. Jiang has delivered 72 keynote, plenary, and invited talks at major academic conferences and published 205 SCI-indexed journal papers.

Dr. Jiang's research interests are the mechanisms and methodologies of ultrafast laser micro/nano manufacturing.

（1）During femtosecond laser pulse irradiation, on a nanometer and femtosecond scale, localized transient changes in material properties play critical roles that classical theories fail to describe. A new plasma model with quantum treatment was proposed and developed that significantly improved the accuracy in estimating ablation depth, enabling the prediction of ablation crater shapes for the first time. Some unexpected predictions were made using the proposed model, which were later experimentally confirmed by dozens of international research groups.

(2) The two-temperature model has been widely used to study the ultrafast laser processing of metals. However, the classical two-temperature models are limited to low laser fluences, at which electron temperatures are much lower than the Fermi temperature. The full-run quantum treatment was used to establish an improved two-temperature model applicable for any electron temperature.

(3) Based on the predictions, a novel ultrafast laser micro/nano fabrication method was proposed. For the first time, localized transient electron dynamics and the corresponding material properties were actively controlled. Fabrication throughput, quality, and precision were significantly improved. For example, recast was reduced by 60%, fabrication throughput was increased by 5~56 times, and aspect ratio limit was extended by 30 times. For the first time, a multitimescale detection system was designed and developed to observe electron dynamics during ultrafast laser-material interactions, providing experimental insights for understanding and improving the novel fabrication method. The proposed method was selected to fabricate a key structure in one of the National S&T Major Projects of China. Novel fiber sensors were designed and fabricated for high-quality sensing and have since been commercialized.

青年创新奖获得者

周　　峰

周峰，1976 年 5 月出生于山东省郓城县。1997 年本科毕业于山东师范大学化学系，2004 年中科院兰州化学物理研究所获得博士学位。2005 年 4 月—2008 年 3 月于英国剑桥大学化学系做研究助理，2008 年 4 月—2013 年 4 月任中科院兰州化学物理研究所"百人计划"研究员。目前为中科院兰州化学物理研究所研究员，固体润滑国家重点实验室副主任，中国化学会会员、理事、青年工作者委员会副主任委员，甘肃省化学会副理事长，中国机械工程学会摩擦学分会润滑材料与摩擦化学专业委员会主任委员，中国科协九大代表，中国青年科技工作者协会理事。从事软物质界面与材料、仿生润滑、减阻降噪防污等研究。发表 SCI 论文 300 多篇，被引用 11000 多次，受邀作国际国内主题报告 20 多次，获得授权中国发明专利 16 件，研制的湿滑材料技术服务于十多家企业。

周峰致力于利用化学的知识解决表界面科学以及摩擦学中的关键科学问题，坚持从基础到应用的全链条研究，发展适合工程应用的减阻润滑材料。在材料表面微纳米结构构筑和化学接枝改性、润湿黏附与摩擦调控等方面做出了有国际影响的创新工作。

一、"润滑"之新解与相互关系研究

"Lubrication"翻译为"润滑"似乎不合适，汉语中的"润滑"应包含润 / 湿和滑两个方面，具有更深刻的内涵。周峰以此为问题的出发点，研究了湿和滑的关系规律，在疏水减阻和亲水润滑方面做出了系统性的创新研究工作。研究了疏水 / 油造成多种固液边界滑移的条件，创造了最高 77% 固液界面的减阻率，通过构筑响应性疏水表面实现了界面黏附和边界滑移的可逆调控；在材料表面接枝亲水性聚合物刷实现固 / 固界面超低摩擦，通过表面接枝响应性聚电解质刷对外界刺激的可逆相互作用，实现了摩擦的可逆调控。由于系统创新的研究工作，周峰受 *Adv. Mater. Interf.* 邀请撰写了首篇摩擦调控研究的综述论文，并受邀在美国摩擦与润滑工程师协会摩擦学前沿大会、国际生物摩擦学大会、国际仿生工程会议以及全国摩擦学大会作主旨或大会报告。

发展了刷型修饰的超高强度水凝胶材料、球刷型润滑材料，发明了光固化水润滑涂层，应用于导管润滑；将含离子液体官能团聚合物用于生物污损防治，并与湿、滑、软、动的仿生理念相结合开发了具有自主知识产权的三类高性能海洋低毒防污涂料，在我国沿海和英国南安普顿进行了长期的实海挂片实验，并于 2013 年起对海洋防污涂层和防腐涂层等多项技术进行了转化生产，取得了良好的经济效益。

二、工程材料表面的润湿及其调控研究

通过揭示自然表面特殊润湿和粘附性原理以及微纳米制造和表面改性技术，构筑了多种超疏液体功能化的表面。总结了特殊润湿材料应用的瓶颈问题，提出"超疏水工程材料"概念，将特殊润湿性现象的研究进一步引向应用，被 *Nature* 作为亮点进行了报道。通过将工程材料表面微纳米形貌调控与表面化学修饰相结合，对微纳米结构化铝合金表面进行氟化物或者疏水聚合物的修饰，获得超疏水性表面，为超疏水工程材料迈向工业应用提供了坚实的基础。在该领域进行了系统的研究工作，发展了在多种工程材料表面获得超疏水、超疏油表面的方法，奠定了工程材料表面润湿黏附行为调控的理论基础；发展了一系列创新性的、适合工程化的表面微纳米结构改性方法，实现了微纳米结构的可控构筑。研究发展了空间润滑油爬行屏障界面材料、流体减阻材料、防结冰材料以及抗油黏附界面材料，与航天科技集团、中国中车集团、中广核等建立了合作关系，开展技术服务。研究工作在 *Adv. Mater.*、*Adv. Funct. Mater.* 等共发表论文 60 多篇，申请中国发明专利 11 件，已获授权 8 件。

三、利用界面组装、表面接枝聚合物刷实现多种工程材料表面的化学修饰

对于自组装界面尤其是聚合物刷界面进行了系统的基础研究，发展了针对各种基材、多种功能的通用表面修饰方法；首次发展了微接触印刷和表面引发聚合相结合制备多元组分图案化表面的方法；利用自组装单分子技术，结合新型组装化学进展，针对不同的工程材料发展了多种聚合物表面接枝技术，对几乎所有材料表面实现了功能化修饰。通过电化学、光化学诱导以及牺牲阳极技术，发展了系列表面引发 ATRP 方法，解决了 ATRP 聚合需要惰性气氛保护、可控性差、单体难于回收利用的难题，产生了重要的国际影响。受英国皇家化学会会刊 *Chemical Society Reviews* 和 *Account of Chemical Research* 的邀请撰写多篇评述论文，共发表研究论文 80 多篇。

四、从离子液体到自约束超分子凝胶润滑剂

致力于将物理化学的知识应用于新型润滑剂的开发。利用界面相互作用的原理理解润滑油及添加剂的作用机制，对于进一步指导分子设计与油品、添加剂/配伍的筛选有重要科学意义。提出离子液体不同于非极性润滑油品的动态作用机理，该研究首次提出了

离子液体润滑剂边界润滑条件下的界面作用机制——偶极作用导致的界面组装，并以此发展了多种功能性的离子液体润滑剂。

创造性地将化学自组装理念用于润滑剂的设计制备，发展了介于润滑油和润滑脂之间的一类中间状态的新型超分子凝胶润滑剂。该润滑剂有望解决润滑油密封难、易爬移以及润滑脂分油的问题，为目前国际上唯一从事这方面研究的课题组。结果在摩擦学专业期刊 *Wear*、*Tribology Letters*、*Tribology International* 以及化学综合期刊 *ChemCommun* 等杂志发表 60 多篇研究论文，其中发表于 *ChemSocRev* 的文章为离子液体润滑剂的首篇综述性文章，产生了重要的国际影响。已授权国家发明专利 6 件。

周峰共培养或联合培养研究生 50 多人，其中 4 人晋升为研究员、1 人获得优青资助、4 人次获得国家奖学金。其个人曾获得 2009 年中国机械工程学会摩擦学分会摩擦学青年学者奖，2011 年中国化学会"青年化学奖"和国家杰出青年基金，2012 年中组部"国家特支计划"的"青年拔尖人才计划"，2013 年国际仿生工程学会"杰出青年奖"，2014 年甘肃省自然科学一等奖（排名第一），2015 年国家自然科学二等奖（排名第一），2016 年第十四届"中国青年科技奖"、首届"中国优秀青年科技人才奖"和英国皇家工程院杰出访问学者"Distinguished Visiting Fellowship"，2017 年科技部中青年科技创新领军人才及中国科学院第十二届"杰出青年"。

Awardee of Youth Innovation Prize, Zhou Feng

Zhou Feng was born in Yuncheng County of Shandong Province in May 1976. In 1997, he graduated from the Shandong Normal University, Department of Chemistry. In 2004, he received a doctorate from Lanzhou Institute of Chemical Physics (LICP), Chinese Academy of Sciences (CAS). From April 2005 to March 2008, he stayed in University of Cambridge, UK, as a research assistant. From April 2008 to April 2013, he took the position as "Hundred Talents Program" researcher in LICP, CAS. Currently he is a research professor and deputy director of the State Key Laboratory of solid lubrication, LICP, CAS. He is vice chairman of Chinese Tribology Institution, Chinese Mechanical Engineering Society.

Zhou Feng works on surface science and new understanding of wetting, adhesion and lubrication, and the development of drag reduction and lubricating materials. He innovated surface modification methods, which includes the generalized surface modification method for a variety of substrates, multi-component patterned surfaces, electrochemical, photochemical and sacrificial anode technology based ATRP. He proposed the concept of superwetting engineering materials and its control. Various super-hydrophobic and super-oil-repellent surface engineering materials were developed. He put forward new insights into "lubrication" and the research on the r̶ ship between wetting and lubrication. The lubrication in Chinese should include two aspects wet and Creatively, the awardee introduced the supra molecular assembly concept for the design of lubrican̶ developed a new types of supramolecular gel lubricants assuming intermediate state in between lu̶ ing oils and greases, which are expected to solve the lubricating oil seal problem, as well as oil ration problem in greases. Zhou Feng published more than 300 SCI papers and was invited as a note and plenary speaker more than 20 times at international conferences. He was granted more th 16 China's invention patents that are serving for more than 10 enterprises.

Zhou Feng has won Tribology Young Scholar Award in 2009; the National Natural Scienc Award (ranked first) in 2015; the 14th "China Youth Science and Technology Award" and the first "China outstanding young science and technology talent award" in 2016; the "Distinguished Visiting Fellowship" of British Royal Academy of Engineering in 2016. Supervised more than 50 postgraduate students, 4 were promoted to professors, one received excellent youth funding from NSFC, 4 graduate students won the national scholarship.

青年创新奖获得者

郑 海 荣

郑海荣，1977 年 11 月出生于安徽省长丰县。2000 年毕业于哈尔滨工业大学，2006 年毕业于美国科罗拉多大学机械工程系获博士学位，2006 年 5 月—2007 年 9 月在美国加州大学戴维斯分校先后任博士后、项目科学家。2007 年 9 月回国至今，在中国科学院深圳先进技术研究院任职，历任副研究员、研究员、医工所所长、副院长。主要从事医学成像物理、技术与仪器研发，在相关超声物理与成像、磁共振成像、图像处理及仪器方面的研究成果在国际学术期刊上发表论文 110 余篇，获得发明专利 60 余项，受邀作国内外学术报告 80 余次。担任 *IEEE Transaction on UFFC* 副编辑、*Ultrasound in Medicine and Biology* 编委、*Physics in Medicine and Biology* 编委、IEEE 高级会员，国家重大科研仪器研制专家委员会委员（2013—2019）、中国超声医学工程学会仪器开发专业委员会副主任委员、中国生物医学工程学会常务理事/青年工作委员会主任、国家重大科研仪器研制专家委员会委员等，为国家杰出青年基金获得者、"973" 项目首席科学家。

郑海荣主要研究领域是超声成像技术与医学成像仪器，在超声辐射力领域发展了一套理论和方法，同时与工程技术密切结合发明了新型超声及快速磁共振成像医疗仪器并得到推广，取得了一系列学术和研究成果。

一、超声辐射力理论与剪切波弹性成像技术设备

提出并实现基于时域有限差分方法计算声辐射力，为面向复杂声场环境的声辐射力研究提供了有效工具，在实验上实现了微观/宏观三维空间对微粒的可编程操控。针对经典散射波理论仅能处理理想情况下柱状、球形散射体在平面波、驻波、Bessel 束等理想声源中所受声辐射力的局限，基于时域有限差分法结合动量张量理论，创建了精确计算复杂声场环境下生物组织所受声辐射力的方法，掌握了声辐射力诱导剪切波的机理与控制方法，解决了剪切波与生物组织微形变控制及其生物力学特性量化关系的核心问题。

（1）1D 剪切波弹性成像肝硬化检测仪。开展了一维超声瞬态弹性成像方法研究，自主研发了我国第一套基于剪切波的超声瞬时弹性成像系统并成功实现转化。建立了基于组织硬度信息的无创早期肝纤维化和肝硬化量化分级评估方法，实现了高灵敏大深度测量新技术，被中华医学会《慢性乙型肝炎防治指南》、欧洲生物医学超声学会联盟发布的《肝脏超声弹性成像临床应用指南》推荐使用。

（2）2D 剪切波彩色弹性成像设备。研发出基于声辐射力的二维超声弹性成像系统，同时与医疗结构合作开展了超声弹性图像信息与病理诊断结果关系的研究，解决了乳腺和甲状腺肿瘤病变等临床精确诊断中的瓶颈问题，形成美国发明专利 1 项，该设备对生物组织硬度的测量精度达到国际领先水平。该技术通过与公司合作形成了第 4 代弹性彩超技术（从黑白 B 超、彩超、造影成像前三代）并实现产业化，此外对于肝硬化、乳腺癌、甲状腺、肌骨、前列腺等部位检查具有重要的医学诊断价值。

从理论上提出并在实验中实现了设计结构声场（声子晶体板）精确筛选微粒的方法。在理论上，通过时域有限差分方法研究了微粒在声子晶体板表面受到的声辐射力，获得可以选择性吸附筛选微颗粒的优化声场，并在实验上实现利用"声筛"结构声场精确"筛选"不同粒径微粒。提出了基于 20 ~ 40MHz 声表面器件耦合微流控芯片的操控技术，实现了声表面芯片—微流道内超声造影剂微泡群和细胞群二维空间内的排列、聚集和定点移动等可编程操控；并以经典模式生物秀丽隐杆线虫（线虫）作为研究对象，发明了一种对超声神经刺激研究具有重要用途的新型超声神经刺激芯片。

二、超声辐射力无创神经调控及深部脑刺激仪器

基于超声波作为一种机械波在特定声学条件下能控制神经元电活动的新原理，开展了超声神经调控研究与仪器研制（国家自然科学基金委重大科研仪器研制项目"基于超声辐射力的深部脑刺激与神经调控仪器研制"）。基于超声辐射力与神经元作用诱发离子通道的开启，实现了对于神经元放电的控制新原理，研制了超声神经调仪器。在国际上率先研制成功了由 3072 阵元 1MHz 面阵超声辐射力发生器等一系列核心部件组成的新型仪器系统，可以实现对非人灵长类动物跨颅骨 5 ~ 10 厘米多核团动态刺激，从而对大脑深部及脑内全空间神经开展无创精准的刺激与调控。实验上初步实现了超声无创神经调控在非人灵长类动物、小鼠、线虫的神经调控能力。该仪器的研制具有重大科学价值和医学价值，相关核心技术未来转化为新型无创超声脑疾病治疗仪器，将有望给大脑及神经精神疾病患者带来福音。

三、3.0 Tesla 快速超导人体磁共振 MR 成像技术与设备

自 2010 年以来，带领团队与联影公司开展深入技术合作，围绕高场 MRI 技术开展紧密合作，攻克梯度、射频、控制和高级成像方法等关键技术，已经转化 30 多项发明专利，并在联影磁共振系统上开发完成了一系列高端应用技术，包括心血管成像中核心的成像序列 bSSFP（平衡稳态自由进动序列）、快速心脏磁共振成像、快速水脂分离和脂肪定量技术、全脑血管壁成像技术 DANTE-MATRIX、云重建系统等。2015 年，成功研制联影 3.0 Tesla 人体快速超导磁共振成像仪，获得国家医疗器械注册证，已经应用到全国 50 多家医院，实现了我国高端医学影像设备的重大突破，打破了国外公司对我国高端影像产品市场的垄断。

四、团队建设及获奖情况

自 2007 年以来，郑海荣主持组建以诺贝尔奖获得者命名的研究单元——劳特伯生物医学成像研究中心，建成了国家发改委国家地方联合高端医学影像技术与装备工程实验室。他带领的医学成像技术与仪器研究团队已形成 150 余人的规模，促进了一批新型生物医学技术的创新和医学转化应用。在其带领和指导下，涌现了一批 80 后副研究员和正研究员，其中多人成长为国家优青、国家重大课题负责人、广东省特支人才、深圳市领军人才及孔雀人才。

郑海荣还同时担任广东省海外留学青年联谊会副会长、广东省青联委员和中科院青联常委，潜心投身创新、服务广大青年科技创新。其个人先后获 2017 年首届全国"创新争先"奖状、2017 国家技术发明二等奖（排名第一）、国家"万人计划"领军人才、2014 年陈嘉庚青年科学奖（技术科学奖）、"广东特支计划"杰出人才（南粤百杰）、中国产学研合作创新与促进奖、中国科学院科技促进发展奖、广东省科学技术一等奖（第一发明人）、深圳市技术发明一等奖（第一发明人）、中国科学院科技促进发展奖等。

Awardee of Youth Innovation Prize,
Zheng Hairong

Zheng Hairong was born in Changfeng County of Anhui Province in November 1977. He received his Ph.D from University of Colorado at Boulder in 2006 and now professor and deputy director of Shenzhen Institutes of Advanced Technology（SIAT）, Chinese Academy of Sciences. He is the founding director of the Paul C. Lauterbur Research Center for Biomedical Imaging. In the past 15 years, Dr. Zheng focus on developing novel acoustic radiation force based multifunctional Ultrasonic technology and system for Imaging/Drug Delivery and neuromodulation, and latterly involved in developing fast high field magnetic resonance imaging system. He invented three biomedical ultrasound instruments, includes 2D ultrasonic particle image velocimetry using of high frame ultrasound imaging technique to track microbubbles within blood flow capable of obtaining 2D/3D velocity vectors and shear stress; invented 2D/3D acoustic manipulation system for tracking cells or particles. 1D/2D superfast shear wave elastography imaging using ultrasonic radiation force to induced deformation and elastic measurement for liver fibrosis and breast cancer diagnosis. The elastography technology has been commercialized and used for thousand hospitals around the world. Dr.Zheng has also developed MR guided 3072-elements ultrasonic neuromodulation systems for non-human primates, providing a non-invasive, dynamic deep brain stimulation tool for neuroscience research and clinical therapy.

He was the invited speaker for the IEEE Ultrasonics Symposium in 2008 and 2016.He has published more than 140 peer-reviewed journal papers, and owned more than 60 Ultrasound/MRI related patents in his research. He received NSF National Outstanding Young Scientist Award and National innovation award of China, and NSFC, respectively in 2013 and 2017. Dr. Zheng has also served as the editorial board member for *Ultrasound in Medicine and Biology* and *Physics in Medicine and Biology*. He is also the associate editor of *IEEE Transactions on UFFC* and the chairman of IEEE EMBS Shenzhen Chapter.

产业创新奖获得者

陈 山 枝

陈山枝，1969 年 2 月出生于浙江省临海市。1997 年毕业于北京邮电大学通信与信息系统专业获工学博士学位。1996 年在比利时安特卫普 Alcatel-Bell 研究中心做访问学者，开展宽带交换合作研究。1997—2001 年任大唐高鸿公司副总工程师、总工程师；2002—2003 年任大唐电信科技股份有限公司副总工程师；2004 年至今在电信科学技术研究院暨大唐电信科技产业集团工作，任副总工程师、总工程师、技术与产品委员会主任，无线移动通信国家重点实验室副主任、主任；2009 年 12 月起任电信科学技术研究院副院长。中国电子学会会士，中国通信学会会士，工信部通信科技委常委，国家杰出青年科学基金获得者，"新世纪百千万人才工程"国家级人选，政府特殊津贴专家。曾任国家"863"计划信息领域专家（1999—2011）、国家科技重大专项三编制专家组成员等。担任 *IEEE Network*、*IEEE Internet of Things Journal*、*China Communications*、《通信学报》等编委。主持完成国家 03 重大科技专项、国家"863"计划、国家自然科学基金委员会等国家级科研项目十余项。

陈山枝长期从事通信理论与技术研究、标准和设备研发，包括宽带交换技术、4G TD-LTE 核心技术和 5G 前沿技术等，是我国宽带高速移动通信领域的技术带头人之一，为 TD-LTE 成为具有国际竞争力的 4G 标准、实现 4G 并跑和 5G 引领国家战略做出了一系列开创性工作和重要贡献。

（1）针对空间复用和波束赋形结合等难题，提出多流波束赋形技术，充分利用 TDD 信道互易性的优势，成为 4G TD-LTE 国际标准的三大标志性核心技术之一。目前，4G TD-LTE 已被中、美、日、韩等 46 个国家 85 家运营商采用，发展了 8.7 亿 TD-LTE 用户，占全球 4G 用户总数的 54%。主持制定大唐基站和芯片等产品的总体技术方案和演进路标，带领团队研制的基站、芯片、仪表等经济效益超 200 亿元，为实现我国主导的 4G TD-LTE 核心技术突破、国际标准制定及提升行业国际竞争力做出了突出贡献。基于 4G 多流波束赋形技术，进一步扩展波束的数量和维度，提出基于 TDD 的大规模天线波束赋形技术，提升 5G 频谱效率 10 倍以上，成为解决 5G 重大挑战的核心技术之一。主持 5G 关键技术验证、样机开发和现场试验，2016 年 4 月在全球首发规模最大的 256 天线阵列，并通过了中国 5G 技术研发试验第一阶段测试，为我国"5G 引领"做出了重要贡献。

（2）针对传统移动性管理存在的功能冗余、系统复杂、性能低下等问题，提出移动性管理理论模型和移动驱动网络（MDN）。应对各种复杂通信应用环境的挑战，提出了高速运动场景、密集无线网络及动态环境下无线自组织网络等移动性管理技术。针对时速高于 350 千米运动场景下（如高铁）的通话差、上网难等问题，提出高速运动场景下无缝覆盖和切换方法，有效解决了 TDD 高速移动通信的工程难题。2008 年首次实现了最高时速 431 千米铁路（上海磁悬浮沿线）的宽带无线移动通信，处于国际领先水平。针对无基础设施网络拓扑变化快、连通性差的难题，提出了动态时变环境下无线自组织网络技术，成为 LTE-V 车联网国际标准核心技术，LTE-V 成为 IEEE 802.11p 的有力竞争者，达到国际领先水平。提出异构融合网络环境下多连接智能协同通信技术，主导制定国际电信联盟（ITU）Y.2609 等系列国际标准。研究成果成功应用在 4G 商用网络及我国高铁宽带移动通信覆盖、智能网联汽车示范区等，有力地支撑了行业信息化跨越式发展，推动了行业进步。

（3）提出多优先级控制高速交换矩阵技术、移动异构组网与网络柔性重组自愈方法，解决了多业务多协议的优先级交换与控制、异构快速协同组网等难题。主持研制宽带多业务接入交换机、现场宽带应急通信系统，应用在宽带数据网、汶川地震、新疆"7.5"事件等，为我国抗震救灾、反恐等做出了重要贡献，社会效益显著。

研究成果在 *IEEE Communications Magazine*、*IEEE Wireless Communications*、*IEEE IoT Journal*、*IEEE Network* 和 *IEEE TVT* 等国际顶级学术期刊上发表 SCI 收录论文 45 篇。最近 4 年发表的论文中，有 2 篇论文入选 ESI 高被引论文；8 篇学术论文在 IEEE Xplore 下载量排名前列，其中 1 篇论文在 IEEE Xplore 逾 400 万在线论文中月下载量多次排在前 30 名，另外 7 篇 IEEE 论文分别在其发表期刊的月下载量多次排在前 50 名。相关成果在 4G 和 5G 研究方向上引起国际同行的高度关注，产生了重要的国际学术影响力。

出版学术专著 5 部（其中英文 3 部），国际著名学术出版机构斯普林格在其网站上高度评价《Mobility Management：Principle，Technology and Applications》是第一本将移动性管理作为单独技术进行系统阐述的专著，创造性地提出了移动性管理参考模型;《User-Centric Ultra-Dense Networks for 5G》是第一本在 5G 中引入以用户为中心的超密集网络的专著，提出"去蜂窝"和"以用户为中心"的创新理念。

主导制定国际标准 11 项，申请发明专利 45 项，其中已授权发明专利 21 项，部分写入 3GPP 和 ITU 国际标准，成为标准必要专利，成功应用在全球 4G 商用网络及我国高铁通信覆盖、大型场馆及火车站等热点通信区域等。

分别获 2016 年度国家科学技术进步特等奖（排名第四）、2015 年度国家技术发明二等奖（排名第一）、2012 年度国家科技进步奖一等奖（排名第四）、2012 年度中国工程院光华工程科技奖青年奖、2001 年度国家科学技术进步奖二等奖（排名第三）和 2012 年度中国通信学会科学技术一等奖（排名第一）。

担任国家重点实验室主任，北京邮电大学、北京理工大学、北京交通大学等高校兼职教授及博士生导师，在无线移动通信方向长期坚持自主创新和国产化，带出了一支具有创新活力和国际影响力的科研团队，其中一名年轻专家成为 ITU 5G 技术评估组主席。培养博士生 25 名，指导博士后 3 名，部分已成为国际标准组织的工作组副组长、技术报告人等。

Awardee of Industrial Innovation Prize, Chen Shanzhi

Chen Shanzhi was born in Linhai City of Zhejiang Province in February 1969. He received his Ph.D. in 1997. Then he joined China Academy of Telecommunications Technology（CATT）and Datang Telecom Technology & Industry Group. Since 2004, he has been CTO, Director of State Key Lab of Wireless Mobile Telecommunications. Besides, he serves as Fellow respectively of The Chinese Institute of Electronics（CIE）, China Institute of Communications（CIC）. He received National Natural Science Foundation of China for Distinguished Young Scholars. Dr. Chen was an expert in Information fields of the National High-Tech R&D（863）Program during 1999—2011 and an expert of the National Science and Technology Major Projects for the New Generation of Broadband Wireless Communication Networks. He used to work as editorial board member of *IEEE Network*, *IEEE Internet of Things Journal*, *China Communications*, *Journal on Communications*.

Dr. Chen has been long engaged in research and development on communication standards and equipment, including broadband switching technology, 4G TD-LTE core technology and 5G cutting-edge technology. He proposed multi-layer beamforming technology, mobility management techniques of high speed movement scenes for 4G, and TDD-based massive beamforming technology, User-Centric Ultra-Dense Networks（UUDN）, Pattern Division Multiple Access（PDMA）for 5G. He did a series of path breaking jobs and made significant contribution to the realization of TD-LTE as international 4G standard and the national strategies of China such as "Peer role in 4G" and "Leading role in 5G", and is hence considered as one of China's broadband mobile communications technology leaders.

Dr. Chen's fruitful results have brought forth 45 papers indexed by SCI and published in top international academic journals including *IEEE Communications Magazine*, *IEEE Wireless Communications*, *IEEE Network*, *IEEE IoT Journal*. Among the papers published in the last 4 years, 2 paper was included by ESI Highly Cited Papers, and 8 papers rank among the top 100 most downloaded IEEE Xplore articles. He has attracted high attention from international peers in the research direction of 4G and 5G, and had major international academic impact.

Dr. Chen has published 5 academic books (3 in English). Dr. Chen has led the formulation of 11 international standards, applied for 45 invention patents among which 21 authorized. Some of the patents were written into 3GPP and ITU international standards, taken as essential IP for standards.

Dr. Chen received several awards for his outstanding contribution, including Grand prize of National Science and Technology Progress in 2016, Second prize of National Technical Invention in 2015, First prize of National Science and Technology Progress Award in 2012, Youth Award of Guanghua Engineering Science and technology Award in 2012, Second prize of National Science and Technology Progress Award in 2001.

产业创新奖获得者

冯仲科

冯仲科，1962 年 5 月出生于甘肃省灵台县。1979 年 9 月—1983 年 7 月在西安矿业学院矿山测量专业学习，毕业后在北京煤炭工业学校、首钢工学院任教。1997 年 9 月调入北京林业大学任教，期间在职攻读博士学位，成为我国第一位森林 GPS 应用研究博士学位获得者。曾应邀到德国弗赖堡大学林学院进行林业 GPS 技术与学术交流。现为北京林业大学测绘与 3S 技术二级教授、博士、博士生导师，地理信息学科负责人、学术带头人、专业负责人，北京林业大学测绘与 3S 技术中心主任，精准林业北京市重点实验室主任，空间信息智能感知国家测绘地理信息局工程技术研究中心主任。

冯仲科任中国地理信息产业协会副秘书长，精准农林业工作委员会主任委员，中国 GPS 应用研究会常务理事，中国测绘学会理事，矿山测量专业委员会副主任委员，中国博士联谊会常务理事，国际矿山测量协会（ISM）第六专业委员会副秘书长，北京测绘学会副理事长，测绘教学研究委员会副主任委员，国家测绘局全国测绘学科指导委员会委员，中国林学会青年工作委员会常委，中国农学会信息学会理事，《北京林业大学学报》副主编，国际测绘杂志 GIM 编委，NREE 杂志主编，Frontiers of Forestry in China、《测绘科学》《农业工程学报》《地理信息世界》《矿山测量》《北京测绘》编委，国家自然科学基金委、国家科技进步奖、北京市自然科学基金、教育部留学基金、北京市科学技术奖评审专家。北京市精品教材《测量学》主编，北京市精品课程《测量学》负责人。科技北京百名领军人才，北京市高等学校优秀青年骨干教师，北京市有突出贡献专家，新世纪国家百千万人才计划国家级人选，北京市农业科技先进个人，北京地区产学研先进个人，首都绿化美化积极分子，中国林业青年科技奖获得者，享受国务院政府特殊津贴。入选济南市客座专业技术拔尖人才、龙江学者奖励计划特聘教授、泰山学者奖励计划特聘专家。俄罗斯自然科学院外籍院士。黑龙江省杰出青年基金获得者，首届中国高校十大 GIS 创新人物奖，首届中国地理信息产业十名杰出人才，全国生态建设突出贡献者，中国绿色新闻十佳人物奖，海峡两岸林业敬业奖，何梁何利科学技术创新奖，北京市优秀教师获得者。

冯仲科多年来主持国家自然科学基金、国家"863"计划、北京市自然科学基金重点项目等20余项；研制中国第一台产业化精密测量型GPS、第一个电子角规、第一台林用视频超站仪，开发软件平台；发表SCI、EI、ISTP收录论文200余篇，授权发明专利50件、实用新型专利4件，软件著作权200余件，荣获国家技术发明二等奖、科技进步奖二等奖及北京市科学技术、省部级科学技术一、二、三等奖近20余项，主讲测量学、3S技术等本硕博课程5门，出版教材和专著9部。

（1）发明测树全站仪，可以在十分钟内花20元成本自动、精准测定一颗活立木的材积。传统方法则通过伐倒、打枝、锯开、运输和树干解析来完成，每棵树平均花三天时间，直接成本1000～3000元，这项破坏性实验在全国每年仅校正材积表就要伐倒约30万棵树。与测树全站仪配套的国家一类样地自动精测、造林决策软件平台、野生动物保护平台、林火管理等都在国家森林资源管理中发挥了重要作用。

（2）发明集测角MEMS、测距EDM野外测树信息自动采集处理于一体的电子测树枪，配合具有软件著作权的近景摄影测树、无人机航摄森林、卫星遥感监测等平台已广泛应用于国家森林资源一类调查、省县二类调查和林场企业三类调查，通过挖掘森林知识实现造林决策，已使各类调查精度提高5%～10%，功效提高1～3倍。

25年来与我国最大的测绘仪器公司南方测绘集团技术合作，主持设计研发的超站仪、电子经纬仪、GPS接收机和CASS软件近年产值超过20亿元人民币，出口产值2亿人民币，使我国从一个依赖进口测绘仪器的大国成长为仪器出口的强国。

冯仲科为我国电子测绘仪器研制与软件开发、矿山仪器防爆、精准林业装备与平台建设、森林环境空间效应与信息化可视表达做出了创造性的科技贡献。

Awardee of Industrial Innovation Prize, Feng Zhongke

Feng Zhongke was born in Lingtai County of Gansu Province in May 1962, the Surveying and Mapping and 3S Technology Professor of Beijing Forestry University with PhD degree. At present holding the office of doctoral supervisor, head of Geographic Information Science, academic leader, director of surveying and mapping and 3S technology center in Beijing Forestry University. Director of Beijing Key Laboratory of Precision Forestry, engineering and technology research center director of National Geographic Information Bureau.

1. Learning and working experience

From September 1979 to July 1983, learned in Mining survey specialty of Xi'an Mining

College; After graduation, taught measurements at the Beijing coal industry school and Shougang Institute of Technology; in September 1997 transferred to Beijing Forestry University to teach, during the period, studied for a doctorate, became the first Ph. D gainer in forest GPS application research in China; Attended the master's degree in advanced studies in China University of Mining and Technology, and invited to forestry GPS technology and academic exchange at the Freiburg University

2. Academic part—time and honorary title

Deputy Secretary—General of China Association for Geographic Information Society, Chairman of the Precision Agriculture and Forestry Committee, Director of China Surveying and Mapping academy. The Expert Reviewer of National Natural Science Foundation of China, Chinese forestry Youth Science and Technology Award winner, the enjoyment of the State Council special government allowance. Selected professor of Longjiang Scholar Award program, distinguished scholar of Taishan Scholar Award Scheme. The first Chinese university top—ten GIS Innovation Award, the geographic information industry China top—ten outstanding talent, the national outstanding contributions to ecological construction, Green news top—ten characters Award in China.

3. Achievements in scientific research

In recent years, Feng Zhongke has presided over the National Natural Science Foundation of China, the National 863 program, and the Beijing Natural Science Foundation of China, with more than 20 projects; He developed the first industrial precise measurement type of GPS in China, the first electronic angle gauge, the first super station instrument with video in forestry; Published SCI, EI, ISTP included more than 200 papers, 50 invention patents and 4 Utility model patents have be authorized; Owned more than 200 software copyrights; Won the second prize of national technology invention award, national scientific and technological progress award second prize and Beijing science and technology award, provincial and ministerial level science and technology award with first, second and third prize for more than 20 items and published 9 books.

Professor Feng has made creative contribution to the development of electronic surveying and mapping instruments, software development, the explosion of mine equipment, the construction of precision forestry equipment and platform, the spatial effect of forest environment and the visualization of informatization in China.

产业创新奖获得者

郭　姣

郭姣，女，1961年11月出生于江西省九江市。1984年毕业于江西中医学院中医学专业，其后于广州中医药大学和第一军医大学（现南方医科大学）获中医诊断学硕士学位和中西医结合临床博士学位。1990年起在广东药学院任教，1997—2001年为香港大学兼职副教授，2001年任广东药学院教授、主任医师，2006年6月任广东药学院副校长，2009年起兼任广东省妇联副主席，2010年6月任广州中医药大学副校长，2013年4月任广东药科大学党委副书记兼纪委书记，2014年4月起任广东药科大学校长。

郭姣为国家中医药管理局中西医结合基础重点学科和广东省中西医结合攀峰重点学科带头人，教育部糖脂代谢病粤港澳联合实验室主任，广东省代谢病中西医结合研究中心主任，国家中医药管理局高脂血症"调肝降脂"重点研究室及脂代谢三级实验室主任，中医诊疗模式创新试点单位学术带头人，全国综合性医院中医示范单位学术带头人，中国中西医结合学会副会长，世界中医药学会联合会代谢病专业委员会会长，粤港澳医药产业协同创新联盟理事会理事长等。三十多年来，带领学术团队在代谢性疾病防治领域取得了突出的创新性研究成果。

一、首提中西医结合"糖脂代谢病"新理论及综合一体化防控策略，极大地提高了代谢病防治水平

郭姣在长期的临床实践和科学研究中发现，代谢病患者常高血糖、高血脂等多种代谢紊乱并存。2008年率团队开展了多中心临床调研，发现高脂血症合并糖尿病、高血压等其他疾病者占84.2%；2012年中国2型糖尿病患者心血管疾病危险因素——血压、血脂、血糖的全国评估研究（CCMR-3B）也表明2型糖尿病患者伴发高血压、血脂异常者占72%。

基于此，郭姣率先提出"糖脂代谢病"理论，创新性地将高脂血症、糖尿病、脂肪

肝、动脉硬化性心脑血管病等作为整体认识和治疗；认为"神经—内分泌—免疫轴紊乱、胰岛素抵抗、慢性炎症、肠道菌群失调"为其核心病机；首提"枢纽肝代谢稳态调节系统"概念及综合一体化防控策略，制定"调肝启枢化浊"治法和方药，形成中西医结合多学科综合诊疗新模式。多中心 RCT 研究表明，总有效率高达 90%，药占比下降 12.3%。获国内外同行认可，形成"世界中医药学会联合会糖脂代谢病综合防控专家共识"。成为国家中医药管理局唯一以创新理论命名的"调肝降脂"重点研究室和中医诊疗模式创新试点单位。被全国高等医药院校规划教材《中医药学概论》《健康管理学》等收录和推广应用。

二、研发系列调肝启枢化浊创新药物，开创药物研发新模式

目前，糖脂代谢病的主流药物是化学药，其作用机理清楚、起效迅速，但存在作用靶点相对单一、肝肾损害、停药易反跳等弊端；而中成药市场份额不足 15%，同时因作用机制不清、物质基础不明、疗效不稳、对病因病机认识未能跟上疾病谱的改变等因素制约了中医药整体观、多靶点等特色和优势的发挥。

郭姣在其创新理论指导下建立了"理论—临床—药效—机制—药学—临床"创新中药系统研发模式，阐明其物质基础与作用机制。研制了以"复方贞术调脂胶囊"（FTZ）为代表的创新中药 6 个，获国家、PCT、欧美发明专利授权 17 项，单项专利授权转让 1780 万元。运用网络药理学、高通量筛选、系统生物学等前沿技术手段，从整体、器官 / 组织、细胞、分子多层次、多水平、多环节阐明 FTZ 等创新中药多靶点、整体、异病同治的作用优势与特色。发现创新中药能同时作用于相关代谢酶、受体及转录调节因子等，综合调节糖、脂的吸收、转运、转化、代谢、排泄全过程，兼具降糖、调脂、抗炎、保护血管内皮、抗脂肪肝、抗动脉粥样硬化等作用，实现了药效媲美主流化学药、综合作用更优的突破，还克服了化学药肝肾损害、停药后反跳等不足。获中国专利优秀奖。研究成果发表在传统医学、代谢病领域国际主流期刊上，学术影响广泛。

二次开发脑心清片、绞股蓝总甙片等 3 个品种，并在全国 203 家三甲医院推广应用，累计新增销售额达 16.1 亿元，开辟了糖脂代谢病综合防治新途径，为中药现代化、国际化提供了新的发展模式。专家鉴定其"理论创新和对中药复方的系统研究达到同类研究国际先进水平"。

三、建立国家级、省部级高水平国际化平台，对中医药产业发展产生了积极的示范效应

创建了多种降糖、降脂、抗动脉粥样硬化等关键技术体系，制定 SOP 200 余项，领衔创建教育部糖脂代谢病粤港澳联合实验室，国家中医药管理局高脂血症"调肝降脂"重点研究室、脂代谢三级实验室，广东省代谢病中西医结合研究中心，中英代谢病国际合作基地，广东省代谢性疾病中医药防治重点实验室等高水平平台 8 个，成为华南地区

该领域标志性平台，引领与辐射作用明显。

依托该平台，首次发现调节糖脂代谢新脂肪激素 A–FABP 促进棕色脂肪适应性产热新机制，拓宽了糖脂代谢病防治路径；首次发现胰岛素抵抗对脂肪和 AT1 信号的非依赖性，拓展了防治糖脂代谢病研究思路；首次发现高胆固醇加速维生素 D2 诱发血管钙化新机制，影响了美国国民的饮食方式，处国际领先水平。论文被权威期刊 *Nature Communications*、*Pharmacological Reviews* 等引用 700 余次，国际影响显著。

培养南粤百杰、珠江学者、珠江新星、研究生等人才 100 余人次。主持编写《华南现代中药城项目建议书》，有效促进了中山市健康产业发展，2016 年华南现代中药城产值达 50 亿元，2016 年中山国家健康医药产业园产值达 500 亿元。校内建有医药高校第一个国家级科技企业孵化器，共孵化企业 160 家，累计注册资本 36 亿元。

以第一完成人先后获国家科技进步奖二等奖、首届全国创新争先奖、何梁何利奖、中国专利优秀奖、吴阶平医药创新奖（中医药界首位）、中华中医药学会科技进步一等奖、广东省科技进步一等奖（2 项，2008 年、2012 年）、广东省丁颖科技奖等科技奖励 9 项；并获全国优秀科技工作者、国务院特殊津贴专家、全国"三八"红旗手、国家卫生计生突出贡献中青年专家、中华中医药科技之星、"南粤百杰"等荣誉。被《人民日报》《中国中医药报》《名医》等媒体报道，成为《中国科技成果》封面人物。

Awardee of Industrial Innovation Prize, Guo Jiao

Guo Jiao, female, was born in Jiujiang City of Jiangxi Province in November 1961. She got her TCM bachelor degree from Jiangxi Chinese Medicine University. Later, she furthered her study in TCM Diagnostics and obtained her master degree from Guangzhou University of Chinese Medicine (GZUCM). After that, she continued her academic training in Integration of Chinese and Western Medicine until she was awarded doctor degree by Southern Medical University.

Guo Jiao has devoted herself to teaching, scientific research and industrialization of integrated Chinese and Western medicine and TCM for more than 30 years. She has taken charge of more than 20 national scientific projects, and has won 9 scientific awards on national and provincial levels.

1. She first put forward the new theory of "gluco–lipid metabolic disease (GLMD)"

Prof. Guo first put forward the new theory–GLMD, innovatively took hyperlipidemia, diabetes, fatty liver, arteriosclerosis, cardiovascular diseases as a whole to recognize and treat. ① She held that the disorder of neuro–endocrine–immune axis, insulin resistance, inflammation and disturbance of intestinal flora are the core pathogenesis of GLDM. ② She first proposed the concept of "Liver–based Regulatory System for Metabolism Homeostasis" and formulated the therapy of Tiao Gan, Qi Shu, Hua Zhuo.

2. She has developed a series of innovative drugs with the function of Tiao Gan, Qi Shu, Hua Zhuo

She developed 6 innovative Chinese Medicine agents which have achieved comparable efficacy and better comprehensive function but overcome the drawbacks of liver and kidney damage and the rebound of mainstream chemical drugs.

3. She has established comprehensive prevention and control strategy of GLMD

She has first established the GLMD specialized subject which centralized TCM, endocrinology, digestion, cardiovascular disease, and health management to the integrated multidisciplinary diagnosis and treatment of GLMD. It has realized the overall management of disease risk assessment and early warning, integrated Chinese and Western medicine, diet and exercise to correct multiple organs damage in GLMD.

4. The innovative achievements made in TCM theories, technologies and products have created active demonstrative effects on the development of TCM industries

She has found eight high-level platforms which have become a landmark in South China. She was in charge of the editing work of "Proposals on the Project of Southern China Modern Herbal City", which effectively promotes the development of health industry in Zhongshan. She took a leading role in the establishment of Guangdong, Hong Kong and Macao Collaboration & Innovation Alliance in Pharmaceutical Industry and was elected chairman of the first term. She set up the first state-level scientific and technological incubator in Guangdong Pharmaceutical University.

产业创新奖获得者

黄 险 波

黄险波，1965 年 3 月出生于河北省保定市。1997 年毕业于北京理工大学获应用化学博士学位。毕业后一直在金发科技股份有限公司任职，现任金发科技股份有限公司首席技术专家、塑料改性与加工国家工程实验室主任、高分子材料资源高质化利用国家重点实验室主任、化工资源有效利用国家重点实验室学术委员会委员、*Advanced Industrial and Engineering Polymer Research* 杂志主编。2016 年推动企业入选国家发改委颁布的"国家第一批创新企业百强工程试点企业"，2017 年牵头组建的"国家先进高分子材料产业创新中心"获国家发改委批复。

黄险波长期致力于热塑性聚合物的高性能、功能化研究及产业化工程技术开发，特别是在通用和工程塑料的阻燃与高性能化、特种工程塑料合成、热塑性连续纤维增强复合材料的开发等方面做出了重要贡献。

一、突破环保型阻燃热塑性树脂关键技术并实现产业化

实现了新型阻燃剂的合成及阻燃体系的设计、优化这一核心技术的突破，并辅之相配套的专用设备及系统集成创新，生产出系列环保阻燃热塑性树脂。

（1）研发了氧杂磷菲等系列新型环保型阻燃剂和新型阻燃复配体系，通过对阻燃、耐候机理的深入研究，解决了添加型阻燃体系会劣化树脂其他性能的技术难题。

（2）利用 XPS 方法研究聚合物凝聚相阻燃机理，为阻燃机理的研究提供了一种全新的表征分析方法。

（3）根据不同产品的特性，自主设计和开发了特殊专用设备元件、组合方式、配套设备及生产集中控制系统，填补了国内专用生产设备及高水平控制系统的空白。

（4）自行设计和研制了反应、分离、吸附一体化高效废气净化装置，解决了塑料加工与改性过程中多组分、高流量、低浓度废气达标排放的难题。

该项成果已成功应用于 PP、HIPS、ABS、PC、PBT、PA、PPE 七大系列树脂，从根本上扭转了高性能阻燃热塑性树脂国外产品一统天下的被动局面，成果经同行专家鉴定达到国际先进水平，2005 年获国家科技进步奖二等奖。承担并全面完成了国家科技支撑计划项目"新型高效环保含氮、含硅氧杂膦菲阻燃剂的制备关键技术开发及产业化"。以上成果出版专著 1 部、获发明专利授权 6 项、发表论文 12 篇。

二、突破车用高性能环保聚丙烯材料关键技术并实现产业化

聚丙烯材料具有密度低、性能优异和易于回收等特点，是车用非金属材料的主要品种。但我国聚丙烯材料在高韧性高模量高流动性、高强度、耐划伤、低微挥发性与聚丙烯高极性五大关键技术尚未取得实质性突破，从而陷入长期依赖进口受制于人的困境，严重阻碍了我国汽车工业的稳步健康快速发展。黄险波带领团队经过 10 多年的研发，成功突破上述关键技术，研发出乘用车内外饰部件、结构件专用料系列产品并实现产业化。

（1）通过特种嵌段共聚物改善聚丙烯 / 弹性体界面来调控弹性体分散形态，采用预分散无机刚性粒子等新技术，解决了长期以来欲提高聚丙烯材料低温韧性往往以牺牲流动性和模量为代价的难题。

（2）发明了多孔材料吸附聚丙烯挥发性有机物和聚硅氧烷钝化无机粉体活性金属离子新技术，解决了材料及其加工过程中产生有害挥发物的技术难题，研发了适用于汽车内饰件的低挥发、低气味改性聚丙烯新材料。

（3）发明了带有二维运动张力辊的高效浸渍设备，解决了高牵引速度下长玻璃纤维单丝有效分散及纤维 / 树脂界面有效结合的关键技术问题。

（4）发明了两种带有高含量极性基团的助剂，大幅提高了聚丙烯材料的极性，解决了聚丙烯保险杠难于免火焰处理喷涂的难题，研制出可直接油漆喷涂的聚丙烯保险杠新材料。

（5）发明了带有亚酰胺结构与含乙烯链的高分子量耐划伤剂，在大幅度提高聚丙烯制件表面润滑性能的同时提高了表面皮层结晶度，使表面抗屈服能力增强，从而提高了耐划伤性能。

应用上述科研成果生产的系列产品性能达到或部分优于国外业界标杆企业的同类产品技术水平，国内市场占有率超过 30%，连续多年位居第一。该项成果经同行专家鉴定达到国际先进水平，2012 年获国家科技进步奖二等奖，并出版专著 1 部、获发明专利授权 6 项、发表论文 2 篇。

三、研究提出了半芳香族聚酰胺聚合新方法并实现产业化

半芳香尼龙作为特种聚酰胺工程塑料家族的主要品种，主要应用于电子电气、特种工业等高科技领域，国内长期依赖进口。黄险波提出了"以水为介质低温悬浮聚合"的新技术方案，解决了传统高温熔融聚合时产发生大量三胺化、分解等副反应的技术难题；

基于此新型聚合工艺，立足国内，设计开发了成套聚合设备，开发出系列半芳香族尼龙及其共聚物产品，并在全球范围内率先建成了万吨级聚合装置及共混改性生产线。产品主要性能指标优于可乐丽、帝斯曼、杜邦等国外公司同类产品，售价仅为进口产品的60%，被木林森、富士康、泰科等国内外企业广泛使用，打破了国外产品的垄断。产品已累计实现销售收入7.4亿元。该项成果经同行专家鉴定达到国际先进水平，并获广州市科技进步一等奖、国家发明专利授权3件、PCT专利1件、中国专利优秀奖1件，发表论文2篇。

四、连续纤维增强热塑性复合材料的研发及产业化

黄险波带领技术团队采用自主研发的设备与工艺，解决了连续纤维在热塑性树脂中的高效浸渍与单丝分散这一核心难题，为复合材料的产业化奠定了坚实的基础。

（1）在国内首次实现了热塑性复合材料在公路护栏产品中从设计制造到实际应用示范工程的重大突破，改变了原有金属护栏的吸能模式，提高了防护性能；采用连续纤维增强热塑性复合材料板连续层压工艺和自动化生产技术，有效提高了产品品质和生产效率。该复合材料护栏性能完全满足国家A（三）级防护标准要求，首次在国内清远市和成都双流县进行了示范应用，得到客户的高度认可，并将在清远"生命防护工程"的公路改造项目中进一步推广。

（2）率先在车用热塑性复合材料轻量化方面实现了重大突破。在国内首次研制出了CFRTP车用备胎盖板、门基板、座椅骨架、全塑尾门等系列产品，并承担科技部重点研发专项"轻量化纯电动轿车集成开发技术"中轻量化四侧门一尾门的总成研制工作。

以上成果获省部级技术发明二等奖1项、国家发明专利19项，发表论文1篇。

黄险波为研发体系建设和人才培养做出了贡献，个人先后获杰出工程师、丁颖科技奖、南粤百杰人才、广州市科学技术突出贡献奖等荣誉。

Awardee of Industrial Innovation Prize, Huang Xianbo

Huang Xianbo was born in Baoding City of Hebei Province in March 1965, and was graduated from Beijing Institute of Technology with a doctorate in applied chemistry in 1997, after which he was working in Kingfa Science and Technology Company Limited. He is the chief technology expert of kingfa, director of National Engineering Laboratory for plastic modification and processing, director of State Key Laboratory of high quality utilization of polymer materials, member of Academic Committee of State Key Laboratory for efficient utilization of chemical resources, and the chief editor of *Advanced Industrial and Engineering Polymer Research*. With his effort,

Kingfa was chosen as one of "The first batch of national innovation enterprises of top 100 pilot enterprises" issued by National Development and Reform Commission in 2016. The National Advanced Polymer Materials Industry Innovation Center built by Huang was also approved by National Development and Reform Commission in 2017.

Huang keeps working on the high performance and functional research of thermoplastics and their development in industry. Especially, he contributes a lot to the flame retardant and high performance research of general and engineering plastics, the synthesis of special engineering plastics, and the development of continuous fiber reinforced thermoplastic composites.

(1) Huang found the solution to the key problem of environmental friendly and flame retardant thermoplastic resin and industrialization. Huang synthesized new retardants and designed a new flame retardant system to produce a series of environmental friendly and flame retardant thermoplastic resins.

(2) Huang solved the key problem of high performance and environmental friendly polypropylene materials for automobiles and industrialization. Huang changed the situation that most polypropylene material was imported from abroad, and developed new car interior and exterior parts and special material for structural parts and made them into industrialization.

(3) Huang put forward a new polymerization method for semi aromatic polyamides.

(4) Huang developed continuous fiber reinforced thermoplastic composites and made them into industrialization.

Dr. Huang contributed to the building of research and development system and personnel training. He has won the outstanding engineer, Ding Ying science and Technology Award, Guangdong 100 talents, Guangzhou science and Technology Award for outstanding contributions and other honors.

产业创新奖获得者

贺　泓

贺泓，1965 年 1 月出生于河北省邯郸市。1994 年在日本东京大学获理学博士学位。中科院生态环境研究中心研究员，国家杰出青年科学基金获得者，中科院百人计划，国家"万人计划"领军人才入选者。2017 年当选中国工程院院士。回国后一直负责国家"863"计划、国家重点研发计划柴油车排放控制项目；担任中科院先导专项"大气灰霾追因与控制"首席科学家、京津冀协同发展专家咨询委员和多个国际期刊主编或编委。发表学术专著 1 部、学术论文 310 余篇。获授权国家发明专利 41 项并在多家企业实施应用。以第一完成人获国家技术发明二等奖（2011）和国家科学技术进步奖二等奖（2014）。

主要研究方向为环境催化和非均相大气化学过程。围绕大气污染物非均相转化过程中的环境催化科学技术问题，重点研究环境催化体系设计及其在大气污染物催化净化方面的应用，组建产、学、研联合团队攻克技术应用难题，取得了柴油车排放污染控制、室内空气净化和大气灰霾成因研究方面从基础研究到工程应用的系列成果，为我国大气污染防治做出了突出贡献。

一、创新柴油车排气净化关键技术与系统，实现行业规模化应用

（1）确立适合我国国情的重型柴油车排放污染控制技术路线，研究建立排气净化技术系统并实现规模化应用。柴油车排放氮氧化物（NOx）和颗粒物（PM）是造成大气灰霾的重要原因，然而有效控制柴油车排放在国际上也没有成熟的技术路线。针对我国柴油含硫高的现实国情，贺泓带领研究团队经过大量实验室模拟、发动机台架和整车试验研究，确立了机内净化 PM、选择性催化还原（NH_3–SCR）净化 NOx 的国 IV/V 重型柴油车达标排放技术路线，研发形成了包含发动机调整匹配、车载自动诊断控制、催化转换器、还原剂供给等单元的柴油机排气净化技术系统。基于对催化剂钒活性中心结构和分

散规律的剖析，主导设计了重型柴油车用钒基 NH_3-SCR 催化剂，实现了 NOx 向目标产物 N_2 的高效转化，降低 NOx 排放 70% 以上；解决了催化剂低温活性差和大尺寸载体上均匀、高强度催化剂涂层技术难题，在中国重汽集团等企业建立了年产 70 万套催化转化器生产线，产品性能满足国 IV/V 重型柴油车排放标准，已装配车辆超过 72 万辆。

（2）设计合成新型非钒基催化剂，满足柴油车排放法规升级需求。基于对 NH_3-SCR 催化反应机制的深入分析，提出 SCR 催化剂氧化／还原与酸性位紧密耦合的原则，设计合成了高性能铁钛和铈钨复合氧化物催化剂，创新方法制备高水热稳定性 Cu 小孔分子筛催化剂并阐明其反常的"快速 SCR"机理，为催化反应体系设计提供了有力依据。重型柴油车示范应用表明，新型非钒基 NH_3-SCR 催化剂较钒基催化剂呈现出更优异的活性、热稳定性与耐高空速特性，为满足柴油车更高排放标准提供了技术储备。

（3）创新氮氧化物选择性催化还原方法，拓展柴油车排气净化技术途径。研制出碳氢化合物选择性催化还原氮氧化物（HC-SCR）的银／氧化铝－乙醇组合体系；首次在银／氧化铝催化剂表面发现了碳氢化合物部分氧化形成的烯醇式物种，证实该物种在 HC-SCR 过程中起关键作用，明确了高效 HC-SCR 体系净化 NOx 的微观机制，为最终实现理想的柴油 -SCR 技术打下了坚实的基础。采用柴油 -SCR 技术可免除还原剂储配并简化车载净化系统，有望成为未来柴油车排气 NOx 催化净化主流技术。

上述成果获 2014 年国家科技进步奖二等奖和 2005 年 GM 中国科技成就奖。

二、突破室温非光催化净化室内空气技术难题，实现新技术的产业化应用

（1）提出室温非光催化净化室内空气新思路，发明室温催化氧化甲醛、催化分解臭氧和催化杀菌新材料。甲醛是我国室内空气中最典型的污染物。尽管催化氧化法是净化室内空气的理想方法之一，但因热催化需要高温而不适用于室内空气净化。贺泓提出室温非光催化净化室内空气新思路，设计并研制出高分散负载型 Pt 基催化剂，确认高度分散的 Pt 是该催化反应的活性中心，首次实现了室温条件下甲醛的催化氧化；发现碱金属助剂作用下可实现 Pt 在载体上的单原子分散，有利于活化氧气和水生成活性表面羟基，从而大大提高室温催化氧化甲醛的反应活性、降低了催化剂成本。针对臭氧污染，开发了室温下高效分解臭氧的锰基催化剂，发现 Mn^{3+} 的含量决定催化剂活性，并通过 Ce 掺杂获得了在高空速、高湿度条件下室温分解臭氧的催化材料。室内空气中还存在一些致病微生物，对人体健康构成威胁。针对臭氧、紫外线、化学药剂杀菌带来的人体或环境危害问题，成功研制出系列载银催化剂，通过催化活化空气中分子氧产生表面活性氧，在室温下实现了快速接触催化杀菌。新方法具有广谱、高效、对人体无害的优势。

（2）实现新技术的产业化应用。开发出上述催化材料及其功能组件的低成本、规模化制备技术，与企业合作实现了相关专利技术的产业化，产品供应市场并应用于 2008 年北京奥运会室内空气质量保障，取得了良好的经济和社会效益。目前，甲醛室温催化净化、臭氧催化分解技术和催化杀菌已在亚都、喜临门、海尔、三菱电机等中外企业的空

气净化产品和工程中得到广泛应用。亚都公司实施了多项以贺泓为第一发明人的专利技术，推出的新型空气净化器已在国内市场累计销售超过 85 万台，惠及千家万户。

上述成果获 2011 年国家技术发明二等奖、2010 年中国专利优秀奖、2008 年科技奥运先进个人 3 项奖励。

三、探索大气中的环境催化，为大气灰霾追因与控制提供理论基础

利用表面 / 界面科学研究方法，重点研究了矿尘、柴油车排放黑碳和 NOx 对灰霾成因的贡献。提出分子氧参与的快速光氧化反应是黑碳大气老化的重要过程，发现黑碳对其表面吸附有机碳的氧化反应具有催化作用；明确了黑碳骨架与分子氧和臭氧反应的活性位点及催化氧化机制。发现黑碳、矿尘、NOx 协同催化 SO_2 向硫酸盐转化的现象，结合烟雾箱模拟和外场观测，提出复合污染条件下二次硫酸盐生成新机制，获得国内外同行的高度认可。以上研究在 *PNAS*、*Sci. Rep.*、*ES&T*、*ACP*、*JGR* 等国际期刊上发表学术论文 50 余篇，相关成果在我国灰霾防治和京津冀协同发展专家咨询工作中发挥了积极作用。

四、人才培养与团队建设

贺泓组织以中科院为主的优势力量，主持了先导专项"大气灰霾追因与控制"的立项和实施，2013 年创建中科院生态环境研究中心大气污染控制中心，2014 年组建的大气污染物的源汇过程与污染源控制技术创新团队入选科技部创新人才推进计划，2015 年作为首席科学家筹建中国科学院区域大气环境研究卓越创新中心。已培养博士生 38 名、硕士生 6 名，其中 7 人分别获得中科院院长特别奖和优秀奖、4 人获中科院优秀博士论文、1 人获第 15 届国际催化大会"青年科学家奖"。

Awardee of Industrial Innovation Prize,
He Hong

He Hong was born in Handan City of Hebei Province in January 1965. He received his doctorate degree at the University of Tokyo in 1994. He is the Chief Scientist of the Center for Excellence in Regional Atmospheric Environment, Deputy Director of Research Center for Eco-Environmental Sciences（RCEES）, Chinese Academy of Sciences（CAS）. He was elected to be the member of the Chinese Academy of Engineering in 2017.

He joined RCEES through the "Hundred Talents Program" of CAS in 2001. His work focused on the fundamental and applied research in environmental catalysis and heterogeneous atmospheric chemistry, with substantial achievements in diesel emission control technologies, catalytic indoor air purification, and haze formation mechanisms.

1. Emission control technologies for diesel vehicles

Professor He established an emission control strategy for heavy-duty diesel vehicles to meet China's category IV and V standards, combining internal-engine reduction of particulate matter and selective catalytic reduction (SCR) for after-treatment of NOx emissions from heavy-duty diesel engines. He was successful in the design and preparation of NH_3-SCR catalysts, and in the production of SCR converters for heavy-duty diesel vehicles through cooperation with China National Heavy Duty Truck Group Co., Ltd. (SINOTRUK).

2. Indoor air catalytic purification at room temperature

Professor He designed and developed a supported noble metal catalyst with single-atom dispersion as well as a method for its preparation, for the first time achieving ambient catalytic oxidation of formaldehyde. The relevant patents and technology were brought to market at home and abroad.

3. Environmental catalytic process and its relationship with haze formation in the atmosphere

Professor He is the Chief Scientist of the project of "Formation Mechanism and Control Strategies of Haze in China", conduct research on the role of environmental catalysis in the atmosphere and its relationship with haze formation. His research established that photochemical oxidation of soot by molecular O_2 is sufficiently fast to result in its chemical ageing in the atmosphere, a process that subsequently influences local air quality and human health. He further determined a new formation mechanism for particulate sulfate in the atmosphere.

Professor He has published more than 310 papers in various peer-reviewed journals. He also published a book *The Principles and Application of Environmental Catalysis*. He has been granted 41 patents as first inventor. He won the National Technology Invention Award (Second Prize) in 2011, and the National Science and Technology Progress Award (Second Prize) in 2014.

He serves as a member of the Expert Consultation Committee of Jing-Jin-Ji Collaborative Development. He is the co-Editor-in-Chief of Catalysis Surveys from Asia, and editorial board member of some international and domestic academic journals.

产业创新奖获得者

金 征 宇

金征宇，1960年5月出生于江苏省扬州市。1982年1月、1988年7月、1992年7月先后在无锡轻工业学院（现江南大学）获工学学士、硕士、博士学位。先后在英国糖业技术研究中心、荷兰WAGENINGEN大学、美国KANSAS州立大学、美国PURDUE大学等从事博士后以及访问教授研究工作。历任江南大学食品学院副院长、院长，江南大学副校长。现任食品科学与技术国家重点实验室主任、教育部食品科学与工程类专业教指委主任、中国粮油学会副理事长、中国食品科学技术学会副理事长、第十二届全国人民代表大会代表。

金征宇长期从事食品工程领域淀粉深加工方向的科研工作。在淀粉深加工基础研究、新产品开发及装备工程化等方面成果突出，以第一或责任作者发表SCI论文165篇，他引3000多次，入围2014年、2015年、2016年农业与生物科学领域中国高被引学者；主编出版专著、教材8部（其中1本英文专著在国外出版）；授权国家发明专利58件（美国专利1件），其中转移专利技术17件；主持设计淀粉工程建设项目13项，产业化效果显著；获得国家科技进步奖二等奖3次（2007年排名第一，2009年排名第二，2011年排名第一）、国家技术发明二等奖1次（2014年排名第一）。

一、淀粉深加工理论创新

围绕淀粉结晶功能化主题，发现淀粉与客体分子组装形成有序化结晶非包合物的调控机制与规律，为淀粉定向衍生化提供了重要理论支撑。在分支环糊精的酶法逆向合成、大环糊精与弹簧糊精的结构解析方面有创新性理论成果。近10年在此方面发表的SCI论文数稳居全球首位，美国 *Science Letter*、*Life Science Weekly* 等权威科技媒体对其中13篇论文研究进展进行了跟踪报道。

二、淀粉新产品开发

基于淀粉衍生物新品种缺乏的现状，开发出一步挤压制备交联类、酯类变性淀粉新工艺，建立了助剂结晶制备抗性淀粉新技术，在国内最大的淀粉衍生物产品生产企业——诸城兴贸玉米开发有限公司分别建成 3 条各年产 3 万吨交联类和酯类变性淀粉生产线、2 条各年产 5000 吨抗性淀粉生产线，年均销售额达 8.6 亿元；创新配合营养米的挤压生产技术，在瑞盛食品建成年产 8000 吨生产线；基于传统环糊精溶解性差的缺陷，创制出高水溶性弹簧糊精、大环糊精、分支环糊精等 10 多种环糊精衍生物，率先在淄博千汇、山东新大建成超千吨级生产线，技术水平居国际领先。

三、挤压装备工程化

针对国产挤压装备适应能力差的问题，与江苏牧羊集团合作二十余年，主持设计完成 21 种不同型号的挤压机用于变性淀粉、配合营养米、营养米粉、饲料用玉米大豆等的挤压工程化生产，为该企业跻身食品加工挤压机产销量全球首位（目前销售 3000 多台套，直接经济效益达 36 亿元）并成为国际 ISO 饲料机械技术委员会秘书处落户单位提供了重要技术支撑。

Awardee of Industrial Innovation Prize, Jin Zhengyu

Jin Zhengyu was born in Yangzhou City of Jiangsu Province in May 1960. He is a professor and director of the State Key Laboratory of Food Science and Technology at Jiangnan University, China, is a distinguished researcher, educator, leader and one of the most prominent scholars in the field of food science and technology. Dr. Jin has worked on chemical and biological modifications of starch before obtaining a scholarship to carry out graduate studies at the Jiangnan University. On completion of his PhD, he worked as a postdoctoral fellow in the Technology Center of British Sugar. In 1997, he moved back to Jiangnan University and appointed in the School of Food Science at Jiangnan University as a lecturer and was promoted to the range of professor in the highest range of that position. His career contributions to the profession include 30 years' innovative research and stellar leadership in food carbohydrate utilization for food product development. Dr. Jin is the author of 165 scientific publications in high-impact journals, holder of 58 patents, editor of 8 books (1 in English) and administrator of numerous prominent positions, including deputy to the National People's Congress, vice-president of Jiangnan University, vice-chairman of Chinese Institute of Food Science and Technology, etc. He is a member of the editorial boards of a number of journals and has organized workshops, symposia, and conferences in the field of food science. Through long-time efforts, he has successfully developed novel processes for the production of many food ingredients, including novel cyclodextrin derivatives, low-digestible starches, enriched rice products and functional sugars, and transferred the technologies to food enterprises for industrialization. Many products have become popular items on the contemporary health-food market. In addition, Dr. Jin was identified as Elsevier Most Cited Chinese Researchers since 2014. He also has previously received awards from the Ministry of Science and Technology, Ministry of Education, Provincial Government, China Light Industry Council and Chinese Institute of Food Science and Technology in recognition of his scientific achievements.

产业创新奖获得者

聂 红

聂红，女，1962 年 12 月出生于云南省昆明市。1985 年毕业于南开大学化学系获硕士学位，2010 年在中国石化石油化工科学研究院获博士学位。1985 年至今一直在中国石化石油化工科学研究院工作（1996 年在法国里昂催化研究所做访问学者半年），1997 年 11 月任加氢催化剂研究室主任，1999 年 12 任教授级高级工程师，2002 年 12 月—2004 年 12 月任副总工程师，2004 年 12 月—2006 年 10 月任院长助理，2006 年 10 月起任副院长。兼任国家石油产品质量监督检验中心主任、炼油工艺与催化剂国家工程研究中心主任、中国石油学会常务理事、中国石油学会石油炼制分会主任、北京石油学会副理事长，博士生导师。

聂红一直从事石油炼制核心技术加氢催化剂与工艺的研发，围绕炼油工业面临的重油高效转化、清洁燃料生产和低碳排放等核心问题，通过不断创新和实践开发出多项具有国际先进水平的技术并成功进行大规模工业应用。

一、开发重油加氢及其与催化裂化双向组合 RICP 技术，提高汽柴油收率成效显著

我国石油资源供给不足、对外依存度高，同时以汽柴油为主的轻质油品需求量大，而轻质油品收率比国际先进水平低，因此提高石油资源利用率事关国家能源安全，也是炼油业关注的焦点和难题。常规重油加氢 - 催化裂化组合技术可以提高重油转化能力，聂红及其团队发现使重油更高效转化的核心是提高多环芳烃转化成轻质油品的选择性，而这需要解决三大技术难题：一是催化裂化产生的 5% ~ 20% 富含多环芳烃的未转化重油（HCO）自身回炼易产焦炭、干气，轻质油品收率低；二是重油中以多环芳烃结构为主的沥青质在加氢和催化裂化过程中均易生成焦炭，影响催化剂活性和轻质油收率；三是重油加氢装置运转周期短，对炼厂整体运转和经济效益影响很大。

作为国家重大产业技术开发专项"重油深加工技术开发"项目负责人，聂红组织并

参与攻关，攻克了难题并形成多项新技术。

一是研究有利于多环芳烃转化成轻质油品的反应路径，提出并首次工业实施了提高轻质油品收率的重油加氢与催化裂化双向组合 RICP 技术。即将催化裂化产生的 HCO 循环到重油加氢装置，与重油混合加氢后再进入催化裂化装置。通过改变 HCO 循环途径，结合催化剂、工艺和工程创新，促进了多环芳烃选择性向轻质油品转化，获得"一箭多雕"的效果：重油加氢装置的进料由于掺入 HCO 黏度降低，加氢脱杂质反应速率提高；同时 HCO 的高芳香性抑制了沥青质析出，降低了加氢催化剂上的积炭；加氢后的 HCO 多环芳烃含量降低，再进入催化裂化装置提高了汽柴油收率。工业应用结果表明，在 HCO 掺入量仅 6% 的情况下，汽柴油收率比常规组合技术高 1.9 个百分点。

二是创新了多项国际先进水平的催化剂制备技术，开发了沥青质高效转化和延长装置运转周期的系列高性能重油加氢处理催化剂。①开发了双通道沥青质高效转化的加氢催化剂，使工业装置上的沥青质转化率较国内同类催化剂提高 40 多个百分点。②创造性开发了活性中心非均匀分布的新型加氢脱金属催化剂，容金属能力提高 24%。③发明了有效孔集中的载体材料制备技术，使制备的加氢脱残炭脱硫催化剂活性高、积炭量降低，是目前国际同类催化剂的最好水平。新催化剂体系可显著延长工业运转周期，在我国台湾中油公司某工业装置上成功运转 703 天，运转周期延长 30%，提高了重油转化效率。

RICP 技术已在 4 家炼厂工业应用，重油加氢催化剂系列在海内外 12 家炼厂工业应用了 44 套次，国内市场占有率第一，具有显著的经济和社会效益。该成果获 2011 年国家科技进步奖二等奖。

二、持续创新开发高效柴油加氢催化剂，满足国家清洁油品生产需求

油品清洁化是国家绿色发展战略的要求。近 20 年，聂红作为负责人一直持续攻关创新，带领团队开发出系列高效加氢催化剂，为企业油品质量升级提供了技术支撑。20 世纪 90 年代，在前辈们开发的 RN-1 催化剂基础上，聂红立足国内两种催化材料创新孔结构互补技术，取代昂贵的国外进口材料，开发了柴油加氢精制催化剂 RN-10，其脱硫活性比当时国内外最好的催化剂高 14% 以上，工业上能够在超出设计负荷 30% 情况下长周期低成本大幅度降低柴油硫含量。进入 21 世纪，油品清洁化要求不断提高且进程加快，硫含量不大于 50ppm、10ppm 的国 IV、国 V 柴油标准要求于 2015 年、2017 年实施，开发难度陡增。2000 年，聂红作为"973"项目中课题负责人认识到实现该目标的关键是要脱除具有空间位阻且反应活性极低的 4, 6- 二甲基二苯并噻吩（4, 6-DMDBT）类硫化物，催化剂制备技术必须有重大突破。通过对反应途径和催化剂构效关系的研究，提出提高加氢活性是消除 4, 6-DMDBT 类硫化物空间位阻的有效途径，并在催化剂制备过程中创造性引入活性金属络合浸渍技术，使双金属活性组元协同硫化，开发出以二类活性相为主的高活性柴油超深度加氢脱硫催化剂 RS-1000，并成功应用于工业装置上，是当时国内少有的能够长周期生产硫含量小于 10ppm、满足国 V 标准柴油的催化剂。随后以络合浸渍技术为基础，相继开发成功了一系列高活性加氢催化剂，显著促进了催化剂制备技术进步，使中国企业可以低成本高效生产国 IV 和国 V 清洁柴油。

RN-10、RS-1000 两种催化剂累计在国内外 50 套次工业装置上应用。2001 年 RN-10 催化剂获国家科技进步奖二等奖，2006 年 RS-1000 催化剂获省部级科技进步奖一等奖。

三、自主开发生物航煤技术并实现工业应用和商业飞行

低碳排放是国家能源发展战略，生物航煤生产技术的开发成为当代热点。作为项目负责人，聂红带领团队解决了餐饮废油等动植物油在加氢过程中放热大、生成水影响催化剂稳定性以及需大幅降低凝点才能满足航煤冰点要求等难题，成功开发出具有完全自主知识产权的加氢法生物航煤生产技术，首次在国内工业装置上生产出合格的生物航煤并商业飞行成功，为中国自己的生物航煤进入航空业奠定了基础。该技术获省部级科技进步奖一等奖。

聂红及其团队力促成果转化并取得优异成绩，其研究成果获国家科技进步奖二等奖 2 项（均排名第一）、省部级科技进步一等奖 7 项，中国专利金奖 1 项、优秀奖 2 项；发表论文 95 篇，专著《加氢处理工艺与工程》（第二版）一部（主编之一）；获授权中国发明专利 128 件、国外发明专利 52 件；2002 年享受政府特殊津贴，获第四届中国杰出青年科技创新奖；2004 年入选"新世纪百千万人才工程国家级人选"；2014 年当选全国优秀科技工作者。

聂红注重年轻人的培养，与团队一起培养研究生 20 余名，其中许多人已成为技术骨干，形成了坚实的技术人才梯队。

Awardee of Industrial Innovation Prize,
Nie Hong

Nie Hong, female, was born in Kunming City of Yunnan Province in December 1962. She has been working at RIPP since 1985. She is now vice president of RIPP, senior engineer with professorship, Ph.D. supervisor, director of National Center for Quality Supervision and Inspection of Petroleum Products, director of National Engineering Research Center of Refining Process and Catalyst, standing director of Chinese Petroleum Society, director of Petroleum Refining Branch of Chinese Petroleum Society.

Nie Hong has been doing the R&D on hydrotreating catalysts and process, which are core technologies in petroleum refining industry. Aiming at main challenges refining industry faced including high efficient conversion of heavy oil, production of clean fuel and low carbon emission, she led the team to develop a number of technologies at internationally advanced level, and successfully commercialized them at a large-scale.

She organized the R&D team and participated in solving key problems to develop the high efficient heavy oil hydrotreating technology (RHT) at internationally advanced level and the novel integrated technology (RICP) by combining it with catalytic cracking process by skillfully facilitating the conversion of polycyclic aromatic hydrocarbons. The yield of light oil increased and the average commercial running period was prolonged. These technologies have made remarkable economic and social benefits. RICP has been applied in 4 refineries, and the series of catalysts for heavy oil hydrotreating have been employed 44 times worldwide.

She leads the team to make continuous innovation and develop high efficient diesel hydrotreating catalysts. RN-10 and RS-1000, the series of diesel hydrotreating catalysts at internationally advanced level, have been commercially applied 50 times worldwide for clean diesel, promptly meeting the national requirements for upgrading the diesel quality.

She led the team to develop a bio-jet fuel production technology. The qualified bio-jet fuel was firstly produced from waste cooking oil in a domestic commercial unit, and the first commercial flight test in March 2015 was successful. This technology provides technological support for reducing greenhouse gases.

Nie Hong and her team have been making great efforts on the commercialization of research achievements, and obtained outstanding success. The research achievements have won two second prize of National Scientific and Technological Progress, seven provincial and ministerial level scientific and technological progress, one gold prize and two excellence award of Chinese Patent. She published 95 papers and compiled one monograph titled *Hydrotreating Process and Engineering* (second edition) as one of the three chief editors. She obtained 128 items of authorized Chinese invention patents and 52 items of foreign invention patents.

区域创新奖获得者

冯　起

　　冯起，1966 年 3 月出生于陕西省榆林市。1995 年毕业于中国科学院兰州沙漠所获理学博士学位，1997—2002 年获日本科技厅和文部省 STA 和 JSPS 基金资助，在日本气象研究所和日本大学文理学部进行合作研究。2003 年回国任中科院寒区旱区环境与工程研究所研究员，2012 年 9 月—2016 年 6 月任中国科学院寒区旱区环境与工程研究所副所长，2016 年 7 月起任中国科学院西北生态环境资源研究院副院长。先后担任中科院内陆河流域生态水文重点实验室副主任、主任，甘肃省水文水资源工程技术中心主任，中科院寒区旱区环境与工程研究所大数据中心主任，昌邑海洋与生物工程中心主任，科技部科技支撑项目首席专家。现为甘肃省沙产业基金会理事长、中国地理学会沙漠分会副理事长、国家"十三五"重点研发计划项目首席专家、联合国工业发展组织咨询专家。

　　冯起从事内陆河流域生态恢复的理论与技术研究。在生态恢复的新原理、新技术以及工程应用转化等方面取得突破，形成从理论支撑、关键技术创新到工程应用的系列成果，突破了世界上生态恢复治理难度最大的寒旱区生态恢复技术难题。

一、阐明了内陆河流域生态环境系统与水文系统的相互作用机制，提出了内陆河流域生态恢复的新技术理论

　　1. 揭示了内陆河流域寒区水文过程与生态环境系统相互耦合机制

　　以方法的突破和数据的积累为支撑，发现以高降水量、低蒸散发量和高径流系数为表征的冰雪冻土带对流域生态系统起主导作用，首次提出流域水汽内循环对生态系统耗水贡献率达 70% 以上，且寒区生态环境对区域水文过程存在逆反馈。这一结论被黄河水利委员会应用到水资源规划工作中，并被国际同行评价为"在生态水文学研究上属于一个创新"。

2.建立干旱内陆河流域荒漠绿洲生态系统蒸散发尺度转换理论，提出了内陆河流域生态保护评估指标体系与预警模型

首次从微观至宏观尺度精确模拟了流域生态系统植被蒸散耗水量，建立了荒漠绿洲植物叶片水分—树干液流—根系吸水的尺度转换方法，奠定了干旱内陆河流域气候水文理论。首次建立了内陆河流域生态保护评估指标体系与预警模型，提出了内陆河流域生态保护的三条红线，被中国科协采纳上报中央。成果获甘肃省科技进步奖二等奖。

3.形成了内陆河流域生态水文研究的理论框架

建立了我国内陆河完整的流域科学观测—试验研究平台，通过对高寒区、平原区和荒漠区的气候、生态、水文要素的长期监测，建立了内陆河流域气候—生态—水文过程模型，阐明了内陆河流域气候变化、生态系统与水文过程的耦合机理，首次建立了气候变化背景下生态水文研究的理论框架。

国际著名生态水文专家 John Landford 院士、环境工程专家 Ravinesh 评价该研究成果处于国际领先水平，成果获甘肃省自然科学一等奖。

二、突破高寒山区植被保育、洪水资源化利用、绿洲节水及风沙防治关键技术，形成内陆河山地 - 平原 - 荒漠系统生态恢复的技术体系

1.建立了高寒山区水源涵养植被保育技术

首次建立了水源涵养增贮潜力的评价体系；提出了乔木型、乔灌混交型、灌木型水源涵养林结构优化模式。针对退化草地，创建了"鼠害防治 + 禁牧封育 + 施肥 + 免耕补播"技术；针对造林成活率低，建立了"低密建植 + 高密锁边 + 人工辅植"的退耕地技术。该技术破解了高寒山区水源涵养林工程建设的"瓶颈"，成果获甘肃省科技进步一等奖。

2.发明了基于生态恢复的浅山区洪水资源化综合利用技术

针对内陆河"水患"与"沙害"威胁并存、洪水难以利用问题，研发了洪水分级疏流—综合拦蓄—渗滤净化技术，提出了洪水资源化—冷水养殖—肥水种植集成技术，开发洪水渗漏—黏土固沙—石堤阻沙—生物防沙综合风沙防御技术体系。该技术创建了以"水害"治"沙害"的生态治理新模式，《瞭望》新闻周刊评价其为"十三五"治水新思路，成果获甘肃省科技进步二等奖。

3.提出了人工绿洲节水灌溉技术与"三带一网"节水型植被防护体系

针对水资源紧缺型人工绿洲，将喷灌、滴灌、管灌等单项节水技术组装配套后，创造性提出了高效混合灌溉系统组装配套技术，节水 10%；提出了配置封沙育草带、前沿阻沙带、植物固沙带和绿洲内部农田防护林网，即"三带一网"的节水型植被防护体系。该体系的实施使绿洲边缘风速平均降低 50% 以上、林网耗水减少 20%。著名生态学家 L.Stringer 评价其构建的绿洲防护体系是"中国干旱区内陆河流域生态建设的成功范式"。商务部已将该技术面向 116 个发展中国家开展培训。成果获内蒙古自治区科技进步二等奖。

4.构建了天然绿洲及外围植被生态恢复与风沙防护技术体系

在绿洲内部，优化了"窄林带宽网格"技术，使林木耗水量减少30%；在荒漠绿洲过渡带，研发了"天然植被保护+雨养植被补植+低耗水树种引种"的封育固沙技术；在绿洲边缘，研发了"高秆作物风障+灌草覆盖阻沙"的技术，集成了荒漠绿洲外围流动沙丘带、机械固沙带、机械化学固沙带、生物固沙带、天然植被保护带、绿洲林草带等"六带一体"的综合防护体系。该模式在降水100毫米以下区域成功应用，为无灌溉条件下的绿洲外围风沙防治提供了成功范式，已被列为"沙漠化研究与治理国际培训班"课程。成果获甘肃省科技进步奖一等奖。

三、解决了生态恢复技术模式向生态治理应用的转化，实现了规模化生态治理工程的应用

在理论研究和技术创新基础上，突破了生态恢复技术模式向实际生态治理工程应用的转化。研发的高寒山区水源涵养植被保育技术成功地应用到"祁连山地区生态治理技术研究及示范"工程，建成生态恢复工程20个，有效解决了高寒山区水源涵养林恢复难度大的工程建设"瓶颈"。

研发的浅山区洪水资源化综合利用技术消除了区域洪水灾害，使可利用水资源量提高2倍以上，得到国际社会的认可。

研发并提出了"六带一体"防沙体系，该体系组成了完整的林、灌、草防护体系，有效阻止了风沙对航天城的侵袭，为我国酒泉卫星发射基地提供了良好的环境保障。

基于上述配套技术体系，形成了干旱内陆河流域生态恢复的水调控关键技术，并在丝绸之路经济带推广应用面积达5.4万平方千米以上。得到澳大利亚政府的认可并授予"奋进奖"，同时得到联合国工业发展组织的高度评价。成果获国家科学技术进步奖二等奖和中国产学研合作创新奖。

Awardee of Region Innovation Prize, Feng Qi

Feng Qi was born in Yulin City of Shaanxi Province in March 1966. In 1995, he graduated from the Lanzhou Institute of Desert, Chinese Academy of Sciences, and received a Ph.D. degree in sciences. From the year of 1997 to 2002, he conducted research collaboration with Japan Meteorological Institute and the Japanese University of Arts and Sciences funded by the Japan Science and Technology Associate (STA) and Japan Science Promotion Society (JSPS). From the year of 2003, he was approved as "Chinese Academy of Sciences hundred people plan", and appointed as professor of Cold and Arid Regions Environmental Engineering Research Institute, Chinese Academy of Sciences. From September 2012 to June 2016, he served as deputy director of the Cold and Arid Regions Environmental Engineering Research Institute, Chinese Academy of Sciences. From July 2016 to present, he acts as vice president of Northwest Institute of Eco-Environmental Resources, Chinese Academy of Sciences, and successively served as the deputy director of key laboratory of Ecohydrology of Inland River Basin, Chinese Academy of Sciences. He also is the deputy director of Key laboratory of Ecohydrology and watershed science, Heihe, and the Director of Hydrology and Water Resources Engineering Technology Center, Gansu Province. He is the Director of Big data Center of Northwest Institute of Eco-Environmental Resources, Chinese Academy of Sciences. He is chief expert of science and technology support project, as the chairman of Sand Industry Foundation in Gansu Province and vice-chairman of Desert Branch, China Geological Society.

Feng Qi is devoted to the theoretical and technical studies of Inland River Basin and Ecological restoration. He made breakthroughs in new principles, new technologies as well as engineering applications transformation of Ecological restoration and other aspects. Through the theoretical foundation and the key technological innovation to engineering applications, he has achieved a series of results. He is known to breaking the world's ecological restoration and management of the most difficult cold and arid ecological restoration technology problems. The main achievements are as follows: ① Clarified the mechanism of the interaction between the ecological environment system and the hydrological system in the inland river basin, he proposed a new technical theory of ecological restoration inland river basin. ② Breakthrough for vegetation conservation in the alpine mountains, flood-water resources use, the key technical of water management and sandstorm control in oases, establishing the technical system of ecological restoration for inland river basin in Alpine-Plain-Desert system. ③ Solved the transformation of ecological restoration technology model to application of ecological management and realized the application of large-scale ecological management and engineering.

区域创新奖获得者

郭 昭 华

郭昭华，1959 年 10 月出生于内蒙古自治区丰镇市。毕业于辽宁工程技术大学采矿工程专业，工学博士，教授级高级工程师，享受国务院政府津贴。1982 年 8 月—1990 年 5 月，在赤峰市平庄矿务局西露天煤矿技术科任技术员、副科长；1990 年 5 月—1995 年 7 月，在准格尔煤炭工业公司黑岱沟露天煤矿任生产作业部经理、副矿长；1995 年 7 月—2014 年 7 月，先后任神华准能公司黑岱沟露天煤矿矿长，神华准能公司副总工程师、总经理助理、总工程师兼安监局局长、副总经理，神华准资公司常务副总经理。现任神华准能集团有限责任公司副总经理、神华准能资源综合开发有限公司常务副总经理兼煤炭伴生资源综合利用研发及工程示范中心主任、内蒙古自治区煤炭伴生资源综合利用工程技术研究中心主任，兼任内蒙古科技大学矿业研究院硕士生导师、内蒙古自治区科学技术协会兼职副主席。

他长期从事露天煤矿开采及煤炭共伴生资源利用技术研发和工程实践，在煤炭露天开采和煤炭燃烧后废渣低成本高值化利用方面做出了一系列开创性的研究工作。

一、研发了厚覆盖层、厚煤层条件下高台阶抛掷爆破 – 吊斗铲倒堆工艺成套关键技术

针对准格尔煤田特点，在世界首创了厚覆盖层（200 米）、厚煤层（34 米）条件下高台阶（60 米）抛掷爆破 – 吊斗铲倒堆剥离工艺技术，并在神华集团黑岱沟露天煤矿主持应用了该成果，使该矿由原设计产能 12Mt/a 提高到核定产能 34Mt/a，成为我国首座年产原煤 30Mt 级的露天煤矿，工效提高 3.2 倍，最高产量 32.89Mt/a，年均创利润 15.8 亿元。实现了高产、高效、安全开采，标志着我国露天煤矿进入了世界一流先进行列。

（1）研究解决了厚覆盖层条件下，进口吊斗铲规格参数及其工艺系统作业参数、下部运煤通道的合理布设等难题；结合露天矿煤层赋存条件和煤层分层开采的技术要求，按照效益最大化原则，通过研究吊斗铲倒堆与排土之间的关系，得出了合理采掘带宽度

为 80 米，高台阶最大高度为 60 米；建立了吊斗铲倒堆作业工艺及运煤通道的理论模型；攻克了厚煤层高强度分层开采、宽采掘带吊斗铲剥离与下部多台阶采煤作业相互协调的理论与技术难题。在世界上首次形成了厚覆盖层、厚煤层、宽采掘带吊斗铲倒堆开采技术。

（2）为保证提高有效抛掷率、减少吊斗铲倒堆作业量及爆破安全，通过研究和反复试验得出了大孔径（310 毫米）抛掷爆破合理的孔网参数、孔间和排间延期时间、起爆方式、装药结构等，研制了与之匹配的系列炸药和制备技术，开发了抛掷爆破设计、模拟和效果分析软件，解决了宽采掘带高台阶抛掷爆破有效抛掷率低和后冲强烈等技术难题，形成了一次爆破炸药量达 1500t 抛掷爆破控制技术。

1）研发了宽采掘带高台阶抛掷爆破技术。通过系统研究，首次形成了爆区宽度 80 米高台阶抛掷爆破的亚临界孔间延时间隔、超临界排间延时间隔、多排倾斜深孔、排间斜线逐孔同向顺序起爆的定向控制爆破专有技术，有效抛掷率达 44.6%，大幅度降低了生产成本。

2）开发了高台阶抛掷爆破设计及其优化软件、模拟软件、效果分析软件，实现了高台阶抛掷爆破计算机优化设计、抛掷爆破前的效果模拟及安全预控分析。

3）研发了适合抛掷爆破的重铵油炸药多种产品配方，使抛掷爆破钻孔数量减少 46.2%、有效抛掷率提高 40%；研发了乳化性能强、稳定性高的乳化炸药关键材料（复合油相）配方；研发了以废机油代替柴油的铵油炸药，使成本降低 14.5%。

4）研发了常压、低转速、低温高效、自动实现安全连锁保护的连续化乳胶基质制备技术及设备，有效保证了生产过程的安全、效率和质量。提前 10 年实现了《工业和信息化部关于民用爆炸物品行业技术进步的指导意见》中民用爆炸物品技术进步要求的三期目标。

（3）黑岱沟露天矿倒堆剥离和采煤台阶总高度达 94 米，抛掷爆破一次装药量达 1500t，单孔最大装药量达 4.5t。为保证高台阶的边坡稳定、作业安全及解决高台阶抛掷爆破振动危害问题，研发了高台阶大孔径预裂爆破技术、高台阶抛掷爆破一次单段起爆药量控制技术和边坡雷达监测实时监控预警安全保障技术。

1）预裂爆破是减少爆破对台阶边坡岩体破坏、降低爆破振动的有效措施。研发了高台阶预裂爆破技术，将抛掷爆破和预裂爆破的孔径统一为 310 毫米；研究得出了大孔径预裂爆破参数、起爆方式、装药结构，预裂效果明显提高。

2）研发了适用于大孔径预裂爆破的超低密度炸药（密度 $0.15 g/cm^3$）及制备技术，使预裂爆破的孔痕率达到 85%，密度范围突破了国内现有低密度炸药（密度 $0.3 g/cm^3$）的技术瓶颈。

3）研发了高台阶抛掷爆破一次单段起爆药量控制技术。通过研究和试验首次提出了将 8ms 单位时间内的累计起爆药量定义为一次单段起爆药量，解决了高台阶抛掷爆破逐孔起爆时单段药量计算和确定技术难题。研究得出抛掷爆破的地震波衰减规律，对解决高台阶抛掷爆破振动危害有重要意义。黑岱沟露天煤矿自 2007 年以来已成功进行了 163 次抛掷爆破，爆破量达 2.55 亿立方米，使用炸药 17.86 万吨，未发生任何爆破技术与安全问题。

4）为保证高台阶局部崩落和滑坡对下部采煤设备和人员的安全，首次在国内研发边坡雷达监测实时监控技术并建立了预警系统，有效解决了高台阶崩落滑坡对作业设备和人员的安全保障难题，应用以来已经成功预警 31 次，未发生安全事故。

二、发明了粉煤灰中有价元素低成本高值化利用的"一步酸溶法"工艺技术

我国大部分煤炭用于热能利用并产生大量废渣，形成污染。为将废渣转换为原料，郭昭华在世界上首次发明了粉煤灰中有价元素低成本高值化利用"一步酸溶法"工艺技术，攻克了盐酸浸出分离纯化、工艺配套材料和设备、环保重大技术难题，创建了粉煤灰中有价元素盐酸法协同溶出、分离纯化及高值化利用工艺技术体系，开辟了生产冶金材料新途径。主持建成了世界首个粉煤灰盐酸浸出法生产 4000 吨 / 年氧化铝及镓工业化装置。自 2011 年 8 月运行六年来，单次最高连续稳定运行 159 天，氧化铝纯度稳定达到 99.0%，镓纯度达到 99.99%，碳酸锂纯度达到 99.41%。该技术工业化仅准格尔煤田就可盘活氧化铝资源 30 亿吨、镓资源 85.7 万吨，可解决我国铝土矿资源紧缺的战略需求问题。

其创新成果先后获国家科技进步奖二等奖 2 项、省部级科技奖 5 项、国际专利 4 项、国家专利 108 项，其中发明专利 62 项；出版专著 2 部，发表论文 39 篇，先后荣获内蒙古自治区"草原英才""内蒙古自治区科学技术特别贡献奖"中华国际科学交流基金会首届"杰出工程师"等荣誉称号。

Awardee of Region Innovation Prize, Guo Zhaohua

Guo Zhaohua was born in Fengzhen City of Inner Mongolia in October 1959. He graduated from Liaoning Technical University in 2008 with a doctor degree in Mining Engineering. Guo Zhaohua has long been engaged in surface coal mining and has researched on coal associated resource utilization technology and engineering practices.

Guo is the first person in the world to develop sets of the high-step（60m）throwing blasting-bucket shovel pile stripping key process technologies under the thick coating（200m）and thick coal seam（34m）conditions. He developed a series of explosives suitable for high-level pre-splitting and throwing blasting, which could adjust the blasting force, detonation velocity and other indexes in real time according to the requirements of each blasthole. The technique firstly throws 30% ～ 45% of the covering directly into scheduled mining Empty area with a high-level thrown blasting, and then pushes the remaining covering with the dragline to achieve the efficient stripping that integrated collection, transportation, abandonment. He presided over the application of the technologies in Shenhua Group Heidaigou opencast coal mine. The mine production capacity increased from the original design capacity of 12Mt/a to the approved production capacity of 34Mt/a and the utility efficiency increased by 3.2 times, the highest yield of 32.89Mt/a, an average annual profit of 1.58 billion yuan, becoming the first annual output of 30Mt class opencast coal mine in China. It realized high yield, high efficiency and safe exploitation, which marked China's opencast coal mine came into the world-class advanced ranks.

Most of coal in china is used for heat utilization. It produces large amounts of waste residue and causes pollution. The waste residue is a high quality raw material for extracting alumina. Guo Zhaohua for the first time invented to extract the valuable elements from fly ash in low cost by 'one-step acid leaching strategy' in the world, overcoming hydrochloric acid leaching, separation, purification, corrosion resistant materials, equipments and environmental protection problems. The system was invented to leach, separate, purificate the useful elements in the fly ash simultaneously. It opened up a new way to produce metallurgical materials, turning waste into treasure. He presided over the construction of the world's first fly ash hydrochloric acid leaching process to produce 4000 tons / year of alumina and gallium pilot plant. The purity of alumina reached 99.0%, the purity of gallium reached 99.99%, the purity of lithium carbonate reached 99.41%. The application of this technology can recycle 3 billion tons of alumina resources and 857000 tons of gallium resources for Zhungeer coal field. What's more, it can relieve the shortage of bauxite resources in China simultaneously.

Guo Zhaohua has obtained 4 international patents, 108 national patents, including 62 invention patents, 2 monographs, 39 published papers, and presided over the formulation of an industrial technical standard.

区域创新奖获得者

郝 小 江

郝小江，1951 年 7 月出生于重庆市。1985 年毕业于中科院昆明植物研究所获理学硕士学位，1986—1990 年在日本京都大学化学研究所留学并获药学博士学位。1991 年回国至今，在中国科学院昆明植物研究所工作任研究员。1995 年 1 月—2006 年 1 月任中国科学院昆明植物研究所常务副所长、所长，首届植物化学与西部植物资源持续利用国家重点实验室主任。1998—2016 年兼任贵州省–中科院天然产物化学重点实验室主任（法人）。

郝小江从事植物天然产物科学研究工作，引领了天然产物化学与植物资源学、与化学生物学的交叉发展方向。通过学科交叉与联合，形成植物资源、化学、生物功能相互衔接和融为一体的天然产物科学研究模式；在新颖复杂结构天然产物的发现、植物系统抗性和防卫的化学物质基础、基于小分子探针的天然产物功能机制等方面取得若干原创性成果，为抗肿瘤、抗病毒、神经保护、抗农作物病虫害提供了先导化合物和候选药物。在 SCI 源学术期刊发表论文 452 篇，他引 4793 次；获授权 PCT 国际专利 1 件、国家发明专利 23 件。他先后领导建设植物化学与西部植物资源持续利用国家重点实验室和省部共建"药用植物功效与利用国家重点实验室"，创建和领导的团队在国际天然产物科学领域产生了一定的影响。

一、发展创新性天然产物科学研究模式

郝小江充分发挥云南植物资源多样性和特殊性的优势，系统研究了 200 余种植物中的 4600 余个化学成分，发现 1300 余个新结构，包括 90 余个新骨架，其中 36 个先后被国际天然产物期刊 *Natural Product Reports* 列为"热点化合物"；在抗肿瘤、抗病毒、神经保护等方面发现生物碱、萜类等 20 余个类型的活性成分，包括 9 个具有自主知识产权的先导化合物，引起国内外学者的关注和跟踪研究。

以中国特有的蔷薇科绣线菊属粉花绣线菊复合群为研究对象，将资源、化学、生物

学研究相结合，在宏观和微观层次揭示了植物种群的若干科学规律，发现了系列具有重要药理活性和生态效应的二萜及其生物碱，并完成了化学合成与结构修饰、资源分布规律的研究；首次证明二萜与生物碱之间的生源关系及其氮源；提出并阐明了该植物复合群的相对独立性以及该复合群历史发生、地理分布、化学成分与细胞染色体、ITS 序列之间进化顺序的对应规律性，揭示了植物种群演化、区系演化以及环境变迁之间的高度协调统一性和相关性。"粉花绣线菊复合群的化学与生物学研究"获得 2003 年度云南省自然科学一等奖。

在我国率先开展了化学结构复杂、骨架奇特多变的虎皮楠生物碱研究。针对该类植物化学成分含量低、碱性强、难分离、骨架环系复杂多样等特点，采用多种现代分离手段和多种波谱技术、单晶衍射及构象互变及过渡态、异构体计算，形成天然产物化学与结构化学、计算化学、分析化学相结合的现代天然产物研究模式；发现新骨架 16 个、新生物碱 92 个，提出了 13 个新骨架生物碱的生源途径假说，成为国际上从事该领域研究的 19 个小组中发现新虎皮楠生物碱最多、发表 SCI 论文最多的研究组。"虎皮楠中新颖结构生物碱的研究"获得 2009 年度云南省自然科学一等奖。

二、建立植物化学防御研究方向

郝小江依据植物化学防御原理，提出"低自毒性植物化学防御分子具备识别病毒和寄主的功能"假说，开展了抗病毒活性天然产物研究。从植物马蓝中发现三类靶向病毒或寄主细胞的植物病毒拮抗剂，诠释了该植物抵御病毒感染的化学本质；以其中的 C_{21} 甾体皂苷为探针，揭示了其特异性抑制烟草花叶病毒亚基因组 RNA 表达、有效抑制病毒复制而对宿主无副作用的新机制，并发现该类 C_{21} 甾体皂苷以该机制显著抑制难以防控的动物甲病毒的复制，治疗指数高达 10000 以上，进而揭示了"正链 RNA 病毒的亚基因组 RNA 可作为抗病毒药物的新靶点"。该研究结果于 2007 年发表在 *PNAS* 上，国际同行专家对该研究结果进行了评述认为："植物化学成分在抗某些 RNA 病毒方面表现出了非常令人鼓舞的成效""是研发抗病毒候选药物的新途径之一""亚基因组 RNA 可能是诱人的抗病毒治疗靶点，该思路已被植物衍生物的纳摩尔浓度的抗动（如甲病毒）植物病毒活性所证实"。以此为起点，郝小江聚焦天然产物的防御功能，相继发现了植物系统获得抗性的化学诱导剂 AHO、烟碱胆碱能受体的高效抑制剂牛筋果素、核盘菌高效抑制剂孕甾烷衍生物等具有开发潜力的植物源农药先导化合物，建立了植物化学防御研究方向。"植物化学防御物质与新农药先导化合物的研究"获得 2013 年度云南省自然科学一等奖，并遴选为云南省 2014 年度十大科技进展之一。

三、形成天然小分子探针的化学生物学研究方向

郝小江基于天然产物与生物体细胞的相容性和酶促合成的特点，以其特殊骨架与有效基团进行小分子探针的优化设计，发展了二萜内酯 S-3、菲啶类 HLY78、大戟二萜

HEP-14 等小分子探针。与李林、陈铨、蒋建东、杨崇林等生物学家的团队合作，先后揭示了特异性调控 Wnt 信号通路、非 BAX/BAK 依赖的线粒体途径诱导细胞凋亡、促进线粒体融合、促进溶酶体生物发生、Fli-1 介导的抗白血病等全新作用机制，为肿瘤、神经系统疾病的治疗提供了新策略、新潜在靶点和先导化合物，形成了以天然小分子为探针的化学生物学研究方向。S-3 促进线粒体融合的研究在国际期刊 *Cell Research* 上发表，同期被德国科隆大学的线粒体研究权威 Mafalda Escobar-Henriques 教授以"融合蛋白：泛素化促进融合"为标题进行专评，"该发现第一次阐明了哺乳动物中融合蛋白的泛素化水平与其线粒体融合活性正相关……更重要的是，S-3 可以使融合蛋白 Mfn1 或 Mfn2 基因缺失的线粒体的表型恢复正常，证实线粒体融合依赖于融合蛋白的泛素化。"大戟二萜 HEP-14 促进溶酶体生物发生的研究结果于 2016 年发表在国际期刊 *Nature Cell Biology* 上，同期的 News and Views 作了专评认为"该研究呈现了蛋白激酶与溶酶体之间一个吸引人的链接，利用这一途径打开了药理学上提高溶酶体活性的通道。"

Awardee of Region Innovation Prize, Hao Xiaojiang

Hao Xiaojiang was born in Chongqing City in July 1951. He obtained his Master degree at Kunming Institute of Botany, Chinese Academy of Sciences in 1985, and PhD degree at Kyoto University in 1990. From 1991 to 1994, he moved to Kunming Institute of Botany, Chinese Academy of Sciences as an associate professor and the Chair of Department of Phytochemistry. Since 1994, he was promoted as a full professor at the current institute. He was the Deputy Director of Kunming Institute of Botany, Chinese Academy of Sciences and the Chair of Open Laboratory of Phytochemistry from 1995 to 1997, and the Director of Kunming Institute of Botany, Chinese Academy of Sciences from 1997 to 2005. He originated the Pilot Knowledge Innovation Project of Chinese Academy of Sciences: Bioresources and Biodiversity Conservation and Development Base in Southwest China in 1998, and founded the State Key Laboratory of Phytochemistry and Plant Resources in West China as the Chair in 2001. In 1998, he founded the Key Laboratory of Chemistry for Natural Products of Guizhou Province and Chinese Academy of Sciences, which was promoted to be the Breeding Base of State Key Laboratory in 2003, and State Key Laboratory of Functions and Applications of Medicinal Plants in 2016.

Hao Xiaojiang has been focusing on studying plant natural products by leading the cutting-edge sciences among natural products, plant resources and chemical biology. After multi-discipline crossing and collaboration, he has created an innovative research system on natural products by integrating plant resources, chemical and biological tools. He has succeeded many original achievements on discovery of novel natural products with complicated structures, identification of chemical mechanism of plant systemic resistance and defense, as well as determination of probe-based functional mechanism of natural products, so as to provide numerous lead compounds and candidates for the anti-cancer, anti-tumor, neuroprotective and agrochemical purposes. With the chronologically origination of State Key Laboratory of Phytochemistry and Plant Resources in West China and State Key Laboratory of Functions and Applications of Medicinal Plants as a founder, Professor Hao has a solid contribution to the international natural products community.

Hao Xiaojiang has published over 439 peer-reviewed SCI papers, which have been cited over 4790 times. He has obtained one PCT patent and 23 China patents. Based on his tremendous results, one candidate drug, phenchlobenpyrrone, has entered the phase II clinical trail for the treatment of Alzheimer's disease. Moreover, he won the First Prize for Natural Sciences in Yunnan Province for three times.

区域创新奖获得者

尼玛扎西

尼玛扎西，1964 年 6 月出生于西藏自治区拉萨市。1988 年毕业于华东师范大学计算机系获工学学士学位，2009 年毕业于四川大学计算机学院获工学博士学位。1988 年至今在西藏大学从事计算机科学与技术学科教学、科研和管理工作，先后任数理系计算机教研室主任、副教授，计算机系副主任，工学院副院长，教务处副处长，现代教育技术中心主任、教授，图书馆和现代教育技术中心馆长、主任，信息科学技术学院院长。入选国家"万人计划"第一批领军人才、全国杰出专业技术人才、新世纪百千万人才工程国家级人选、西藏自治区学术技术带头人、青海省"昆仑英才"引智人才，被中国青年报誉为"西藏 IT 之父"。兼任教育部高校图书情报工作指导委员会委员、中国高等教育学会教育信息化分会理事、中国教育和科研计算机网（CERNET）西藏核心节点主任、《计算机应用》杂志社第九届编委会常务编委。

尼玛扎西从事藏文信息技术研究近三十年，在信息技术标准制订、基础理论研究、关键技术和软件研发等领域做出了一系列开创性工作。获得国家科学技术进步奖二等奖、中国标准创新贡献奖一等奖、西藏自治区科学技术一等奖等近 10 项省部级以上科研奖励。获 1 项国家发明专利、13 项软件著作权，并申请国家发明专利 4 项、美国发明专利 3 项。

一、研究制定《信息交换用藏文编码字符集》国际和国家标准

藏文上下左右拼写，是一种具有二维结构的拼音文字。在《信息交换用藏文编码字符集》国际和国家标准制定之前，藏文信息处理将藏文的上下拼写结果视作一个独立的处理单元并自定义编码，致使藏文信息处理困难且无法交换，严重制约了藏语文的信息化和现代化。1994 年年底—1997 年 7 月，在国家相关部委的组织下，尼玛扎西带领研究团队主持研究制定《信息交换用藏文编码字符集》国际标准。当时，在技术上非常重要的 ISO/IEC 10646 基本多文种平面（Basic Multilingual Plane，BMP）编码空间所剩不多，而且其他一些国家和机构也在研究制订《信息交换用藏文编码字符集》国际标准，竞争十分激烈。研究团队先后向 ISO/IEC JTC1/SC2/WG2 提交 6 份《信息交换用藏文编码字符集》标准提案，最终的提案在深入分析藏文相关文法及文字构成规律的基础上，借鉴其他文字的编码技术，创新性地提出使用藏文基本字符和组合用字符编码所有藏文的技术方案。该方案虽然只规定了藏文的基本字符和组合用字符集合、编码表示及其实现规则，但是可以编码几乎所有的藏文，奠定了藏文信息技术发展的技术基础。1997 年 7 月，提案被 ISO 组织正式确定为《信息交换用藏文编码字符集》国际标准，使藏文成为我国第一个制定完成编码国际标准的少数民族文字。1998 年 1 月 1 日起，该标准作为《信息技术信息交换用藏文编码字符集基本集》（GB 16959—1997）国家标准在全国颁布实行。自此，全球藏文信息处理都遵循上述标准。

二、填补藏文信息技术领域一系列研究空白

研发西藏自治区第一个藏汉英文信息处理系统并广泛应用于公文处理、教材编撰、古籍整理等领域；承担西藏自治区第一个"863"项目，研发藏文 Windows 平台；与国内专业软件公司合作研发国内外第一套全藏文办公软件，填补了国内外相关领域空白；完成国内藏文期刊、现代图书和学位论文数字化以及藏文文献资源服务平台和藏文全文检索系统研发，建设国内外第一个藏文文献资源服务平台——中国西藏知网；完成微软总部 RFP 资助项目，研发藏汉双语同步远程教学及资源发布与管理系统，首次将藏文信息技术应用于现代远程教育。

三、构建藏语自然语言处理基础理论

首次将形式语言和自动机理论引入藏语自然语言处理和藏语计算语言学领域，研究了藏文拼写形式文法，从信息技术的角度揭示了藏文拼写文法的内在规律，构建了藏文拼写形式语言和自动机理论，提出了解决计算机藏文自动拼写检查、自动排序、自动校对和智能输入等领域长期以来未能有效解决的技术难题的新方法，专著《藏文拼写形式语言及其自动机研究和应用》由科学出版社出版。计算机领域著名科学家评价该专著"兼具有系统性和理论深度"，实现了"藏文知识、计算机科学技术和藏文信息技术应用三者深度融合"。

研究了计算机藏文输入技术的数学原理，推导出计算机藏文无重码键盘布局规则，提出实现藏文快速智能输入的方法，并应用信息论证明了方法的最优性，为研发各种藏文快速智能输入法奠定了理论基础。

四、突破藏语自然语言处理关键技术

研究藏汉双向统计机器翻译关键技术，研发藏语自动分词与词性标注系统、藏汉双向机器翻译系统等系列软件。通过对藏文动词时态、动词及物性和格助词的处理，并研

究基于中介语言的汉藏统计翻译模型和直接翻译模型的融合，有效解决了汉藏平行语料不足导致的数据稀疏问题，使藏汉双向机器翻译的平均翻译可读性达到 65% 以上。通过修订和完善《信息处理用藏语词类标记规范》，研究未登录词识别技术，使藏语自动分词和词性标注系统的分词准确率达到 95%。应用藏汉双向机器翻译和藏语自动分词技术研发多文种搜索引擎，实现了藏汉英跨语言搜索和多文种呈现技术。藏汉双向机器翻译系统通过网站和 iOS、Android 操作系统 App 面向社会提供服务，用户遍布国内外，是全球最具影响力的藏汉双向机器翻译系统。

五、开辟藏文通信技术研究方向

首次提出藏文编码标准与索引技术结合的移动电话藏文编码方法，解决了藏文编码标准在系统资源有限的数字移动电话上应用的技术难题。首次设计移动电话藏文键盘布局，解决了在有限键位上科学安排藏文字符的技术难题。与电信运营商和移动电话制造商合作，先后研发全球第一款全藏文数字移动电话和车载移动电话和基于 Android、Symbian 和 Windows Mobile 智能移动电话操作系统藏文软件包、第一款藏文 Android 操作系统和基于该操作系统的藏汉双语智能移动电话。应用所取得的技术成果进行技术集成创新，开辟了藏文通信技术研究方向。2005 年 8 月之前，国内外无任何手持移动设备支持藏文信息处理。经过十几年的努力，尼玛扎西营造了藏文通信技术研发环境，奠定了相关技术基础，目前各种智能移动电话操作系统支持藏文处理逐渐成为常态。仅以中国电信集团西藏分公司为例，推广应用相关成果实现了数亿元的销售收入。

六、规划教育信息化，培养信息技术人才

1997 年，主持建设 CERNET 西藏核心节点，使之成为西藏第一个因特网接入服务机构。1999 年至今，负责西藏大学校园计算机网络和数字化校园规划、建设和运行管理。在近 30 年的从教历程中，指导和培养了一批计算机专业领域的本科生和研究生。

Awardee of Region Innovation Prize, Nyima Tashi

Nyima Tashi was born in Lhasa City of Tibet Autonomous Region in June 1964. He got his bachelor degree of engineering from Department of Computer Science and Technology, East China Normal University in 1988 and the doctor degree of engineering from College of Computer Science, Sichuan University. Since 1988, he has been engaged in the teaching, research and management of computer science and technology in Tibet University. He has served as director of Computer Teaching and Research Department, associate professor of computer science, deputy director of Computer Department, associate dean of School of Engineering, deputy director of Academic Affairs, director of Modern Education Technology Center, professor of computer science, director of Library and Modern Education Technology Center, director of College of Information Science and Technology. He was elected to the first batch of leading talent of national "Ten Thousand People Plan", the national outstanding professional and technical personnel, the national candidate of New Century Hundred, Thousand and Ten Thousand of Talent Engineering, the leader of Tibet Autonomous Region Science and technology, the talent of "KunLun YingCai" of Qinghai province. He was praised by China Youth Daily as "the father of IT in Tibet". He is a member of the Guidance Committee of the Library and Information Work of the Ministry of Education, a director of the China Higher Education Society Information Technology Branch, the director of Tibet core node of China Education and Research Computer Network, a standing editorial board of "Computer Application" magazine.

Nyima Tashi has been doing research about Tibetan information technology for almost 30 years. He has done a series of groundbreaking jobs in the fields of the development of Tibetan information technology standards, basic theory research, key technologies and software development. He researched and developed international and national standards of Tibetan coded character set for information interchange, filled a series of research blank in the Tibetan information technology field, structured the basic theory of natural language processing in Tibetan language, broke through key technology of the Tibetan natural language processing, started the direction of Tibetan communication technology research, and plans and constructs education informationization. He received nearly 10 provincial and ministerial levels above research awards including the second prize of National Science and Technology Progress Award, the first prize of China Standard Innovation Contribution Award and the first prize of Tibet Autonomous Region Science and Technology Award. He owns one national invention patent and 13 software copyrights. Besides, he applied for 4 national invention patents and 3 US invention patents.

区域创新奖获得者

杨　斌

　　杨斌，1965 年 5 月出生于云南省墨江县。1987 年毕业于东北工学院（现东北大学）有色金属冶金系，1990 年毕业于昆明工学院（现昆明理工大学）冶金系获硕士学位后留校任助教、讲师，1994—1998 年在昆明理工大学冶金系攻读博士学位，1998 年晋升为副教授，次年破格晋升为教授。2007 年受国家公派到莫斯科国立钢铁及合金学院有色金属教研室进行访问。现任昆明理工大学副校长、博士生导师、二级教授，真空冶金国家工程实验室常务副主任，复杂有色金属清洁利用国家重点实验室副主任，云南省有色金属真空冶金重点实验室主任；国家万人计划科技创新领军人才，新世纪百千万人才工程国家级人选，享受国务院政府特殊津贴专家，云南省科技领军人才，科技部、教育部和云南省创新团队带头人，云南省中青年学术和技术带头人；兼任中国真空学会常务理事，中国有色金属学会稀有金属冶金学术委员会委员，*Journal of Alloys and Compounds*、*RSC Advances*、*Journal of Hazardous Materials*、*Vacuum* 等多个国际专业期刊的通讯审稿人。

　　杨斌从事冶金科学与工程的科研教学工作 30 年。发明了复杂锡合金真空蒸馏新技术、从含铟粗锌中高效提炼金属铟技术等一系列技术，在我国 14 个省区 70 余家企业推广应用，并出口至美国、英国、西班牙、马来西亚等国家，累计形成年处理 45 万吨复杂合金的规模，年产值超过百亿元人民币，推动了有色金属冶金行业的科技进步。撰写专著和国家规划教材 3 部，发表论文 100 余篇，其中被 SCI、EI、ISTP 收录 70 余篇；获授权专利 19 件，其中美国授权专利 1 件；获国家科学技术奖励二等奖 3 项、国家级教学成果一等奖 1 项、省部级科学技术一等奖 6 项。先后获得全国优秀科技工作者、中国有色金属工业优秀科技工作者、云南省兴滇人才奖、云南省有突出贡献的优秀专业技术人才、云南省创先争优优秀共产党员、云南省教育功勋奖等荣誉。

一、发明了复杂锡资源清洁高效综合利用技术

针对多金属锡资源综合利用的难题，提出了还原熔炼—真空精炼新工艺，发明了复杂锡合金真空蒸馏新技术，研制出真空蒸馏专用装备，实现了复杂锡资源的清洁高效利用。

新工艺与原有的氯化法、电解法和加剂造渣法工艺相比，能够处理任意成分的锡基合金，深度脱除锡基合金中的铅（Pb < 30ppm），锑、砷脱除率大于80%，锡直收率由89%提高到97%，金属回收率大于99%，生产成本降低20%，危险固废量减少80%。开发成功大型化、连续化、自动化和系统化的真空冶金成套装备，与德国、英国、俄罗斯的装备相比，处理能力提升5倍（达15000吨/年），连续运行时间由15天延长至180天以上，节能30%。

2005年以来，相关技术成果在全球最大的锡冶炼企业云南锡业集团、广西华锡集团等国内56家企业应用，并输出到美国ECS、英国CE、西班牙CRM、马来西亚MSC和我国台湾瑞大鸿等6家企业，从复杂合金中生产锡、铅、锑、铋、锌、铜、银、砷等金属产品，年处理40万吨物料。技术覆盖我国所有锡冶炼厂，还拓展到铅铋锑冶炼行业处理贵铅、贵铋、贵锑等物料。成果入编"锡冶炼厂工艺设计规范"国家标准、《有色金属真空冶金》国家规划教材、《中国工业史—有色金属卷》及《中国大百科全书》。"复杂锡合金真空蒸馏新技术及产业化应用"获2015年度国家科技进步奖二等奖。

二、发明了从高铁闪锌矿中提炼金属铟的技术

针对高铁闪锌矿冶炼过程金属铟回收率低、资源浪费严重的问题，提出了"深度脱硫—还原挥发—真空蒸馏—电解精炼"提炼铟的工艺，建成了多金属锌矿资源综合利用的示范工程。

高铁闪锌矿是富含铟的典型矿物，是我国特有矿物。传统湿法工艺处理高铁闪锌矿，铟回收率不足60%，过程产出浸出渣、净化渣和含重金属废水，铁、铜、镉、铅等有价金属综合利用率低。杨斌根据精矿中铟、锌、铁等元素的赋存状态，揭示了Me-S-O、Me-C-O体系的高温物理化学规律以及锌基合金挥发特性，发明了从含铟粗锌中高效提炼金属铟的关键技术。与加拿大、芬兰、比利时的湿法提铟工艺相比，无需溶剂萃取和化学除杂工序，且从高铁闪锌矿（In > 0.05%）中生产金属铟（> 99.995%）的铟回收率由60%提高至80%以上。自2004年，该技术在云南、广西和湖南5家企业应用，年产120吨铟、5万吨锌，占我国原生铟产量的30%。此外，在云南铜业建成国家高技术产业发展示范工程。"从含铟粗锌中高效提炼金属铟的技术"获2009年度国家技术发明二等奖。

三、发明了从冶炼渣中回收稀散稀贵金属新技术

稀散稀贵金属在冶炼过程中进入冶炼渣，回收利用难度大。为此，杨斌开发了硒渣、镉渣及硬锌资源化新技术，从冶炼渣中提炼出硒和镉，高效富集锗、铟、银、金，开辟

了冶炼渣资源化生产稀散稀贵金属的新途径。

发明了真空蒸馏提取硒新技术和装备，硒渣经过真空蒸馏得到产品硒（＞99%），金银铜等元素富集于蒸馏渣。2004年在云南铜业集团建成生产线，累计产出金属硒1600余吨、富集金银超过20吨；开发了"海绵镉熔炼—连续真空蒸馏—无氧铸锭"技术和装备，2011年在云南冶金集团建成年产800吨精镉（Cd＞99.995%）的生产线，金属镉回收率大于98%。

作为主要完成人之一，参与了"硬锌真空蒸馏提锌和富集锗铟银"的技术研究及产业化工作，1997年在广东韶关冶炼厂建成5条生产线，解决了锗铟银高效富集等难题。至今已累计处理硬锌72000吨，回收金属锗超过200吨，金属回收率大于98%，获2003年度国家技术发明二等奖。

Awardee of Region Innovation Prize, Yang Bin

Yang Bin was born in Mojiang County of Yunnan Province in May 1965. He received his bachelor's degree from School of non-ferrous metals metallurgy, Northeastern Institute (now Northeastern institute of technology) in 1987. He continued to study graduate courses at School of metal metallurgy, Kunming Institute (now Kunming University of Science and Technology), and in 1990, he received his master degree and stayed to teach as a teaching assistant. He obtained his PhD degree in 1998 and was elected as an associated professor in 1998. In 1999, he was been a professor, and selected as PhD supervisor in 2003. In 2007, he studied in The National University of Science and Technology "MISiS" of Russia (formerly Moscow Institute of Steel and Alloys State Technological University) as government-sponsored visiting scholar. He is the vice President of Kunming university of science and technology, executive deputy director of National Engineering Laboratory for Vacuum Metallurgy, deputy director of State Key Laboratory of Complex Nonferrous Metal Resources Clean Utilization. He is a person selected into the Country's "10000 Talents Plan", a person selected for New Century Talents Project, an expert gaining the special government allowance, the Leader of Innovation Teams of Ministry of Science and Technology and Ministry of Education, the winner of Leading Talent of Yunnan Province. He is also the Excellent fellow with Great Contribution to Yunnan Province, Academic and Technological Leader of Yunnan province. Executive Directive of China Vacuum Society, Deputy Director of Vacuum Metallurgy Division of China Vacuum Society, member of Rare Metal Metallurgy Academic Council of China Non-ferrous Metal Academy, Paper reviewers of *Journal of Alloys and Compounds*, *RSC Advances*, *Journal of Hazardous Materials*, *Vacuum*.

Prof. Yang has dedicated to the research and education of metallurgical science and engineering more than 30 years. He has taught a verity of courses successively, such as New Metallurgical Technology, Vacuum Metallurgy, Introduction of Metallurgical Engineering. He was known for a series of high-tech vacuum metallurgy achievement: "New technology and Equipment of Purify Tin" "a novel technology of clean metallurgy of effective extraction of indium from crude Zinc containing Indium" and "Recovering Zinc and Enriching Ge, In, Ag from Hard Zinc by Vacuum Distillation". There were more than 70 companies located in 14 provinces that have applied these technologies in our county. Furthermore, many developed counties had imported the production lines. The increase output value has surpassed one billion yuan, achieved significant economical, social and environmental benefits. He has published three academic monographs and textbooks, and more than 70 pieces of papers indexed by SCI and EI. The whole technology reached top level in the world. He has awarded two second National Invention Second Prizes (ranking first and third, respectively), one second National Science and Technology Progress Prize (ranking first), one first prize of national teaching achievement and six provincial first prizes.

附　　录

APPENDICES

何梁何利基金评选章程

（2007 年 5 月 15 日何梁何利基金信托委员会会议通过）

一、总则

第一条 何梁何利基金（以下称本基金）由何善衡慈善基金会有限公司、梁铢琚博士、何添博士、利国伟博士之伟伦基金有限公司于 1994 年 3 月 30 日捐款成立。2005 年 10 月 12 日经香港高等法院批准。基金捐款人，除了何善衡慈善基金会有限公司及利国伟博士之伟伦基金有限公司外，梁铢琚慈善基金会有限公司和何添基金有限公司各自分别为已故梁铢琚博士及已故何添博士之遗产承办人指定之慈善机构，以便根据本基金信托契约之条款行使有关权力或给予所需批准。

第二条 本基金的宗旨是：

（一）促进中国的科学与技术发展；

（二）奖励取得杰出成就和重大创新的科学技术工作者。

二、评奖条件

第三条 本基金奖励和资助致力于推进中国科学技术取得成就及进步与创新的个人。

第四条 本基金奖励和资助具备下列条件的中华人民共和国公民：

（一）对推动科学技术事业发展有杰出贡献；

（二）热爱祖国，积极为国家现代化建设服务，有高尚的社会公德和职业道德；

（三）在我国科学技术研究院（所）、大专院校、企业以及信托委员会认为适当的其他机构从事科学研究、教学或技术工作已满 5 年。

第五条 获奖候选人须由评选委员会选定的提名人以书面形式推荐。

提名人由科学技术领域具有一定资格的专家包括海外学者组成。

三、奖项

第六条 本基金设"何梁何利基金科学与技术成就奖""何梁何利基金科学与技术进步奖""何梁何利基金科学与技术创新奖"，每年评奖一次。

第七条 何梁何利基金科学与技术成就奖授予下列杰出科学技术工作者：

（一）长期致力于推进国家科学技术进步，贡献卓著，历史上取得国际高水平学术成就者；

（二）在科学技术前沿，取得重大科技突破，攀登当今科技高峰，领先世界先进水平者；

（三）推进技术创新，建立强大自主知识产权和自主品牌，其产业居于当今世界前列者。

何梁何利基金科学与技术成就奖获奖人每人颁发奖励证书和奖金100万港元。

第八条 何梁何利基金科学与技术进步奖授予在特定学科领域取得重大发明、发现和科技成果者，尤其是在近年内有突出贡献者。

何梁何利基金科学与技术进步奖按学科领域分设下列奖项：

（一）数学力学奖

（二）物理学奖

（三）化学奖

（四）天文学奖

（五）气象学奖

（六）地球科学奖

（七）生命科学奖

（八）农学奖

（九）医学、药学奖

（十）古生物学、考古学奖

（十一）机械电力技术奖

（十二）电子信息技术奖

（十三）交通运输技术奖

（十四）冶金材料技术奖

（十五）化学工程技术奖

（十六）资源环保技术奖

（十七）工程建设技术奖

何梁何利基金科学与技术进步奖获奖人每人颁发奖励证书和奖金20万港元。

第九条 何梁何利基金科学与技术创新奖授予具有高水平科技成就而通过技术创新和管理创新，创建自主知识产权产业和著名品牌，创造重大经济效益和社会效益的杰出贡献者。

何梁何利基金科学与技术创新奖分设下列奖项：

（一）青年创新奖

（二）产业创新奖

（三）区域创新奖

何梁何利基金科学与技术创新奖获奖人每人颁发奖励证书和奖金20万港元。

第十条 本基金每年各奖项名额如下：

何梁何利基金科学与技术成就奖不超过5名；何梁何利基金科学与技术进步奖、何梁何利基金科学与技术创新奖总数不超过65名（原则上科学与技术进步奖和科学与技术创新奖名额的比例为3比1至2比1）。而奖金总额不超过该年度信托委员会审议通过的奖金总额。

具体名额根据年度资金运作情况和评选情况确定。

四、评选委员会

第十一条　本基金成立由各相关领域具有高尚道德情操、精深学术造诣、热心科技奖励
　　　　　事业的专家组成的评选委员会。

　　　　　评选委员会委员经过信托委员会批准、颁发聘任书后，独立行使职能，负责评选工作。

第十二条　评选委员会委员最多不超过20人，其中主任一人、副主任二人、秘书长一人，
　　　　　由内地学者和海外学者出任。

　　　　　评选委员会委员内地学者和海外学者的比例，原则上每四名委员中，内地学者为三
　　　　　人，海外学者为一人。

　　　　　评选委员会主任、副主任由基金信托契约补充条款规定的信托委员兼任。其中主任
　　　　　由补充契约所指明的与科技部有关的信托委员兼任，副主任二人分别由补充契约所
　　　　　指明的与教育部有关的信托委员和补充契约所指明的国际学者信托委员兼任。评选
　　　　　委员会秘书长由信托委员会任命并征得捐款人同意的人选担任。

　　　　　评选委员会委员每三年更换四分之一（不包括主任、副主任及秘书长）。

　　　　　此外，评选委员会委员的聘任，贯彻相对稳定和适度更新的原则。其办法由评选委
　　　　　员会制定。

　　　　　评选委员会办公室设在北京，挂靠科学技术部。

第十三条　评选委员会根据评选工作需要，可组织若干专业评审组、奖项评审组，根据提
　　　　　名人的提名推荐材料对被提名人进行初评，产生获奖候选人，提交评选委员会终评。

　　　　　专业评审组、奖项评审组的评委由评选委员会任命。

第十四条　本基金各奖项获奖人由评选委员会会议评定。

　　　　　何梁何利基金科学与技术进步奖、何梁何利基金科学与技术创新奖的获奖人，由评
　　　　　选委员会根据专业评审组、奖项评审组的评选结果，评选审定。

　　　　　何梁何利基金科学与技术成就奖获奖人，由评选委员会全体会议，根据评选委员提
　　　　　名评选产生。评选委员会设立预审小组，必要时对候选人进行考察和听证。

第十五条　评选委员会会议贯彻"公平、公正、公开"原则，实行一人一票制，以无记
　　　　　名形式表决确定获奖人。何梁何利基金科学与技术进步奖、何梁何利基金科学与技
　　　　　术创新奖的候选人，获半数赞成票为获奖人。何梁何利基金科学与技术成就奖的候
　　　　　选人，获三分之二多数赞成票为获奖人。

第十六条　评选委员会在评定获奖人名额时，应适当考虑奖种、学科和区域之间的平衡。

五、授　　奖

第十七条　评选委员会评选结果揭晓前须征求获奖人本人意愿，并通知捐款人及信托委
　　　　　员会。遵照捐款人意愿，获奖人应承诺于获奖后，继续在国内从事科学研究和技术

工作不少于三年。

第十八条　本基金每年适当时候举行颁奖仪式，由评选委员会安排向何梁何利基金各奖项获得者颁发证书和奖金，并通过新闻媒体公布获奖人员名单及其主要贡献。

六、出版物和学术会议

第十九条　本基金每年出版介绍获奖人及其主要科学技术成就的出版物。

出版物的编辑、出版工作由评选委员会负责。

第二十条　本基金每年举办学术报告会、研讨会，由评选委员会委员、获奖人代表介绍其学术成就及相关学科领域的进展。

根据基金财政状况，本基金各专业领域专题学术讨论会可在海外举办。

本基金学术报告会、研讨会由评选委员会负责组织。

七、附　　则

第二十一条　本基金评选委员会每年例会一次，总结当年工作，部署下一年度工作，研究和决定重大事宜。

第二十二条　本章程由本基金评选委员会解释。

第二十三条　本章程自 2007 年 5 月 15 日施行。

REGULATIONS OF HO LEUNG HO LEE FOUNDATION ON THE EVALUATION AND EXAMINATION OF ITS PRIZES AND AWARDS

(Adopted at the meeting of the Board of Trustees on May 15, 2007)

I General Provisions

Article 1　Ho Leung Ho Lee Foundation (hereinafter referred to as " the Foundation") was established on March 30, 1994 in Hong Kong with funds donated by the S H Ho Foundation Limited, Dr. Leung Kau-Kui, Dr. Ho Tim and Dr. Lee Quo-Wei's Wei Lun Foundation Limited. With the approval of the High Court of Hong Kong, apart from S H Ho Foundation Limited and Wei Lun Foundation Limited (donors of the Foundation), Leung Kau-Kui Foundation Limited and Ho Tim Foundation Limited have respectively been nominated by the estates of the late Dr. Leung Kau-Kui and Dr. Ho Tim to and they can as from October 12, 2005 exercise the powers or give the necessary approvals under the terms of the Foundation's trust deed.

Article 2　Purposes of the Foundation are:

(1) to promote the development of science and technology in China;

(2) to reward the scientific and technical personnel with outstanding achievements and great innovations.

II Criteria for Awards

Article 3　The Foundation shall grant awards and prizes to individuals who are devoted to the achievements, progress and innovations of China's science and technology.

Article 4　The Foundation shall grant awards and prizes to the citizens of the People's Republic of China who meet the following criteria:

(1) Having made outstanding contributions in promoting the development of science and technology;

(2) Being patriotic, vigorously working for the modernization drive of the country, and preserving lofty social morality and professional ethics;

(3) Being with at least five years of scientific researches, teaching or technical working experience in China's science and technology research institutes, institutions for higher learning and universities, enterprises and other organizations which the Board of Trustees regards as appropriate.

Article 5　Candidates for the awards and prizes of the Foundation shall be recommended in writing by nominators identified by the Selection Board.

Nominators should be qualified experts (including those overseas) in various fields of sciences and technology.

III　Awards and Prizes

Article 6　The Foundation sets three annual prizes. They are the Prize for Scientific and Technological Achievements of Ho Leung Ho Lee Foundation, the Prize for Scientific and Technological Progress of Ho Leung Ho Lee Foundation, and the Prize for Scientific and Technological Innovation of Ho Leung Ho Lee Foundation.

Article 7　The Prize for Scientific and Technological Achievements of Ho Leung Ho Lee Foundation shall be awarded to the outstanding science and technology personnel as follows:

(1) Those who have devoted to scientific and technological progress in China for a long time, having made significant contributions and world–class academic achievements.

(2) Those who have made great breakthroughs in the frontline of science and technology, attaining high levels in science and technology and leading the trend in specific areas in the world.

(3) Those who have made great efforts in pushing forward the technology innovation and have built up powerful self intellectual property and brand of its own so that its industry ranks the top of today's world.

Each winner of the Prize for Scientific and Technological Achievements of Ho Leung Ho Lee Foundation will receive a certificate and the amount of the prize of HK $ 1000000.

Article 8　The Prize for Scientific and Technological Progress of Ho Leung Ho Lee Foundation is for those who have made important inventions, discoveries and achievements in specific subject areas, especially having remarkable contributions in recent years.

The following prizes of the Prize for Scientific and Technological Progress of Ho Leung Ho Lee Foundation are set up by subjects:

(1) Award for Mathematics and Mechanics

(2) Award for Physics

(3) Award for Chemistry

(4) Award for Astronomy

(5) Award for Meteorology

(6) Award for Earth Sciences

(7) Award for Life Sciences

(8) Award for Agronomy

（9）Award for Medical Sciences and Materia Medica

（10）Award for Paleontology and Archaeology

（11）Award for Machinery and Electric Technology

（12）Award for Electronics and Information Technology

（13）Award for Communication and Transportation Technology

（14）Award for Metallurgy and Materials Technology

（15）Award for Chemical Engineering Technology

（16）Award for Resources and Environmental Protection Technology

（17）Award for Engineering and Construction Technology

Each winner of the Prize for Science and Technological Progress of Ho Leung Ho Lee Foundation will be awarded a certificate and the amount of the prize of HK $ 200000.

Article 9   The Prize for Scientific and Technological Innovation of Ho Leung Ho Lee Foundation is for the outstanding contributors who have made high level achievements in science and technology, created industry with self intellectual property and famous brands through technology and management innovation, and thus have created great economic and social benefits for the society.

The following prizes of the Prize for Scientific and Technological Innovation of Ho Leung Ho Lee Foundation are set up:

（1）Award for Youth Innovation

（2）Award for Industrial Innovation

（3）Award for Region Innovation

Each winner of the Prize for Scientific and Technological Innovation of Ho Leung Ho Lee Foundation will be awarded a certificate and the amount of the prize of HK $ 200000.

Article 10   Annual quotas of awardees of each prize of Ho Leung Ho Lee Foundation are as follows:

There should be no more than 5 awardees each year for the Prize for Scientific and Technological Achievements of Ho Leung Ho Lee Foundation; and the total number of the winners of the Prize for Scientific and Technological Progress of Ho Leung Ho Lee Foundation and the Prize for Scientific and Technological Innovation of Ho Leung Ho Lee Foundation should be no more than 65 (The proportion of the awardees of the Prize for Scientific and Technological Progress of Ho Leung Ho Lee Foundation and the Prize for Scientific and Technological Innovation of Ho Leung Ho Lee Foundation is in principle from 3 to 1 to 2 to 1) . And the total amount of all the Prizes awarded should not exceed the total amount of prize moneys of the year as approved by the Board of Trustees for that year.

The number of winners of each prize should be decided according to the situation each year of the operation of the Foundation's funds and the results of evaluation and selection for the year.

IV Selection Board

Article 11   A Selection Board shall be constituted under the Foundation, consisting of scholars who are highly respected in ethics, with accomplishments in academic researches and devotion to the work of award of science and technology prizes.

Members of the Selection Board shall independently exercise the powers and are responsible for the evaluation work after they have been appointed with the approval of the Board of Trustees and received the letters of appointment.

Article 12   The total number of the members of the Selection Board should be no more than 20. Among them, there will be one Chair, two Vice Chairs and one Secretary-General. Both local and overseas scholars could be members of the Selection Board.

For every four members of the Selection Board, the ratio between local and overseas scholars should in principle be 3 to 1.

The Chair and the two Vice Chairs of the Selection Board should also be members of the Board of Trustees as stated in the Foundation's Supplemental trust deed. Among them, the Chair should be the member of the Board of Trustees who is related, as stated in the Foundation's Supplemental trust deed, to the Ministry of Science and Technology. And the two Vice Chairs should respectively be the member of the Board of Trustees who is related, as stated in the Foundation's Supplemental trust deed, to the Ministry of Education and the international scholar member of the Board of Trustees as mentioned in the Foundation's Supplemental trust deed.

Secretary General of the Selection Board should be appointed by the Board of Trustees with the agreement of the donors as well.

The members of the Selection Board shall be altered a quarter every 3 years (except Chair, Vice Chair and Secretary General.)

Besides, the appointment of the members of the Selection Board should be in line with the principles of comparative stability and proper renewal. The Selection Board will be responsible for formulation of the ways of selection.

The office of the Selection Board is located in Beijing and affiliated to the Ministry of Science and Technology of China.

Article 13   Several specific professional evaluation panels or prize evaluation panels may be set up under the Selection Board when it is necessary. The first round of evaluation is done according to recommendation materials submitted by the nominators with a candidate list as the results. This list will be submitted to the Selection Board for a final evaluation.

Members of the professional evaluation panels and prize evaluation panels shall be appointed by the Selection Board.

Article 14   Winners of the prizes of the Foundation are evaluated and decided by the Selection Board.

The Selection Board shall evaluate and determine the winners of the Prize for Scientific and Technological Progress of Ho Leung Ho Lee Foundation and the Prize for Scientific and Technological Innovation of Ho Leung Ho Lee Foundation on the basis of results of the work of the professional evaluation panels or the prize evaluation panels.

The Prize for Scientific and Technological Achievements of Ho Leung Ho Lee Foundation should be decided on a plenary meeting of the Selection Board and on the basis of the nomination of the Selection Board. The Selection Board may set up preliminary evaluation panel to exercise the right of examination and hearing of the candidates when necessary.

Article 15　The Selection Board shall work with the principles of "Fairness, Justness and Openness" and "One Member One Vote". Decisions on winners of prizes of the Foundation are made in a way of anonymous ballot by the members of the Selection Board. The endorsement of at least half of the members of the Selection Board is a must for a candidate to win the Prize for Scientific and Technological Progress of Ho Leung Ho Lee Foundation and the Prize for Scientific and Technological Innovation of Ho Leung Ho Lee Foundation; while at least two-third of favorable votes of the total number is a must for candidates to win the Prize for Scientific and Technological Achievements of Ho Leung Ho Lee Foundation.

Article 16　The Selection Board should take the balance between types of prize, between subjects and between regions into consideration in the process of evaluation.

V　Awarding

Article 17　The Selection Board must ask for the winners' willingness prior to any public announcement of the results of evaluation and selection, and notify both the donors and the Board of Trustees. According to the wishes of the donors, the winners are required to stay in China and continue to carry on scientific researches or technological work for no less than 3 years after receiving the prizes.

Article 18　An award granting ceremony will be held each year at a proper time, in which the winners shall be granted with certificates and prizes as arranged by the Selection Board. The list of awardees and their major contributions will be publicized through media.

VI　Publications and Academic Seminars

Article 19　The Foundation shall make a publication yearly to introduce the awardees and their major scientific and technological achievements.

The Selection Board is responsible for editing and publication of the publications.

Article 20　The Foundation shall organize academic seminars every year, in which members of the Selection Board and representatives of the awardees introduce their academic achievements and updated progress in the related areas and make relevant reports where appropriate.

Should the financial situation of the Foundation permits, the academic seminars of specific subjects of the Foundation may be held abroad.

The Selection Board is responsible for the organization of the reports and seminars.

VII Supplementary Provisions

Article 21　The Selection Board of the Foundation holds a meeting annually to summarize the work of the year, to plan the work of the following year and to study and decide on the relevant important issues.

Article 22　The Selection Board of the Foundation shall have the right of explanation of the Articles of this regulation.

Article 23　This regulation becomes effective on May 15. 2007.

关于何梁何利基金获奖科学家
异议处理若干规定

（2009 年 5 月 20 日何梁何利基金信托委员会会议通过）

一、总　　则

为了正确处理对何梁何利基金获奖人提出异议的投诉事件，弘扬科学精神，崇尚科学道德，抵御社会不正之风和科研不端行为，提升何梁何利基金科学与技术奖的权威性和公信力，制定本规定。

二、基本原则

处理对获奖人投诉事件，贯彻以事实为依据，以法律为准绳的原则，遵循科学共同体认同的道德准则，区别情况，妥善处置。

三、受　　理

涉及对获奖科学家主要科技成果评价、知识产权权属以及与奖项有关事项提出异议的署名投诉信件，由评选委员会受理，并调查处理。

匿名投诉信件，原则上不予受理。但涉及获奖人因科研不端行为受到处分、学术资格被取消或与其学术著作、奖项评选相关重要情况的，应由评选委员会跟进调查核实处理。

四、调　　查

评选委员会受理投诉后，由评选委员会秘书长指定评选委员会办公室专人按以下工作程序办理：

1. 将投诉信函复印件送交该获奖人的专业评审组负责人，征求意见。

2. 专业评审组负责人有足够理由认为投诉异议不成立，没有必要调查的，评选委员会秘书长可决定终止处理。

专业评审组负责人认为投诉异议有一定依据，有必要进一步调查的，由评选委员会办公室向获奖人所在部门或单位发函听证。

3. 获奖人所在部门或单位经调查，认为投诉异议不成立或基本不能成立的，应请该单位出具书面意见。评选委员会秘书长可据此决定终止处理。

获奖人所在部门或单位根据投诉认为获奖人涉嫌科研不端行为的，评选委员会应建议该部门或单位根据国家有关规定调查处理，并反馈查处信息。

4. 调查结果应向信托委员会报告。

五、处理决定

获奖人所在部门或单位经调查认定获奖人确属科研不端行为，并做出相应处理的，评选委员会秘书长应当参照《中华人民共和国科学技术进步法》第七十一条规定，提出撤销其奖励决定（草案），经评选委员会主任批准后，提交信托委员会审议。

六、公　　告

因获奖人科研不端行为，撤销其奖励的决定经信托委员会审议通过后，由评选委员会在何梁何利基金年报上公告，并通知本人，返回奖励证书、奖金。

信托委员会对获奖人撤销奖励的决定是终局决定。

七、附　　则

本规定自 2009 年 6 月 1 日起试行。

附:《中华人民共和国科学技术进步法》第七十一条:

"违反本法规定，骗取国家科学技术奖励的，由主管部门依法撤销奖励，追回奖金，并依法给予处分。

违反本法规定，推荐的单位或者个人提供虚假数据、材料，协助他人骗取国家科学技术奖励的，由主管部门给予通报批评；情节严重的，暂停或者取消其推荐资格，并依法给予处分。"

REGULATIONS ON HANDLING THE COMPLAINT LODGED AGAINST THE PRIZE-WINNER WITH HO LEUNG HO LEE FOUNDATION

(Adopted at the meeting of the Board of Trustees on May 20, 2009)

I General Principle

For the purpose of handling properly the objection lodged against the prize-winner with Ho Leung Ho Lee Foundation, promoting scientific spirits and upholding scientific ethics, preventing social malpractice or misconduct in scientific research, and improving the public credibility and authority of Ho Leung Ho Lee Foundation with respect to awards for science and technology, the Selection Board hereby formulates the regulations as stipulated below.

II Basic Principle

The Selection Board shall handle the complaint lodged against any prize-winner in accordance with the principle of taking the facts as the basis and taking the law as the criterion, and deal with each case properly by following the moral standard recognized by the scientific community.

III Acceptance

For any duly signed letter of objection against a prize-wining scientist with respect to the appraisal of his major scientific and technological achievement, the ownership of intellectual property right and other prize-related matter, the Selection Board shall be responsible for acceptance of the letter of objection and for further investigation and handling thereof?

The Selection Board shall, in principle, not accept a letter of objection written or sent in an anonymous manner. However, if it is mentioned in the letter of objection that, due to misconduct of the prize-winner in the scientific research, the discipline measure is imposed against him, or his academic qualification is cancelled, or there is any other important matter concerning his academic publication and prize selection, such a letter of objection must be accepted by the Selection Board, followed by further investigation, verification and handling.

IV Investigation

Upon acceptance of a letter of objection, the Secretary General of the Selection Board shall designate a special person in the Office of Selection Board to handle the letter of objection according to the procedures as follows:

1. A copy of the letter of complaint shall be sent to the person-in-charge of the specialized evaluation team determining to grant the award to the prize-winner for soliciting his comment.

2. When the person-in-charge of the specialized evaluation team concludes with sufficient reason that the objection cannot be established and it is not necessary to make further investigation, the Secretary General of the Selection Board can make a decision as to terminate the handling of the letter of objection.

When the person-in-charge of the specialized evaluation team deems that the objection can be established on basis of facts but should be proved by further investigation, the office of the Selection Board shall issue a notification to the working unit of the prize-winner to request his presenceat a hearing to be held.

3. If the working unit of the prize-winner deems that the objection cannot be established or basically cannot be established after investigation, the working unit is obligated to produce a formal document in writing to state its opinion. Then the Secretary General of the Selection Board has the right to make a decision as to the termination of the handling of the letter of objection.

In case the working unit of the prize-winner deems that the prize-winner commits malpractice or misconduct in proof of the letter of objection, the Selection Board is obligated to propose that the working unit carry out investigation in accordance with government regulations before making a response by sending a feedback to the Selection Board.

4. The investigation results should be reported to Ho Leung Ho Lee Foundation's Board of Trustees.

V Decision

Once the working unit of the prize-winner proves with further investigation that the prize-winner commits malpractice or misconduct, and takes discipline measure against the prize-winner, the Secretary General of the Selection Board should draft a proposal, in accordance with Article 71 of the *Law of the PRC on, Science and Technology Progres*s, on withdrawal of the prize awarded to the prize-winner. The proposal needs to be further approved by the Director of the Selection Board before being submitted to Ho Leung Ho Lee Foundation's Board of Trustees for deliberation.

VI Announcement

The Selection Board shall announce its decision with respect to withdrawal of the prize from the prize-winner, due to his malpractice or misconduct, in its annual report with approval of the Ho Leung Ho Lee Foundation's Board of Trustees, and shall notify the prize-winner that the prize and prize-winning certificate are to be cancelled. The decision to withdraw the prize from the prize-winner made by Ho Leung Ho Lee Foundation's Board of Trustees shall be final.

VII Appendix

These regulations shall enter into trial implementation on June 1, 2009.

Appendix: Article 71 of the *Law of the People's Republic of China on Science and Technology Progress* stipulates as follows:

The competent authority shall, in accordance with law, withdraw a prize and a bonus and take disciplinary action against anyone who is engaged in fraudulent practice for winning the National Science and Technology Prize.

For anyone or any working unit, which offers false data, false material, or conspire with others in fraudulent practice for winning the National Science and Technology Prize, the competent authority shall circulate a notice of criticism of such malpractice or misconduct; if the circumstances are serious, the competent authority shall suspend or cancel the working unit's eligibility for recommendation of any prize-winning candidate, and shall punish it in accordance with law.

关于何梁何利基金评选工作
若干问题的说明

何梁何利基金是由香港爱国金融实业家何善衡、梁铢琚先生、何添先生、利国伟先生于1994年3月30日在香港创立的，以奖励中华人民共和国杰出科学技术工作者为宗旨的科技奖励基金。截至2010年，已有901位获奖科学家获得此项殊荣。经过16年的成功实践，何梁何利基金科技奖，已经成为我国规模大、层次高、影响广、在国内外享有巨大权威性和公信力的科学技术大奖。为便于科技界、教育界和社会各界进一步了解基金宗旨、基本原则、评选标准和运行机制，在2010年10月颁奖大会期间，何梁何利基金评选委员会秘书长段瑞春就基金评选章程、评选工作以及社会各界所关心的有关问题，做了如下说明。

一、什么是何梁何利基金评选章程？

何梁何利基金评选章程是评选工作的基本准则。评选章程以基金《信托契约》为依据，由何梁何利基金信托委员会全体会议审议通过和发布。第一部评选章程诞生于1994年3月30日基金成立之时，保障了评选工作从一开始就步入科学、规范、健康的轨道运行。1998年5月11日适应香港九七回归和国内形势发展，对评选章程做过一次修订。2007年5月15日基金信托委员会会议决定再次修改评选章程，其主要目的，一是根据2005年10月12日香港高等法院批准生效的《补充契约条款》，对评选章程有关条款做相应修改，使之与基金《信托契约》及其《补充契约条款》保持一致。二是将评选委员会适应我国创新国策、改革评选工作的成功经验上升为章程，使之条文化、规范化、制度化，进一步提升各奖项的科学性、权威性。

二、根据《补充契约条款》，评选章程做了哪些重要修改？

何梁何利基金是依据香港法律创立的慈善基金。当初，根据香港普通法原则，实行信任委托制度，由捐款人与信托人签订《信托契约》，经香港终审法院批准成立。信托委员会是基金的最高权力机构，决定基金投资、评选和管理等重大事项。自1994年3月基金成立以来，当年四位创立者中，梁铢琚先生、何善衡先生、何添先生都在九旬高寿与世长辞。我们永远缅怀他们的崇高精神。由于他们的离去，《信托契约》有关捐款人的权利与义务主体出现缺位，从法律意义上影响到基金决策程序的进行。2005年10月，经香港高等法院批准《信托契约补充条款》将基金"捐款人"统一修订为原捐款人或者其遗产承办人指定的慈善基金，从而实现了捐款人从老一辈爱国金融家向其下一代的平稳过渡。依据此项修订，现基金捐款人为4个法人，即何善衡慈善基金有限公司、梁銶琚慈善基金有限公司、何添基金有限公司、利国伟先生和其夫人的伟伦基金有限公司。为此，评选章程也做了相应修改。

三、何梁何利基金奖励对象应当具备什么条件？

何梁何利基金奖励对象为中华人民共和国公民，获奖人应具备下列三个条件：一是对推动科学技术事业发展有杰出贡献；二是热爱祖国，有高尚的社会公德和职业道德；三是在国内从事科研、教学或技术工作已满5年。

1994年3月30日，何梁何利基金成立时，香港、澳门尚未回归祖国。鉴于当时历史状况，评选章程关于奖励对象为中华人民共和国公民的规定，仅适用祖国内地科技工作者，不包括在香港、澳门地区工作的科技人员。在"一国两制"的原则下，香港和澳门先后于1997年7月1日和1999年12月20日回归祖国。祖国内地与港澳特区科技合作与交流出现崭新局面。而今，香港、澳门特别行政区科技人员，是中华人民共和国公民中的"港人""澳人"，符合章程的要求。为此，自2007年起，何梁何利基金奖励对象扩大到符合上述条件的香港特别行政区、澳门特别行政区科学技术人员。

四、现行评选章程对基金奖项结构是如何规定的？

在中央人民政府和香港特区政府的关怀和指导下，16年来，何梁何利基金已经形成了科学合理的奖项结构和严谨、高效、便捷的评选程序。始终保持客观、公正、权威和具有公信力的评选纪录。现行评选章程规定基金设"科学与技术成就奖""科学与技术进步奖""科学与技术创新奖"。

每年，"科学与技术成就奖"不超过5名，授予奖牌、奖金100万港元；"科学与技术进步奖"和"科学与技术创新奖"总数不超过65名，分别授予相应的奖牌、奖金20万港元，其中，"科学与技术进步奖"和"科学与技术创新奖"的数量按三比一至二比一的比例，由评选委员会具体掌握。

五、"科学与技术成就奖"的评选标准是什么？

根据评选章程，符合下列三类条件的杰出科技工作者，均可获得"科学与技术成就奖"。一是长期致力于推进国家科学技术进步，贡献卓著，历史上取得国际高水平学术成就者；二是在科学技术前沿，取得重大科技突破，攀登当今科技高峰，领先世界先进水平者；三是推进技术创新，建立强大自主知识产权和自主品牌，其产业居于当今世界前列者。符合上述标准的获奖人选，既包括毕生奉献我国科技事业、其卓越成就曾达到世界一流水平的资深科学家，也包括以科学研究或技术创新领域的重大突破或突出业绩，使我国取得世界领先地位的中青年杰出人才。在征求意见过程中，我国科技界对此普遍赞同，认为这样修订丝毫没有降低了标准，而是使得基金的科技大奖进一步向国际规范靠拢，为在研究开发和创新第一线拔尖人才的脱颖而出注入强大精神动力，也使基金科技奖励更加贴近建设创新型国家的主旋律。

六、"科学与技术进步奖"的评选标准是怎样规定的？

评选章程规定，"科学与技术进步奖"授予在特定学科领域取得重大发明、发现和科技成果者，尤其是在近年内有突出贡献者。需要说明的，一是这里所说的"特定学科"包括：数学力学、物理学、化学、天文学、气象学、地球科学、生命科学、农学、医学和药学、古生物学和考古学、机械电力技术、电子信息技术、交通运输技术、冶金材料技术、化学工程技术、资源环保技术、工程建设技术等17个领域，每一领域设一个奖项。原评选章程用"技术科学奖"涵盖了机电、信息、冶金、材料、工程、环保等技术领域，修订后的章程从学科领域之间平衡考虑，将其分别设立奖项。二是"科学与技术进步奖"评选政策，重在考察被提名人"近年内"的突出贡献。所谓"近年内"是指近10年内。三是随着科学技术飞速发展，新兴学科、交叉学科、边缘学科层出不穷。这些学科的被提名人宜按其最主要成就、最接近学科领域归类。关注新兴、交叉、边缘学科优秀人才，是评选委员会的一项政策。有些确实需要跨学科评议的特殊情况，将作为个案协调处理，但不专门设立新兴学科、交叉学科、边缘学科等奖项。

七、"科学与技术创新奖"的评选标准是怎样规定的？

设立"科学与技术创新奖"是基金评选工作的重要改革。评选章程规定："科学与技术创新奖"授予具有高水平科技成就而通过技术创新和管理创新，创建自主知识产权产业和著名品牌，创造重大经济效益和社会效益的杰出贡献者。这里需要说明的是，创新，是一个经济学的范畴，指的是有明确经济、社会目标的行为。有人解释为"科学思想在市场的首次出现"。何梁何利基金为适应我国提高自主创新能力，建设创新型国家的重大决策设立这个奖项，评选章程所称的"科学与技术创新"，首先，要以高水平的科学技术成就为起点，实现科技成果转化为现实生产力，完成科技产业化的过程。第二，就创新活动而言，是指在高水平科技成就基础上的技术创新和管理创新，包括原始创新、集成创新和在他人先进技术之上的再创新，但应有自主知识产权产业和著名品牌，创造出重大经济效益和社会效益，对于创新成果在教育、节能环保、生态平衡、国家安全、社会公益事业等领域产生的巨大社会效益，将和可计量的经济效益一样，获得评选委员会的认可。第三，任何一项重大创新都是团队作战的成果，"科学与技术创新奖"的得主，可以是发挥核心作用的领军人物，也可以是实现技术突破的关键人物。当然，这里所说的领军人物本身要有科技成就，而不只是行政管理和组织协调工作。

八、怎样理解"科学技术创新奖"所分设的奖项？

根据评选章程，"科学技术创新奖"分设青年创新奖、产业创新奖和区域创新奖等三个奖项。青年创新奖授予在技术创新和管理创新方面业绩突出、年龄不超过 45 周岁的优秀科技人才；区域创新奖授予通过技术创新、管理创新和区域创新，对区域经济发展和技术进步，尤其是对祖国内地、边远、艰苦地区和少数民族地区发展做出突出贡献的人物；产业创新是指通过创新、创业，大幅度推进技术进步和产业升级，包括对传统产业技术改造和新兴产业的腾飞跨越做出贡献的优秀人才。分设上述三个奖项，是评选政策的安排，其本身并不是相互独立的创新门类。因此，"科学技术创新奖"仍然按照创新奖的基本要求统一评选，适当注意三类奖项的结构平衡，不按区域创新奖、产业创新奖、青年创新奖分组切块进行评审。

九、"科学与技术进步奖"和"科学与技术创新奖"评选标准有何差别？

从原则上讲，"科学与技术进步奖"按照学科领域设置，"科学与技术创新奖"基于创新业绩设置，二者有交叉和关联之处，又有重要区别，评选标准的政策取向和侧重有所不同。《评选章程》要求"科学与技术进步奖"获奖人必须是重大发明、发现和科技成果的完成人或主要完成人。而"科学与技术创新奖"的获奖人是在高水平科技成就基础上的创新实践者。前者，重在考察其发明、发现和其他科技成就的水平及其在国内国际的学术地位；而后者，重点考察其产业高端技术创新和管理创新的业绩，包括经济社会效益、自主知识产权和著名品牌建设。当然，"科学与技术创新奖"得主的领军人物本身要有高水平的科技成就，而不只是战略决策、行政管理和组织协调工作。

十、"科学与技术进步奖""科学与技术创新奖"获奖人能否获得"科学与技术成就奖"？

何梁何利基金的宗旨是鼓励我国优秀科学技术工作者，无所畏惧地追求科学真理，勇攀当代科学技术高峰。已经获得"科学与技术进步奖""科学与技术创新奖"的科技工作者，在获奖后，再接再厉，开拓进取，在科学技术前沿取得新的重大科技突破，领先世界先进水平者；或者在产业高端做出新的重大技术创新，建立强大自主知识产权和自主品牌，使得我国产业跃居当今世界前列者；如果在前次获奖后取得的新的杰出成就达到"科学与技术成就奖"标准，可以推荐为"科学与技术成就奖"被提名人的人选，按照《评选章程》规定程序参评，也有望摘取"科学与技术成就奖"的桂冠。

十一、评选委员会按照怎样的程序进行各奖项评选工作？

每年，基金评选委员会按照下列程序开展评选工作：

（一）提名

每年年初，评选委员会向国内外 2000 多位提名人发去提名表，由其提名推荐获奖人选，并于 3 月 31 日前将提名表返回评选委员会。评选办公室将对提名材料进行形式审查、整理、分组、印刷成册。

（二）初评

每年 7 月中旬，评选委员会召开当年专业评审会，进行"科学与技术进步奖""科学与技术创新奖"的初评。其中，"科学与技术进步奖"初评，按照学科设立若干专业评审组进行；"科学与技术创新奖"成立一个由不同行业和领域专家组成的评审组进行初评。经过初评，以无记名投票方式，产生一定差额比例的候选人，提交评选委员会会议终评。

（三）预审

根据《评选章程》，"科学与技术成就奖"候选人由评选委员会委员在初评结束后提名。每年 8 月，评选委员会成立预审小组进行协调、评议，必要时进行考察和听证，产生"科学与技术成就奖"候选人，并形成预审报告，提交评选委员会会议终评。

（四）终评

每年 9 月中旬评选委员会召开全体会议进行终评。对候选人逐一评议，最后，根据基金信托委员会确定的当年获奖名额，进行无记名投票表决。"科学与技术进步奖""科学与技术创新奖"的候选人，获半数以上赞成票为获奖人。"科学与技术成就奖"的候选人，获三分之二多数赞成票为获奖人。

（五）授奖

每年 10 月的适当时候，何梁何利基金举行颁奖大会，向获奖人颁发奖牌、奖金。

十二、何梁何利基金获奖人有哪些权利和义务？

《世界人权宣言》宣布："人人对他所创造的任何科学、文学或艺术成果所产生的精神的和物质的权利，享有受保护的权利"。知识产权是精神权利和经济权利的总和，其本原和第一要义，是给人的智慧、才能和创造性劳动注入强大精神动力。科技奖励是确认和保护精神权利的重要制度，何梁何利基金"科学与技术成就奖""科学与技术进步奖""科学与技术创新奖"获奖人的权利是，享有何梁何利基金获奖科学家的身份权、荣誉权；享有接受何梁何利基金颁发的奖金的权利，该奖金个人所有；有从第二年起成为基金提名人，向基金提名推荐被提名人的权利。根据基金《信托契约》和评选章程，获奖人有义务在获得基金奖励后继续在中华人民共和国从事科学与技术工作不少于三年，为我国科技进步与创新做出更多贡献。

十三、评选委员会委员和专业评委是怎样产生的？

评选委员会是何梁何利基金评选工作的执行机构，通过全体会议审议、决定各奖项获奖人，行使最终评选决定权。根据评选章程，评选委员会由最多不超过20名委员组成。评选委员会主任由科技系统的信托委员担任，副主任委员两人，分别由教育部系统的信托委员和补充契约所指明的国际学者信托委员担任。评选委员会秘书长由信托委员会任命并征得捐款人代表同意的人选担任。

评选委员会委员由信托委员会任命，委员名单通过何梁何利基金出版物、网站公布。

按《评选章程》规定，评选委员会委员的聘任条件是，第一，要具备高尚道德情操，能够公正履行评选委员的职责；第二，要具备精深学术造诣，能够对其所属领域科技成就做出科学性和权威性评价；第三，要热心祖国科技奖励事业，愿意为之做出无私奉献；第四，评选委员会委员的结构配置，原则上每一领域有一名委员，国内评委和海外评委按照三比一的比例安排；第五，评选章程还规定了评选委员会委员的更新和替换制度，以保障评选委员会的生机和活力。

每年7月何梁何利基金召开专业评审会议，进行初评。初评是评选工作的第一道关口。其十多个"科学与技术进步奖"评审组和"科学与技术创新奖"的专业评委，由评选委员会根据工作需要，从250人左右的评审专家库或历年获奖科学家中，按《评选章程》规定的上述条件遴选。

十四、怎样理解基金公平、公正、公开的评选原则？

科学精神的精髓是求实、求是、求真。科技奖励评选工作必须坚持以诚信为本，践行实事求是的方针。何梁何利基金从一开始就贯彻"公平、公正、公开"的评选原则，保持良好的评选记录，得到社会各界的高度评价和充分肯定。所谓公平，体现在所有被提名者，不论职务、职位、学衔、资历，也不论年龄、民族、性别，在评选章程确定的评选标准面前一律平等。所谓公正，是指评选工作严格按照章程确定的评选标准和评选程序进行，无论初评的专业评委，还是终评的评选委员会委员，有权做出独立判断，按一人一票的制度行使表决权，最终依据评委共同体的意志决定获奖人，不受任何单位或个人的干扰。所谓公开，是指何梁何利基金评选章程、评选标准及其解释、评选委员会委员、逐年获奖人材料等，通过年报、网站等向社会公开，接受社会公众的监督和指导。自2006年起，评选委员会在部分省市和部门建立联络员，加强同社会各界的联系。何梁何利基金评选实践经验凝练到一点，就是贯彻"公平、公正、公开"的评选原则，是何梁何利基金的指导方针，是评选委员会的工作纪律，是基金的立业之本，权威之根，公信力之源泉，是一个具有国内和国际影响力的科技大奖的生命线。今后，基金将一如既往恪守"三公"原则，本着对科学负责、对基金负责、对科技共同体负责的精神，做好评选工作，使何梁何利基金科学与技术奖经得起历史的检验。

十五、何梁何利基金有无异议处理程序？

为了弘扬科学精神，崇尚科学道德，抵御社会不正之风和科研不端行为，提升何梁何利基金科学与技术奖的权威性和公信力，基金于 2009 年 5 月 20 日制定并发布了《关于何梁何利基金获奖科学家异议处理若干规定》，自发布之日起试行。

根据该项决定，凡涉及对获奖科学家主要科技成果评价、知识产权权属以及与奖项有关事项提出异议的署名投诉信件，由评选委员会受理，并调查处理。匿名投诉信件，原则上不予受理。但涉及获奖人因科研不端行为受到处分、学术资格被取消或与奖项评选相关重要情况的，应跟进调查核实，酌情处理。

评选委员会的处理原则是，以事实为依据，以法律为准绳，遵循科学共同体认同的道德准则，区别情况，正确处置。经调查，认定获奖人确属科研不端行为，将参照《中华人民共和国科学技术进步法》第七十一条规定，报基金信托委员会审议并做出相应的处分决定，直至公告撤销其奖励的决定，并通知本人，返回奖励证书、奖金。

十六、何梁何利基金未来发展目标是什么？

在中央人民政府和香港特别行政区政府的指导下，在我国科技界、教育界和社会各界的共同努力下，何梁何利基金已经成为我国规模大、权威性高、公信力强的社会力量奖励，成为推进我国科技进步与创新的强大杠杆，在国内外影响和声誉与日俱增。在历年颁奖大会上，党和国家领导人亲临颁奖，发表重要讲话，给予基金同仁极大鼓舞和力量。何梁何利基金同仁将不负众望，不辱使命，承前启后，继往开来，在新的起点上总结经验，开拓创新，突出特色，丰富内涵，朝着办成国际一流的科技奖励的方向迈进，为祖国的科技进步和创新，为建设富强民主、文明和谐的社会主义现代化国家而不懈努力！

EXPLANATIONS ON SEVERAL ISSUES ON THE SELECTION WORK OF HO LEUNG HO LEE FOUNDATION

Ho Leung Ho Lee Foundation ("the Foundation") is a scientific and technological award foundation established on March 30. 1994 in Hong Kong by patriotic Hong Kong financial industrialists Ho Sin Hang, Leung Kau-Kui, Ho Tim, Lee Quo-Wei for the purpose of awarding prominent scientific and technological workers of the People's Republic of China. Up to 2010, there were 901 scientists who received this special honor. Within the 16 years of successful practice, HLHL Foundation Scientific and Technological Awards have become major scientific and technological awards of large scale, high standard and extensive influence in China that enjoy enormous prestige and public trust both domestically and abroad. In order for the circle of science and technology, the circle of education, and other various social circles to further understand the Foundation's purpose, basic principles, award selection criteria and operation mechanisms, Mr. Duan Ruichun, secretary general of the Selection Board of HLHL Foundation, made the following explana-tions during the awards ceremony in October 2010 with respect to the Foundation's selection regulation, selection work and other issues that various social circles are concerned about.

I. What Is the Regulation of Ho Leung Ho Lee Foundation on the Selection of the Award Winners of Its Prizes?

The Regulation of Ho Leung Ho Lee Foundation on the Selection of the Award Winners of Its Prizes ("Selection Regulation") is the fundamental guideline of the award selection work. The Selection Regulation is based on the Foundation's Trust Agreement and deliberated, adopted and published by the plenary meeting of HLHL Foundation Broad of Trustees. The birth of the first selection regulation on March 30. 1994, the very day when the Foundation was established, guaranteed the operation of the selection work in a scientific, regulated and healthy track from the very beginning. On May 11. 1998, a revision was made to the Selection Regulation to adapt to the return of Hong Kong to China and the development of domestic situation. On May 15. 2007, it was resolved at the meeting of the Foundation's Broad of Trustees that another revision would be made to the Selection Regulation. The main purpose of the revision was that, on the one hand, relevant modifications would be made to certain terms and conditions in the Selection Regulation in accordance with the Supplementary Terms to the Trust Agreement which took effect upon approval by the Hong Kong SAR High Court on October 12. 2005 so that the Foundation's Trust Agreement became consistent with its Supplementary Terms to the Trust Agreement while, on the other hand, the successful experience of the Selection Board in adapting to China's national innovation policy and reforming its selection work was elevated to become part of the selection regulation so that the experience was embodied in agreement terms, standards and systems to further improve the scientific and authoritative features of different award categories.

II. What Are the Important Modifications to the Selection Regulation Made in Accordance with the Supplementary Terms of the Trust Agreement?

HLHL Foundation is a charity foundation established in accordance with the laws of the Hong Kong SAR. In its early days, the trust system was established in accordance with the principles in Hong Kong's common law and the foundation was established upon the approval of the Hong Kong Supreme Court after the donors and the trustees signed the Trust Agreement. The Board of Trustees is the supreme body of power of the Foundation that decides on major matters of the foundation in investment, award selection and management. After the foundation was established in March, 1994, Mr. Ho Sin Hang, Mr. Leung Kau-Kui and Mr. Ho Tim of the four founders, whose sublime and noble spirits we will all cherish forever, passed away in their nineties. Due to their decease, the main parties to the rights and obligations of donors in the Trust Agreement became absent, which affected the operation of the Foundation's decision-making procedures in terms of law. In October 2005, it was uniformly revised in the Supplementary Terms of the Trust Agreement, upon the approval of the Hong Kong SAR High Court, that the "donors" of the Foundation became the charity foundations designated by the original donors or their estate administrator. Thus a peaceful and smooth transition was achieved with respect to donors from the old generation patriotic financers to the charity foundations run by their next generation. According to the revision, the current donors of the Foundation are four legal persons, namely the S. H. Ho Foundation Limited, the Leung Kau-Kui Foundation Limited, the Ho Tim Foundation Limited, and the Wei Lun Foundation Limited of Mr. Lee Quo-Wei and his wife. And the relevant modifications were made to the Selection Regulation accordingly.

III. What Conditions Need the Winners of the Awards of HLHL Foundation Have?

The winners of the awards of HLHL Foundation shall be the citizens of the People's Republic of China. And they also need to meet the following three conditions: First, they shall have made prominent contributions in the development of the undertakings in science and technology. Second, they shall love the motherland and exhibit noble social ethics and good professional ethics. Third, they shall have engaged in scientific and technological research work, teaching work or technical work for no less than five years in China.

When HLHL Foundation was established on March 30. 1994, Hong Kong and Macao were not returned to the motherland yet. In view of the historical situation then, the provision in the Selection Regulation that the winners of the awards shall be citizens of the People's Republic of China only applied to scientific and technological workers in China's mainland and scientific and technological workers in Hong Kong and Macao were excluded. Then Hong Kong and Macao were returned to the motherland under the principle of "one country, two systems" respectively on July 1st, 1997 and December 20. 1999. And a brand new situation emerged in the cooperation and exchange between the mainland of China and the Hong Kong and Macao SARs. Now, the scientific and technological workers in the Hong Kong and Macao SARs are "Hong Kong people" and "Macao people" among the citizens of the People's Republic of China and thus meet the conditions in the Selection Regulation. Therefore, the scope of the scientists eligible to the awards of HLHL Foundation was expanded from 2007 to include scientific and technological personnel in the Hong Kong and Macao SARs who meet the above conditions.

IV. What Are the Provisions on the Structure of the Award Categories in the Prevailing Selection Regulation?

Under the care and guidance of the Central People's Government and the government of the Hong Kong SAR, HLHL Foundation has formed during 16 years a scientific and rational structure of the award categories and a selection regulation of meticulousness, high efficiency, convenience and swiftness. It has always retained its objective, fair, authoritative selection performance and won good public trust. As provided in the prevailing Selection Regulation, the Foundation sets up the Prize for Scientific and Technological Achievements, the Prize for Scientific and Technological Progress, and the Prize for Scientific and Technological Innovation.

Each year there will be no more than five winners of the Prize for Scientific and Technological Achievements. Each of them will be given a medal and a prize of HKMYM one million. The total number of the winners of the Prize for Scientific and Technological Progress and the Prize for Scientific and Technological Innovation will not exceed 65. Each winner will be given a corresponding medal and a prize of HKMYM 200000. Among these, the proportion of the winners of the Prize for Scientific and Technological Progress to those of the Prize for Scientific and Technological Innovation will range from 3 : 1 to 2 : 1. The proportion will be determined by the Selection Board on the basis of specific situation.

V. What Are the Selection Criteria on the Prize for Scientific and Technological Achievements?

According to the Selection Regulation, all outstanding scientific and technological workers who meet the following three conditions are eligible to be honored with the Prize for Scientific and Technological Achievements. The first condition is that the scientist has been committed for a long time to promoting the scientific and technological achievements of the state in China and he or she has made eminent contribution and obtained high–level international academic achievements in his career. The second condition is that the scientist has obtained major scientific and technological breakthroughs in the frontiers of science and technology, mounted the peak of the science and technology of the present age, and obtained achievements of a world–leading standard. Third, the scientist has promoted technological innovation and established powerful independently–owned intellectual property and brand. And the industry in which the scientist works is one of the leading industries in the world. The candidates who meet the above standards include both senior scientists who have devoted their whole life to Chinese scientific and technological undertakings and obtained eminent achievements that were once first–rate in the world and youth and middle–aged outstanding talents who have made major breakthroughs or prominent achievements in the area of scientific and technological research and technical innovation so that China got a world–leading position in the area. During the process of opinion solicitation, the Chinese scientific and technological circle expressed general approval of the revision and indicated that such revision lowered the standard by not a slight bit while pushing the Foundation's awards one step further and closer to international standards. It injected powerful spiritual impetus for top–level talents to excel in the frontline of research and development and innovation. The revision also drew the Foundation's scientific and technological awards more closer to the mainstream ideology of building an innovative country.

VI. What Are the Provisions on the Selection Criteria of the Prize for Scientific and Technological Progress?

It is provided in the Selection Regulation that the Prize for Scientific and Technological Progress will be honored to scientists who have made major inventions, discoveries and scientific and technological results in particular disciplinary areas, particularly those who have made prominent contributions in recent years. First, it needs to be noted that the "particular disciplines" stated here include 17 disciplines, namely mathematics and mechanics, physics, chemistry, astronomy, meteorology, earth sciences, life sciences, agronomy, medical sciences and materia medica, paleontology and archeology, technology of machinery and electronics, information technology, communication and transportation technology, metallurgical materials technology, chemical engineering technology, resources and environment protection technology, and engineering and construction technology. One award category is established for each of these areas. In the original selection regulation, the Award of Technical Sciences is set up to cover various technical areas including machinery, electronics, information, metallurgy, material science, engineering and environment protection. The revised procedure sets up different award categories for these areas out of the consideration on the balance between various disciplinary areas. Second, the selection policy on the Prize for Scientific and Technological Progress focuses on examining and reviewing the prominent contribution of the nominees "within recent years". And "within recent years" refers to within the recentten years. Third, as emerging disciplines, interdisciplines, and fringe disciplines come up one after another with the rapid development of science and technology, the nominees from these disciplines should desirably be classified according to their most important achievements and the closest disciplines to which these belong. To pay more attention to the excellent talents from emerging disciplines, interdisciplines and fringe disciplines is one policy of the Selection Board. The special cases that truly need cross–disciplinary review and deliberation will be processed through coordination as separate cases. But no prize category will be established particularly for emerging disciplines, interdisciplines and fringe disciplines.

VII. What Are the Provisions on the Selection Criteria of the Prize for Scientific and Technological Innovation?

Setting up the Prize for Scientific and Technological Innovation is an important reform of the Foundation's selection work. It is provided in the Selection Regulation that " the Prize for Scientific and Technological Innovation will be awarded to scientists who have high–level scientific and technological accomplishments and who have established an industry with independently–owned intellectual property and famous brand, created significant economic and social benefits, and made prominent contribution". It needs to be noted here that, as a term in economics, innovation refers to acts with specific economic and social goals. Some people defines it as the "first presence of an idea in science on the market". HLHL Foundation set up the innovation award to adapt to China's important decision to improve the ability to independent innovation and build an innovative country. For the purpose of the Selection Regulation, to make "scientific and technological innovation" first needs to make high–level scientific and technological achievements as its starting point to realize the transformation of scientific and technological achievements into real productive force and complete the process of scientific and technological industrialization. Second, innovation activities refer to technological and managerial innovations on the basis of high–level scientific and technological achievements. These include original innovation, integration innovation and re–innovation on the basis of other people's advanced technology. And such innovations should create independently–owned intellectual properties and famous brands and create significant economic and social benefits. Besides, the Selection Board also accepts and approves, in the same way as measurable economic benefits, the enormous social benefits created by innovation results in the areas of education, energy preservation and environment protection, ecological balance, national security, and social public interest undertakings. Third, as any major innovation is the result of teamwork, the winner of the Prize for Scientific and Technological Innovation may be either a leading person that plays the key role or a key person who has achieved technical breakthroughs. Naturally, the leading person here needs to have his or her own scientific and technological accomplishments in addition to conducting administrative management, organization and coordination work.

VIII. How Should the Award Categories Set Up in the Prize for Scientific and Technological Innovation Be Understood?

In accordance with the Selection Regulation, the Prize for Scientific and Technological Innovation includes three award categories of the Award for Youth Innovation, the Award for Region Innovation and the Award for Industrial Innovation. The Award for Youth Innovation will be given to excellent scientific and technological talents not older than 45 years old who have achieved prominent performance in technical and managerial innovation. The Award for Region Innovation will be given to people who have made prominent contributions to regional economic development and technological progress through technical, managerial and regional innovations, particularly those who have made contributions to China's inland, remote regions, regions of harsh conditions, and regions of ethic minorities. The Prize for Industrial Innovation will be given to excellent talents who have made contributions through innovation and entrepreneurship to greatly promote technical progress and industrial upgrading, which include both the technical transformation of traditional industries and the leap-forwards of emerging industries. The above three award categories are set up according to the arrangement in selection policy. These do not define mutually-independent types of innovation. Therefore, the selection of the winners of the Prize for Scientific and Technological Innovation will be conducted as a whole part in accordance with the basic requirements on the Prize while proper attention will be paid to retain the structural balance between these three award categories. Selection and evaluation will not be conducted in a manner that the Award for Region Innovation, the Award for Industrial Innovation and the Award for Youth Innovation are separated and form different groups.

IX. What Are the Differences in the Selection Criteria of the Prize for Scientific and Technological Progress and the Prize for Scientific and Technological Innovation?

In principle, the Prize for Scientific and Technological Progress has award categories set up in accordance with different disciplines while the Prize for Scientific and Technological Innovation has award categories based on innovation results. The two prizes have overlaps and connections while there are important differences between them. And the policy orientations and stresses in their selection criteria are also different. The Selection Regulation requires that the winners of the Prize for Scientific and Technological Achievements must be completers or major completers of major inventions, discoveries and scientific and technological research results while the winners of the Prize for Scientific and Technological Innovation are scientists in innovative practices on the basis of high-level scientific and technological achievements. The former focuses on examining the standard and value of a scientist's invention, discovery or other scientific and technological achievement and its domestic and international academic status. The latter focuses on examining a person's performance in high-end industrial technical and managerial innovations, including economic and social benefits, independently-owned intellectual properties and building of famous brands. Naturally, the winners of the Prize for Scientific and Technological Innovations need to have high-level scientific and technological achievements as leading persons in addition to just conducting strategic decision making, administrative management, organization and coordination work.

X. Can the Winners of the Prize for Scientific and Technological Progress and the Prize for Scientific and Technological Innovation Be Honored with the Prize for Scientific and Technological Achievements?

The purpose of HLHL Foundation is to encourage excellent Chinese scientific and technological workers to dauntlessly pursue the truth of science and courageously mount the peaks in modern science and technology. The scientific and technological workers who have won the Prize for Scientific and Technological Progress and the Prize for Scientific and Technological Innovation may continue to forge ahead and break new grounds. And they may achieve new important breakthroughs in the frontiers of science and technology and lead in the cutting edge area of the world. Or they may make new important technical innovations in the high-end areas of an industry and create powerful independent intellectual properties and independent brands so that China's relevant industries become industrial leaders in the world. If such scientists' new outstanding achievements obtained after the previous prize winning meet the criteria for the Prize for Scientific and Technological Achievement, these scientists may be recommended as candidates to be nominated to the Prize for Scientific and Technological Achievements. They will participate in the evaluation in accordance with the procedures as provided in the Selection Regulation. And it is hopeful that they may become the laureates of the Prize for Scientific and Technological Achievements.

XI. In Accordance with What Procedures Will the Selection Board Conduct the Selection Work for Various Award Categories?

Each year, the Foundation's Selection Board will carry out selection work in accordance with the following procedure:

A. Nomination. In the beginning of each year, the Selection Board will send nomination forms to over 2000 domestic and foreign nominators. The nominators will recommend candidates for award winners and return the nomination form to the Selection Board by March 31st. The Selection Office will conduct the formal examination, arranging, assorting, and printing of the nomination materials and bind them into booklets.

B. Preliminary Evaluation. In the middle of July each year, the Selection Board will hold the year's specialized evaluation meeting and conduct the preliminary evaluation for the Prize of Scientific and Technological Progress and the Prize for Scientific and Technological Innovation. In the preliminary evaluation, that of the Prize for Scientific and Technological Progress will be conducted with a number of specialized evaluation groups formed according to different disciplines. The preliminary evaluation of the Prize for Scientific and Technological Innovation will be conducted by an evaluation group consisting of experts from different industries and areas. After the preliminary evaluation, candidates will be determined with a proportion of competitive selection by means of secret ballot and submitted to the meeting of the Selection Board for final evaluation.

C. Preliminary Review. In accordance with the Selection Regulation, the candidates of the Prize for Scientific and Technological Achievements will be nominated by the members of the Selection Board upon the conclusion of the preliminary evaluation. Each August, the Selection Board will form a preliminary evaluation group to conduct coordination and evaluation. Inspection tours and hearings will be made when necessary. Then the candidates for the Prize for Scientific and Technological Achievements will be determined and a preliminary review report will be prepared and submitted to the meeting of the Selection Board for final evaluation.

D. Final Evaluation. In the middle of September each year, the Selection Board will hold a plenary meeting to conduct final evaluation. Candidates will be evaluated one by one. And finally a secret ballot will be made on the selection in accordance with the numbers of prize winners of the year determined by the Trust Board of the Foundation. The candidates for the Prize for Scientific and Technological Progress and the Prize for Scientific and Technological Innovation will become prize winners with over half of the votes in favor. The candidates for the Prize for Scientific and Technological Achievements will become prize winners with over two thirds of the votes in favor.

E. Award Ceremony. At a proper time in October each year, HLHL Foundation will hold an award ceremony to present medals and prizes to the winners.

XII. What Are the Rights and Obligations of the Winners of the Awards of HLHL Foundation?

The *Universal Declaration of Human Rights* states that "Everyone has the right to the protection of the moral and material interests resulting from any scientific, literary or artistic production of which he is the author. " Intellectual property rights are the sum of both spiritual and economic rights. Its origin and primary significance is to inject powerful spiritual drive to people's wisdom, talent and creative labor. Scientific and technological awards are important systems to recognize and protect spiritual rights. The rights of the winners of the Prize of Scientific and Technological Achievements, the Prize for Scientific and Technological Progress, and the Prize for Scientific and Technological Innovation of HLHL Foundation are the enjoyment of the right of status and the right of honor of the prize-winning scientists of HLHL Foundation, the enjoyment of the right to accept the prize money granted by HLHL Foundation which shall be owned personally by the prize winners, and the right to become a nominator of the Foundation from the year next to the prize winning to recommend nominees to the Foundation. In accordance with the Foundation's Trust Agreement and Selection Regulation, the prize winner is obligated to continue to engage in scientific and technological work in the People's Republic of China for three years after prize winning so as to make more contribution to China's scientific and technological advancement and innovation.

XIII. How Are the Members of the Selection Board and the Specialized Evaluators Selected?

The Selection Board is the implementing body of the selection work of HLHL Foundation. It conducts deliberation through plenary meeting, decides on the winners of the award categories, and exercises the right of decision in final evaluation. In accordance with the Selection Regulation, the Selection Board consists of no more than twenty members at the most. The chairman of the Selection Board shall be a member of the Board of Trustees for the circle of science and technology. The two vice chairmen of the board shall be a member of the Board of Trustees from the bodies under the Ministry of Education and a member of the Board of Trustees who is an international scholar as specified in the Supplementary Terms to the Trust Agreement. The secretary general of the Selection Boards shall be appointed by the Board of Trustees upon the consent of the representatives of the donors.

The members of the Selection Board are appointed by the Board of Trustees. And the list of such members will be published through the publications and website of HLHL Foundation.

As provided in the Selection Regulation, the conditions for the appointment of a member of the Selection Board are: First, the person needs to have noble ethics and the ability to fairly perform the duties of the member of the Selection Board. Second, the person needs to have sophisticated academic accomplishment and the ability to make scientific and authoritative evaluation on the scientific and technological achievements in his or her own specialized field. Third, the person needs to have enthusiasm on the motherland's undertakings in scientific and technological awards and the willingness to make selfless contributions to these undertakings. Fourth, with respect to the structural distribution of the members of the Selection Board, there shall be one member from each area in principle and the proportion between domestic and overseas members shall be 3 : 1. Fifth, the Selection Regulation provides for the renewal and replacement system of the members of the Selection Board so as to ensure the liveliness and vigor of the board.

Each July, HLHL Foundation holds a specialized evaluation meeting to conduct the preliminary evaluation. The preliminary evaluation is the very first step in the selection work. About a dozen of evaluation groups for the Prize for Scientific and Technological Progress and the specialized evaluators of the Prize for Scientific and Technological Innovation will be selected by the Selection Board on the basis of working needs and in accordance with the above conditions as provided in the Selection Regulation from an evaluation expert pool containing about 250 persons or the prize winners in previous years.

XIV. How Should People Understand the Foundation's Selection Principles of Fairness, Justice and Openness?

The essence of the scientific spirit is to be practical, honest and truth-seeking. The selection work for the scientific and technological awards must adhere to the principle of sincerity and follow the guideline of doing things with a realistic and pragmatic approach. HLHL Foundation persistently carries out the selection principle of fairness, justice and openness from the very beginning. It retains good selection records and wins high praises and full recognition from various social circles. The principle of fairness is embodied in the provision that all the nominees, regardless of their jobs, positions, academic titles or work experiences and also their age, ethnic group or gender, areequal with respect to the selection criteria determined in the Selection Regulation. The principle of justice refers to the provision that the selection work is carried out strictly in accordance with the selection criteria and procedures determined in accordance with the Selection Regulation. Any person as either a specialized evaluator in the preliminary evaluation or a member of the Selection Board in final evaluation has the right to make independent judgment and exercise the right to vote under the system of one vote for one person. The prize winners are eventually determined according to the common will of all the evaluators free from the intervention of any entity or individual. The principle of openness refers to the practice that HLHL Foundation's Selection Regulation, Selection Criteria, and their explanations and the information about the members of the Selection Board and the prize winners of different years are published to the society through annual report and website to receive supervision and guidance from the public in the society. From 2006, the Selection Board has appointed liaison persons in some governmental departments, provinces and cities to strengthen its contact with various social circles. One viewpoint that can summarize the practical experience of the award selection of HLHL Foundation is to carry out the selection principle of "fairness, justice and openness." It is the guideline of HLHL Foundation, the working discipline of the Selection Board, and the cornerstone of the Foundation, the root of its authoritativeness and the source of its public trust. It is the lifeline of this major scientific and technological award with both domestic and international influence. From now on, the Foundation will adhere to this three-word principle as always. It will carry out the selection work well with the spirit of being responsible to science, to the Foundation, and to the scientific and technological community so that the scientific and technological awards of HLHL Foundation can stand the test of the history.

XV. Does HLHL Foundation Have Dispute Handling Procedures?

With a view to carrying forward the spirit of the science, advocating the ethics of the science, guarding against the unhealthy tendencies in the society and the improper conducts in scientific and technological research, and enhancing the authoritativeness and public trust of HLHL Foundation's scientific and technological awards, the Foundation formulated and published on May 20th, 2009 *Several Provisions on Handling the Disputes on the Prize-Winning Scientists of Ho Leung Ho Lee Foundation*. It took effect from the date of publication.

In accordance with the resolution on the document, the Selection Board will accept, investigate and handle all the signed complaint letters on the disputes with respect to the evaluation of the main scientific and technological research results, the ownership of relevant intellectual properties, and the matters about award categories related to a prize-winning scientist. In principle, anonymous complaint letters will not be accepted and handled. However, where such anonymous complaint letters involve the information that a prize winner has been punished due to improper conducts in scientific and technological research, that his academic title or qualification was cancelled, or other information related to the award evaluation, follow-up action shall be taken to investigate and verify. Such disputes shall then be handled according to actual situation.

The complaint handling principle of the Selection Board is to take facts as the basis and the law as the criterion, follow the ethical principles commonly accepted by the science community, distinguish different situations, and handle correctly. Where it is determined upon investigation that a prize winner really involves in improper conducts in scientific and technological research, the case will be referred to the Board of Trustees of the Foundation for deliberation with reference to the provisions in Article 71 of the *Law of the People's Republic of China on*, *Science and Technology Progress*. The board will make resolutions on corresponding punishment up to that of a public announcement to cancel its reward. The person involved will be notified of the decision and required to return his certificate and prize money.

XVI. What Are the Goals of HLHL Foundation on Its Future Development?

Under the guidance of the Central People's Government and the government of the Hong Kong SAR and with the joint efforts of China's scientific and technological circle, education circle and various social circles, HLHL Foundation has already become an awarding organization founded with social resources that is of large scale, high authoritativeness, and strong public trust in China. It becomes a powerful lever to push forward China's scientific and technological advancement and innovation. Its domestic and foreign influence and reputation also grow constantly. China's state and CPC leaders attended in person the award ceremonies in the previous years. They presented the awards and delivered important speeches to give great encouragement and power to our colleagues working with the Foundation. The people of HLHL Foundation will live up to the expectations of the people and their own commitment. They will build on the past and usher in the future. They will summarize their experiences and move on from a new starting point. They will explore and innovate, highlight the Foundation's features, enrich its connotations, and advance in the direction of making it an internationally first-rate scientific and technological award. They will work hard and relentlessly for the motherland's scientific and technological advancement and innovation and for building China into a wealthy, democratic, civilized and harmonious socialist modern country!

何 梁 何 利 基 金 捐 款 人 简 历

捐款者何善衡慈善基金会有限公司之创办人
何 善 衡

何善衡博士，1900 年出生，广东番禺市人。

何博士于 1933 年创办香港恒生银号，其后又创办恒昌企业及大昌贸易行。1952 年恒生银号改为有限公司，1959 年改称恒生银行，何氏一直担任董事长一职。1983 年，于恒生银行成立 50 周年时，何氏因年事关系，改任恒生银行名誉董事长至病逝。

何博士经营之业务包括银行、贸易、信托、财务、酒店、保险、地产、船务、投资等。

何博士热心慈善公益不遗余力。1970 年设立何善衡慈善基金会，资助国内外慈善事业，包括地方建设、教育、医疗、科学等，帮助社会造就人才，尤其对广州市及其家乡一带贡献很多。1978 年创办恒生商学书院，免费提供教学，并曾任多所学校校董。1971 年获香港中文大学荣誉社会科学博士衔，1983 年获香港大学荣誉法律博士衔，1990 年及 1995 年分别获广州市中山大学荣誉顾问衔及名誉博士学位，1993 年获广州市荣誉市民及番禺市荣誉市民称谓。

何善衡博士于 1997 年 12 月 4 日在香港病逝，享年 97 岁。

梁 铢 琚

梁铢琚博士，1903 年出生，广东顺德人。

梁博士为恒昌企业之创办人，曾任恒生银行董事、大昌贸易行副董事长，亦为美丽华酒店企业有限公司、富丽华酒店有限公司、Milford 国际投资有限公司等董事以及恒生商学书院校董等。

梁博士早年在穗、港、澳等地经营银号和贸易，为大昌贸易行创办人之一，为工作经常往返国内各大商埠及海外大城市，或开设分行，或推进业务，并与合伙股东制订运作规章，积极培育人才；梁博士领导华商参与国际贸易，并于 20 世纪 60 年代协助香港政府重新厘定米业政策，对香港的安定繁荣有卓越贡献。

梁博士宅心仁厚，精于事业，淡薄声名，热心公益。数十年来对社会福利、教育、医疗事业捐助良多，堪称楷模。较为显著者包括捐款建成纪念其先父之圣高隆庞女修会梁式芝书院，纪念其先母之保良局梁周顺琴学校，香港大学梁铢琚楼，香港中文大学梁铢琚楼，香港浸会学院"梁铢琚汉语中心"，岭南学院梁铢琚楼，广州中山大学捐建两千两百座位的梁铢琚堂与梁李秀娛图书馆，赞助杨振宁博士倡议之中山大学高级学术研究中心基金会及中国教育交流协会留学名额，为清华大学设立"梁铢琚博士图书基金"，中国人民解放军第四军医大学"梁铢琚脑研究中心"，清华大学建筑馆——梁铢琚楼。

在香港的其他教育捐助包括：顺德联谊总会梁铢琚中学，顺德联谊总会梁李秀娛幼稚园（屯门），顺德联谊总会梁李秀娛幼稚园（沙田），香港励志会梁李秀娛小学，恒生商学书院，劳工子弟学校新校，九龙乐善堂陈祖泽学校礼堂，乐善堂梁铢琚学校，乐善堂梁铢琚书院，香港大学黄丽松学术基金，香港女童军总会沙田扬坑营地及梁李秀娛花园；在医疗卫生方面包括：医务卫生署土瓜湾顺德联谊总会梁铢琚诊所，香港防癌会，香港放射诊断科医生协会，玛丽医院"梁铢琚糖尿病中心"，玛丽医院放射学图书博物馆教学资料和医院员工的福利，香港大学医院在山东省为胃癌研究工作经费，支持张力正医生在葛量洪医院的心脏病手术和医疗的发展经费及捐助圣保禄医院设立心脏中心并以"梁铢琚心脏中心"命名；在社会福利捐献包括：九龙乐善堂梁铢琚敬老之家，东区妇女福利会梁李秀娛晚晴中心，香港明爱，西区少年警讯活动及跑马地鹅颈桥区街坊福利会等。向宗教团体的捐助包括：资助基督教"突破机构"开设青年村——信息站；赞助"志莲净苑"重建基金及大屿山"宝莲禅寺"筹募兴建天坛大佛基金等。

多年来，梁博士对家乡顺德的地方建设，科技教育，医疗事业亦大量资助，其中包括捐资成立国家级重点中学梁铢琚中学，中学的科学楼并增置教学仪器，北头学校，梁铢琚图书馆及图书，增设杏坛医院 230 张病床、独立手术室及分科设备仪器等，杏坛康乐活动中心，北头大会堂及北头老人康乐中心，北头乡每户开建水井一口，修葺北头主路及河道两岸，北头乡蚕房四座，梁铢琚夫人保健中心（即妇产幼儿医院），梁铢琚夫人幼儿园及梁铢琚福利基金会。

1987 年梁博士荣获香港中文大学颁授荣誉社会科学博士学位，1990 年被广州中山大学聘为名誉顾问，1992 年获顺德市颁授为首位荣誉市民，1994 年国务院学位委员会批准清华大学授予梁博士名誉博士学位；同年 4 月，国务院总理李鹏为梁博士题词"热心公益，发展教育"，以赞扬其贡献。1995 年 6 月 21 日，香港大学向已故梁铢琚博士追授名誉法学博士文凭。

在海外方面，梁博士亦曾捐助英国牛津大学，苏格兰 Aberdeen 大学医学院与加拿大多伦多颐康护理中心。

梁铢琚博士于 1994 年 11 月 10 日在香港病逝，享年 91 岁。

何　　添

　　何添博士于 1933 年加入香港恒生银行有限公司（前为恒生银号），于 1953 年任董事兼总经理，1967—1979 年任恒生银行副董事长。何添博士于 2004 年 4 月退任恒生银行董事，同时获该行委任为名誉资深顾问。何添博士曾任多个上市公司董事职位，包括美丽华酒店企业有限公司（董事长）、新世界发展有限公司、新鸿基地产有限公司，熊谷组（香港）有限公司及景福集团有限公司。

　　何添博士积极参与公职服务，他为香港中文大学联合书院永久校董、香港中文大学校董会校董、恒生商学书院校董、邓肇坚何添慈善基金创办人之一、香港何氏宗亲总会永久会长、旅港番禺会所永久名誉会长及金银业贸易场永远名誉会长。

　　何添博士于 1982 年获香港中文大学颁授荣誉社会科学博士学位；1997 年获香港城市大学颁授名誉工商管理学博士学位；1999 年获香港大学颁授荣誉法律博士学位；于 1988 年、1993 年、1995 年及 2004 年分别获广州市、番禺市、顺德市及佛山市授予荣誉市民的称号；又于 1996 年 11 月出任中华人民共和国香港特别行政区第一届政府推选委员会委员。

　　何添博士于 2004 年 11 月 6 日在香港病逝，享年 95 岁。

捐款者伟伦基金有限公司之创办人
利　国　伟

　　利国伟博士于 1946 年加入香港恒生银行有限公司（前为恒生银号），1959 年 12 月任该行董事，1976 年 1 月任副董事长，1983—1996 年 2 月做执行董事长，1996 年 3 月至 1997 年 12 月任非执行董事长，1998 年 1 月至 2004 年 4 月任名誉董事长，退任后续任名誉资深顾问。

　　在公职方面，利国伟博士 1963—1982 年为香港中文大学司库，1982—1997 年为该大学校董会主席，并于 1994 年 11 月 30 日起被该校委为终身校董。利博士亦曾先后任香港李宝椿联合世界书院创校主席及名誉主席。此外，亦曾任江门市五邑大学名誉校长。

　　利国伟博士曾先后任香港行政局议员 7 年，立法局议员 10 年，银行业务咨询委员会委员 14 年，教育委员会主席 7 年，教育统筹委员会主席 5 年。

利国伟博士历年获香港及海外多所大学颁授荣誉博士学位，这些学校分别为香港中文大学（1972）、英国候尔大学（University of Hull）（1985）、英国伯明翰大学（University of Birmingham）（1989）、香港大学及香港城市理工学院（即现时之香港城市大学）（1990）、香港理工学院（即现时之香港理工大学）及香港浸会学院（即现时之香港浸会大学）（1992）、英国伦敦市政厅大学（London Guildhall University）（1993）、清华大学及香港公开进修学院（即现时之香港公开大学）（1995）。利博士于 1971 年及 1995 年分别获选为英国银行学会及美国塔傅思大学（Tufts University）院士，并于 1991 年、1993 年、1995 年、1996 年及 2003 年分别获选为英国牛津大学圣候斯学院（St Hugh's College, Oxford University）、爱丁堡皇家医学院（Royal College of Physicians of Edinburgh）、香港心脏专科学院、香港内科医学院以及英国剑桥李约瑟研究所荣誉院士，并于 1993 年获广州市政府、开平市政府及江门市政府颁授荣誉市民名衔。此外，利博士在南华早报及敦豪国际（香港）有限公司主办之 1994 年香港商业奖中获业成就奖。利博士于 1995—2003 年受聘为中国老教授协会名誉会长，并于 1997 年荣获香港特别行政区政府颁授"大紫荆勋章"，2006 年获香港证券专业学院授予荣誉会员衔。

多年来，利国伟博士对其原籍之开平地方建设、教育及医疗事务多所资助，对江门市亦捐赠不少。此外，对清华大学、上海市和广州市之其他机构亦分别做出捐献。

利国伟博士于 2013 年 8 月 10 日在香港病逝，享年 95 岁。

BRIEF INTRODUCTION TO THE DONORS TO
HO LEUNG HO LEE FOUNDATION

Brief Biography of Dr. S. H. Ho

Dr. S. H. Ho, the founder of the S. H. Ho Foundation Ltd. which donated to Ho Leung Ho Lee Foundation, born in 1900, was a native of Panyu, Guangdong Province. He cofounded Hang Seng Ngan Ho in Hong Kong in 1933 and later, the Hang Chong Investment Co Ltd. and the Dah Chong Hong Ltd. In 1952, Hang Seng Ngan Ho was incorporated and in 1959, was renamed Hang Seng Bank Ltd. From 1960 until 1983, Dr. Ho served as Chairman of the Bank. In 1983, on the 50th anniversary of the Bank, he became its Honorary Chairman until he passed away.

Dr. Ho was involved in a wide range of businesses, including banking, trade, trusteeship, financing, hotels, insurance, property, shipping and investment.

Dr. Ho was a philanthropist who was committed to promoting charitable causes. In 1970, he founded the S. H. Ho Foundation Ltd to support charitable causes in China and overseas, including regional construction, education, medical services, scientific research and the training of new talent. His contributions to Guangzhou and his homeland were particularly notable. In 1978, he founded the Hang Seng School of Commerce to provide free education to aspiring youths. He also sat as director on many school boards. In 1971, he was conferred the Honorary Degree of Doctor of Social Science by The Chinese University of Hong Kong and in 1983, an Honorary Degree of Doctor of Laws by The University of Hong Kong. In 1990, he became an Honorary Adviser to the Zhongshan University in Guangzhou and was conferred the Honorary Doctorate's degree by that University in 1995. He was made an Honorary Citizen of Guangzhou and of Panyu in 1993.

Dr. S. H. Ho passed away peacefully in Hong Kong on December 4. 1997 at the age of 97.

Brief Biography of Dr. Leung Kau-Kui

The late Dr. Leung Kau-Kui was born in 1903, a native of the City of Shunde in Guangdong Province. Dr. Leung made his mark in the businesses of foreign exchange and trading in Guangzhou, Hong Kong and Macau early in his career. He was a pioneer in leading Chinese businessmen to participate in international trades.

Throughout his career, Dr. Leung held directorships in various companies. He was a director of the Hang Seng Bank, founder of Hang Chong Investment Co. Ltd., and one of the founders and Vice-Chairman of the Dah Chong Hong Ltd. —a leading Chinese-owned trading firm in Hong Kong during the colonial days. He was also a director of Miramar Hotel and Investment Co. Ltd. Furama Hotel Co. Ltd., Milford (International) Investment Co. Ltd., and a director of the Hang Seng School of Commerce.

Dr. Leung travelled regularly and extensively to cities in China and overseas to set up branches for Dah Chong Hong Ltd. as well as to promote and develop businesses for his partners. During the 60's, he helped to restructure the import procedures of rice to Hong Kong from Thailand contributing significantly to the stability and prosperity of Hong Kong.

Benevolent, enterprising and self-effacing, Dr. Leung was a committed contributor to charitable causes. He gave generously to education, medical social services and religious organisations. Among the charitable causes which he had supported were: the Missionary Sisters St. Columban Leung Shek Chee College in memory of his late father, the Po Leung Kuk Leung Chou Shun Kam Primary School in memory of his late mother, The University of Hong Kong's K K Leung Building, The Chinese University of Hong Kong's Leung Kau-Kui Building, Lingnan College's Leung Kau-Kui Building, the Hong Kong Baptist College's (now the Hong Kong Baptist University) School of Continuing Education Leung Kau-Kui Hanyu Institute, K. K. Leung Architectural Building of Beijing's Tsinghua University, Guangzhou's Zhongshan University's Leung Kau-Kui Hall and Leung Lee Sau Yu Library, and The K. K. Leung Brain Research Centre of the Fourth Military Medical University in Xian, China. He also sponsored the Foundation of Zhongshan University Advanced Research Centre and the China Educational Exchange Association's Scholarships for Overseas Studies, both of which were promoted by Professor Yang Chen Ning. He also set up the Book Foundation of Dr. Leung Kau-Kui for Tsinghua University.

In Hong Kong, his other contributions were supports given to: Shun Tak Fraternal Association Leung Kau-Kui College, Shun Tak Fraternal Association Leung Lee Sau Yu Kindergarten (Tuen Mun), Shun Tak Fraternal Association Leung Lee Sau Yu Kindergarten (Shatin), The Endeavourers Leung Lee Sau Yu Memorial Primary School, Hang Seng School of Commerce, the assembly hall of Lok Sin Tong Chan Cho Chak Primary School, Lok Sin Tong Leung Kau-Kui Primary School, Lok Sin Tong Leung Kau-Kui College, Dr. Raymond Huang Foundation of the University of Hong Kong, S. T. F. A. Leung Kau-Kui Clinic of the Medical and Health Department, The Hong Kong Anti-Cancer Society, Queen Mary Hospital's Leung Kau-Kui Diabetes Centre and donations to upgrade the Radiology Library/Museum as well as teaching materials and staff welfare of the Hospital. He also contributed to the Department of Medicine of the University of Hong Kong to do research work on gastric cancer in Shandong Province, China. Dr. Leung also made generous contributions to the religions bodies, which included assisting the Christian Break-through Organization in establishing and donating to the Youth Village-Information Centre, redevelopment foundation of the Buddhist Chi Lin Nunnery, as well as the construction fund of the Buddha Statue at Po Lin Monastery on Lantau Island.

Dr. Leung was generous and zealous in promoting education in science and technology and medical services in his hometown, Shunde. In particular, he was the first donor working to improve the public amenities of his native Beitou Village. Notable projects which he supported in Shunde included multipurpose halls, hospitals, child care and nursery centres, schools, kindergartens, libraries, sports and recreational centres as well as welfare institutions.

Dr. Leung received an Honorary Degree of Doctor of Social Sciences from The Chinese University of Hong Kong in 1987 and became an Honorary Adviser to Guangzhou's Zhongshan University in 1990. In 1992, the government of Shunde named him an Honorary Citizen. He was conferred an Honorary Doctorate by Tsinghua University in 1994. In April 1994, Premier Li Peng praised him for his enthusiastic support of charitable causes and development of education in China.

Dr. Leung had also donated to overseas institutions such as the Oxford University of United Kingdom, the medical school of Aberdeen University in Scotland, and the Yee Hong Geriatric Centre in Toronto, Canada.

Dr. Leung passed away peacefully in Hong Kong on November 10. 1994 at the age of 91.

Brief Biography of Dr. Ho Tim

Dr. Ho Tim joined Hang Seng Bank Ltd (formerly Hang Seng Ngan Ho) in Hong Kong in 1933, was appointed its Director and General Manager in 1953 and Vice-Chairman from 1967 to 1979. In April 2004, he retired from the Board of Hang Seng Bank Limited and was named one of the Bank's Honorary Senior Advisers. Dr. Ho held directorships in a number of listed companies. He was the Chairman of Miramar Hotel and Investment Co. Ltd.; a Director of New World Development Co. Ltd., Sun Hung Kai Properties Ltd., Kumagai Gumi (Hong Kong) Ltd. and King Fook Holdings Ltd.

Dr. Ho was active in public service. He was a Permanent Member of the Board of Trustees of the United College of The Chinese University of Hong Kong, a Council Member of The Chinese University of Hong Kong, a Board Member of the Hang Seng School of Commerce, one of the founders of the Tang Shiu Kin and Ho Tim Charitable Fund, Permanent President of the Ho's Clansmen Association Ltd., Honorary President of the Panyu District Association of Hong Kong and Honorary Permanent President of the Chinese Gold & Silver Exchange Society.

In 1982, The Chinese University of Hong Kong conferred on Dr. Ho the Honorary Degree of Doctor of Social Science; in 1997, an Honorary Doctorate Degree of Business Administration by The City University of Hong Kong; and in 1999, an Honorary Degree of Doctor of Laws by The University of Hong Kong. He was made an Honorary Citizen of Guangzhou, Panyu, Shunde and Foshan in 1988, 1993, 1995 and 2004 respectively by the respective municipal governments. He was appointed a member of the Selection Committee of the First Government of the Hong Kong

Special Administrative Region of the People's Republic of China in November 1996.

Dr. Ho Tim passed away peacefully in Hong Kong on November 6. 2004 at the age of 95.

Brief Biography of Dr. Lee Quo-Wei

Dr Lee Quo-Wei, the founder of Wei Lun Foundation Limited which donated to Ho Leung Ho Lee Foundation, joined Hang Seng Bank (formerly Hang Seng Ngan Ho) in Hong Kong in 1946. He was appointed a Director of the Bank in December 1959 and elected Vice-Chairman in January 1976. He became Executive Chairman of the Bank from 1983 until February 1996; non-executive Chairman from March 1996 to December 1997. He was appointed Honorary Senior Advi-sor of the Bank after his appointment as Honorary Chairman from January 1998 to April 2004.

Dr Lee was well-known for his active involvement in public services. He had been Treasurer of the Chinese University of Hong Kong from 1963 to 1982, the Chairman of the Council of the University from 1982 to 1997 and a Life Member of the Council of the University since 30 November 1994. He was the Founding Chairman and later the Honorary Chairman of the Li Po Chun United World College of Hong Kong as well as the Honorary President of Jiangmen's Wuyi University.

He was a member of the Executive Council in Hong Kong for 7 years and a member of the Legislative Council for 10 years. He was also a member of the Banking Advisory Committee for 14 years, Chairman of the Board of Education for 7 years and Chairman of the Education Commission for 5 years.

Several universities in Hong Kong and overseas had conferred Honorary Doctorate Degrees on Dr Lee, including The Chinese University of Hong Kong in 1972, University of Hull (United Kingdom) in 1985, University of Birmingham (United Kingdom) in 1989, University of Hong Kong in 1990, City Polytechnic of Hong Kong (presently known as the City University of Hong Kong) in 1990, Hong Kong Polytechnic (now the Hong Kong Polytechnic University) and Hong Kong Baptist College (now the Hong Kong Baptist University) in 1972, London Guildhall University (United Kingdom) in 1993, Tsinghua University (Beijing of China) and the Open Learning Institute (now the Open University of Hong Kong) in 1995. Dr Lee was also elected to a fellowship of the Chartered Institute of Bankers, London in 1971 and Tufts University (USA) in 1995 as well as honorary fellowships of St Hugh's College, Oxford University; Royal College of Physicians of Edinburgh; Hong Kong College of Cardiology; and Hong Kong College of Physicians; and Needham Research Institute, Cambridge in 1991, 1993, 1995, 1996 and 2003 respectively. In 1993, he was made an Honorary Citizen of Guangzhou, Kaiping and Jiangmen by the three municipal governments. In the 1994 South China Morning Post/DHL Hong Kong Business Awards, he was awarded Businessman of the year. Dr Lee had been engaged Honorary President of

China Senior Professors Association from 1995 to 2003. In July 1997, he was awarded the Grand Bauhinia Medal by the Hong Kong Special Administrative Region Government. In 2006, he was elected Honorary Fellow for the year by the Hong Kong Securities Institute.

Over the years, Dr Lee had donated generously to his homeland Kaiping, helping to improve infrastructure, education and medical services. He had also made significant contributions to Jiangmen. In addition, he had made donations to Tsinghua University in Beijing and other institutions in the cities of Shanghai and Guangzhou.

Dr Lee Quo—Wei passed away peacefully in Hong Kong on August 10. 2013 at the age of 95.

何 梁 何 利 基 金 信 托 人 简 历

朱 丽 兰

朱丽兰，女，1935年8月出生于上海。教授，原科学技术部部长，现任全国人大常委会委员、全国人大教科文卫委员会主任委员。曾就读于上海中西小学，毕业于第三女中。1956年在苏联敖德萨大学高分子物理化学专业学习，1961年获优秀毕业生文凭。回国后在中国科学院化学研究所工作到1986年。长期从事高分子反应动力学、高分子材料剖析及结构表征研究。所承担的高分子材料剖析、性能结构形态关系的研究项目曾分别获国家级重大科研成果奖及应用成果奖，多次在国内外发表学术论文。曾任中国科学院化学研究所研究室主任和所长职务。

1979—1980年，在德国费拉堡大学高分子化学研究所做访问学者。在科研工作中，发展了一种新的染色技术用于制备样品，被称为一种突破，在国内外同行中享有较高声誉。

1986—2001年，曾任国家科委副主任、常务副主任、科学技术部部长。任国家科委、科技部领导期间，组织制定并实施了国家高技术研究发展计划（"863"计划）、国家发展基础研究的攀登计划以及高技术产业化的火炬计划等。倡导和推行新的专家管理机制，提出了一系列适应当代高技术发展规律并结合中国国情的管理理论与政策、方法，出版了专著《当代高技术与发展战略》《发展与挑战》等，并获中国材料研究学会成就奖。由于在推动国际科技合作以及促进中国国家高技术研究发展与产业化方面成绩卓著，1993年获美洲中国工程师协会颁发的杰出服务奖；1998年获德国联邦总统星级大十字勋章。

朱丽兰曾任中国工程院主席团顾问，中国科学院学部主席团顾问，国家科技领导小组成员，中央农村工作领导小组成员，国家信息化领导小组成员，国家奖励委员会主任委员等职。现任中国化学会常务理事会理事，中国对外友好协会常务理事，中国自然辩证法研究会理事，中国材料研究学会理事，并被聘为北京理工大学、国家行政学院、清华大学、中国科学院化学研究所兼职教授。

朱丽兰是国际欧亚科学院院士、亚太材料科学院院士。

岳　毅

岳毅现任中银香港（控股）有限公司及中国银行（香港）有限公司（"中银香港"）副董事长兼总裁，同时担任集友银行有限公司董事长、中银集团人寿保险有限公司董事长、中银香港慈善基金董事长等职务。

岳毅是资深的银行家，拥有37年的银行经验，深具战略思维、国际化视野和开拓创新意识。在他的领导下，中银香港进一步明确了战略定位和发展战略，更加主动地融入国家战略，积极推进由本地城市银行向跨境区域性银行的转型。

岳毅现任香港银行公会主席、香港中国企业协会会长、香港中资银行业协会会长、经济发展委员会委员、外汇基金咨询委员会成员以及香港贸易发展局理事会成员。他亦是银行业咨询委员会和发钞咨询委员会成员，香港银行同业结算有限公司、香港银行同业结算服务有限公司及香港印钞有限公司董事，财资市场公会议会成员，港日经济合作委员会特邀委员，香港银行学会副会长，海上丝绸之路协会特别顾问。

在加入中银香港前，岳毅曾先后于中国银行集团境内外多家机构担任不同职务，曾从事和分管个人金融、公司金融、金融市场、投资银行、风险管理等多个不同业务领域，曾荣获《亚洲银行家》杂志评选的"年度中国零售银行家"。岳毅获武汉大学金融学专业硕士学位。

杜　占　元

杜占元，1962年7月生，湖南华容人。1985年7月参加工作。美国马萨诸塞大学植物与土壤科学系植物生理化学专业毕业，研究生学历，哲学博士学位，农艺师。

现任教育部副部长、党组成员。

1978—1982年，湖南农学院基础课部生理生化专业学生；1982—1985年，北京农业大学农学系植物生理生化专业硕士研究生；1985—1989年，国家科委中国农村技术开发中心农业处干部、负责人；1989—1993年，美国马萨诸塞大学植物与土壤科学系植物生理生化专业博士研究生；1993—1994年，国家科委综合计划司计划处干部、主任科员；1994—1997 年，国家科委综合计划司计划处副处长（其间：1996—1997 年，在美国杜克大学法学院和商学院进修科技政策与商业管理）；1997—1998 年，国家科委综合计划司计划处处长；1998—2000 年，科技部发展计划司计划协调处、成果处处长；2000—2001 年，科技部发展计划司副司长；2001—2006 年，科技部发展计划司司长（其间：2003—2004 年在中央党校一年制中青年干部培训班学习）；2006—2008 年，科技部农村科技司司长；2008—2010 年，科技部副部长、党组成员；2010 年起任教育部副部长、党组成员。

郑 慧 敏

郑慧敏女士为恒生银行副董事长兼行政总裁、恒生银行（中国）及恒生集团内若干附属公司之董事长、恒生指数顾问委员会主席，以及何梁何利基金信托委员会委员。郑女士亦为汇丰控股集团总经理及香港上海汇丰银行董事。

郑女士于 1999 年加入汇丰集团，曾出任个人理财服务及市场推广业务多个要职。郑女士于 2007 年获委任为香港个人理财服务主管；于 2009 年为亚太区个人理财服务董事；及于 2010 年为亚太区零售银行及财富管理业务主管。郑女士于 2014 年被委任为汇丰集团环球零售银行业务主管，至 2017 年出任恒生银行副董事长兼行政总裁。

郑女士现时亦出任下列机构的职务：

● 香港公益金董事
● 中国银联国际顾问
● 第十二届江苏省政协委员
● 中国（广东）自由贸易试验区深圳前海蛇口片区暨深圳市前海深港现代服务业合作区咨询委员会委员
● 香港银行学会副会长

郑女士过往的职务包括：

● 美国花旗银行市场总监
● 香港按揭证券有限公司董事
● 汇丰集团多间公司董事

郑女士毕业于香港大学，并取得社会科学学士学位。郑女士为 Beta Gamma Sigma 香港大学分会终身荣誉会员。

杨 纲 凯

杨纲凯教授，1948 年 7 月生于上海市，现任香港中文大学敬文书院院长、物理系教授，香港特别行政区教育统筹委员会委员、课程发展议会主席。曾任香港特别行政区大学教育资助委员会委员及香港研究资助局主席、亚太物理联会秘书长、副会长。自 1973 年起任职香港中文大学，曾任物理系主任、理学院院长、研究院院长、副校长。1965—1972 年就读美加州理工学院，主修物理，1969 年获学士学位，1972 年获博士学位。1972—1973 年在美国普林斯顿大学从事教学及研究。

杨教授长期从事理论物理学研究，包括基本粒子、场论、高能唯象、耗散系统及其本征态展开，对光学、引力波等开放系统的应用做出贡献，其主要研究成果载于有关国际杂志，包括 "Microscopic derivation of the Helmholtz force density" Phys Rev Lett 47，177；"Late-time tail of wave propagation on curved spacetime"，Phys Rev Lett 74，4588；"Quasinormal modes of dirty black holes"，Phys Rev Lett 78，2894；"Quasinormal-mode expansion for waves in open systems"，Rev Mod Phys 70，1545 等。1999 年被选为美国物理学会院士，2004 年被选为国际欧亚科学院院士。

BRIEF INTRODUCTION TO THE TRUSTEES OF
HO LEUNG HO LEE FOUNDATION

Brief Biography of Professor Zhu Lilan

Professor Zhu Lilan, female, born in Shanghai in August 1935, is the member of the Standing Committee of the National People's Congress, the director of the Science, Education, Culture and Health Commission of the National People's Congress, former minister of the Ministry of Science and Technology of China. From 1956 to 1961, Professor Zhu studied in the Aodesa University of former Soviet Union majoring in macromolecule physical chemistry. After graduated from the university as an excellent student, Professor Zhu worked in the Institute of Chemistry, Chinese Academy of Sciences till 1986. For a long time, Professor Zhu had been conducted the research of macromolecule reactivity dynamics, macromolecule material analysis and structure token. The research project had got the national award of Grand Research Achievements and Award of Application Achievements. During this period, Professor Zhu served as the director of the research department and the director of the Institute of Chemistry, Chinese Academy of Sciences.

From 1979 to 1980, Professor Zhu was a visiting scholar in macromolecule institute in Fleberg University in Germany. In her research, she developed a kind of new dyeing technique for the sample producing, which was considered a break through at that time and won high reputation in the research circle.

From 1986 to 2001, Professor Zhu was appointed vice-minister of the State Science and Technology Commission and minister of the Ministry of Science and Technology of China. During this period, Professor Zhu organized the formulating and implementation of the National High-Tech Development Plan (863 Plan), National Climbing Plan for the Basic Research, and Torch Program for the High-Tech Industrialization. Professor Zhu advocated and implemented the new expertise management mechanism, put forward a series of management theories and policies which suit to the development of high-tech and the situation of China, published her monograph *High-tech*, *Development Strategy in the Contemporary Era*, *Development and Challenge*. Owing to her outstanding contribution to promoting international science and technology cooperation and the development of China's high-tech research and industrialization, Professor Zhu was awarded the Outstanding Service Prize in 1993 by the American Association of Chinese Engineers, and the Germany Federal President Star Great Cross Medal in 1998.

Professor Zhu has been the counselor of Chinese Academy of Engineering Presidium, the counselor of Chinese Academy of Science Presidium, the member of State Science and Education Steering Group, member of Central Rural Work Steering Group, member of State Informationaliza-tion Steering Group, director-commissioner of State Award Commission. Professor Zhu is now the member of China Chemistry Society Administrative Council, the administrative member of the board of the Association of China Foreign Friendship Relations, the member of board of China Nat-ural Dialectic Seminar, the director of China Material Seminar. Professor Zhu is also the concurrent Professors of Beijing University of Science and Technology, National Administration College, Tsinghua University, Chemistry Institute of Chinese Academy of Sciences. Professor Zhu is the academician of International Europe and Asia Academy of Science, and the academician of Asian and Pacific Material Academy of Science.

Brief Biography of Mr. Yue Yi

Mr Yue Yi is the Vice Chairman and Chief Executive of BOC Hong Kong (Holdings) Limited and Bank of China (Hong Kong) Limited ("BOCHK"). He is also Chairman of Chiyu Banking Corporation Limited, BOC Group Life Assurance Company Limited and BOCHK Charitable Foundation.

As a veteran banker with 37 years of experience, Mr YUE is a strategic thinker with international vision and innovative spirit. Under his leadership, BOCHK has further defined its strategic position and development to align with the important national strategies and proactively drive its transformation from a local bank into a regional bank.

Mr YUE is Chairman of Hong Kong Association of Banks, President of Hong Kong Chinese Enterprises Association, and Chairman of Chinese Banking Association of Hong Kong. He is also a member of both the Economic Development Commission and Exchange Fund Advisory Committee, and a council member of Hong Kong Trade Development Council. Mr YUE sits on both the Banking Advisory Committee and Bank Notes Issue Advisory Committee and serves as a director of Hong Kong Interbank Clearing Limited, HKICL Services Limited and Hong Kong Note Printing Limited. He is also a council member of Treasury Markets Association, an honorary member of Hong Kong-Japan Business Co-operation Committee, Vice President of Hong Kong Institute of Bankers, and a special advisor of Maritime Silk Road Society.

Before joining BOCHK, Mr YUE assumed various senior management positions at the domestic and foreign institutions of Bank of China Group, covering personal finance, corporate finance, financial markets, investment banking and risk management. Mr YUE was named the Retail Banker of the Year in China by the *Asian Banker*. Mr YUE obtained his Master's Degree in Finance from Wuhan University.

Brief Biography of Mr. Du Zhanyuan

Du Zhanyuan, born in July 1962 in Huarong, Hunan Province, started to be employed in July 1985. He graduated from the specialty of plant biology and biochemistry in the Department of Plant and Soil Sciences in the University of Massachusetts in the USA. He has postgraduate education and holds the titles of Ph. D. and agronomist.

He is currently vice minister of education of China and member of the ministry's CPC committee.

1978—1982, student in the specialty of biology and biochemistry of the department of basic courses in the Hunan College of Agriculture;

1982—1985, postgraduate of master program of the specialty of plant biology and biochemistry in the Department of Agriculture in the Beijing Agricultural University;

1985—1989, cadre and person-in-charge of the section of agriculture in the China Rural Technology Department Center of the State Science and Technology Commission;

1989—1993, postgraduate of doctorate program in the specialty of plant biology and biochem-istry in the Department of Plant and Soil Sciences of the University of Massachusetts, USA;

1993—1994, cadre and principal staff member of the planning section in the Department of Comprehensive Planning of the State Science and Technology Commission;

1994—1997, deputy chief of the planning section in the Department of Comprehensive Plan-ning of the State Science and Technology Commission (During the period of 1996—1997 in this period, he studied science and technology policies and business administration in the Schools of Law and Business in the Duke University, USA.);

1997—1998, chief of the planning section in the Department of Comprehensive Planning of the State Science and Technology Commission;

1998—2000, chief of sections of planning and coordination and of research results in the De-partment of Development and Planning of the Ministry of Science and Technology;

2000—2001, deputy director of the Department of Development and Planning in the Ministry of Science and Technology;

2001—2006, director of the Department of Development and Planning in the Ministry of Sci-ence and Technology (During the period of 2003—2004, he studied in the one-year middle-aged and young cadre training program in the Party School of the CPC Central Committee.);

2006—2008, director of the Department of Rural Science and Technology in the Ministry of Science and Technology;

2008—2010, vice minister of science and technology and member of the ministry's CPC com-mittee;

In 2010, vice minister of education and member of the ministry's CPC committee.

Brief Biography of Ms Louisa Cheang

Ms Louisa Cheang is Vice–Chairman and Chief Executive of Hang Seng Bank, and Chairman of Hang Seng Bank (China) and various subsidiaries in Hang Seng Group. She is Chairman of Hang Seng Index Advisory Committee of Hang Seng Indexes, and a Member of the Board of Trustees of the Ho Leung Ho Lee Foundation. She is also a Group General Manager of HSBC and a Director of The Hongkong and Shanghai Banking Corporation.

Ms Cheang joined HSBC in 1999, and has worked across a wide range of Personal Financial Services and Marketing positions. She was appointed Head of Personal Financial Services, Hong Kong in 2007; Regional Director of Personal Financial Services, Asia Pacific in 2009; and Regional Head of Retail Banking and Wealth Management, Asia Pacific in 2010. Ms Cheang became Group Head of Retail Banking, HSBC in 2014 prior to her appointment as Vice–Chairman and Chief Executive of Hang Seng Bank in 2017.

Ms Cheang currently also holds the following appointments:

- Board Member of The Community Chest of Hong Kong

- International Advisor of China Union Pay

- Member of The Twelfth Jiangsu Provincial Committee of the Chinese People's Political Consultative Conference

- Member of the Consulting Committee of Qianhai & Shekou Area of Shenzhen, China (Guangdong) Pilot Free Trade Zone, and Qianhai Shenzhen–Hong Kong Modern Service Industry Cooperation Zone of Shenzhen

- Vice President of The Hong Kong Institute of Bankers

Her previous appointments include:

- Marketing Director of Citibank N.A.

- Director of The Hong Kong Mortgage Corporation Limited

- Director of various subsidiaries in HSBC

Ms Cheang graduated from the University of Hong Kong receiving a Bachelor of Social Sciences degree. She was made a Chapter Honoree of Beta Gamma Sigma of The University of Hong Kong Chapter.

Brief Biography of Professor Kenneth Young

Professor Kenneth Young was born in July 1948 in Shanghai, China. He joined The Chinese University of Hong Kong in 1973, and has been Chairman, Department of Physics and later Dean, Faculty of Science, Dean of the Graduate School, and Pro-Vice-Chancellor/Vice-President. He is currently Master of CW Chu College and professor of physics at The Chinese University of Hong Kong, Hong Kong SAR, China. He was also a member of the Hong Kong University Grants Committee, and chairman of its Research Grants Council. He was formerly Secretary and then Vice-President of the Association of Asia Pacific Physical Societies. He pursued studies at the California Institute of Technology, USA, 1965—1972, and obtained a BS in Physics (1969) and a PhD in Physics and Mathematics (1972). Before returning to Hong Kong, he held a research appointment at Princeton University, USA, 1972—1973.

His research interests include elementary particles, field theory, high energy phenomenology, dissipative systems and especially their eigenfunction representation and applications to optics, gravitational waves and other open systems. Publications include for example "Microscopic derivation of the Helmholtz force density" Phys Rev Lett 47, 177; "Late-time tail of wave propagation on curved spacetime", Phys Rev Lett 74, 4588; "Quasinormal modes of dirty black holes", Phys Rev Lett 78, 2894; "Quasinormal-mode expansion for waves in open systems", Rev Mod Phys 70, 1545. He was elected Fellow, American Physical Society in 1999 and Member, international Eurasian Academy of Sciences in 2004.

何 梁 何 利 基 金 评 选 委 员 会 成 员 简 历

评选委员会主任
朱 丽 兰

朱丽兰，女，1935年8月出生，浙江湖州人，教授。现任中国发明协会理事长，澳门特别行政区科技奖励委员会主任。曾任国家科委副主任（1986年）、国家科学技术部部长（1998年），全国人大常委会教科文卫委员会主任委员（2001年），中国工程院主席团顾问，中国科学院学部主席团顾问，国家科教领导小组成员，国家科技奖励委员会主任委员，澳门特别行政区科学技术委员会顾问等职。

在中国科学院化学所从事高分子材料剖析及结构形态表征、反应动力学研究期间，承担了多项国家、国防重点科研攻关项目，曾获国家级、省部级重大科研成果奖及应用成果奖。担任全国人大常委会教科文卫委员会主任委员期间，负责组织完成《科技进步法》《义务教育法》的修订和实施；组织实施一批关系到社会、民生、科技、文化、卫生等重要法律的立法调研与修法任务，为法制建设奠定重要基础。

发表了多篇有关高技术发展现状及对策和管理方面的文章，出版了《当代高技术与发展战略》《发展与挑战》等专著。曾获中国材料研究学会成就奖。由于在推动中国高技术发展及国际科技合作方面成绩显著，获美洲中国工程师协会颁发的杰出服务奖、德国总统颁发的德意志联邦共和国大十字勋章、乌克兰总统二级勋章。

评选委员会副主任
杜 占 元

杜占元，1962年7月出生。先后就读于湖南农业大学、中国农业大学并获得学士学位和硕士学位；1993

年在美国马萨诸塞大学植物与土壤科学系植物生理生化专业获得博士学位。长期在国家科技部、教育部工作，曾任科技部副部长，现任教育部副部长。

在农业生物领域具有很深的科研造诣，在植物生理研究的国际刊物上发表论文若干篇，并曾获得美国东北园艺学会研究生优秀论文奖第一名。对科技管理和技术创新经济方面有深入研究，在科技部任职期间，曾参与国家"十五""十一五"科技发展规划以及科技支撑计划的制订等。在国内科技管理刊物和报纸上发表论文多篇，并合作编著了《中小企业与技术创新》和《中国制造业发展报告》等学术型专著，对国家科技战略和国际学术前沿有全面深刻的了解和把握。近年来，在研究推动高校科技、研究生教育、教育信息化等方面做了大量工作。

任教育部副部长期间，主要分管高校科技、学位管理与研究生教育、教育信息化等工作，对科技管理工作有着深入的研究，在科技工作、高层次人才培养、教育信息化等方面具备丰富的管理经验。

评选委员会副主任
杨 纲 凯

杨纲凯，1948 年 7 月生于上海市。自 1973 年起任职香港中文大学，曾任物理系主任、理学院院长、研究院院长、副校长。现任香港中文大学敬文书院院长、物理系教授，香港特别行政区教育统筹委员会委员、课程发展议会主席。曾任香港特别行政区大学教育资助委员会委员及香港研究资助局主席，亚太物理联会秘书长、副会长。1965—1972 年就读美国加州理工学院，主修物理，1969 年获学士学位，1972 年获博士学位。1972—1973 年在美国普林斯顿大学从事教学及研究。

长期从事理论物理学研究，包括基本粒子、场论、高能唯象、耗散系统及其本征态展开，对光学、引力波等开放系统的应用做出贡献，其主要研究成果载于有关国际杂志，包括 Microscopic derivation of the Helmholtz force density, Phys Rev Lett 47, 77; Late time tail of wave propagation on curved spacetime, Phys Rev Lett 74, 2414; Quasinormal mode expansion for linearized waves in gravitational systems, Phys Rev Lett 74, 4588; Quasinormal modes of dirty black holes, Phys Rev Lett 78, 289 等。1999 年被选为美国物理学会院士，2004 年被选为国际欧亚科学院院士。

评选委员会秘书长
段 瑞 春

段瑞春，1943年2月出生。上海交通大学工学学士，中国科学院研究生院理学硕士，北京大学法学硕士；20世纪90年代，任国家科委政策法规与体制改革司司长、国务院知识产权办公会议办公室主任，2000—2007年任国务院国有重点大型企业监事会主席。现任中国科学技术法学会会长、中国产学研合作促进会常务副会长。

我国知识产权、科技政策和企业创新领域著名专家，具有自然科学、经济管理和法律科学复合型知识结构。曾主持起草我国《技术合同法》《科学技术进步法》《国家科技奖励条例》等法律法规；参加多项知识产权法律的制定和修改工作；担任中美、中欧、中俄科技合作知识产权谈判首席代表、中国"入世"知识产权谈判主要代表；《国家知识产权战略》总报告评审组组长；何梁何利基金《信托契约》《评选章程》主要制定者之一。

其研究成果于1992年获得国家科委科技进步奖一等奖、1993年获得国家科技进步奖二等奖，均为第一完成人。2004年获我国技术市场建设功勋奖，2008年获中国科技法学杰出贡献奖。撰写出版《国际合作与知识产权》《技术合同原理与实践》《技术创新读本》《科技政策多维思考》等多部著作。

评选委员会委员
马 永 生

马永生，1961年10月生于内蒙古自治区呼和浩特市。石油地质学家、沉积学家。1980至1990年先后就读于中国地质大学（原武汉地质学院）和中国地质科学院，获博士学位。现任中国石化集团公司副总经理、总地质师。2009年当选中国工程院院士。

长期从事中国油气资源勘探理论研究和生产实践，在中国海相碳酸盐岩油气勘探理论和技术方面取得了多项创新性成果，成功指导发现了普光、元坝等多个大型、特大型天然气田，为国家重大工程"川气东送"提供了扎实的资源基础。他在非常规天然气领域的前瞻性研究，为中国第一个页岩气田——涪陵页岩气田的发现做出了重要贡献。他的科研成果对缓解我国天然气供需矛盾、发展地区经济与环境保护起到了重要的促进作用。

获国家科技进步奖一等奖 2 项；2007 年获何梁何利科学与技术成就奖，同年获第十次李四光地质科学奖；2013 年被评为国家首批"万人计划"杰出人才。由于他在石油工业界的杰出成果，2017 年国际小行星中心将国际编号为 210292 号小行星命名为"马永生星"。

评选委员会委员
朱 道 本

朱道本，1942 年 8 月生于上海，原籍浙江杭州。有机化学、物理化学家，中国科学院化学研究所研究员，1997 年 10 月当选为中国科学院院士。

1965 年毕业于华东化工学院，1968 年华东化工学院有机系研究生学习后到中国科学院化学研究所工作。曾任中国科学院化学研究所副所长、所长、中国化学会理事长、国家自然科学基金会副主任。现任中国科学院学术委员会副主任、中国科学院有机固体重点实验室主任等职。

20 世纪 70 年代开始有机固体领域的研究，在有机晶体的电导、铁磁性、分子薄膜与器件、C60 及其衍生物的结构性能等研究都引起了国际同行的关注。发表论文 500 余篇，研究成果曾获国家自然科学奖二等奖 4 项，中国科学院自然科学奖二等奖 2 项。

评选委员会委员
杨 祖 佑

杨祖佑，1940 年出生。获美国康奈尔大学博士学位。先后任普度大学航空宇宙工程系主任，工学院院长；曾兼任美国国家科学基金会智能制造工程中心共同主任，同时任阿姆斯特朗（首位登陆月球者）杰出宇航讲座教授。现任美国圣塔芭芭拉加州大学校长（1994 年始任），美国国家工程院院士，美国航天、机械学会 Fellow，中国工程院海外院士。兼任美、中、印、日、加"三十米望远镜"计划（简称"TMT"计划）主席，太平洋滨 42 所大学联盟主席（包括北大、清华、复旦、科大、浙大、南京），美国总统科学奖章评委，科维理科学基金会理事，曾任美国大学联盟（AAU，包括 62 所顶尖研究型大学）主席，芬兰千禧科技奖评委。共获七所大学荣誉博士。

长期致力于教学及科研。从事宇航结构、颤振、控制转型至地震、制造、材料（LED）及生物工程等方面的研究，亲任博士论文主席指导 60 篇，发表期刊论文 200 余篇，学术会议论文 200 余篇，有限元教科书一本（被四十余所美国大学采用，有中文、日文版）。

曾获 2008 美国航天学会结构、振动，材料奖（SDM Award），美国工程教育学会最高李梅金质奖章以及十余次最佳教学奖。

评选委员会委员
沈 祖 尧

沈祖尧，1959 年 10 月出生。香港大学内外全科医学士学位，加拿大卡尔加里大学博士学位（生命科学），香港中文大学医学博士学位。为英国皇家内科医学院院士、泰国皇家医学院院士、澳洲皇家内科医学院院士、美国肠胃病学学院院士、美国肠胃学会院士、香港内科医学院院士及香港医学专科学院院士，并担任二十多个专业学会委员。中国工程院院士，欧亚科学院院士。

曾任中大医学院内科学系讲师及内科及药物治疗学讲座教授，内科及药物治疗学系系主任，医学院副院长，以及逸夫书院院长等职。

为肠胃研究权威，研究范围包括肠胃出血、幽门螺杆菌、消化性溃疡、肝炎以及与消化系统相关的癌症。为领导全球肠胃科研究的先驱，自 2004 年起带领 15 国专家展开大肠癌筛查研究，拟定清晰普查指引，于 2008 年获授美国防癌基金会桂冠奖。其医学服务卓越研究成就，获 2008 年国家科技进步奖二等奖及多项本港及国际奖项。

著作甚丰，曾在顶尖国际期刊发表论文 700 多篇，著作及编辑的书籍超过 32 种，并为超过 15 份知名学术期刊担任审阅委员，亦多次获颁最佳论文奖。

评选委员会委员
张 立 同

张立同，女，1938年4月出生于重庆，著名航空航天材料专家。1961年毕业于西北工业大学。1989—1991年在美国NASA空间结构材料商业发展中心作高级访问学者。现任西北工业大学教授、博士生导师、超高温结构复合材料技术国家重点实验室学术委员会副主任。1995年当选中国工程院院士。

致力于航空航天材料及其制造技术研究，在薄壁复杂高温合金和铝合金铸件的无余量熔模精密铸造技术及其理论基础研究中取得丰硕成果。揭示了叶片变形规律、粗糙度形成规律和陶瓷型壳中温和高温软化变形机理。创新发展了高温合金无余量熔模铸造技术、铝合金石膏型熔模铸造技术、高温合金熔模铸造用中温和高温抗蠕变陶瓷型壳材料、高温合金泡沫陶瓷过滤净化材料技术等。相关成果成功用于航空发动机和飞机构件生产中。

突破大型空间站用陶瓷基复合材料技术，建立了具有自主知识产权的制造工艺、制造设备与材料环境性能考核三个技术平台，打破了国际技术封锁。

获国家技术发明奖一等奖1项，国家科技进步奖一、二、三等奖4项，国家级教学成果奖二等奖1项，获授权国家发明专利64项。

评选委员会委员
张 恭 庆

张恭庆，1936年5月29日出生于上海。1959年毕业于北京大学数学系，毕业后留校工作至今。1978年作为我国改革开放后第一批赴美访问学者赴美进修。现为北京大学教授、中国科学院院士、发展中国家（第三世界）科学院院士、高校数学研究与人才培养中心主任，还担任多个国际核心刊物的编委。

著名数学家。发展无穷维Morse理论为临界点理论的统一框架，并首次将其应用于偏微分方程的多解问题，其著作成为该领域的基本文献。发展了集值映射的拓扑度理论以及不可微泛函的临界点理论，使之成为研究数学物理方程以及非光滑力学中的一类自由边界问题的有效方法。

曾荣获全国科技大会奖（1978）、国家自然科学奖三等奖（1982）、国家自然科学奖二等奖（1987）、陈省身数学奖（1986）、有突出贡献的中青年科学家（1984）、第三世界科学院数学奖（1993）、华罗庚数学奖（2009）、北京大学国华奖、方正教学特等奖（2011）等。

评选委员会委员
陈 佳 洱

陈佳洱，1934年10月1日生于上海。中国科学院院士、第三世界科学院院士。现任北京大学物理学教授，国家重点基础研究计划（"973"计划）专家顾问组副组长，国际科联中国协调委员会副主席等职。

曾任北京大学校长和研究生院院长、国家自然科学基金委员会主任、中国科学院数理学部主任和中科院主席团成员以及中科院研究生院物理科学学院院长等职。

长期致力于低能粒子加速器及其应用的教学与科研工作，善于把握学科前沿发展与国家需求的结合，前瞻性地部署物理研究与人才培养，开拓发展我国的射频超导加速器、超灵敏加速器质谱计、射频四极场加速器、高压静电加速器等，是我国低能粒子加速器的奠基者和领头人之一。

陈佳洱长期在北京大学和国家自然科学基金委等单位担任领导工作，并曾担任国家中长期科技规划领导小组成员等职，为我国科学技术中长期规划的制定与相关的科教事业的发展做出了重要贡献。

评选委员会委员
郝 吉 明

郝吉明，1946年8月出生于山东省，著名环境工程专家。1970年毕业于清华大学，1981年获清华大学硕士学位，1984年获美国辛辛那提大学博士学位。现任清华大学教授、博士生导师、教学委员会副主任、环

境科学与工程研究院院长，兼任国家环境咨询委员会委员、中国环境与发展国际合作委员会委员。2005年当选中国工程院院士，2018年当选美国国家工程院外籍院士。

致力于中国空气污染控制研究40余年，主要研究领域为能源与环境、大气污染控制工程。主持全国酸沉降控制规划与对策研究，划定酸雨和二氧化硫控制区，被国务院采纳实施，为确定我国酸雨防治对策起到主导作用。建立了城市机动车污染控制规划方法，推动了我国机动车污染控制进程。深入开展大气复合污染特征、成因及控制策略研究，发展了特大城市空气质量改善的理论与技术方法，推动我国区域性大气复合污染的联防联控。长期开展大气污染控制关键技术研究，在燃煤烟气除尘脱硫脱硝、机动车污染控制等领域做出贡献。

获国家科技进步奖一等奖1项、二等奖2项，国家自然科学二等奖和国家技术发明二等奖各1项，国家教学成果一等奖2项。2006年获国家教学名师称号，获2015年度哈根－斯密特清洁空气奖及2016年IBM全球杰出学者奖。

评选委员会委员
钱 绍 钧

钱绍钧，1934年生于浙江平湖。1951年考入清华大学物理系，后在北京俄语专科学校和北京大学物理系、物理研究室（现技术物理系）学习。现任原总装备部科技委顾问，研究员，中国工程院院士。曾任核试验基地副司令员、司令员，国防科工委科技委常任委员。

长期从事核试验放射化学诊断工作，参与了由原子弹到氢弹、由大气层到地下的一系列核试验，建立完善多项诊断方法和技术，显著提升测量精度。多次参加国防科技和武器装备发展战略研究，参与组织国家中长期科学技术发展规划专题研究。指导开展国防应用基础研究，努力促进与国家基础研究的协调链接。指导军用核技术发展，长期跟踪研究国际态势及主要国家政策演变，参与军备控制研究和"全面禁止核试验条约"谈判。

出版译著1部，主编专著2部，撰写科技论文和重要科技档案多篇，获国家科技进步奖特等奖、二等奖各1项，国家发明奖二等奖、三等奖各1项，军队科技进步奖多项。

评选委员会委员
徐 立 之

徐立之，1950 年 12 月 21 日出生于上海，成长于香港。分子遗传学家。曾任香港大学校长，现任香港科学院首任院长。1979 年在美国匹兹堡大学获博士学位。其后于美国田纳西州 Oak Ridge 国家实验室及加拿大多伦多病童医院遗传系进行博士后研究，后任多伦多病童医院研究所遗传系主任及首席遗传学家，同时兼多伦多大学教授及 H. E. Sellers 囊状纤维症讲座教授。

长期致力于遗传学研究，在囊性纤维化致病基因的定位、分离及突变分析以及对这种常见基因缺陷疾病的分子发病原理研究中取得重大成果。获得加拿大勋章、加拿大国会 Killam 奖、大紫荆勋章、加拿大皇家学院院士、伦敦皇家学院院士、美国国家科学院外籍院士、国际创新基金会院士等多个奖项及荣誉。

评选委员会委员
高 文

高文，1956 年出生。1988 年获哈尔滨工业大学计算机应用博士学位，1991 年获日本东京大学电子学博士学位。北京大学信息学院教授，博导。2011 年当选中国工程院院士。

主要研究领域为数字媒体技术。长期以来从事计算机视觉、模式识别与图像处理、多媒体数据压缩、多模式接口以及虚拟现实等的研究，在视频编码与分析、手语识别与合成、人脸识别、数字图书馆等领域有精深造诣。主持"973"计划（首席）、"863"计划、国家自然科学基金等国家级项目二十余项；担任数字音视频编解码技术标准（AVS）工作组组长，为视频编码国家标准与国际标准的创立和推广做出主要贡献。曾任 IEEE ICME 2007 和 ACM MM 2009 旗舰会议主席。

有科学著作 5 部，在国际期刊上发表论文百余篇。作为第一完成人，在视频编码与系统等研究领域成果曾 5 次获得国家科技进步奖二等奖，1 次获国家技术发明奖二等奖。

评选委员会委员
桑 国 卫

桑国卫，1941年11月生，浙江湖州人。临床药理学家，中国工程院院士。中国药学会理事长，"十一五""十二五""十三五"国家"重大新药创制"重大专项技术总师，工信部"医药工业'十三五'发展规划"专家咨询委员会主任，中国药品生物制品检定所资深研究员，上海中医药大学名誉校长。曾任十一届全国人大常委会副委员长、农工民主党中央主席。

对长效注射与口服甾体避孕药及抗孕激素的药代动力学、种族差异及临床药理学做了系统研究，取得多项重大成果。近年来，在新药的安全性评价、质量控制和临床试验等方面进行了卓有成效的工作，为加强我国GLP、GCP平台建设做出了重要贡献。

获全国科技大会奖2项，国家科学技术进步奖二等奖3项，部委级科技进步奖一等奖1项、二等奖4项。1997年获何梁何利科学与技术进步奖（医学药学奖）。2008年获吴阶平—保罗·杨森奖特殊贡献奖。2014年获国际药学联合会药学科学终身成就奖。

评选委员会委员
曹 雪 涛

曹雪涛，1964年7月出生，山东济南人，1990年毕业于第二军医大学。现为中国医学科学院院长、中国工程院院士、医学免疫学国家重点实验室主任，兼任中国免疫学会理事长、全球慢性疾病防控联盟主席、亚洲大洋洲免疫学会联盟主席等。担任 *Cell* 等杂志编委。

主要从事天然免疫识别及其免疫调节的基础研究、肿瘤免疫治疗应用性研究。发现了具有重要免疫调控功能的树突状细胞新型亚群；独立发现了22种免疫相关分子；系统研究了天然免疫识别与干扰素产生调控的新机制；探讨了表观分子在炎症与肿瘤发生发展中的作用；建立了肿瘤免疫治疗新途径并开展了临床试验。

以第一完成人获国家自然科学奖二等奖1项，中华医学科技奖一等奖1项，军队科技进步奖一等奖1项，上海市自然科学奖一等奖3项，已获得国家发明专利16项，获得两个国家Ⅱ类新药证书。研究成果入选 2011 年中国十大科技进展。获得光华工程奖、长江学者成就奖、中国青年科学家奖、中国十大杰出青年等。以通讯作者发表 SCI 收录论文 220 余篇，包括 *Cell*、*Science*、*Nature Immunology*、*Cancer Cell*、*Immunity* 等。论文被 SCI 他引 5600 多次；编写和共同主编专著 8 部；培养的博士生中有 11 名获得全国百篇优秀博士论文。

评选委员会委员
程　　序

程序，1944 年出生，江苏无锡人。1965 年毕业于北京农业大学（现中国农业大学）农学系，后入中国农业科学院作物育种栽培研究所从事研究工作。现为中国农业大学教授，博导。曾就职于北京市农科院、农业部等单位。主要研究方向为可持续农业与农村发展、农业生态与生态农业以及生物能源等。

曾主持农业现代化规律和实验基地建设（实验基地：北京市房山区窦店村）以及生态农业两个研究项目。1985 年率先引进农业可持续发展的理论，此后开始研究中国条件下农业可持续发展的途径。重点放在农牧交错生态脆弱带的生态恢复途径，以及探索可持续的集约化农业模式的研究两个方面。

作为第一完成人，先后被授予北京市科技进步奖一等奖及国家星火科技奖（等同科技进步奖）一等奖。累计获省部级科技进步奖二、三等奖 7 项，1988 年被批准为国家级有突出贡献的中青年专家。

著有《可持续农业导论》和《中国可持续发展总纲第 13 卷：中国农业与可持续发展》两部专著。

评选委员会委员
曾　庆　存

曾庆存，1935 年 5 月生于广东省阳江市（原阳江县）。1956 年毕业于北京大学物理系。1961 年在苏联科学院应用地球物理研究所获副博士（现称博士即 Ph. D）学位。回国后先后在中国科学院地球物理研究所和大气物理研究所工作。1980 年当选中国科学院院士。现为中国科学院大气物理研究所研究员。

　　主要研究领域为大气科学和地球流体力学。致力于大气环流和地球流体动力学基础理论和数值模式及模拟、地球系统动力学模式、数值天气预报和气候预测理论、气候动力学和季风理论、大气边界层动力学、卫星遥感理论方法、应用数学和计算数学以及自然控制论等的研究工作。在国际上最早提出半隐式差分法和平方守恒格式，最早成功将原始方程应用于实际数值天气预告（1961）和研制成大气海洋耦合模式并用作跨季度气候预测（1990，1994），提出系统的卫星大气遥感理论（1974）以及自然控制论理论方法（1995）。

　　曾获国家自然科学奖二等奖 2 项和三等奖 1 项，中国科学院自然科学奖一等奖 6 项和杰出贡献奖 1 项。出版专著包括《大气红外遥测原理》《数值天气预报的数学物理基础》《短期数值气候预测原理》《千里黄云——东亚沙尘暴研究》等。发表学术文章约百篇。

BRIEF INTRODUCTION TO THE MEMBERS OF THE SELECTION BOARD OF HO LEUNG HO LEE FOUNDATION

Zhu Lilan, Director of the Selection Board

Zhu Lilan, female, was born in August 1935 and is of the origin of Huzhou, Zhejiang Province. At present, she is the Chairman of the China Association of Inventions and the Chairman of the Committee of Science and Technology Awards of Macau Special Administrative Region. She was the vice-minister of the State Science and Technology Commission (1986), the Minister of the Ministry of Science and Technology (1998), the Director of the Education, Science, Culture and Public Health Committee of the National People's Congress (2001), the counselor of Chinese Academy of Engineering Presidium, the Advisor of the Presidential Committee of CAS Academic Board, the Member of the State Leading Group of Science, Technology and Education, the Director of the State Committee of Science and Technology Awards and the Advisor of the Macao Science and Technology Council.

When analyzing polymer materials and researching morphological structure and reaction dynamics in the Institute of Chemistry of the Chinese Academy of Sciences, Zhu Lilan undertook several national and national defense key science and technological projects and was granted the statelevel and provincelevel significant scientific and technological result awards and application result awards. When being the Director of the Education, Science, Culture and Public Health Committee of the National People's Congress, she organized the amendments to and implementation of the Science and Technology Progress Law and the Compulsory Education Law; and organized a series of investigations for making the laws and amending the important laws concerning such matters as society, people's life, science and technology, culture and health, which has provided an important basis for legal construction.

Zhu Lilan has published several articles and books on the status quo of hi-tech development and the corresponding strategies and management measures, including *Modern Hi-tech. Development Strategy in the Contemporary Era* and *Development and Challenge*. She was granted the Achievement Award by the Chinese Materials Research Society. Thanks to her significant contribution to the development of China's hi-tech development and international scientific and technological cooperation, Zhu Lilan obtained the Distinguished Service Award granted by the Chinese Institute of Engineers, USA, the Grand Cross Medal of the Federal Republic of Germany granted by German President and the Medal No. 2of Ukraine President.

Du Zhanyuan, Deputy Director of the Selection Board

Du Zhanyuan was born in July 1962. He got his bachelor's degree from Hunan Agricultural University and master's degree from China Agricultural University. He got his doctoral degree on Plant Physiology & Biochemistry from the Plant & Soil Science Department of University of Massachusetts in the US in 1993. He worked for the Ministry of Science and Technology and the Ministry of Education of the People's Republic of China and served as Deputy Minister of the Ministry of Science and Technology. He is now Deputy Minister of the Ministry of Education.

He is well established in the field of agriculture & biology and has published several essays on plant physiology in international science journals. He won the top award during an essay competition for postgraduates of the Northeast Horticultural Society in the U.S. He has conducted indepth study of science and technology management and technological innovation economy. During his tenure at the Ministry of Science and Technology, he participated in the formulation of the 10th and 11th Scientific and Technological Development Plans and Technological Cornerstone Plans. He has also published numerous essays in Chinese magazines, journals and newspapers on the subject of science management and coauthored academic monographs such as *Small and Medium-Sized Enterprises and Technological Innovation and China Development Report on Manufacturing Industry*. He has full knowledge and deep understanding of China's national science and technology strategies and the cutting edge development of international academia. In recent years, he has been dedicated himself to promoting technology in higher education institutions, development of postgraduate education and application of information technology in education.

As Deputy Minister of the Ministry of Education, his responsibilities cover science and technology in higher education institutions, degree management and postgraduate education and application of information technology in education. He has conducted in-depth research programs on science and technology management with rich managerial experience in the areas of science and technology, cultivation of high-caliber talent and application of information technology in education.

Kenneth Young, Vice Director of the Selection Board

Born in July 1948 in Shanghai, Kenneth Young has been working at The Chinese University of Hong Kong (CUHK) since 1973, and has held the position of Chairman of the Department of Physics, Dean of the Faculty of Science, Dean of the Graduate School and Pro-Vice-Chancellor/ Vice-President. At present, Kenneth Young is Master of the CW Chu College and professor of physics at CUHK. He is also a member of the Education Commission (EC) and the Chairman of the Curriculum Development Council of the Hong Kong SAR. He was a member of the Hong Kong University Grants Committee and Chairman its Research Grants Council. He was the Secretary and later Vice-President of the Association of Asia Pacific Physical Societies. Kenneth Young studied at the California Institute of Technology from 1965 to 1972 and obtained the BS in physics in 1969 and the PhD in physics and mathematics in 1972. He was engaged in teaching and research at Princeton University from 1972 to 1973.

Kenneth Young has been engaged in physics research for a long time, on topics including elementary particles, field theory, high energy phenomenology, dissipation system and their eigenfunctions expansion, with applications to such open systems as optics and gravitational waves. Some of his publications include "Microscopic derivation of the Helmholtz force density", Phys Rev Lett 47, 77; "Late time tail of wave propagation on curved spacetime", Phys Rev Lett 74, 2414; "Quasinormal mode expansion for linearized waves in gravitational systems", Phys Rev Lett 74, 4588; "Quasinormal modes of dirty black holes", Phys Rev Lett 78, 289. Kenneth Young was elected as a Fellow of the American Physical Society in 1999 and an academician of International Eurasian Academy of Science in 2004.

Duan Ruichun, Secretary-General of the Selection Board

Duan Ruichun, born in February 1943, is a bachelor of engineer from Shanghai Jiaotong University, a master of science from Graduate University of Chinese Academy of Science and a master of law from Peking University. In the 1990s, he was the Director of the Policy, Law and System Reform Department of the State Science and Technology Commission and the Director of the Intellectual Property Working Meeting Office of the State Council. From 2000 to 2007, he was the Chairman of the Board of Supervisors for Key Large State-Owned Enterprises of the State Council. At present, Duan Ruichun is the Chairman of the China Association for Science and Technology and the permanent vice chairman of the China Association for Promotion of Cooperation among Industries, Universities & Research Institutes.

As a famous expert in Chinas intellectual property rights, scientific and technological policies and enterprise innovation, Duan Ruichun possesses interdisciplinary knowledge in natural science, economic management and legal science. He has led the drafting of many Chinese laws and regulations such as the Technology Contract Law, the Scientific and Technological Progress Law and the Regulation on National Awards for Science and Technology; he has participated in drafting of and amendments to many laws on intellectual property rights; he was the chief representative of the Intellectual Property Negotiations for Scientific and Technological Cooperation between China and the United States and the main representative of intellectual property negotiations in the process of Chinas entry into WTO; he was the Leader of the Review Team of the general report of the National IP Strategy; and he was one of the main person formulating the Trust Deed and the Selection Articles of the Ho Leung Ho Lee Foundation.

Due to his research results, Duan Ruichun was granted the first prize of the Science and Technology Progress Award by the State Science and Technology Commission in 1992 and granted the second prize of the Science and Technology Progress Award in 1993. He was granted the recognition award of Chinas technology market in 2004 and the significant contribution award of the China Law Association on Science and Technology in 2008. He has written and published several books such as *International Cooperation and Intellectual Property Rights*, *Principles and Practice of Technology Contracts*, *Guidelines on Technology Innovation* and *Multi-Dimensional Thinking of Scientific and Technological Policies*.

Ma Yongsheng, Member of the Selection Board

Ma Yongsheng, a petroleum geologist and sedimentologist, was born in Hohhot City of Inner Mongolia in October 1961. He obtained his bachelor's and master's degrees from China University of Geosciences(previously known as Wuhan College of Geology)and received his Ph.D. from Chinese Academy of Geological Sciences in 1990. He is now the Vice President and Chief Geologist of China Petroleum & Chemical Corporation(Sinopec Group). He has been elected as academician of Chinese Academy of Engineering in 2009.

Over the past few decades, he devoted his career to the research and application of the petroleum and natural gas exploration theory. He has made great contributions to the marine carbonates hydrocarbon exploration theory with a number of leading technological and theoretical achievements. For instance, he led the successful discovery of several giant natural gas reservoirs in China, such as the Puguang and Yuanba gas fields, establishing solid foundations for the Sichuan-to-East China Gas Transmission Project. His pioneering research in unconventional natural gas contributed significantly to the discovery of Fuling shale gas field in Chongqing, China's first large-scale shale gas field. His research accomplishments have also remarkably facilitated the mitigation of natural gas supply-demand imbalance, as well as the promotion of regional economy and environmental protection in China.

Ma has won the 1st Prize of the National Science & Technology Progress Award twice. In 2007, he won the Scientific & Technological Achievements Award granted by the Ho Leung Ho Lee Foundation. In the same year, he won Li Siguang Geoscience Prize for the 10th time. In 2013, he was selected as one of China's first six outstanding scientists supported by the National Ten-Thousand Talents Program. For his distinguished achievement in the petroleum industry, the Minor Planet Center named No. 210292 asteroid officially after him as "Ma Yongsheng Planet" in 2017.

Zhu Daoben, Member of the Selection Board

Zhu Daoben, born in Shanghai in August 1942, came from Hangzhou, Zhejiang Province. As an organic and physical chemist, he is a researcher from the Institute of Chemistry of the Chinese Academy of Sciences. In October 1997, He was elected as an academician of the Chinese Academy of Sciences.

He graduated from East China Institute of Chemical Technology in 1965 and completed his postgraduate program at the Organic Chemistry Department of the Institute in 1968. Then he began his career at the Institute of Chemistry of the Chinese Academy of Sciences. Throughout his career, he has served as Deputy Director and Director of the Institute of Chemistry, Director-general of Chinese Chemical Society and Deputy Director of the National Natural Science Foundation. Currently, he is Vice Director of the Academic Committee of the Chinese Academy of Sciences and Director of the Key Laboratory of Organic Solids.

Since 1970s, Zhu has been involved in the research of organic solids and attracted international attention in the fields of conductance of organic crystal, ferromagnetism, molecular membranes and devices, structure performance of C60 and its derivatives. He has published over 500 papers. His research findings have won four National Natural Science Awards (Grade II) and two Natural Science Awards (Grade II) of the Chinese Academy of Sciences.

Henry T. Yang, Member of the Selection Board

Henry T. Yang was born in 1940. He obtained a PHD from Cornell University. He has served as Dean of the Aerospace Engineering Department and Head of the Engineering College of Purdue University. He used to be a co-director of the Smart Manufacturing Engineering center of the National Science Foundation (U. S.) and an outstanding professor of Armstrong (the first Moon lander) Astronautics Lectures. Currently, he is President of University of California Santa Barbara (since 1994), an academician of American Academy of Engineering, a fellow of both American Institute of Aeronautics and Astronautics and American Society of Mechanical Engineers, an overseas academician of Chinese Academy of Engineering and an academician of the Taiwan Academia Sinica. He is the chairman of the Thirty-metre Telescope Program (TMT Program) jointly sponsored by the United States, China, India, Japan and Canada. He is the chairman of the Association of Pacific Rim 42 Universities (including Peking University, Tsinghua University, Fudan University, University of Science and Technology of China, Zhejiang University and Nanjing University), a member of the Selection Board of the United States Presidential Medal of Science and a member of council of the Kavli Foundation. He used to be the Chairman of Association of American Universities (AAU) that consists of 62 top universities and a member of the Selection Board of Finnish Millennium Technology Grand Prize. He has been conferred seven honorary doctoral degrees.

He has been involved in teaching and research in aerospace structure, oscillation, control transition to earthquake, manufacturing, material (LED) and biological engineering. He has served as doctoral supervisor for sixty dissertations. He has published over 200 papers in journals, over 200 papers for academic conferences and one textbook on finite element (used by over forty American universities and translated into Chinese and Japanese).

He won the SDM Award granted by the American Institute of Aeronautics and Astronautics in 2008. He won Benjamin Garver Lamme Gold Metal, the highest one granted by the American Society for Engineering Education, and over ten excellent awards for education.

Joseph Jao-Yiu Sung, Member of the Selection Board

Joseph Jao-Yiu Sung was born in October 1959. He obtained a Bachelor degree in medicine from Hong Kong University, a PHD in life science from Calgary University and another PHD in medicine from the Chinese University of Hong Kong. He is an academician of the Royal College of Physicians of London, the Royal College of Medicine of Thailand, the Royal College of Physicians of Australia, American College of Gastroenterology, American Society of Gastroenterology, the College of Physicians of Hong Kong and Hong Kong Academy of Medicine. He is a member of over twenty academic committees. He is an academician of the Chinese Academy of Engineering and the Eurasian Academy of Sciences.

He used to be a lecturer in the Department of Medicine in the Faculty of Medicine of the Chinese University of Hong Kong, a professor and then Dean of the Department of Medicine and Therapeutics, Deputy Dean of the Faculty of Medicine and Head of Shaw College.

He is an authority and pioneer in gastroenterological research. His research covers gastrointestinal bleeding, Helicobacter pylori, peptic ulcer, hepatitis and cancer in digestive system. Since 2004, he has led experts from fifteen countries to conduct screening and research of colorectal cancer. He formulated a clear guideline for general survey, so he won the Laurel Award of American Cancer Fund in 2008. He won the National Science and Technology Progress Award (Grade II) in 2008 and a number of other awards in Hong Kong and the world for his achievements in medical research.

As a prolific scientist, he has published over 700 papers in top international journals, written and compiled over thirty-two books, served as a reviewer for over fifteen renowned academic periodicals and won many prizes for the best papers.

Zhang Litong, Member of the Selection Board

Zhang Litong, female, born in Chongqing in April of 1938, is a famous expert in aerospace materials. She graduated from Northwestern Polytechnical University in 1961. She was a senior visiting scholar in the Business Development Center of Spatial Structure Materials of NASA of the US from April 1989 to January 1991. Now, she acts as a professor and doctoral supervisor of Northwestern Polytechnical University and the deputy director of the Academic Committee of National Key Laboratory on Ultra-temperature Structure Composite Material Technology. She was elected as an academician of the Chinese Academy of Engineering in 1995.

She has been devoting himself to the research of aerospace materials and the technologies of manufacturing aerospace materials for many years and has achieved abundant research results in marginless melted module precise casting technologies and their fundamental theory research of thin-wall complex high-temperature alloy and aluminum alloy castings. She reveals the blade deformation rules, roughness generation rules and middle/high-temperature softening deformation mechanism of ceramic shells. Through independent innovation, she develops marginless melted module casting technology of high-temperature alloy, plaster-mold melted module casting technology of aluminum alloy, technology of middle/high-temperature creep-resisting ceramic shell materials for melted module casting of high-temperature alloy, and technology of foamed ceramic filtering and purifying materials for high-temperature alloy. Relevant achievements have been applied to production of aero-engines and aircraft components successfully.

After returning to China, she establishes three technology platforms with independent intellectual property rights (manufacturing process, manufacturing equipment and material and environment performance assessment), breaking international blockade on technologies.

She was awarded with one first-class prize of National Award for Technological Invention, four first-class, second-class and third-class prizes of National Award for Scientific and Technological Progress, one second-class prize of State-level Teaching Award. She is authorized with 64 national invention patents.

Zhang Gongqing, Member of the Selection Board

Zhang Gongqing was born on May 29. 1936 in Shanghai. After he graduated from the Department of Mathematics of Peking University in 1959 he worked in his university. In the year of 1978, as one of the first visiting scholars since the reform and opening-up, he made further study in the United States. Now he is a professor of Peking University, an academician of Chinese Academy of Sciences, an academician of the Academy of Sciences for the Developing World, the Director of the Research and Talent Training Center for Teaching and Learning Mathematics in Universities and Colleges, and he also serves as a member in the editorial board of many international core academic journals.

As a famous mathematician, he develops infinite dimensional Morse theory into a unified framework of the critical point theory, and is the first one to employ Morse theory as a tool to study multiple solutions to partial differential equations. His monograph is the fundamental literature of the related field. He also develops the topological degree theory of set-valued mappings and the critical point theory of non-differential functional, making them a kind of free boundary problem in the study on equations of mathematical physics and on non-smooth mechanics.

He won the Award of National Science & Technology Conference (1978), the third prize of the State Natural Sciences Award (1982), the second prize of the State Natural Sciences Award (1987), Chen Xingshen Mathematics Prize (1986), the title of the Young Scientist with Outstanding Contributions (1984), the Third World Academy of Sciences Award in Mathematics (1993), Hua Luogeng Mathematics Prize (2009), Guohua Award of Peking University, and Special Award for Teaching presented by Founder Group (2011), etc.

Chen Jiaer, Member of the Selection Board

Chen Jiaer, born on October 1. 1934 in Shanghai, is an academician of Chinese Academy of Sciences, an academician of the Academy of Sciences for the Developing World. He is currently a professor of physics at Peking University, the vice director of the Advisory Group of the National Basic Research Program of China (or 973 Program), and the vice chairman of the China Coordination Committee of the International Council of Scientific Unions.

He was the president of the Peking University and the dean of the Graduate School of Peking University, the director of the Committee of the National Natural Sciences Foundation, the director of the Division of Mathematics and Physics of the Chinese Academy of Sciences (CAS), a member of the CAS presidium, and the dean of the School of Physics of the Graduate University of CAS.

For a long time he has been devoting himself to the teaching and scientific research of the low-energy particle accelerator and its application. He is good at combining the cutting-edge development of an academic subject with national demands and planning the research in physics and talent training in a forward-looking way. He pioneered the development of RF superconducting accelerator, ultra-sensitive accelerator mass spectrometry, RF quadrupole field accelerator and electrostatic accelerator in China. He is a founder and one of the leaders in researching and developing low-energy particle accelerator in China.

Chen Jiaer was a long-time leader in Peking University and the Committee of the National

Natural Science Foundation, and was also a member of the Leadership Group of Medium and Long Term Planning for Development of Science and Technology. He made important contribution to the formulation of the National Medium and Long Term Planning of Development of Science and Technology and the development of relevant science and education causes in China.

Hao Jiming, Member of the Selection Board

Hao Jiming, a well-known expert in environmental engineering, was born in Shandong Province in August 1946. He graduated from Tsinghua University in 1970. He earned a master degree from Tsinghua University in 1981, and obtained a PhD from University of Cincinnati in 1984. At Tsinghua University, he is a professor, tutor for doctoral candidates, deputy director of the teaching committee, and director of the Research Institute of Environmental Science and Engineering. He is also a member on the National Environmental Consultation Committee and China Council for International Cooperation on Environment and Development. He was elected as academician of the Chinese Academy of Engineering in 2005, and was elected as foreign academician of the National Academy of Engineering in the U.S. in 2018.

Hao Jiming has dedicated himself to the research in controlling air pollution in China for more than 40 years. His main fields of research include energy and environment, and air pollution control engineering. He is in charge of national acid deposition control planning and the research in countermeasures against acid deposition. His research result on dividing the areas for controlling acid rain and carbon dioxide has been adopted by the State Council, playing a guiding role in formulating China's policies on preventing and treating acid rain pollution. He has developed the planning and methods for controlling pollution caused by motor-driven vehicles in urban areas, promoting the control of the pollution caused by motor-driven vehicles in China. He has conducted in-depth research in the characteristics, causes and control policy on air compound pollution, further developed the theoretical and technological methods on improving the air quality in mega cities, and promoted the joint efforts to prevent and control the regional air compound pollution in China. He has conducted the research in the key technologies for controlling air pollution for a long period of time, and has made contributions in the fields such as dust control, desulfurization and denitration in coal-fired flue gas, and control of the pollution caused by motor-driven vehicles.

Hao Jiming won one first-prize and two second prizes of National Award for Scientific and Technological Progress, one second prize of National Award for Natural Science and two second prizes of National Award for Technical Invention, and two first prizes of National Award in Teaching Achievement. He was granted the title of national famous teacher in 2006. He won the Haagen-Smit Clean Air Award in 2015, and the IBM Global Faculty Award in 2016.

Qian Shaojun, Member of the Selection Board

Qian Shaojun was born in 1934 in Pinghu, Zhejiang Province. In 1951, he was admitted to the Department of Physics of Tsinghua University, and later studied Beijing Russian Language College, Department of Physics and the Research Section of Physics (now the Department of Technical Physics) of Peking University. He currently works as a consultant and research fellow of the Committee of Science and Technology of General Armament Department of the PLA, a research fellow and an academician of the Chinese Academy of Engineering. He used to be the deputy commander and the commander of the Nuclear Test Base, and was a standing member of the Committee of Science and Technology in the State Commission of Science and Technology for National Defense Industry.

He has been long engaged in the radiochemical diagnostic work of nuclear test and participated in a series of atomic bomb and hydrogen bomb nuclear tests conducted in the atmosphere or underground, in which he remarkably enhanced the measurement accuracy by establishing and improving many diagnostic approach and technology. For many times he took part in the study on the development strategy of science and technology and weaponry and equipment for national defence and participated in organizing the special research in national medium and long term scientific and technical development planning. He guided the basic study on applying research results in national defense, and worked hard to make such basic study consistent with the national basic research programs. He was put in charge of developing nuclear technology for military use, kept track of long-term changes with international situations and the policy evolvement of some leading nations, and instructed and took part in the study of arms control. He participated in the negotiation of the Comprehensive Nuclear Test Ban Treaty and guided the preparatory work for the performance of the treaty after it was signed.

His published works include a translated work, two monographs, wrote many scientific and technical papers and important scientific and technical articles for archival purpose. He won the Top Prize of the State Scientific and Technological Progress Award and the second prize of the State Scientific and Technological Progress Award once, the second prize of the State Award for Inventions and the third prize of the State Award for Inventions once, and the Military Progress Prize in Science and Technology many times.

Lap-Chee Tsui, Member of the Selection Board

Lap-Chee Tsui was born in Shanghai on December 21. 1950 and grew up in Hong Kong. He is a molecular geneticist. He was the Vice-chancellor and President of The University of Hong Kong, and is now the first president of Hong Kong Academy of Science. He obtained the doctoral degree at University of Pittsburgh in 1979. Later he carried out post–doctoral research at Oak Ridge National Laboratory in Tennessee and at the Department of Genetics of The Hospital for Sick Children in Toronto. Then he acted as the Geneticist–in–Chief and Head of the Genetics and Genomic Biology Program of the Research Institute at the Hospital for Sick Children in Toronto, and meanwhile acted as a professor with University of Toronto and holder of the H.E. Sellers Chair in Cystic Fibrosis.

Having been dedicated to the genetic research on a long–term basis, he has made great achievements in the mapping, isolation and mutation analysis of the pathogenic gene of cystic fibrosis, as well as in the research of the pathogenesis of such common gene–defect diseases.

He has successively won a number of awards and honors, including Order of Canada, Killam Research Fellowships, Grand Bauhinia Medal, Distinguished Scientist of the Medical Research Council of Canada, Fellow of the Royal Society of Canada, Fellow of the Royal Society of London, Member [Foreign Associate] of National Academy of Sciences of USA, and Fellow of World Innovation Foundation.

Gao Wen, Member of the Selection Board

Gao Wen, male, was born in 1956. He received his doctorate in computer application from Harbin Institute of Technology in 1988, and earned a doctorate in electronics in Tokyo University In 1991. Now he is a professor of the School of Information of Peking University, tutor for doctoral candidates. In 2011, he was elected the academician of the Chinese Academy of Engineering.

His main area of research is digital media technology. He has long been engaged in the research in many fields including computer vision, pattern recognition and image processing, Multimedia data compression, and multi–model interface and virtual reality. He is a scientist of profound accomplishments in video coding and analysis, sign language recognition and synthesis, human face identification, and digital library. He was put in charge of more than twenty state–level research programs like 973 program (chief leader), 863 program and programs of the National Natural Science Foundation. He served as the leader of the Audio Video Coding Standard (AVS) Workgroup, making main contribution to the establishment and popularization of the international standards with independent intellectual property of China. He was the president of the Flagship Conference of the IEEE ICME 2007 and ACM MM 2009.

He completed five scientific monographs and has more than one hundred papers published in international academic periodicals. As the main participant in completing the research project of video coding and system, he won the second prize of the State Scientific and Technological Progress Award for five times and the second prize of the State Technological Invention Award for one time for his achievements in this regard.

Sang Guowei, Member of the Selection Board

Sang Guowei was born in Huzhou, Zhejiang in November 1941. He is a clinical pharmacologist, an academician of the Chinese Academy of Engineering, Chairman of Chinese Pharmaceutical Association, Chief Engineer for the important specific techniques for the national "development of important new medicines" in the "11th Five-Year Plan", "12th Five-Year Plan" and "13th Five-Year Plan". He is also the director of the Expert Consultation Committee of the "Development Program of the Pharmaceuticals Industry in the 13th Five-Year Plan" of the Ministry of Industry and Information Technology, senior research fellow of National Institute for the Control of Pharmaceutical and Biological Products (NICPBP), honorary president of Shanghai University of Traditional Chinese Medicine (SHUTCM), and was the vice chairman of the 11th National People's Congress Standing Committee, and chairman of Chinese Peasants' and Workers' Democratic Party.

He has systematically studied the pharmacokinetics, race differences and clinical pharmacology of steroidal contraceptives and antiprogestogens for long-acting injection and for oral taking, and made a number of important achievements. He has done fruitful work in terms of safety evaluation, quality control and clinical trial etc. for new drugs in recent years, and has made great contributions in strengthening China's construction of the GLP and GCP platforms.

He has won two National Scientific Conference Awards (in 1978), three Second Prizes of National Science and Technology Progress Award (in 1987, 1997 and 2008), one First Prize and four Second Prizes of Science and Technology Progress Award at the ministerial and commission levels, the Science and Technology Awards of the Ho Leung Ho Lee Foundation in 1997(Medical-Pharmaceutical Award), the Special Contribution Award of the Wu Jieping-Paul Janssen Medical-Pharmaceutical Award in 2008, and the Lifetime Achievement Award in Pharmacy Science of the Federation International Pharmaceutical (FIP) in 2014.

Cao Xuetao, Member of the Selection Board

Cao Xuetao, was born in July 1964 in Jinan City, Shandong Province. In 1990, he graduated from the Second Military Medical University. He is the President of Chinese Academy of Medical Sciences (CAMS), member of the Chinese Academy of Engineering, and the Director of National Key Laboratory of Medical Immunology. Concurrently he is the President of the Chinese Society for Immunology, Chairperson of Global Alliance of Chronic Diseases (GACD), and President of the Federation of Immunological Societies of Asia-Oceania (FIMSA). He also serves as a member of the editorial board of magazines including Cell.

He is mainly engaged in fundamental research on innate immune recognition and relevant immune regulation, and applicability research on tumor immunotherapy. He has found a new dendritic cell (DC) subset with an important immune regulation function, independently identified 22 immune-related molecules, systematically studied innate immune recognition and the new mechanism for interferon production regulation, explored apparent molecular action on inflammation and cancer development and progression, established new approaches for tumor immunotherapy, and carried out relevant clinical trials.

He won the second-class prize of National Science and Technology Awards as the primary participant of a research project, a first-class prize of Chinese Medical Science and Technology Awards, a first-class prize of Military Science and Technology Progress Awards, three first-class prizes of Shanghai Science and Technology Progress Awards. He has obtained 16 national invention patents and two national category-II new medicine certificates. His research result was selected as one of the top ten results representing the scientific and technological progress in China in 2011. He was presented with Guanghua Engineering Science and Technology Award, Cheng Kong Scholar Achievement Award, China Young Scientist Award, and others. As corresponding author, he published over 220 papers in SCI-cited journals including Cell, Science, Nature Immunology, Cancer Cell, Immunity and others. His papers have been non-self-cited for over 5600 times in SCI-cited journals; he has written and served as a co-chief-editor for eight monographs. Of all the doctoral candidates under his tutorship, 11 have been presented with the awards of "national 100 excellent dissertations for doctoral degrees."

Cheng Xu, Member of the Selection Board

Cheng Xu, born in 1944, is of the origin of Wuxi, Jiangsu Province. He graduated from the Department of Agronomy of Beijing Agricultural University (Now China Agricultural University), later he worked in the Institute of Crop Breeding and Cultivation of the Chinese Academy of Agricultural Science. He is currently a professor of the China Agricultural University, and a tutor for doctoral candidates. He worked in the Beijing Academy of Agricultural Science and the Ministry of Agriculture. His major fields of research include sustainable agriculture and rural development, agricultural ecology and ecological agriculture.

He was put in charge of two research projects: one is the construction of the Agricultural Modernization and Experimental Base (location: Doudian village, Fangshan County, Beijing) and the other is Ecological Agriculture Program. In 1985, he took the lead in introducing the theory of sustainable agricultural development. From then on he started to study the way to realize sustainable agricultural development in China. He focused his research on the ecological restoration in the fragile farming-pastoral transitional zones and the exploration of the sustainable intensive agriculture.

As the main participant in completing the research project, he won the first prize of the Beijing

Science and Technology Progress Awards and the first prize of the National Sparkle Technology Award (equivalent to Science and Technology Progress Award) . He was totally presented with seven second or third prizes of science and technology progress awards at provincial and ministerial level. In 1988, he was approved as a National Young & Middle–Aged Expert with Outstanding Contribution.

His works include *An Introduction to Sustainable Agriculture* and *General Program on Sustainable Development in China Volume* 13: *Agriculture in China and the Sustainable Development.*

Zeng Qingcun, Member of the Selection Board

Zeng Qingcun, born on May, 1935 in Yangjiang County, Guangdong Province, graduated from the Department of Physics of Peking University in 1956. In 1961, he completed his Licentiate (namely Ph. D now) in the Institute of Applied Geophysics of the Soviet Academy of Science. After he returned to China he worked in the Institute of Geophysics and then the Institute of Atmospheric Physics of the Chinese Academy of Sciences (CAS) . He was elected as an academician of the Chinese Academy of Sciences in 1980. Currently he is a research fellow of the Institute of Atmospheric physics of the CAS.

His major research field includes atmospheric sciences and geophysical fluid dynamics. He has been devoting himself to the study of the basic theory and numerical model and simulation of general atmospheric circulation and fluid dynamics, earth system dynamics model, numerical weather prediction and climatic prediction theory, climate dynamics and monsoon theory, dynamics of atmospheric boundary layer, theoretical method of satellite remote sensing, applied mathematics and numerical mathematics, and natural cybernetics. He is the first one in the world to put forward half–implicit difference scheme and square conservative scheme, applied the original equation into the actual numerical climate prediction (1961), developed the marine–atmosphere coupled mode for the extra–seasonal climate predictions (1990, 1994), and put forward the systematic theory of satellite remote sensing (1974) and the Theoretical method of natural control (1995) .

He won the second prize of the State Natural Sciences Award twice and the third prize of the State Natural Sciences Awards once, the first prize of the Natural Science Award of the CAS six times and Outstanding Contribution Award once. His monographs include *Principles of the Atmospheric Remote Sensing in Infrared*, *Mathematical Physics Foundations of the Numerical Weather Prediction*, *Principles of the Short–term Numerical Climatic Prediction*, *Yellow Clouds Stretching Thousands of Miles—The research on Dust–storm in East Asia.* He has also published hundreds of academic articles.

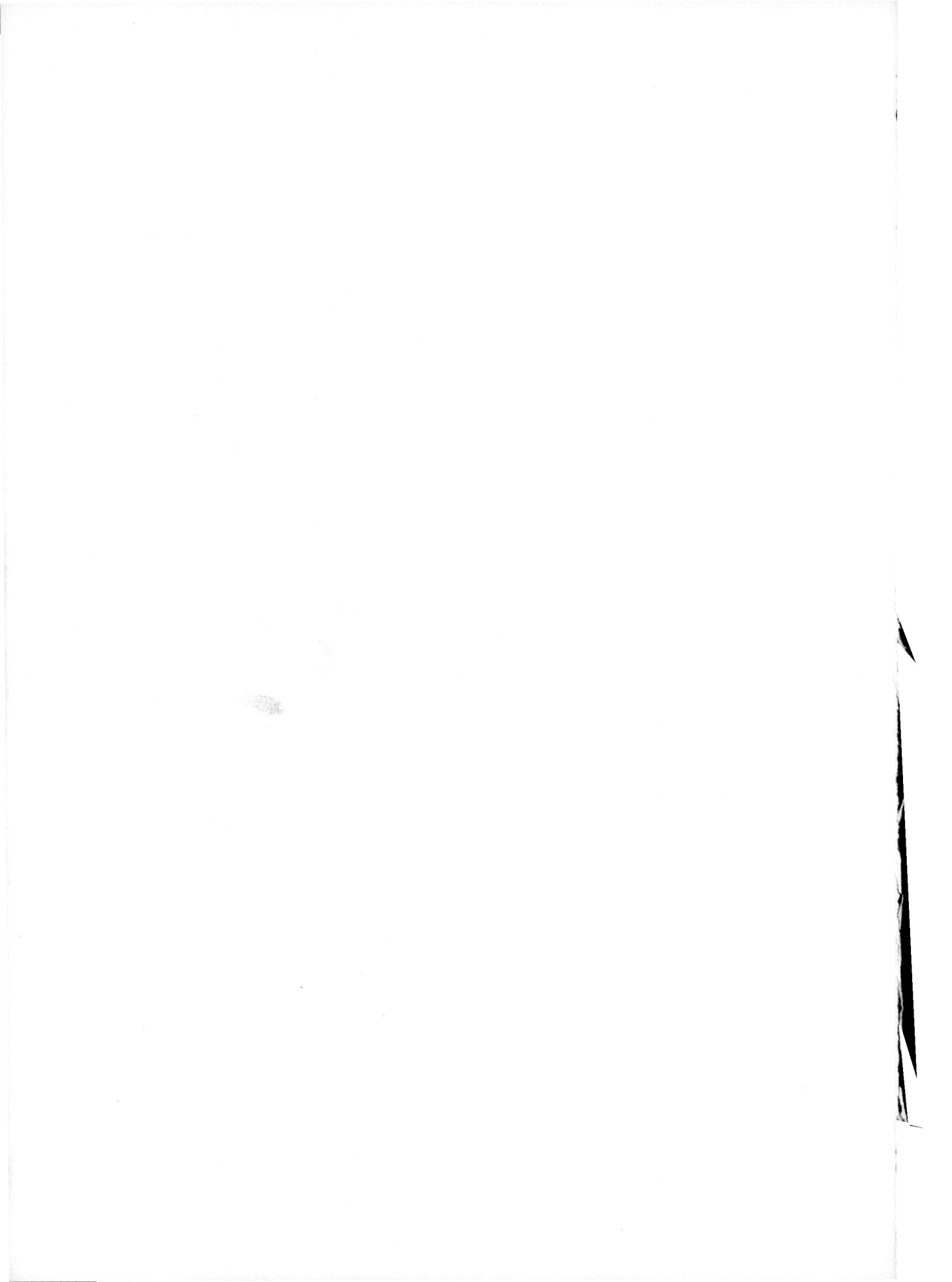